<u>INTERDEPENDENCE</u>

AN
INTRODUCTION
TO
INTERNATIONAL
RELATIONS

NTERDEPENDENCE

AN INTRODUCTION TO INTERNATIONAL RELATIONS

HOYT PURVIS
University of Arkansas

HBJ
Harcourt Brace Jovanovich College Publishers
Fort Worth   Philadelphia   San Diego   New York   Orlando   Austin   San Antonio
Toronto   Montreal   London   Sydney   Tokyo

Acquisitions Editors: Drake Bush and David Tatom
Manuscript Editor: Julia Ross
Senior Project Editor: Kay Kaylor
Designer: Don Fujimoto
Art Editor: Louise Sandy
Production Manager: Mandy Van Dusen

ISBN: 0-15-500005-5
Library of Congress Catalog Number: 92-70090
Printed in the United States of America
2 3 4 5 6 7 8 9 0 1   039   9 8 7 6 5 4 3 2 1

PREFACE

The increasing linkages that connect the world's peoples and nations make the study of international relations, and the understanding of those linkages, more important than ever. The emergence of the global economy, the impact of communications and technology, and the sweeping changes affecting the world as we move toward the beginning of the twenty-first century bring new dimensions and new issues to world affairs and to the study of international relations.

Interdependence: An Introduction to International Relations gives major emphasis to those new dimensions and issues while stressing the fundamental concepts and principles in international relations. It covers the dramatic and significant developments that have altered the world's political landscape in recent years, but also gives thorough treatment to the historic factors influencing world politics and to the traditional characteristics of international affairs.

The growing interdependence among nations is a theme that resonates throughout this book. As it focuses on the factors that draw peoples and nations together, it also gives attention to the issues that cause or may may cause division in the contemporary world.

Part I provides both the foundation and the framework for viewing, understanding, and analyzing world affairs. Part II examines in some detail the major issues confronting the world and those likely to be important in the years ahead, and uses these issues to elaborate on points made in Part I. Particular attention is given to such issues as the environment; population; weapons proliferation; North-South relations; regionalization and the international political economy; ethnic/nationalist factors in international relations; and the growing significance of communications and technology, including the powerful role the media can play in international politics.

Throughout *Interdependence,* illustrative examples and brief studies explain and amplify main points and themes, including key concepts and theories.

An important feature is a series of profiles of individual leaders. Also, city portraits of Berlin and Mexico City illustrate some historic, contemporary, and continuing issues in world affairs. The profiles emphasize the importance individual leaders can have in international relations and, along with the city portraits, strengthen the basic points covered in the proximate chapters. The profile essays deal with the character, style, ideas/policies, and historical significance of the individuals and their countries. In a broad sense, the model for these profiles was a series written by Walter Bagehot in the nineteenth century about British leaders and statesmen. While it is immodest to suggest a comparison to Bagehot, it would be improper not to pay tribute to the example he provided.

Among the other features of this textbook are a number of maps, with detailed captions, and other illustrations designed to assist readers and complement the text. Key terms and concepts are defined in context throughout the book and are included in a comprehensive glossary at the end of the book. An overall bibliography and suggestions for further reading at the end of most profiles are also provided.

Anyone who tries to simplify international relations is not doing the subject proper justice and risks ignoring the subtleties and great variety of forces that influence the interplay among nations. However, I have attempted to make *Interdependence* as practical as possible, stressing basic points in a "real world" context and discussing the complex issues that confront the world in a clear and comprehensive manner.

We are living in a time of extraordinary change and new directions in world affairs, and, considering the regularity with which such change has been occurring, it would be impossible for any book on international relations to be up-to-the-minute, even if that were desirable. However, this textbook does take into account not only the landmark changes in Europe, as symbolized by the fall of the Berlin Wall and the unification of Germany, but also the collapse of Soviet communism, the 1991 Persian Gulf War and related events, and the seemingly contradictory trends of integration and disintegration at work in the world of the 1990s. These developments and analyses of their significance are incorporated throughout the book, leading up to the consideration in the concluding chapter of the future world order and of international issues for the twenty-first century.

This book is the product of many years of study, teaching, and involvement in international relations. My own interest in the subject began to intensify when, while an undergraduate at the University of Texas, I participated in a student exchange program at the University of Chile. Graduate study in France served to strengthen my interest. It was further intensified during my years of working, teaching, and writing in the field of international relations. I have been fortunate enough to travel to almost all of the countries discussed in this book and to spend lengthy periods in Africa, Asia, Europe, and Latin America.

The actual work on this book was done in a variety of locales. As befits a book on international relations, I worked in Germany, Costa Rica, Panama, and Britain. Additionally, sojourns in various parts of the United States have also been helpful. Time spent in Austin; Washington; Phoenix; San Francisco; and at Blue Mountain Lake, New York, was valuable in various ways. While I benefited from these brief changes of venue, I did most of the work at home in Fayetteville, Arkansas.

Appreciation and acknowledgment should go to numerous individuals and institutions, far too many to mention here.

In addition to my home base, the Fulbright Institute of International Relations at the University of Arkansas, institutions that have been supportive include the Foreign Ministry of the German Federal Republic; the Deutscher Akademischer Austauschdienst (German Academic Exchange Service); and the Instituto Centroamerico de Asuntos Internacionales (Central American Institute for International Affairs) in San Jose, Costa Rica. Special appreciation also goes to Harriet Barlow and the staff of the Blue Mountain Center.

Any acknowledgments must also include an expression of gratitude to J. William Fulbright and Robert C. Byrd for the opportunities they provided me in my years as a United States Senate staff member, and to my staff colleagues during those years. The experience I had working on international issues was invaluable.

I have also benefited from the many colleagues I have worked with over the years and from my students, who are a constant source of education. Specifically, in terms of the work on this book, I express appreciation to friends and colleagues Donald R. Kelley, Margaret Scranton, Kathy Hirsch, and Raymond Eichmann for their comments on sections of the manuscript. Additionally, I appreciate the helpful suggestions of the reviewers, notably Richard H. Foster of Idaho State University and James W. Peterson of Valdosta State College.

A number of individuals at Harcourt Brace Jovanovich deserve acknowledgment for their assistance, particularly Drake Bush, the editor with whom I originally discussed this book and who helped guide it to completion. Others at HBJ who were helpful in various ways include Don Fujimoto, Kay Kaylor, Julia Ross, Louise Sandy, David Tatom, and Mandy Van Dusen.

Special thanks go to everyone at the Fulbright Institute for all of the help and support I have received while working on this project. I am deeply indebted to Elizabeth (Betty) Skinner for her extremely valuable assistance in preparing this manuscript, and to Sivagami Natesan.

I also want to express special appreciation to Ellen Gilchrist for her interest and encouragement.

Finally, this book is dedicated to my daughters, Pamela and Camille. It is their generation that will be the primary audience for this book, and it will, I hope, significantly strengthen their generation's interest in and understanding of the world in which we live.

HOYT PURVIS

CONTENTS

Part II Global Issues and Concerns

PART I

Dimensions of the Contemporary World

CHAPTER ONE

Introduction: Linkage and Power in an Interdependent World

In the age of intercontinental nuclear weapons, the issues of war and peace, which are at the center of international relations, should be matters of concern to citizens of every nation. Much of the world's technological capability and a substantial portion of the world's resources are channeled into the development and production of increasingly sophisticated and powerful weapons and for other security-related purposes.

Critical as these issues are, many of the world's citizens may be more concerned with problems or conflicts that are much more immediate and tangible to them than the threat of nuclear war. The problems may be food shortages or even famine, or overcrowded or inadequate living conditions. Problems such as these may be exacerbated by or contribute to the political, ethnic, and religious conflicts that plague various regions of the world.

It may not be readily apparent to those who are caught up in these predicaments, but these conflicts and problems are often influenced by events in or actions by other nations, and, in turn, these issues almost always have international implications. For example, Vietnam, Nicaragua, and Afghanistan are all countries that have been torn by struggles which had international as well as domestic dimensions.

The reality in today's world is, as a former president of Mexico succinctly stated, "Everything is part of everything else."

This is true not only with problems, with conflict and turmoil, but with progress, with economic development and commerce.

The interconnections among the world's nations and peoples are increasingly obvious but frequently overlooked, even when they have very direct effects. There are many examples of these interconnections:

- A farmer in Iowa or the Canadian plains grows wheat that eventually is used for bread in Russia.
- Workers in a Japanese-owned plant in Mexico make television sets which are sold in the United States.
- A Venezuelan watches an American-made movie, dubbed in Spanish, on a video recorder manufactured in Korea.
- A Frenchman at a sidewalk cafe in Paris drinks coffee or cocoa that came from crops in the Ivory Coast or Brazil.
- Using a computer made in Germany, an Italian government worker communicates with her colleagues at the European Economic Community (Common Market) headquarters in Brussels.
- A Philippine airline, using American-made planes, transports a Chinese official to London to discuss selling clothes made in China to British stores.
- Oil from Saudi Arabia is used for the fuel which enables a Dutch ship captain to drive his Japanese car to the port of Rotterdam so he can sail his cargo ship of electronic equipment and chemicals to Greece and North Africa and return with a load of bauxite, lignite, or iron ore.
- A customer interested in doing business with the world's largest companies might order clothes from a United States firm—the largest apparel maker is Levi Strauss—but the materials could well come from Japan, which has the three top textile makers. Planning a dinner party? The food and beverages could come from United States companies, but Unilever, a British-Dutch company, produces Lipton Tea and Ragu spaghetti sauce, Nestle (Swiss) makes chocolates, and Grand Metropolitan, another British company, owns Pillsbury and Burger King. For music at the party, Yamaha (Japan) is the world's largest piano company.
- A study of the components of a European Ford Escort car, assembled in either Britain or Germany, indicated that parts could come from as many as 15 different countries, including, for example, cylinder head from Italy, heater hose from Austria, speedometer from Switzerland, brakes from France, fan belt from Denmark, tires from Belgium, and starter from Japan.

Obviously, these are merely a few examples of the international connections.

Consider also factors and real and potential developments such as these:

- Following the disaster at the nuclear power plant in Chernobyl in the Soviet Union, radiation emissions reached a number of countries, offering a dramatic demonstration of how meaningless national boundaries are in such circumstances. It was also a vivid reminder of the devastating effects that even a small nuclear weapon could have.

- Many Third World (sometimes called less-developed or developing) countries borrowed large amounts from Western financial institutions to finance development projects in their countries. When there was an international economic downturn, many of the Third World nations could not meet their repayment obligations. Not only did this cause problems for those who made the loans, but, because of the debt problem, Third World nations reduced their purchases of products from the industrialized countries. Since debtor nations had to devote nearly all of their export earnings to servicing debt (paying interest), they were unable to continue importing goods from abroad. Overall, the debt problem affected citizens of many nations. In the United States, not only did it affect many in banking and finance but it also had an impact on many others whose livelihood was tied to exports, including farmers and a variety of manufacturers.

- Terrorists hijack an airliner in a location or for a cause that may seem relatively obscure to those who are victimized, or to the millions around the world who watch news of the events on television, including live, on-the-spot coverage from the airport where the airliner and its passengers are held. Because of the technological capabilities of modern communication, news of such events can have an almost instantaneous impact in many nations.

- Arms are sold by one nation to another, and the recipient nation then uses them against a third nation, which is an ally of the nation that originally sold the weapons.

- The datelines of the news stories that make headlines shift from one region to another, sometimes reading like destinations on a round-the-world flight itinerary. Ethiopia, Argentina, Iran, Korea, New Zealand, Uganda, Poland, Iraq, and Sweden have all been the subjects of major news stories in recent years.

- The Middle East and Persian Gulf region has 60 percent of the world's oil reserves, but only 4 percent of the world's population. Many countries outside the region—Japan being a notable example—are heavily dependent on Middle Eastern oil. On the other hand, many of the oil-exporting countries rely on imports for much of their food.

- Airborne pollutants from industrial plants are easily carried beyond national boundary lines; for example, "acid rain" (or acid deposition) has been a subject of friction between the United States and Canada. Toxic waste after a chemical fire in Switzerland resulted in major problems downstream on the Rhine river in Germany and the Netherlands. A slogan used by some environmentalists, "Everyone lives downstream," has a definite ring of truth in today's world.

■ A group of refugees from Sri Lanka, who had fled their country because they claimed they were being persecuted, arrived in Canada after being transported on a West German ship. There have been a number of instances of "boat people" escaping oppression or political turmoil in various countries. In recent years the United States has drawn political refugees from many countries, including Vietnam, Cambodia, Cuba, and El Salvador.

■ Ethnic and religious conflicts can spill across national borders. In past centuries there were major religious wars. Late in the twentieth century, there were still conflicts, for example, between Muslims and Hindus in Asia or between Sunni and Shiite Muslims in the Near East.

Six nations have confirmed that they have successfully exploded nuclear devices—the United States (1945), the Soviet Union (1949), Britain (1952), France (1960), the People's Republic of China (1964), and India (1974). Others—including Israel, South Africa, and Pakistan—are believed to have nuclear capability or the ability to attain it. Still other countries would like to acquire nuclear weapons or may attempt to cross the nuclear threshold. The proliferation of nuclear weapons makes international relations less predictable and almost certainly more dangerous. The acquisition of nuclear weapons by unstable regimes could add a new and perilous dimension to international relations.

In a number of ways the nations of the world are increasingly linked together. Technological breakthroughs, such as satellite communications, point toward further diminution of barriers between nations. However, despite these transnational influences, divisions persist within and among nations, and localized conflicts can rapidly escalate and draw in other nations. Studies have indicated that wars waged to regain lost territory and revolutions undertaken by ethnic minorities in the interest of self-determination have accounted for 70 percent of all international conflicts. Military spending and the development and acquisition of weapons has continued unabated, and the total annual expenditure of all countries for weapons has climbed toward the $1 trillion mark.

NATION-STATES AND INTERCONNECTIONS

Regional groupings are becoming more important in world affairs, especially in an economic sense, and some of the trends discussed earlier in this chapter are rendering national boundaries less meaningful than in the past. Nonetheless, the nation-state system provides the basis for the structure and organization of the contemporary world. And, as will be discussed in following chapters, nationalism is one of the most powerful forces at work in international relations. Yet, it is important to understand that not all nations developed from natural groupings of peoples. Many nations are amalgamations of different ethnic or tribal groups. Where ethnic or tribal loyalties do not coincide with political lines on a map, nationalism is often a troublesome factor.

In some instances national boundary lines were drawn in an arbitrary fashion and resulted from conquest by forces from another continent. In 1884, the great powers of Europe met at the Berlin Conference to agree on the partitioning of Africa. The boundaries of African nations, as drawn by Europeans, did not necessarily enclose communities with common history and ties.

Boundaries for some Middle East nations have also resulted from lines drawn on a map by outside powers. A critic said that boundaries were created by the "spiteful pencil and scissors of imperialism." According to one story, Winston Churchill of Britain was drawing Jordan's eastern border with Saudi Arabia when his elbow was jogged, resulting in an angular jut in the desert boundary known as "Winston's Elbow." A further problem resulted when some of the colonial empires collapsed in the Middle East and elsewhere and they left behind nation-states in which the dominant ethnic groups suppressed or ignored minorities.

The Kurds—spread across Turkey, Iran, Iraq, Syria, and the Soviet Union—are one of a number of distinct peoples left without a nation-state of their own following the collapse of the Ottoman and British Empires in the region.

THE EXAMPLE OF LEBANON

A notable example of arbitrary borders is Lebanon, which has been one of the world's most troubled nations in recent years. The case of Lebanon illustrates a number of important points about conflicts in today's world and the interconnections among nations.

At the end of World War I, the winning British and French divided the Arab lands of the defeated Germany's ally, the Ottoman (Turkish) empire. Under a League of Nations mandate, the territory which now comprises Syria and Lebanon was placed under French control. Lebanon, as designed by the French, was made up of a bewildering array of religious and cultural communities combined into one "nation." In 1943, Lebanon declared itself independent of France, and power was divided among six major religious groups—three of them Christian and three Moslem. But the attempted balance of so many ethnic and religious groups resulted in an extremely fragile political structure. The precarious balance was jeopardized by the insistence of some Muslim groups that, since they had become the majority of the population, they should have greater political power. Further tension resulted from the conflict between traditionalism and modernism, a conflict that also could be seen in Iran and a number of Third World countries. Beirut, the capital city, had become a center of international banking and business and tourism, but much of the population had its roots in the rural life of the country and was alienated from the more cosmopolitan life of the urban elite.

Still greater strains were placed on Lebanon by the influx of tens of thousands of Palestinians after the Arab-Israeli wars, and gradually Lebanon was drawn into the regional conflict. Some of the Palestinians used Lebanon as a base to attack Israel, and this invited reprisal from Israel. In the early 1970s the Palestine Liberation Organization (PLO) was expelled from Jordan by King Hussein, and some of its leaders relocated in Lebanon. Armed Palestinian groups came into conflict with Lebanese militias, and the situation gradually deteriorated into civil war and anarchy. By 1977, much of the country was in ruins and foreign or foreign-supported forces dominated various sections. Syria controlled one area; Israeli-supported forces dominated another; and the PLO had its strongholds. In 1978, Israel sent a large force into southern Lebanon in response to a series of PLO raids. The United Nations, which had long been struggling with the problems of the Middle East, managed to get agreement on establishment of a United Nations multination "peace-keeping" force in Lebanon. Although the United Nations force did provide a buffer between the various contending factions, it did not end hostilities.

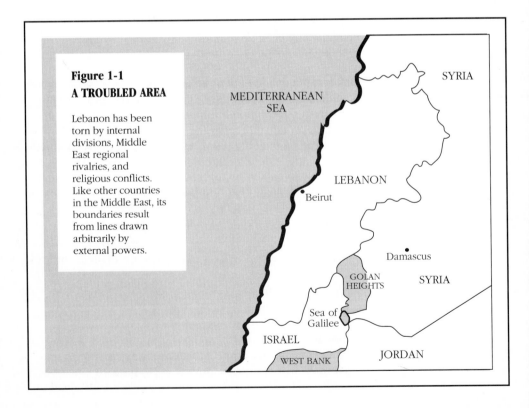

Figure 1-1
A TROUBLED AREA

Lebanon has been torn by internal divisions, Middle East regional rivalries, and religious conflicts. Like other countries in the Middle East, its boundaries result from lines drawn arbitrarily by external powers.

Attempts to mediate a settlement in Lebanon continued, including an effort undertaken by the United States. But tensions remained high, and there were several instances of PLO shelling of northern Israel and Israeli retaliation. Then on June 3, 1982, an incident in London set in motion a new and bloodier round of fighting in Lebanon. The Israeli ambassador to Britain was shot and critically wounded and, in response to what it believed to be a PLO−inspired assassination attempt, Israel launched heavy air strikes against PLO targets in Beirut and in southern Lebanon. (Those involved in the London attack were apparently trained in Iraq, part of a Palestinian faction opposed to the PLO, and supported by Libya and Syria.) The PLO, in turn, shelled towns and villages in northern Israel. The next step was a major invasion of Lebanon by Israel.

At the time of the explosive events in Lebanon, the international stage was already crowded. Argentina and Britain were locked in an improbable but bloody war over control of the Falkland (or Malvinas) Islands in the South Atlantic off the Argentine coast. When the Israeli invasion was launched, many international leaders were preoccupied with the Falklands war, and heads of the major industrial democracies were in France, attending the annual economic summit meeting.

Initially, Israel's stated goal was to clear out PLO forces located close to the Israeli border. But the Israelis pushed on, driving all the way to Beirut. In some of the heaviest fighting in the history of air warfare, Israel (using American-supplied planes) shot down dozens of Syrian jets (supplied by the Soviet Union) and attacked antiaircraft missile batteries. Israel also kept the pressure on the PLO command in Beirut, until finally the PLO agreed to leave Lebanon.

The PLO withdrawal, supervised by an international force, hardly brought an end to the troubles in Lebanon. Within a few days, the newly elected president of Lebanon had been assassinated, and hundreds of Palestinian refugees were massacred by the Lebanese Christian militia. The international outcry over the massacre resulted in a return of a multinational force, including a contingent of United States Marines, and troops from Britain, Italy, and France, to try to bring some stability to Lebanon. Efforts to resolve the multifaceted problems in Lebanon made little headway, and increasingly the Americans were drawn into the conflict. There was a devastating attack on the United States Embassy, and later 241 Marines were killed in a truck-bomb attack on their compound. A similar attack on French forces killed 59. Within months afterwards, the multinational force had withdrawn. Neighboring Syria assumed a more important role in Lebanon, but the situation became even more labyrinthine. There were a number of contending forces and groups which controlled various regions.

Again and again in the twentieth century change burst upon the Middle East, dividing it along new lines of ideology, alliance, or religion. Colonial rule was replaced by shifting Cold War loyalties; republicans vied with monarchs; Islamic fundamentalists with modernizers; and often the region was divided against itself, as in the Gulf War. (The problems of the Middle East are discussed further in Chapter 7.)

TERRORISM AND ARMS SALES

Lebanon was also at the center of a series of terrorist and hostage-taking episodes with international implications. In June 1985, there was a highly publicized event involving an American-owned airliner (Trans World Airlines) which was hijacked by radical Shiite Muslims while on a flight from Athens to Rome. The hijackers eventually demanded that the plane be taken to Beirut. Some of the passengers were released at Beirut, but one American was killed and 39 Americans spent 17 days in captivity. The saga of the TWA plane and the hostages was the subject of intensive international media coverage, with video, photographs, and news reports transmitted around the world.

The radicalized Shiites in Lebanon, encouraged by coreligionists in Iran, were also believed to be involved in several episodes in which foreign hostages were taken, including Germans, French, and British, as well as American. In some cases those taking the hostages tied their actions to demands for the release of prisoners being held in other countries for terrorist actions.

The holding of American hostages by groups in Lebanon believed to have connections with Iran was a factor in the decision by the Reagan White House to sell arms to Iran, hoping to gain release of the hostages. The major stated rationale for selling American weapons to Iran in 1985–86 was to keep the United States competitive with the Soviet Union in a battle for influence with those who might gain power in Iran after Ayatollah Khomeini. In yet another international twist, some of the profits from the arms sales to Iran were used to help fund the "*contra*" forces fighting against the Sandinista-controlled government in Nicaragua.

Iran was badly in need of military equipment to pursue its lengthy war against Iraq during the 1980s. Not only was that war extremely costly to the participating nations in both human and material terms, but it represented a threat to regional stability in the Persian Gulf area. Many nations around the world, including Japan and much of Western Europe, are heavily dependent upon oil from the Persian Gulf region. Both Iran and Iraq found direct or indirect support from a number of countries, as well as individual arms dealers. Later, Iraq used some of the weapons and military strength it acquired in a bid for greater regional power, a move that again threatened the world's oil supply. Some of the nations that earlier directly or indirectly aided Iraq were part of the coalition of nations arrayed against Iraq in 1990–91.

CHAIN LINKAGE

The chain of events and developments growing out of and related to the problems in Lebanon, a nation of only 3 million people, provide a tragic example of how events in one nation can affect others, and of how strongly interconnected international relations can be. With so many nations becoming involved in or affected by the spiraling series of developments arising out of the problems in Lebanon and neighboring Middle East nations, this experience serves as a classic illustration of the phenomenon of *chain linkage* in today's world.

Chain linkage can also be seen when the policies or actions of one nation toward another or on a particular issue, have a major bearing on relations with other nations.

"Politics everywhere, it would seem, are related to politics everywhere else," wrote James N. Rosenau, one of the first to focus attention on such linkages and the convergence of national and international systems. "Where the functioning of any political unit was once sustained by structures within its boundaries, now the roots of its political life can be traced to remote corners of the globe," said Rosenau. "Modern science and technology have collapsed space and time in the physical world and thereby heightened interdependence in the political world."[1]

Obviously, nations have always had power and ability to affect others. But in today's world of complex interrelationships, there can be so many more dimensions and ramifications to a nation's actions or policies. There are a variety of ways in which one nation's actions (or inactions) can have an impact on others—and a variety of sources of power and influence which a nation can employ, directly or indirectly. Military power, economic power, and resource power are only the most obvious sources of potential strength or influence in international relations. Geopolitical factors can also be important. (The concept of geopolitics will be discussed in Chapter 3.) The location of a country, its proximity to other countries or to key strategic areas can become important considerations in the foreign policies of other nations, particularly the great powers.

Asian Chain Reaction

In 1979, the Soviet Union invaded Afghanistan, which borders the Soviet Union on the south. The Soviets did not want to risk a potentially hostile or troublesome government in a neighboring country. One element of the United States' response to this action was to attempt to strengthen ties with Pakistan. Located adjacent to Afghanistan, Pakistan was seen by the United States as attaining increased geopolitical importance. American aid to Pakistan, particularly military assistance, was vastly increased. (Initially, Pakistan's leaders rejected a proposed aid package as "peanuts.") Although the United States had long been accused of "tilting" toward Pakistan in Pakistan's ongoing rivalry with India, relations between the United States and Pakistan had often been strained. (Pakistan was established as a nation in 1947; it had been part of the former British Indian Empire. When India gained independence from Britain, Pakistan became a separate, predominantly Muslim nation, while India was Hindu-dominated. Still later, the Bengalis of East Pakistan, encouraged and aided

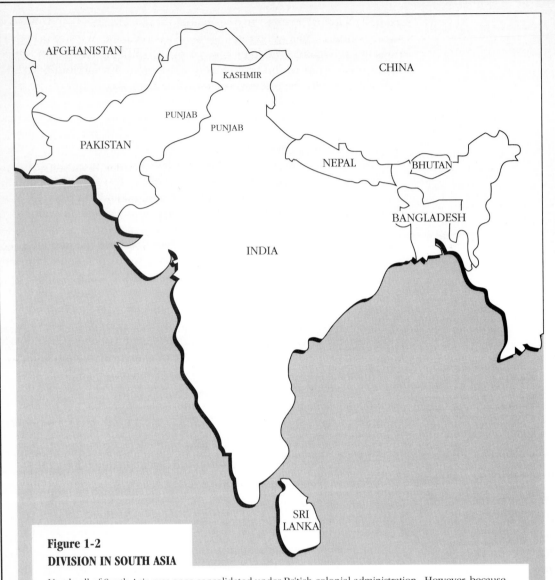

Figure 1-2
DIVISION IN SOUTH ASIA

Nearly all of South Asia was once consolidated under British colonial administration. However, because no agreement could be reached on unified independence, the subcontinent was partitioned. Pakistan was established as a separate, predominantly Muslim nation in 1947, breaking away from India, predominantly Hindu. In 1971 Bangladesh (formerly East Pakistan) became independent with India's support. Pakistan and India have often been at odds; three wars were fought in the years after independence. There have been a variety of continuing disputes about territorial claims. Additionally, a number of ethnic conflicts have kept tensions high in the region, which is one of the world's most heavily populated. Kashmir and the Punjab area in the north and northeast have been especially troublesome. Sri Lanka has also been torn by communal strife, with major implications for India. There have also been boundary disputes between China and India.

by India, succeeded in breaking away to form a third country, Bangladesh.) Just a few months before the United States stepped up aid to Pakistan in 1980, a mob had stormed and burned the American embassy in Pakistan. That incident, which came on the heels of the takeover by Iranian militants of the American embassy in Teheran, was set off by erroneous radio reports that Americans were involved in an attack on a religious site in the Muslim holy city of Mecca in Saudi Arabia.

Providing military aid to Pakistan further complicated United States relations with India. Much larger than Pakistan, India is an important country, second only to China in population, and a democracy with many common interests with the United States. However, India had tended to look to Moscow for some of its military equipment, and in 1971 signed a defense treaty with the Soviets. Moreover, India viewed the United States as having usually sided with Pakistan in conflicts between the two South Asian countries. After the Soviet invasion of Afghanistan, India was one of the few countries that was not critical of the Soviets, although India did eventually direct some criticisms toward the Soviet presence in Afghanistan.

There are still further dimensions to these geopolitical gyrations. One reason for the development of closer ties between the Soviet Union and India was that following a split between the Soviets and China, which began to develop in the late 1950s, India became of increasing importance to Moscow. The Soviets were supportive of India in its conflicts with Pakistan and China. The communist government in China has had close relations with Pakistan, and Pakistan served as an intermediary when China and the United States moved toward reopening relations in the 1970s.

These examples of chain linkage and geopolitical considerations and influences offer further indications of how actions or policies by one nation toward another can have ramifications for other nations and for relations between other nations.

NATIONAL INTERESTS AND INTERDEPENDENCE

It is important to remember that each nation has its own priorities and interests (the concept of national interests will come up repeatedly in this book) and its own agenda, and often these will not coincide with and may be in conflict with those of other nations. Likewise, each nation's policies are influenced by the national heritage, by history and culture.

However, nations cannot live in isolation. This is true not just because of the reach of technology, communications, and transportation in the modern world, or because modern weaponry renders every nation potentially vulnerable, but because most countries cannot exist as self-contained units. Dependency on oil has created a vulnerability in many nations to disruptions in the international oil supply. It is not just that goods and resources are needed from other countries; many nations are also dependent upon their ability to export commodities and products—selling to other countries in order to sustain their own economies. For example, developing countries need to export so that they can obtain the foreign exchange to buy equipment and technology needed to help spur their economic advancement.

Trade: Domestic and International Policies

Domestic political pressures in some of the highly industrialized countries often lead to a push for protectionist policies, and some of the rising industrial powers have used direct and indirect forms of protectionism to shield their developing industries. Protectionism involves the use of tariffs (taxes on imports), quotas, preferential tax treatment, or other means of reducing imports and giving an advantage to domestic producers.

In the 1930s, in response to depressed economic conditions, many nations raised their tariffs, which, in turn, had the effect of deepening the international depression, demonstrating world economic interdependence. By resorting to "beggar-thy-neighbor" policies in an attempt to protect their own economies, nations actually undermined the global economy. The fallout from this deterioration of the international economy contributed to the rise of Nazism in Germany and militarism and expansionism in Japan and helped bring on World War II.

After World War II, the General Agreement on Tariffs and Trade (GATT) was established, a sort of international code of commercial conduct subscribed to by the United States and most other nations. (Chapters 9 and 10 provide a detailed look at international trade issues.) Most other nations generally express support for the concept of international "free trade," consistent with the principles of GATT. However, workers, management, and owners of industries adversely affected by imports may bring considerable pressure for protectionist action, aimed at protecting their jobs and investments. In the United States, for example, there have been calls for protectionist measures for textiles, shoes, electronics, and automobiles, all threatened by import competition. Some United States political and labor leaders opposed the United States–Mexico (North American) free-trade agreement because they said it would result in many United States workers losing their jobs. Lower wages in Mexico, it was said, would mean that more companies would set up factories in Mexico. Proponents of the agreement said it would help both nations; making Mexico more prosperous would, in turn, mean more good jobs in the United States, as Mexico would be able to buy more United States products. This situation is symptomatic of a world in which individual nations depend, for their prosperity, upon the prosperity of others to a much greater degree than in the past.

Trade policies can have a clear and direct effect on the lives of a nation's citizens; thus, domestic considerations may become an important factor in a nation's international economic policies. By no means are economic affairs the only area of international relations where domestic political considerations can be significant factors in shaping foreign policy.

National Political Factors

It is not at all unusual for national political leaders to take international actions in order to shore up their positions at home or to divert attention from domestic problems. Frequently, at least in the short term, citizens will tend to rally around their national leaders when the nation is perceived to be involved in an international crisis or threatened by other nations. Nationalism can be a very powerful force in such cases.

When Argentina invaded the Falklands (Malvinas) in 1982, the generals who were ruling Argentina were facing mounting problems at home, with increasing economic difficulties and political discontent. British control of the islands had long been a sore point with Argentina, and a successful takeover would probably have strengthened the shaky position of the Argentine leaders. However, they may have failed to take British nationalism into account. For British Prime Minister Margaret Thatcher, it was an opportunity to assert Britain's resolve and to demonstrate her own toughness.

Beginning in the late 1960s, representatives of the United States and the Soviet Union spent considerable time discussing and negotiating arms control issues. The timing of and support for such agreements owed much to the domestic political environment in each of the countries, environments subject to influence by a variety of matters outside the realm of bilateral relations. Another important factor influencing such agreements has been the political climate in Western Europe, where the United States and Soviets were long engaged in a continuing public relations competition to attempt to sway European opinion. As relations improved between the major military powers, arms control issues became less dominant in bilateral relations and Russian and American leaders found economic issues and matters originating in Europe and elsewhere dominating their attention in summit meetings and high-level discussions.

As noted earlier, each nation has its "agenda" and priorities and those agendas and priorities can be revised due to a variety of domestic and international factors. As will be discussed in Chapter 4, although domestic political considerations and national political factors can significantly affect a nation's foreign policy, in today's interdependent world it becomes increasingly difficult to separate domestic and international influences and interests. South Africa and its racial policies became a more important issue in the United States after organized protests in this country and intensive media attention helped push the subject of United States policy on South Africa onto the national political agenda. Another important consideration when it comes to American policies on South Africa is the attitude of other African nations. Some of the African countries have conditioned their relations with the United States and other non-African nations on the policies of those nations on issues related to South Africa.

A new kind of linkage developed in the 1980s and was evident in Latin America and most dramatically in Eastern Europe. As one nation achieved greater political liberty, this brought pressure for similar change in nearby nations. Modern communications, as discussed in Chapter 12, contributed significantly to this momentum for change.

THE TRIANGULAR RELATIONSHIP: SHIFTING POWER AND PERCEPTIONS

National interests and priorities are not static, and as one nation's perceptions of its interests shift, or as domestic political tides turn, changes in its foreign policies may well affect perceptions and policies in other nations. One of the most significant and fascinating examples of these shifts can be seen in the triangular relationship between China, the Soviet Union, and the United States.

For some years after the communists took power and established the People's Republic of China (P.R.C.) in 1949, the United States had no relations with the communist government. Instead, the United States recognized the government set up on the island of Taiwan by Chiang Kai-shek and some of his Nationalist colleagues after they had fled the mainland. There were "two Chinas," and the United States recognized the Taiwan government as the "official" government of China. Here was another example of domestic political considerations influencing foreign policy. Strong political forces in the United States opposed any relations with the mainland government, and feelings grew stronger when the United States and the People's Republic of China fought on opposite sides in the Korean War in the early 1950s. There was an assumption in Washington that the Chinese Communists were closely aligned with the Soviet Union and that they presented a united, monolithic communist front. However, as noted earlier, there was a break between the two communist giants, which was becoming evident by the early 1960s, shattering the notion of monolithic communism. The United States was slow to comprehend or accept that such a rift had truly occurred. Sino-American relations, although relatively close at times, have been plagued by misperceptions at many points in history. As John Stoessinger has written, "For an entire generation, two great nations perceived each other through dark screens that often produced caricatures out of realities. They learned to fashion images that were based upon their deepest fears." [2]

In the 1960s, United States officials depicted American involvement in Vietnam as necessary to stop Chinese efforts to take over Southeast Asia, with China being seen, in effect, as a Soviet agent. That assessment overlooked not only the civil component of the struggle in Vietnam but the growing differences between Moscow and Beijing, and the historic antipathy between China and Vietnam.

As the United States and the Soviet Union competed for influence in the Third World countries of Asia, Africa, and Latin America, China sought to identify itself with the Third World and to become a leader of the so-called "nonaligned nations," those in neither the Soviet nor American camps. In 1964, China had exploded its first nuclear device, a further indication of its independence and significance on the world scene. However, beginning in the late 1960s, China's attention was almost exclusively turned inward for a time, as the country went through the upheaval of the Cultural Revolution, which was, in part, aimed at reducing all foreign influences within the country. (A somewhat comparable development occurred in Iran a decade later when one of the goals of the Islamic fundamentalists who led the revolution there was to rid the country of Western influences.) As the Cultural Revolution got underway in China, the government called home most of its ambassadors, stopping diplomatic contact with much of the world. But, within a few years, Chinese diplomacy took a sharp turn in another direction. After a long period of antagonism, China and the United States moved toward reconciliation, as dramatized by President Richard Nixon's visit to China in 1972.

China's Changes

An important factor in China's motivation for the turnabout in relations with the United States was its concern about what it referred to as Soviet *hegemony* (attempts by one state to dominate or exercise control over another). Historic differences and tensions between China and the Soviet Union resurfaced, and there was a series of border clashes. The 1968 Soviet invasion of Czechoslovakia, another communist state, heightened China's fear of the Soviets.

The end of the war in Vietnam in 1975 and of the United States role there was followed by open hostility between China and Vietnam, which had become an ally of the Soviets. China and Vietnam had been traditional antagonists, but that had been forgotten during the years of American involvement in Vietnam. In 1978, after the war, the reunified Vietnam, with support from the Soviets, overran Cambodia, China's ally. Chinese troops invaded northern Vietnam early in 1979 "to teach Vietnam a lesson," although the brief war was inconclusive. When the Soviet Union invaded Afghanistan late in 1979, this strengthened Chinese opposition to the Soviets, and contributed to closer Sino-American relations. China also joined with its long-time friend, Pakistan, in serving as a source of aid to Afghan rebels.

For a time, the United States and the Chinese (mostly the United States) spoke of a "strategic relationship," and there was some military cooperation between the two nations. In the early years of the Reagan Administration, a strongly anti-Soviet policy helped push President Reagan toward a more cooperative relationship with China, a country he had once condemned.

China was particularly interested in obtaining advanced technology from the United States and from other nations in order to assist in modernizing its economy. The Chinese learned of the problems that result when a nation attempts to close itself off from the world, as China had done for some time. Zhao Ziyang, one of the new generation of Chinese leaders who favored an "open door" policy for the nation, said, "We are still at a quite backward stage because we lost too much time in the past. Closing one's country to external contacts results only in increasing backwardness."

Although China and the United States continued to have good relations, the Chinese resisted being drawn too close to the Americans. China sought to cast itself in a more independent role once again, not becoming too dependent on any one country, and gradually adopting a less-rigid posture toward the Soviets.

However, in 1989, when China's relations with the United States were steadily expanding and contacts with the Soviets were increasing, the repression of the "pro-democracy" reform movement by the Chinese leadership was widely criticized in the West and put a damper on China's international relations. Zhao Ziyang, who had been a leader in China's economic reform effort, was forced from power, but the Chinese leadership sought to maintain its international economic ties. (China's policies and leaders are discussed in the Profile: "Mao Zedong, Deng Xiaoping, and China.")

Although China had a history of upheavals in the twentieth century, including the Cultural Revolution of the late 1960s and early 1970s and some examples of brutal government repression, the country had often been isolated from the rest of the world. Those earlier events were not heavily reported by the world press, and there were relatively few eyewitness accounts by foreign correspondents. In 1989, China was much less isolated, and advanced telecommunications technology resulted in news and images of developments in China being transmitted instantaneously around the world. In effect, the whole world was watching when the government cracked down on the protesters. This was another example of how telecommunications can affect international relations in today's world, a subject which is discussed at length in Chapter 12. International public reaction to the events in China was so strong that many governments were compelled to condemn the Chinese government, and some restricted official relations or took other actions, such as imposing trade or aid restrictions.

A Complex Triangle

Meanwhile, the United States and the Soviets had been improving relations, a trend that began in the final years of the Reagan presidency. The superpowers were moving away from the Cold War–like harshness, which marked the first Reagan years, toward a relationship closer to the *détente* (relaxed tensions), which had characterized the 1970s.

As relations in the United States–Russia–China triangle have gone through these complex shifts, each has tried to gain the pivotal position, each has tried to be the balancer. American officials and analysts, for example, spoke of "playing the China card," by which they meant that the United States could exploit the Sino-Soviet split and help end Sino-American hostility by taking advantage of the common adversarial relationship with the Soviets. The "China card" was also intended to help moderate Soviet international behavior. Another way of looking at the United States policy was to see it as an effort to strike a balancing position between the two communist powers, giving each of them a greater stake in better relations with the United States.

This triangular relationship provides an illustration of what is sometimes referred to as a tripolar international system. Another form of tripolar system is the distribution of international economic power in which the United States, Japan, and Western Europe are the three dominant powers. Seeing the world in tripolar terms is only one of a number of ways of conceptualizing international relations, as will be explored in Chapter 3.

In more specific terms, the policy shifts by China and the United States can be seen as illustrating how nations act to advance their perceived interests, even when it means overlooking previous differences or ideological conflicts. This could be described as an example of realistic power politics or *realpolitik*. The United States came to view China—despite major policy differences between the two—as making a positive contribution to balancing world power. When China's government cracked down on the prodemocracy movement in 1989 and maintained a hard line against expressions of domestic opposition, there was pressure from the United States Congress to impose severe limitations on United States–China relations. However, President George Bush, backed by some leading foreign policy analysts, resisted this, believing that the United States should keep channels of communication with China open and not push to a breaking point with Beijing. Bush emphasized China's geopolitical importance and took what could be considered a "realist" rather than an "idealist" approach.

POWER, CONFLICT, AND INTERCONNECTIONS

Viewing the world in balance-of-power terms is one of the basic approaches to studying and conceptualizing international relations. Late in the twentieth century, most agree that a *multipolar* system is developing, a system in which the United States, Russia, China, Japan, and the major European countries all constitute important forces in the world. Under certain circumstances, nations rich in a particular resource, such as oil, can exercise considerable power as well, especially when they join forces. There are, in fact, several fulcrums of power and influence in the modern world, the most significant being economic, political, and, of course, military. The rise of new economic powers such as Japan and Germany has added a new dimension to world politics. However, the rivalry between the United States and the Soviet Union was long at the forefront of world affairs, especially because of the massive military strength of the two superpowers.

During the Cold War period, the rivalry between the military superpowers cast a long shadow. There was a tendency to view almost everything that happened in international relations in recent decades in terms of the superpower rivalry. The competition between the United States and the Soviet Union permeated world affairs. Throughout the Cold War period this rivalry constituted a fundamental conflict underlying international relations, in many respects not just a conflict between two nations, but an ideological conflict between communism and capitalism, sometimes called the East-West conflict. This conflict, in turn, has been a factor not only in regional clashes discussed in Chapter 7 (in such areas as Southeast Asia, the Middle East, Central America, and Southern Africa) that have plagued the world but has also had an influence on or become entangled in other basic conflicts that underlie international affairs.

The movement in the late 1980s away from communism and toward more democratic governments and market economies reduced the old East-West rivalry and intensified the move in the direction of multipolarism rather than bipolarism in the world's power balance. The balance of power has become more subtle, and economic power is an increasingly significant factor in global affairs. The dollar (North America), the Deutsche mark (Germany and Europe), and the yen (Japan) symbolize this emerging economically based power balance.

Although the need for economic cooperation across borders has given impetus to more *integration* among nations, especially on the regional scale, the seemingly contradictory trend of *disintegration* is also at work. The weakening or collapse of communism helped unbridle nationalist aspirations in certain areas, and some former political entities have broken up. Some of the old, artificial countries are being pulled apart as smaller governmental units come together in supranational organizations, driven by the reality of economic interdependence.

The end of the Cold War and the push for greater economic and political freedom have brought new dimensions to international relations, but even though the Cold War rivalry and conflicts have dissipated, other basic conflicts still underlie international affairs. These conflicts are:

■ **The Haves vs. the Have-Nots.**   Sometimes seen as a North vs. South conflict (referring to the generally richer nations of the Northern hemisphere and the generally poorer countries of the Southern hemisphere), this conflict basically revolves around economic issues and the disparities between rich and poor nations, discussed in detail in Chapters 10 and 11.

■**Imperialism vs. Nationalism.**   Although the colonial era has formally ended, and the forces of nationalism have scored victories in many battles for national independence, the issue of dependence and external dominance remain important in world politics. In the Third World, many believe that we are in an era of neocolonialism and neoimperialism, that the more powerful nations exert undue influence over the less-developed countries. Meanwhile, arbitrary borders sometimes left behind by collapsed empires or colonial powers have often been the source of long-held grievances, which at times erupt in nationalist fervor with international impact.

■**Traditionalism vs. Modernization.**   This is the social and cultural component of this set of conflicts. The advances in transportation and communications capabilities that have tied the world more closely have in some cases exacerbated problems in developing countries, where external cultural influences may collide with traditional life styles. The growing urbanization of the world also contributes to this schism. Resistance to modern intrusions may have a religious base, such as in Iran, and this resistance may be manifested in civil conflict, as well as in a xenophobic attitude (fear or distrust of foreigners).

All of these interrelated points of conflict and contention have been referred to in this chapter and will be discussed at length in the following chapters. They are all sources of instability or potential instability and, in an interdependent world, these issues inevitably have international implications. There are more than 160 sovereign nations in the world, and the actions of any one of them can have meaning for all of us.

NOTES

1. James N. Rosenau (ed.), *Linkage Politics* (New York: The Free Press, 1969), p. 2.
2. John G. Stoessinger, *Nations in Darkness*, 4th ed., (New York: Random House, 1986), p. 93.

CHAPTER TWO

The Framework of International Relations

World War II was a cataclysmic period in world affairs. From 1939 to 1945, at various times and in various ways, many of the world's nations and peoples were caught up in the war. Europe, including the Soviet Union, and the Pacific were the primary theaters of war, but there was also heavy fighting in Asia and North Africa. A number of nations that were not themselves scenes of major battles were, nonetheless, drawn into the fighting.

The war in Europe ended in May 1945 with the surrender of Nazi Germany. Following the dropping of the atomic bomb by the United States on the Japanese cities of Hiroshima and Nagasaki in August 1945, Japan surrendered on September 2, 1945, bringing World War II to an end.

The world that emerged after the war was to be vastly different from the world that existed prior to 1939. The once-powerful European states, which had dominated international affairs for years, were seriously weakened and no longer at the apex of the international power structure. The ending of World War II opened the curtains on a new international scene, which was to bring new trends, new forces, new powers, and new rivalries into place. A new framework of international organizations, institutions, and arrangements came into being. The developments during the final stages of the war and the years immediately after have had a major impact on the evolution of international affairs in the decades since.

To understand the world and the international structures that emerged from World War II, it is necessary to understand some of the history, some of the events and forces that went before.

There has been an established pattern, in the aftermath of past wars, of efforts to create structures of international order and to prevent further wars, as will be seen by reviewing some of the major developments of the past 350 years.

THE PEACE OF WESTPHALIA AND THE STATE SYSTEM

The agreements which were known as the Peace of Westphalia in 1648 marked the end of the devastating Thirty Years War in Europe and inaugurated the modern European state system and the framework of an international system of nation states. It also marked the end of the era of religious warfare and of the Holy Roman Empire as an effective institution.

The chief participants in the Westphalia negotiations were the allies, Sweden and France, and their opponents, Spain, the Holy Roman Empire and the various parts of the empire, together with the newly independent Netherlands. France emerged as the more dominant power, and although sovereignty of the German states was recognized, the agreements were generally disadvantageous to Germany. Sovereignty, which involved the primacy of the state over its territory, was becoming an increasingly important concept. The various monarchies of the time agreed to honor each other's sovereignty over their respective territories. The Peace of Westphalia was supposed to be upheld by shifting alliances among the various European dynasties, which created a sort of incipient balance of power, and it was a forerunner of subsequent agreements which are discussed in this chapter.

The Peace of Westphalia did not, of course, bring lasting peace to Europe. It did reduce sources of potential conflict, but, periodically, ambitious national leaders would still seek to extend their dominance across the continent. And, although the Peace of Westphalia is generally credited as marking the beginning of the modern state system and the present system of international politics, Europe was still evolving into a real pattern of nation states, and nationalism had not yet become a major factor in international affairs. Nonetheless, the outlines of the international system which would prevail for three centuries had been drawn.

VIENNA AND THE BALANCE OF POWER

The Congress of Vienna (1814–15) followed the Napoleonic Wars in Europe, and in many respects determined the international balance of power for the next four decades and beyond.

The gathering in Vienna is considered to have been one of the most brilliant international assemblies in history. It was a precursor of today's summit meetings. Most of the rulers of Europe took part, and a number of lesser potentates, ministers, and claimants were present. The chief negotiators included Prince Klemens Metternich of Austria; Czar Alexander I of Russia; Karl von Hardenberg and Wilhelm von Humboldt of Prussia; Viscount Castlereagh and the Duke of Wellington for Great Britain.

France was represented by Charles-Maurice de Talleyrand, who, by skillfully exploiting differences among the victorious allies, managed to obtain a strong voice in the negotiations.

Metternich was the guiding spirit of the Congress and a skillful diplomat. He became identified with such important concepts in international relations as balance of power and realpolitik and these were important factors in the Vienna deliberations. Henry Kissinger (see Profile) studied Metternich and this period and is believed to have been greatly influenced by what he learned. Kissinger wrote, "Their goal was stability, not perfection, and the balance of power is the classic expression of the lesson of history that no order is safe without physical safeguards against aggression." [1]

The French Revolution and the Napoleonic Wars had swept away the structure of Europe. The Vienna participants were concerned with restoring previous dynasties and territories, but they were also seeking to achieve a balance of power for the preservation of peace.

The concept of balance of power will be discussed further in Chapter 3. The term is used in different ways, but the fundamental notion is that nations seek to preserve international order by maintaining an approximate equilibrium of power, thus preventing the preponderance of any one state.

Although the Congress of Vienna did establish some alliances and mechanisms for settling disputes and upholding its decisions, territories had been bartered without much reference to the wishes of their inhabitants, a problem that has occurred repeatedly in the affairs of nations. Further revolution, shifting empires, and growing national aspirations gradually broke down the framework that had been created at Vienna.

VERSAILLES AND THE LEAGUE OF NATIONS

When World War I ended in 1918, it was followed by the Versailles Peace Conference. This time the United States was a participant in postwar negotiations, having entered the war in 1917 and helped defeat Germany and its allies. The Versailles Conference led to creation of the League of Nations, which was supposed to deter further aggression and war through collective action. The League of Nations did achieve some success in dealing with minor disputes in the 1920s, but it failed to curb powerful aggressors or to protect its weaker members from attack. It was never a well-balanced, truly supranational organization, and proved unable to deal with economic problems or to enforce its decisions. Moreover, the United States, despite the efforts of President Woodrow Wilson at Versailles in fostering the League, never became a member. Many of those countries which did join the League were increasingly concerned with their own national interests and priorities—a point that is central to an understanding of the interaction among nations—and those took precedence over the League's efforts at coordination.

The League could not be held responsible for World War II, but it failed to prevent it. A number of factors contributed to the climate for war. Totalitarian, militaristic regimes arose in Germany, Italy, and Japan, and their ascendance was due at least in part to the worldwide economic depression of the early 1930s. The depression sharpened national rivalries, increased fear and distrust, and made people more susceptible to the promises of demagogues such as Hitler in Germany or Mussolini in Italy. Germany believed that it had been treated vengefully and harshly at Versailles, and wanted to regain lost territory and military power. The democracies, on the other hand, desired peace and tried to work out settlements which would appease Hitler and stave off another world war. Instead, this only emboldened the ruthless German dictator.

The League of Nations was unable to promote disarmament, and by 1939, when World War II began, the League had lost almost all of its prestige and influence.

THE UNITED NATIONS

The failure of the League of Nations was very much on the minds of world leaders as they began to plan for a post–World War II world. Planning for the United Nations had actually been underway since the early stages of World War II. British Prime Minister Winston Churchill and United States President Franklin Roosevelt had agreed that a "permanent system of general security" should be established after the war. At a series of meetings during the war they formulated plans for the United Nations. The name United Nations had been coined by Roosevelt in 1941 to describe the countries fighting against the Axis Powers. The need for an international organization to replace the League was first stated officially in October 1943 at the Moscow Conference. Britain, the United States, the Soviet Union, and China agreed to establish an international organization for peace and security. At the Dumbarton Oaks conference (in Washington, D.C.) in 1944, delegates representing the United States, the British Commonwealth, and the Soviet Union published proposals for the organization to be known as the United Nations. Further discussions were held at the Black Sea resort of Yalta (Soviet Union) in February 1945 when, among a number of important decisions, Churchill, Roosevelt, and Soviet Premier Joseph Stalin agreed to ask China and France to join them in sponsoring the founding conference of the United Nations. At that meeting, the United States and Great Britain also agreed to recognize the autonomy of Outer Mongolia and to admit the Ukraine and Belorussia to the United Nations as full members. This was later to become a point of dispute because these were actually considered to be republics of the Soviet Union, yet Belorussia and the Ukraine became voting members of the United Nations. They were not, however, members of the Security Council, the most important organ within the United Nations. (Greater controversy would result from other decisions at Yalta—agreements which had the effect, in the view of some analysts, of opening the way for Soviet domination of Eastern Europe in the postwar period.)

The founding conference of the United Nations opened in San Francisco in April 1945. Delegates from 50 nations drafted the United Nations Charter, which was signed on June 26, and ratified by the required number of states on October 24. The first meeting of the General Assembly, in which all the member states are represented, was held in London in January 1946. Within a short time a decision was made to locate the headquarters in New York. The principal buildings there—the Secretariat, the General Assembly, and the Conference Building—were completed in 1952.

UNITED NATIONS STRUCTURE AND FUNCTIONS

The major organs of the United Nations, as specified in the charter, are the General Assembly, the Security Council, the Economic and Social Council, the Trusteeship Council, the International Court of Justice, and the Secretariat. In addition to these principal organs, there are a group of subsidiary organs established to deal with particular aspects of the United Nation's responsibilities—the United Nations Children's Fund (UNICEF) and United Nations Conference on Trade and Development are two well-known examples. A number of other bodies function as United Nations specialized agencies, but are not specifically provided for in the charter. These are autonomous entities ranging from the Food and Agriculture Organization (FAO), headquartered in Rome, to the International Labor Organization (ILO), based in Geneva.

The basic purposes of the United Nations, as set forth in the charter, are maintenance of international peace and security, development of friendly relations between states, and achievement of cooperation in solving international economic, social, cultural, and humanitarian problems. The charter also expresses a strong hope for the equality of all people and for the expansion of basic freedoms.

The administrative functions of the United Nations are handled by the Secretariat, which is headed by the secretary-general. The first secretary-general was Trygve Lie of Norway. He and his successors have all been from countries other than the major powers. The secretary-general has more than a merely administrative role because of his authority to bring situations to the attention of various United Nations organs, and especially because he can function as an impartial party in attempting to conciliate various international conflicts. The relative effectiveness and activism of the secretary-generals has varied according to their individual styles and the political climate of the period.

The General Assembly meets in a regular annual session beginning in late September, and prominent world leaders, including American presidents, sometimes use this platform to address major international issues. In 1988, Soviet leader Mikhail Gorbachev made a highly significant speech to the General Assembly, outlining changes in Soviet international policy.

There are also occasional special sessions of the Assembly. It has a large number of committees, but may not conduct studies or take action on matters before the smaller Security Council, unless requested by the Council to do so. Routine matters in the Assembly are decided by a majority vote, but a two-thirds majority of those voting is required for such matters as admission of new members, revision of the charter, and budgetary and trusteeship questions.

The Security Council

The General Assembly was seen by the United Nations architects as primarily a deliberative body, dealing with general political, social, and economic questions. The Security Council, on the other hand, was designed as the United Nation's "action" arm, with primary responsibility for preserving peace. Unlike the General Assembly, it was given enforcement power and a compact structure, with only 15 (originally 11) members, and, in theory, it is a continuously functioning body. There are five permanent members—the United States, the Soviet Union (Russia), Great Britain, France, and China, the victorious powers in World War II. (Until 1971, the Republic of China held the seat. During the Chinese revolution in 1949, the Republic of China government fled the mainland for Taiwan, but continued to be recognized by the United States and the United Nations as the official government of China. In 1949 the triumphant Chinese Communists had proclaimed the People's Republic of China, which was finally recognized by the United Nations in 1971.) The ten nonpermanent members of the Security Council are elected for two-year terms by the General Assembly, which is required to consider the contribution countries have made to peace, as well as geographical equity in choosing Council members. Customarily there are five nonpermanent members from African and Asian nations, one from Eastern Europe, two from Latin America, and two from Western Europe and elsewhere. The presidency of the Council is rotated on a monthly basis among the member nations.

A central feature of the Security Council has been the veto power held by each of the permanent members. The veto was provided for because it was believed that resolution of major crises would require agreement among the leading powers. Instead, the veto for many years symbolized the division and conflict between the United States and the Soviet Union.

The United States, Soviet Union, and Collective Security

Clearly, the United Nations did not evolve as was originally hoped and envisioned. As relations between the United States and its allies and the Soviet Union and its allies became more polarized, so did matters within the United Nations. In the early years the Soviet side was usually badly outnumbered in both the General Assembly or the Security Council. In the Council the Soviets cast more than 100 vetoes in the first 25 years of the United Nations.

There were, however, some early instances of Soviet cooperation with the United States and other powers that allowed for United Nations successes in resolving conflict or preserving peace. These included the 1946 settlement of the complaint by Syria and Lebanon that France and Great Britain were illegally occupying their territory; the 1947 partitioning of Palestine; helping to settle fighting by Pakistan and India over Kashmir in 1949; and withdrawal of the Netherlands from its former colony of Indonesia in 1949, following several years of fighting between the Indonesian movement for independence and Dutch government forces.

Increasingly, however, conflict between the Soviet Union and the other members of the Big Five came to overshadow the United Nations. With the Security Council often thwarted by the Soviet veto, the United States and its allies made an effort to expand the role of the General Assembly. That was during the period when the United States and Britain could expect strong backing from British Commonwealth and Latin American countries and usually had a comfortable majority in the Assembly. However, the General Assembly remained limited in what it could do, other than pass resolutions and issue pronouncements.

Ironically, one of the major "collective security" actions in United Nations history was probably possible only because of a Soviet boycott. At the time of the Korean crisis in 1950, the Soviets were boycotting the Security Council because of the refusal of the General Assembly to admit the People's Republic of China as a member. The Soviets would almost surely have cast a veto had they been present, but in their absence the Security Council approved sending a United Nations combat force to Korea to repel the attack by communist North Korea on South Korea. Subsequent resolutions authorizing various actions by the United Nations forces were approved by the General Assembly, so as to avoid a possible Soviet veto. In truth, the United Nations action in Korea was primarily carried out by troops from the United States and a few allied countries, under the flag of the United Nations.

THE UNITED NATIONS AND A CHANGING WORLD

From 50 nations in 1945, the United Nations has grown to more than 165 members. In the late 1950s and early 1960s, the United Nations began to undergo dramatic change and new issues came to dominate the agenda. The central factor contributing to this change in the United Nations was decolonization. As more and more nations, particularly in Asia and Africa, gained their independence and joined the United Nations, the political dynamics of the organization shifted significantly. These newly independent nations frequently differed with the United States, which now began to find itself in the minority on certain issues, as the new members sometimes joined with the Soviet bloc to form a solid majority in the General Assembly.

Reflecting the changing character of the United Nations, the organization began to devote major attention to the remaining colonial areas and to the problems of the newly independent nations. In 1960, 14 new members were admitted to the organization, all but one of them from Africa. It was in 1960 that the United Nations became actively involved in the Republic of the Congo (formerly the Belgian Congo and later called Zaire). United Nations Secretary General Dag Hammarskjold, who had been elected in 1953, took the lead in initiating and directing the United Nations's vigorous role in the Congo. With rival factions battling for control of the newly independent nation, the United Nations sought to resolve the conflict. Early in 1961, Patrice Lumumba, one of the factional leaders and for a brief time premier of the independent republic, was killed under mysterious circumstances. The Soviet Union accused Hammarskjold of being an "accomplice" in the murder, and demanded the withdrawal of United Nations forces from the Congo and the removal of Hammarskjold as secretary general. Hammarskjold remained on the job, however, until he died in a plane crash in Northern Rhodesia (now Zambia) while on a mission to the Congo in September 1961. United Nations troops remained in the Congo until 1964, and probably helped save the new nation from being recolonized or partitioned by pro-Soviet and pro-Belgian factions.

In the wake of the Congo controversy and Hammarskjold's death, the Soviets were pushing for a "troika" plan, in which the secretary general's office would be headed by three persons, one representative each from Eastern, Western, and neutralist states. As is discussed later in this chapter, the world was increasingly being viewed in terms of this tripartite division. The Soviet plan was not adopted, but Soviet pressures did help put a rein on the activism of the Secretariat for a long period.

United Nations and Southern Africa

More and more, United Nations efforts were directed toward such targets as Portuguese colonialism, until Portugal, the last European power to hold a large colonial empire, began to free its colonies in 1974. The United Nations also regularly criticized the racial policies of the white minority governments of South Africa and Rhodesia. (Rhodesia officially became Zimbabwe in 1980 when the black majority gained control of the country. Zimbabwe became a United Nations member that same year.) South Africa remained a major target of condemnatory resolutions, and the organization voted to apply a variety of economic sanctions against South Africa and also sought to remove Namibia (South West Africa) from South African control. South West Africa had been controlled by Germany before World War I. Afterwards, the territory was administered by neighboring South Africa under a League of Nations mandate. South Africa continued to control South West Africa after the United Nations was founded, but South Africa refused to acknowledge United Nations authority over the area. Increasingly, the United Nations objected to South Africa imposing its *apartheid* (racial separation) policies over South West Africa, and in 1966 the United Nations revoked the original mandate from the League of Nations. South Africa remained adamant in its refusal to accept United Nations authority. In 1971, the International Court of Justice, in one of a series of rulings on the area, declared that South Africa was occupying the area illegally. The International Court of Justice, usually referred to as the World Court, is the United Nations's judicial branch. Its 15 members are elected by the United Nations and the Court sits in The Hague, Netherlands. All of these pronouncements served to further isolate South Africa in the international community, but for many years brought about no significant change. Finally, Namibia became an independent nation in 1990, after considerable United Nations effort. (See Chapter 7 for further discussion of Southern Africa.)

Change, Conflict, and Development

Although the United Nations helped draw attention to the problems within Southern Africa, the prolonged inability to bring about change contributed to the organization's growing reputation for ineffectiveness. In its early years the United Nations also gave considerable attention to the issue of disarmament, and, periodically, the topic reappeared on the agenda; however, as was the case with the League of Nations before it, the United Nations had little to point to in terms of accomplishments in this area, and weaponry was growing all the more sophisticated and destructive. During the 1960s and 70s, the United Nations played relatively secondary roles in a series of crises—the Arab-Israeli wars, the India-Pakistan war of 1971, the Vietnam War, and the Cuban Missile Crisis.

As the United Nations focused less on peacekeeping and security issues, and with the impetus provided by the large number of newly independent nations, attention increasingly turned to economic and technological development. The United Nations and its agencies did have significant impact in certain areas such as disease control, aid to refugees, and technological cooperation. And the emphasis on hunger, human rights, and literacy helped stimulate interest and action on these enduring problems. However, the General Assembly became more and more a forum for discussion of development issues and what came to be called North-South relations. In 1964, the developing nations (or less-developed nations) formed an economic caucus, the Group of Seventy-Seven or G-77 (which now numbers 127 members), to represent their interests in international economic affairs and their push for what they believed would be a more equitable international economic order. (See Chapter 8.)

Reflection of Rivalry

What happened in the United Nations was a reflection of the divisions, the rivalries, the polarization that occurred in the post–World War II international system. As noted earlier, as relations between East and West became more polarized, so did matters within the United Nations. The primary trends and conflicts in world affairs—the evolution of the Cold War, the end of the colonial era, the troubled emergence of the Third World—were clearly visible within the United Nations.

Within a short time after the end of World War II, the lines were being drawn between East and West, between Communist and noncommunist or anticommunist, between the Soviet Union and its allies and the United States and those nations associated with it. There were, as has been pointed out, a few examples of Soviet-American cooperation in the early days of the United Nations, but more and more the international body became a forum of conflict between the two dominant powers in the postwar world.

The wartime alliance against fascism between the Americans and the Soviets quickly dissolved after the war, and increasingly the two nations became bitter rivals. Actually, the antagonism between the two was not new. As historian Walter LaFeber has pointed out, a half century of Russian-American enmity preceded the wartime partnership, and the two nations had held drastically different views of how the world should be organized.[2]

THE COLD WAR

The origins and causes of the Cold War are the subject of endless debate and analysis. There is also argument over whether this global antagonism was inevitable and over why the United Nations did not succeed in its intended purpose of fostering cooperation and preventing deep divisions among the world's nations. There has been a great deal of what Daniel Yergin has referred to as "onus-shifting"—with each side attempting to place blame on the other for the division of Europe and the development of the Cold War.

In the United States the tendency has been, not surprisingly, to assign all responsibility for the Cold War to the Soviets, while the Soviet Union laid all the blame on the United States and its European allies. Both views are tragically oversimplified. While from the American perspective it is possible to see a number of actions and events on the part of the Soviets that led to the Cold War, it can also be argued that certain American actions heightened tensions. Indeed, what occurred was a sadly familiar pattern in international relations which can be called the "action-reaction" cycle. One nation's actions are seen as hostile or threatening or, in any case, requiring a strong response. That process characterized what came to be called the Cold War.

Soviet determination to maintain dominance over Eastern Europe was a central factor in the Cold War, but over the years the Cold War rivalry was to involve political and diplomatic maneuvering, psychological and propaganda warfare, strong ideological conflict, the arms race, and a number of peripheral conflicts, all of which fell short of direct warfare between the United States and the Soviets.

Indeed, the term Cold War refers to nonmilitary conflict, as contrasted to a "hot" or "shooting" war. Although often attributed to Walter Lippmann, the noted American columnist, the term was apparently originated by Herbert Bayard Swope in a speech he wrote for Bernard Baruch, an American statesman. It is interesting to note that it was Baruch who, in 1946, presented a plan for international control of atomic energy. The Baruch Plan was rejected by the Soviets, who vetoed the proposal in the United Nations Security Council. Under the Baruch Plan, the United States would have given up its monopoly on atomic weapons. However, the Soviets wanted to develop their own atomic weapons—and were already in the process of doing so—and believed the Baruch Plan was intended to leave only the United States with the capability for making atomic weapons. In any case, Baruch said in a 1947 speech, not long after his plan was rejected, "Let us not be deceived—today we are in the midst of a cold war."[3]

The Iron Curtain

There was, of course, no formal declaration of war for the Cold War. However, three speeches can be cited as having the effect of declaring cold war, or at least they can be interpreted that way in retrospect. The first of these was in February 1946, when Soviet leader Joseph Stalin delivered a menacing speech, invoking Marxist-Leninist doctrine, and suggesting that as long as capitalism existed, war was inevitable.

A few weeks later, Britain's Winston Churchill delivered his famous "Iron Curtain" speech. Speaking at Westminster College in Fulton, Missouri, Churchill said, "From Stettin in the Baltic to Trieste in the Adriatic, an Iron Curtain has descended across the continent. Behind that line lie the capitals of the ancient states of central and eastern Europe." Churchill called for Anglo-American cooperation, with the support of atomic weapons, and outside the framework of the United Nations, saying, "The safety of the world . . . requires a new unity in Europe from which no nation should be permanently outcast." This was seen by the Soviets as a threat to their control in Eastern Europe, as an indication that the British and Americans were intent on confrontation with the Soviet Union.

Not long after the Iron Curtain speech, the Soviets took a series of steps demonstrating their unwillingness to cooperate with the capitalist nations on economic matters. They rejected the terms of a $1-billion American loan, and also refused to join the World Bank and International Monetary Fund. (The international financial institutions are discussed in Chapter 9.)

Truman Doctrine

The next major pronouncement that signaled the onset of the Cold War came in March 1947, when President Harry Truman, in a landmark ad-

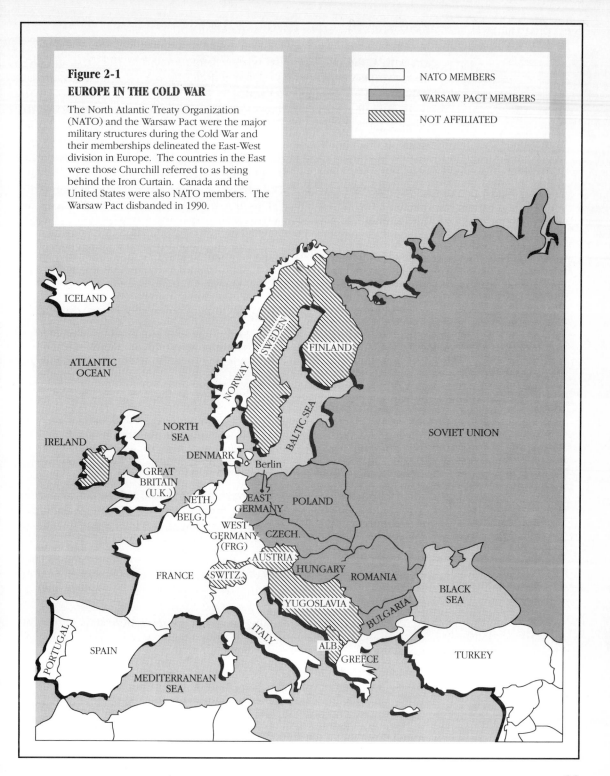

Figure 2-1
EUROPE IN THE COLD WAR

The North Atlantic Treaty Organization (NATO) and the Warsaw Pact were the major military structures during the Cold War and their memberships delineated the East-West division in Europe. The countries in the East were those Churchill referred to as being behind the Iron Curtain. Canada and the United States were also NATO members. The Warsaw Pact disbanded in 1990.

NATO MEMBERS

WARSAW PACT MEMBERS

NOT AFFILIATED

ICELAND

ATLANTIC OCEAN

SWEDEN

NORWAY

FINLAND

BALTIC SEA

SOVIET UNION

IRELAND

NORTH SEA

DENMARK

Berlin

GREAT BRITAIN (U.K.)

NETH.

EAST GERMANY

POLAND

BELG.

WEST GERMANY (FRG)

CZECH.

FRANCE

SWITZ.

AUSTRIA

HUNGARY

ROMANIA

YUGOSLAVIA

BULGARIA

BLACK SEA

PORTUGAL

SPAIN

ITALY

ALB.

GREECE

TURKEY

MEDITERRANEAN SEA

dress to Congress, launched what became known as the Truman Doctrine. Truman's speech and related actions charted the course for American foreign policy for decades.

The specific purpose of President Truman's address to Congress was to request aid for Greece and Turkey. He described the need for the aid in grave terms, and said, "I am fully aware of the broad implications involved if the United States extends assistance to Greece and Turkey." Truman said that one of the primary objectives of United States foreign policy was "the creation of conditions in which we and other nations will be able to work out a way of life free from coercion." Although the clear implication of Truman's message was that Turkey and Greece were threatened with the prospect of Soviet/communist domination, he did not make specific reference to the Soviet Union. However, he was more explicit when he later recalled, in his memoirs, the factors that led to the United States commitment to Greece and Turkey:

> . . . The alternative was the loss of Greece and the extension of the Iron Curtain across the eastern Mediterranean. If Greece was lost, Turkey would become an untenable outpost in a sea of communism. Similarly, if Turkey yielded to Soviet demands, the position of Greece would be endangered . . . Greece and Turkey were still free countries being challenged by communist threats both from within and without . . . The ideals and the traditions of our nation demanded that we come to the aid of Greece and Turkey and that we put the world on notice that it would be our policy to support the cause of freedom wherever it was threatened.[i]

Earlier in 1947, the British Government had notified the United States that London could not provide the support needed by Greece and Turkey. Britain had traditionally exercised power and influence in the eastern Mediterranean region, but the reality was that Britain had been economically devastated by the war, and was no longer in a position to play the role of a major power. Indeed, this abdication of the British role in the eastern Mediterranean foreshadowed the breakup of the vast British Empire.

With the British notice to the United States, the American government was galvanized into action. During a remarkable period often referred to as the "Fifteen Weeks," the United States embarked upon a new course in world affairs, symbolized by the Truman Doctrine, the Marshall Plan, and the policy of containment.

J. William Fulbright, long a leading foreign policy figure in Congress, termed the Truman Doctrine a seminal development in American foreign policy. He said this was true because President Truman based his appeal to Congress not primarily on specific circumstances of those two countries at that time but on sweeping ideological (anticommunist) grounds.

Actually, Truman did focus on specific circumstances of Greece and Turkey, while acknowledging that broader implications were involved. Fulbright, who voted for the original aid package for Greece and Turkey, conceded that the Truman Doctrine "may have made sense for its time and place," but says that "it came to be recognized as the basic rationale, from the American standpoint, for the Cold War."[5]

Fulbright and others have also noted the significance of the decision by the United States to act outside the framework of the United Nations on the Greek-Turkish question. Some members of Congress protested about this at the time, but to no avail. This reliance on unilateral action rather than attempting to work through a multilateral organization (the United Nations) was to become characteristic of much of American foreign policy, though there would be exceptions, such as the Korean war, as has already been discussed. Similarly, the action by the United States on Greece and Turkey and proclamation of the Truman Doctrine indicated a United States willingness to intervene directly in the affairs of other nations—as, for example, in the civil war in Greece—with anticommunism as the basis for such actions.

Differing Interpretations

While from the American perspective, as was pointed out earlier, the tendency was to view United States actions as necessary responses to Soviet or Soviet-inspired moves, there are some who challenge that interpretation. Indeed, critics—sometimes referred to as "revisionists"—offer an interpretation that suggests that the United States did as much or more to bring on the Cold War than did the Soviets. American historians and analysts such as William Appelman Williams and D. F. Fleming[6] challenged the orthodox view of the origins of the Cold War. (Subsequent chapters will examine the underlying factors influencing Soviet foreign policy and the development of the superpower rivalry.) The revisionist view maintains that American policymakers in the post–World War II period greatly exaggerated the ability and the intention of the Soviets to engage in expansionist policies. Further, and this point will be dealt with in more detail in Chapter 4, it is argued that the United States failed to take into account the Soviet view of national security, based on the historical experience of the peoples of the Soviet Union. The Soviets, it is said by the revisionists, were primarily concerned with security against further invasion or intervention from outside, and wanted to assure friendly governments on their Western borders and to guard against a resurgent Germany.

American leaders did have genuine fears about Soviet expansionist tendencies, however, and there was a belief that an expansionist-minded totalitarian state had to be opposed sooner rather than later, a conviction based on the experience with the German Nazis, when the allies were slow to react.

Thus, through a series of steps and statements by the major players, the lines had been drawn between the East and West. The Iron Curtain served, in the view of the West, as the demarcation point between the communist world and the noncommunist or "free" world. The two camps, led by the Soviets and Americans, were locked into prolonged conflict and competition.

REBUILDING EUROPE

Having launched the Truman Doctrine, the United States next moved to deal with another major concern of the post–World War II period— the reconstruction of war-torn Western Europe. What resulted was the Marshall Plan, also a landmark in international relations. The Marshall Plan, named after American Secretary of State George C. Marshall, ranks as one of the most magnanimous humanitarian efforts ever made by one nation on behalf of others. At the same time, it was an action that the United States undertook for reasons of economic and geopolitical self-interest.

The plan was outlined in a speech by Marshall at Harvard on June 5, 1947. He said,

> It is logical that the United States should do whatever it is able to do to assist in the return of normal economic health in the world without which there can be no political stability and no assured peace. Our policy is directed not against any country or doctrine but against hunger, poverty, desperation, and chaos.⁷

The original Marshall aid proposal extended to the entire European continent, including the Soviet satellites and European Russia. However, the United States probably did not expect the Eastern countries to participate and were not surprised when Soviet leaders opposed the plan. The Soviets characterized it as an American attempt to control the Eastern economies. A possibility for cooperation had been lost, and East and West were further embarked on their separate courses of development.

To help integrate and implement the Marshall Plan, the 16 participating European countries formed a Committee on European Economic Cooperation (which can be seen as a forerunner of the later European Economic Community). The actual European Recovery Program (Marshall Plan) was in effect for three years, through 1951, and was in most respects highly successful. The participating countries received $13.3 billion in aid, a very substantial figure in the dollar values of that time, but a relatively small amount when considered in a broader historical context and in light of the Marshall Plan's impact. Although it was essentially an economic enterprise, involving a substantial transfer of financial and technical resources from the United States, it also helped solidify political, cultural, and security ties between Western Europe and the United States. The Marshall Plan was especially successful in providing the foundation for the remarkable resurgence in the economies of Western Europe which was to occur over the following years.

CONTAINMENT

American actions were giving shape and substance to the policy which came to be known as containment, and which became a fundamental factor in international relations.

George Kennan, who was a State Department expert on Soviet affairs, is generally thought of as the architect of the containment policy. It was Kennan, who, as the pseudonymous "Mr. X," authored an article titled "The Sources of Soviet Conduct" in the July 1947 edition of the journal, *Foreign Affairs*. The article has been viewed as the blueprint for American Cold War policy, the intellectual/philosophical rationale for United States international strategy. The Truman Doctrine and containment were generally considered to be examples of policies based on *realpolitik* or the "realistic" view of international affairs—in this case the basis for policy being the belief that the Soviet Union was an imperial nation seeking world power.

Kennan's article has been subjected to a variety of interpretations, and Kennan himself has expressed regret about some of the interpretations that have been attached to the article, which called for a "long-term, patient but firm and vigilant containment of Russian expansionist tendencies." In Kennan's view, the policy of containment would "promote tendencies which must eventually find their outlet in either the break-up or the gradual mellowing of Soviet power."[8]

Later, in his memoirs, Kennan said that perhaps the most serious of several deficiencies in the "X-article" was the failure to make clear that his notion of the containment of Soviet power "was not the containment by military means of a military threat, but the political containment of a political threat."[9] It was Kennan's view that the United States should not resort to bluster and excessive reliance on the military in meeting the Soviet challenge. Much to his dismay, even with the Truman Doctrine, Washington began stressing the military aspects of containment, rather than the careful blend of political, diplomatic, economic, and military pressures which he thought should be applied. As Coit Blacker has written, "Containment soon came to mean a kind of generalized resistance to communism in all its forms rather than opposition to the further territorial and/or political aggrandizement of the Soviet Union."[10]

The Truman Doctrine and the Marshall Plan were the first major manifestations of the containment policy. There was hope that these actions might send a sufficiently strong signal to the Soviet Union that it would head off a further polarization in world affairs. In 1948, however, the deterioration in United States–Soviet relations was accelerated. A Soviet-backed faction succeeded in taking over the government in Czechoslovakia in February. This, in the words of United States President Harry

Truman, "sent a shock through the civilized world." The disappearance of the last semblance of a democratic government in Eastern Europe was followed by one of the most dramatic episodes of the Cold War—the Berlin blockade. (See Berlin city portrait.)

The Berlin Challenge

The former capital city of Germany had been divided into four sectors at the end of World War II, each administered by one of the four victorious European powers (the United States, Soviet Union, Great Britain, and France). There were numerous disagreements between the Soviets and the other three nations about the administration of Berlin. Germany itself had also been divided into four sectors, with the Soviets controlling the East and the three Western countries each responsible for a section of West Germany. Access to Berlin, however, required crossing through East Germany. On June 24, 1948, the Soviets stopped all surface traffic between Berlin and the Western zones of Germany. Electric power in West Berlin, generated in the Eastern sector, was also cut off. Faced with this effort to isolate West Berlin—and with all railways, roads, and waterways blocked—the Western powers decided that the only solution was to supply the inhabitants of the threatened area by an airlift.

The challenge of the Berlin Airlift was daunting. Was it feasible to satisfy the economic needs of a city of more than two million inhabitants exclusively by air? At the peak of the airlift, one plane landed in West Berlin every one to two minutes. In April 1949 they flew in nearly 13,000 tons in a single day. In the nearly 11 months of the Airlift, the Western allies flew more than 270,000 delivery flights and took 1.82 million tons of supplies—primarily coal and food—to Berlin. They even transported the equipment for a power plant.

Recognizing the failure of this crude pressure on West Berlin, the Soviets ended the blockade in May 1949. A short time later, the Federal Republic of Germany (West Germany) and the German Democratic Republic (East Germany) officially came into being, formalizing the political division of the former Reich and the delineation between the Western and Eastern (communist) camps which would remain in effect for 40 years.

Further Polarization

At about the time the Berlin Blockade ended, the Western allies were also formalizing the North Atlantic military alliance, with the signing of the North Atlantic Treaty by the United States, Canada, and 10 European nations. The member nations of the North Atlantic Treaty Organization (NATO) agreed to regard an attack on any one of them as an attack on all. It represented an affirmation of the security ties between Western Europe and North America and assured that the United States would play an active role in European defense. (NATO and the Warsaw Pact, which was the Soviet–East European military grouping, are discussed further in Chapter 6.)

Two other events of 1949 were to have major impact on international relations and to further the polarization between the Americans and Soviets. In the summer of 1949 the Soviets ended the brief American monopoly on atomic weaponry when they tested their first atomic bomb. This event had the effect of setting off what was to become the arms race between the superpowers. Within a short time, the United States had begun work on a more advanced weapon, the hydrogen bomb.

Later in 1949, the long civil war in China ended with a victory for the Communists. The "fall" of China had major repercussions in the United States, where many interpreted the developments in China as a great and threatening victory for international communism and a "loss" for the United States. American foreign policy was significantly shaped by the experience. Some argued that the United States should have done more to prevent the fall of the nationalist government in China, although it might have required a major and lengthy American intervention. Nonetheless, it led to a "tougher" American approach in the years that followed. There was also a tendency among some American officials to view Communist China as virtually a Soviet colony, which did not prove to be the case.

CONFLICT IN KOREA

The first prolonged military struggle between East and West began in 1950, following the attack by North Korea against South Korea. The role of the United Nations forces in this conflict has already been described. Although the Soviet Union did not take part in the fighting, it did provide supplies and advisers for the North Koreans. There is no strong evidence that the Soviets did actually orchestrate the North Korean invasion, but at the time the action was viewed by the United States as part of a Soviet global strategy.

Whether or not it was part of the Cold War, the fighting in Korea was a "hot war," large-scale conventional warfare that eventually pitted United States forces (fighting under the United Nations flag with South Korea and troops from 15 other nations) against Chinese and North Korean troops, China having entered the war in support of North Korea. It was not a "declared" war by the United States; Congress never approved a formal declaration of war, and the conflict was referred to as a "police action." Nonetheless, the commitment of large numbers of American forces indicated the willingness of the United States to use military means to back up the policy of containment and the principles associated with the Truman Doctrine. However, the United States did not seek to extend the war beyond Korea, even though some American leaders favored invading China. The war continued for three years, with substantial casualties on both sides, before an armistice was signed, based on the prewar 38th parallel dividing line between North and South Korea.

UNITED STATES– SOVIET RIVALRY

Joseph Stalin died in 1953, the same year that the Korean War ended. He had come to symbolize a hard-line Soviet foreign policy, aimed at expanding Soviet influence and consolidating its control in Eastern Europe. At home, his regime was notorious for its repressive, strong-arm tactics, including brutal purges within his own government. With the death of Stalin, a very gradual change began to occur in Soviet policies and in United States–Soviet relations. At several points there was a lessening of tension between the superpowers and signs of a thaw in the Cold War. There were still many points of contention and conflict, however, and at times relations were bitter and frosty. The superpower rivalry, which was often played out in the Third World, remained as the centerpiece of international relations. The arms race continued apace, with the quantity and the destructive capability of the weapons steadily growing.

Although the United Nations and other international bodies had relatively little impact in restraining the arms race, there were some important breakthroughs, such as the Treaty on the Non-Proliferation of Nuclear Weapons (1970), which sought to prohibit the spread of nuclear weapons among non-nuclear nations. The Americans and the Soviets also began an on-again/off-again process of arms control negotiations, which finally began to yield some results in restricting the arms race. (See Chapter 6 for more discussion on arms control.)

THE EVOLVING FRAMEWORK

This, then, was the international framework that evolved in the decades following World War II, an international system that was dominated in many ways—directly and indirectly—by the superpowers. The formal international structure, based in the United Nations, had many strengths, but was often limited in its effectiveness and inhibited by the conflicting goals of the major powers. There were a number of economic, political, and security structures and alliances and groupings, some of them regional in nature, with nations linked through geographical, ideological, or economic commonalities. These structures were in many cases influenced by or a result of the East-West division. The gradual emergence of the Third World as a force in world affairs, albeit a limited one in many respects, brought to light a North-South division as well. Although the North-South issues frequently dominated debate in the United Nations, the menacing shadow of the superpowers, with their nuclear arsenals, seemed always to be on the horizon. In effect, while the Security Council was often paralyzed by East-West differences, the General Assembly was frustrated by North-South differences.

Economic Structures

For the most part, East and West went their separate ways economically, although that began to change somewhat in the late 1980s. The international financial institutions associated with the United Nations were generally dominated and heavily influenced by the United States, other industrialized Western nations, and Japan. Indeed, in the economic sphere, these nations, sometimes referred to as the First World, stood far ahead of the rest of the world. The First World (including the United States, Canada, Western Europe, Japan, Australia, and New Zealand) was predominant in the world economy, exercising much greater economic strength than the communist Second World (Soviet Union, Eastern Europe) or the Third World (most of the nations of Africa, Asia, and Latin America). The First World nations were clustered in the Organization for Economic Cooperation and Development (OEDC), designed to help coordinate policy and to assist poorer nations, and in a variety of other economic groupings. One of the most important of these is the Group of Seven (G-7), composed of Japan and the Western economic powers, which convenes the annual economic summits. (See Chapters 5 and 8.)

As Third World countries became more of a political force in international organizations, they sought to gain more influence in economic affairs, but with limited success. Mention has already been made of G-77, the organization of Third World nations seeking a reordering of the world economy.

A few of the Third World nations did, however, become more significant factors in the international economy as their economies grew stronger. (These nations are sometimes referred to as newly industrializing countries or NICs.) And, at certain points, groups such as the Organization of Petroleum Exporting Countries (OPEC), were able to alter the international economic balance, although that was an exception. (See Chapters 7 and 8.) In Europe, the European Community (Common Market) became an increasingly important factor, and developed into the world's largest trading bloc, far more potent than the Council on Mutual Economic Assistance (COMECON), which had been composed of the Soviet Union, Eastern Europe, Cuba, and Mongolia. The European Community is important not only as a supranational economic structure but it and related organizations also have growing political significance. (International economic structures and development are discussed in detail in Chapter 8.)

A NEW ERA?

By the late 1980s, there were indications of changing attitudes toward the United Nations by the superpowers, and signs of a revitalization within the organization, which had been plagued by a variety of problems, including financial difficulties, partially because of the lack of support from the Soviets and Americans. The United Nations Charter predated the development of nuclear weapons and the East-West and North-South divisions, developments that greatly affected the organization's capacity to fulfill the role of international peacekeeper which had been envisioned by its founders.

Clearly, an essential element in the effectiveness of the United Nations is the active support and commitment of the major powers, something that was often lacking during the first four decades of the organization's life. The United Nations has usually been least successful when there has been disagreement among the permanent members of the Security Council, who must approve all peacekeeping operations.

While the work of the United Nations specialized agencies in areas such as health and literacy is widely acknowledged, the organization has often been seen as irrelevant or as a minor factor in dealing with international conflicts. Indeed, some argued that the major questions of international peace and security were simply beyond the capacity of the United Nations and that its primary usefulness was limited to the economic and social fields.

The bipolar balance of power during the Cold War period, with the United States and the Soviet Union as the dominant factors in world affairs, had a profound impact on the United Nations and on the international structure, even though there were other important dimensions in international affairs, especially when Third World nations began assuming a more important role. As the United Nations neared its fiftieth year of existence, the shifts in the balance of power—the reduction in the international role of the Soviets and the move toward multipolarity—also have significant impact on the international framework and open new possibilities for international organizations.

However, the reshaping of patterns of power and influence has increased the United Nations's potential for playing a key role in resolving conflicts. This has been demonstrated by a series of actions in recent years, including the United Nations's success in helping to extract the Soviet military from Afghanistan, bringing about a cease-fire in the Iran-Iraq war, and in negotiating settlements to conflicts in Angola and Namibia (South West Africa).

"The changes in the Soviet Union have been critical to the emergence of a stronger United Nations," President Bush told the United Nations General Assembly in 1990. "The U.S.–Soviet relationship is finally beyond containment and confrontation, and now we seek to fulfill the promise of mutually shared understanding."[11]

However, others pointed to what they saw as inherent limitations in the United Nations. Jeane Kirkpatrick, who served as United States delegate to the United Nations during the Reagan administration, said, "The biggest single problem with the U.N. is that it involves in every decision too many nations that don't have a stake in the outcome . . . That's a prerequisite for irresponsible decision-making."[12]

In 1990–91 the United Nations was a center for diplomatic activity and a forum for consideration of decisions on international action against Iraq for its invasion of Kuwait. In this case the center of gravity shifted back toward the Security Council, where it had been in the early years, and away from the General Assembly. The relative unity within the Security Council over condemnation of and action against Iraq was indicative of prospects for a stronger role for the international organization.

The United Nations received important recognition when the United Nations peacekeeping forces—known as the "blue helmets"—were awarded the 1988 Nobel Peace Prize. First deployed in 1948 on an observer mission between Israel and its Arab neighbors, the blue helmets were utilized in various areas—Cyprus, Lebanon, the India-Pakistan border—to serve as buffer forces or to monitor cease-fire or treaty compliance. Perhaps the most successful peacekeeping operation was that in the former Belgian Congo (Zaire), discussed earlier in this chapter. The Nobel Prize brought some much-needed attention to the United Nations role. When a peacekeeping effort is successful, it doesn't make much news. Despite the divisions that have often made its work difficult and despite its limited ability to bridge those divisions, the United Nations has been successful in many respects. It is firmly established and it does provide a structural framework for international cooperation.

With the influence of the East-West rivalry considerably reduced as a factor in international relations and in international organizations, some significant barriers to cooperation and progress are removed. At the same time, the growing importance of regional, economically based organizations, such as the European Community, adds an increasingly important dimension to the framework of international relations. A number of communist-bloc structures became irrelevant or outmoded with the changes occurring in Eastern Europe in recent years. In some cases these nations began moving into association with what had previously been "Western" organizations. However, even with significant improvement in East-West relations, subsequent chapters will make clear that significant problems, conflicts, and potential conflicts remain to be dealt with, and an agenda of new issues is emerging, presenting a considerable challenge to the United Nations and other international organizations.

NOTES

1. Henry Kissinger, *Nuclear Weapons and Foreign Policy* (New York: Harper and Row, 1957).
2. Walter LaFeber, *America, Russia, and the Cold War*, 5th ed. (New York: Alfred A. Knopf, 1985).
3. William Safire, *Safire's Political Dictionary* (New York: Random House, 1978), pp. 127–29. See also: Peter Calvocoressi, *World Politics Since 1945*, 5th ed. (New York: Longman, 1987), pp. 6–7.
4. Harry S Truman, *Memoirs, Volume II: Years of Trial and Hope* (Garden City, New York: Doubleday, 1956), pp. 100–101.
5. J. William Fulbright, *The Crippled Giant* (New York: Random House, 1972), pp. 17–22.
6. See: William Appelman Williams, *The Tragedy of American Diplomacy*, Rev. ed. (New York: Delta Books, 1962); D. W. Fleming, *The*

Cold War and Its Origins 1917–60. 2 vols. (Garden City, New York: Doubleday, 1961). Also: Daniel Yergin, *Shattered Peace: The Origins of the Cold War and the National Security State* (Boston: Houghton Mifflin: 1977); Richard A. Melanson, *Writing History and Making Policy—The Cold War, Vietnam, and Revisionism* (Lanham, Maryland: University Press of America, 1983).

7. Address by Secretary of State George C. Marshall at the commencement exercises of Harvard University, Cambridge, Massachusetts, June 5, 1947; text reprinted in Joseph M. Jones, *The Fifteen Weeks* (New York: Viking, 1955); and Charles L. Mee, Jr., *The Marshall Plan: The Launching of Pax Americana* (New York: Simon and Schuster, 1984), p. 272.

8. "X" (George F. Kennan), "The Sources of Soviet Conduct," *Foreign Affairs* 25, July 1947, pp. 575–76, 582.

9. George F. Kennan, *Memoirs, 1925–1950* (Boston: Little, Brown, 1967), p. 358.

10. Coit Blacker, *Reluctant Warriors* (New York: W. H. Freeman, 1987), p. 65.

11. Address by President George Bush, "The UN: World Parliament of Peace," before the United Nations General Assembly, New York, October 1, 1990, Department of State Current Policy No. 1303.

12. Quoted in Doyle McManus, "Bush's Vision of a 'New World Order' Still Unclear," *Los Angeles Times*, February 18, 1991.

CHAPTER THREE

Concepts, Theories, and Analysis in International Relations

When viewed broadly, international relations can be seen as a matter of conflict and cooperation, with the conflict or cooperation often driven by efforts to attain or retain power or by the forces of nationalism or ideological or religious movements. Power, as already noted, is not necessarily a matter of military strength, but may well involve economic or political power or a combination thereof. The basic concepts and theories through which we analyze and characterize international relations generally relate to or grow out of these fundamental operating principles.

Since the development of the nation-state system, rising out of the Westphalian state system (discussed in Chapter 2), nations and the behavior of nations—with their concern for national security and national interests—have commonly provided a basis for analyzing international relations. However, in recent years other perspectives have emerged, and transnational behavior and the role of nonstate actors have received increasing attention in international relations theory and analysis. The rise of supranational units of government, such as the European Community (see Chapter 8), adds a new dimension to international relations.

REALISM AND POWER

A primary approach to viewing world politics has involved the concept of *realism* or the realist theory or paradigm. (A paradigm is a framework, pattern, or model.) The realist approach proceeds from the premise that states are the most important actors and major units of analysis, and that power is the central factor in international relations. Hans J. Morgenthau, one of the foremost exponents of realism, summed up the "power ap-

45

proach" in his seminal book, *Politics Among Nations*, published in 1948. Morgenthau wrote: "International politics, like all politics, is a struggle for power. Whatever the ultimate aims of international politics, power is always the immediate aim." [1]

Power generally refers to influence and/or control exercised by one nation over other nations or over international events. The realist theory of international relations is based on the notion that nations (through their leaders) will act in terms of interest defined as power. Realist theory stresses the importance of national interest in influencing a nation's behavior. The concept of national interest will be explored further in this and subsequent chapters. However, it should be understood that one of the realities in contemporary world politics is not only the fact that the interests of nations may come into conflict but that interests may be viewed in a variety of ways. Indeed, there may be conflicts and divisions within nations about where that nation's interests may lie. This was true in the United States, for example, in the debate over the American role in Vietnam and what truly served the interests of the nation. The basic objective of a nation's foreign policy is to uphold the national interests. The concept of national interest can be a rather generalized one, normally centering on a nation's vital needs or concerns—such as national survival, sovereignty and territorial integrity, and military and economic security. Policies based solely on these concerns, with little attention to moral factors, are seen as examples of realism in foreign policy.

Realism has often been seen as military/security oriented, placing a strong emphasis on military strength. The realist approach became predominant in the years following World War II, and in some respects realism can be seen as the opposite of *idealism*, and as a reaction to the failure after World War I to prevent the rise of fascism, the onset of World War II, and the development of the Cold War. Idealism was associated with the efforts after World War I, led by Woodrow Wilson (discussed in Chapter 2) to establish a new international order through the Treaty of Versailles and the League of Nations, envisioning international cooperation and morality in the behavior of nations.

Although realism is associated with the post–World War II period, it has deep historical roots. An early "realist" was Niccolò Machiavelli, whose name has come to symbolize crafty and unscrupulous political tactics. Actually, Machiavelli (1469–1529), an Italian scholar and diplomat, has been called the first writer to describe the world of politics as it actually operates rather than in an ideal or theoretical fashion. In his best-known work, *The Prince*, Machiavelli argued that morality gives way to whatever it takes to gain and maintain power. The German term *realpolitik* is sometimes used to identify this approach to international diplomacy, which is based on power politics rather than on moral or ethical considerations. Realpolitik is closely associated with the *balance of power* concept, which was discussed in the opening chapters. Balance-of-power politics is seen as a fundamental manifestation of realpolitik. As noted in the previous chapter, the term is used in a variety of different ways, but balance of power basically refers to an equilibrium of power among nations, with no nation having a preponderant position.

BALANCE OF POWER AND ALLIANCES

Realpolitik and balance of power are traditional concepts in international relations. In fact, Thucydides (471–400 B.C.), who has been referred to as the first to employ the realist approach, describes the cause of war between Athens and Sparta and their allies in balance-of-power terms. His classic *The Peloponnesian War* can be considered as one of the earliest examples of analysis of international relations (or relations among states). Thucydides wrote:

> . . . the point was reached when Athenian strength attained a peak plain for all to see and the Athenians began to encroach upon Sparta's allies. It was at this point that Sparta felt the position to be no longer tolerable and decided by starting this present war to employ all her energies in attacking and, if possible, destroying the power of Athens.[2]

The balance of power was a primary consideration in seventeenth-, eighteenth-, and nineteenth-century international relations, particularly among the European nations. This was especially true of Metternich and others at the Congress of Vienna in 1814–15.

In the post–World War II period, realists argued that a balance of power was the key to prevention of further conflict. One way to maintain the balance of power is through alliances, which are normally an integral part of international relations. In most cases, nations will enter into alliances based on their perceptions of how their interests and security will be best served. Alliances usually involve pledges of mutual military assistance in case one or more alliance members is attacked or threatened. Frequently, alliances are formalized through treaties agreed to by the participating nations. In more recent times the best-known alliance has been the North Atlantic Treaty Organization (NATO), which served to balance off or deter the military power and ambitions of the Soviet-led Eastern bloc of Warsaw Pact nations. This situation was part of what is sometimes referred to as a bipolar balance of power. (The concept of bipolarity was discussed in Chapter 2 and will be further discussed later in this chapter.)

A major purpose of most alliances is to deter other nations or alignments of nations. Henry Kissinger has defined deterrent power as the ability to prevent certain threats or actions from being carried out by posing an equivalent or greater threat.[3] Such deterrent capability on the part of alliances is consistent with the basic balance-of-power theory. Alliances are supposed to create balances so that one grouping will not gain superiority over another. Alliances do not necessarily eliminate the possibility of war, however. Indeed, President Woodrow Wilson and others argued after World War I that the system of alliances and the emphasis on balance-of-power actually contributed to the outbreak of that war. Wilson and his supporters believed that the balance-of-power/alliance system should be replaced by a "community of power" and *collective security*, which was to be centered in the League of Nations. Wilson was determined to go beyond the "old diplomacy" of alliances and balance of power to build a peace that would combine power and morality. However, as John Lewis Gaddis points out, this approach, unfortunately, neglected the realities of power.[4] Realists would contend that the Wilsonian approach presumed a harmony of interests among states, with relations among them governed by ideals and morality, while, in truth, they were determined by national interests and power.

Failure of the United States to join the League was one of a variety of factors that hindered its chances for success. And while the League did not discriminate against any nation, the Versailles Treaty, which established the League, was notable for its harshness toward Germany. Many believe that this sowed the seeds of future conflict. By the late 1930s, Germany, Italy, and Japan were all intent on pursuing their expansionist goals, and while their actions were condemned by the League, there was no collective security response.

Just as generals sometimes seem to be fighting the last war instead of the one in which they are actually involved, diplomats have sometimes created the conditions for war by managing as if in the last prewar crisis instead of the one in which they are involved. That is not to suggest that important lessons are not to be learned from history; to the contrary, there are important lessons to be learned. It was George Santayana, the American philosopher, who said that those who do not know the past are condemned to repeat it. Thucydides, the Greek historian who is considered to be the father of the study of international relations, expressed the hope that his history would be found profitable by "those who desire an exact knowledge of the past as a key to the future, which in all probability will repeat or resemble the past."[5] What is important, of course, is to learn the right lessons from history, and that is part of what we hope that study and analysis of international relations can teach us. Ernest R. May, who has studied the uses and misuses of history by policymakers, has concluded that they often use it badly. They do not, according to May, look carefully enough at history. However, he believes that policymakers can benefit from history, if they engage in critical and systematic analysis.[6]

Bipolarity and Beyond

By the end of World War II, the *bipolar* system was taking shape, and a new balance of power developing. Bipolarity refers to a balance-of-power system in which major power is centered in two rival camps. In the years following World War II, it became clear that the United States and the Soviet Union were the two dominant powers, with a number of other nations clustered around them in a bipolar configuration. During the Cold War, the division became more rigid. The monopoly of nuclear weapons by the superpowers underscored the bipolar structure of the world. However, a variety of factors contributed to a gradual breakdown of rigid bipolarity and to a dispersal of power, beginning in the 1960s and accelerating thereafter. This dispersal of power, much of which is economically based, is discussed in later chapters.

Historian Paul Kennedy gained considerable attention in the late 1980s with his book *The Rise and Fall of the Great Powers*, in which he sought to trace and to explain how various world powers had risen and fallen over five centuries. He discussed the development of the bipolar world during and after World War II. But, wrote Kennedy:

> . . . for all the focus upon the American-Russian relationship and its many ups and downs between 1960 and 1980, other trends had been at work to make the international power system much *less* bipolar than it had appeared to be in the earlier period. Not only had the Third World emerged to complicate matters, but significant fissures had occurred in what had earlier appeared to be the two monolithic blocs dominated by Moscow and Washington.⁷

REALISM AND IDEALISM/MORALISM

Realism or realpolitik had strong American adherents in the post–World War II period, and, indeed, has continued to be a major strain in American thinking on foreign policy and international relations. Leading American advocates of realism and balance of power have included such figures as Kissinger and Zbigniew Brzezinski, both of whom served in high-ranking government positions. Others, including Walter Lippmann and George F. Kennan, have been identified with realism, although their views are not easily categorized. All of these individuals recognized that power has various components, and that American values sometimes conflicted with the realpolitik approach. Policymakers are often forced to make hard choices between conflicting considerations.

Kennan was strongly identified with the origins of America's activist "containment" policy, which was aimed at limiting the Soviet Union's "expansionist tendencies." Often this policy was pictured in "moral" terms as a kind of crusade against communism, which was seen by many in the West as an immoral system of government. In more recent times, Kennan set forth a view that the United States should use its resources prudently, and argued that a truly "moral" foreign policy would avoid the "histrionics of moralism," and, instead, be based on setting a good example for the world, rather than judging others or telling them what to do. He particularly distrusted, as did Morgenthau, a messianic impulse in international politics, or policies driven by ideological crusades rather than careful calculation of national interest. Kennan called for

> a policy founded on recognition of the national interest, reasonably conceived, as the legitimate motivation for a large portion of the nation's behavior, and prepared to pursue that interest without either moral pretension or apology. It would be a policy that would seek the possibilities for service to morality primarily in our behavior, not in our judgment of others. It would restrict our undertakings to the limits established by our own traditions and resources. It would see virtue in our minding our own business wherever there is not some overwhelming reason for minding the business of others.[8]

This approach could be called pragmatic realism, and some might even see in it evidence of the American tendency toward isolationism, which largely disappeared when the United States became a world power. Mikhail Gorbachev might also be thought of as a pragmatic realist. Although undoubtedly a superpower in military terms, the Soviet Union lagged in other areas when Gorbachev came to power. Gorbachev recognized that it was important to strengthen the Soviet economy and society in order to be internationally competitive and he sought to restrain Soviet spending for military and foreign affairs, although he was overtaken by his own reform efforts. (See Gorbachev Profile.)

Most American leaders in recent decades have wanted to be considered as realists. Kissinger, in particular, disdained morality as a principal factor in international relations. However, morality and idealism became strong elements in American foreign policy during the administration of President Jimmy Carter, especially through an emphasis on human rights. While the human rights policy was admirable and scored some important gains, Carter's idealism ran into more practical ("realistic") considerations in international affairs. Nations that were seen as important to United States security interests—South Korea, Pakistan, and the Philippines, for example—were also reported to be human rights violators. Carter found himself in a dilemma; it was very difficult to apply the policy evenly. Later, Carter said that he "did not fully grasp all the ramifications" of his human rights policy and how it would conflict with other goals. Although Carter defended his policy, he acknowledged, "Our country paid a price for its emphasis on human rights."[9]

One of those who criticized Carter was Jeane Kirkpatrick, who served as ambassador to the United Nations under President Reagan. Kirkpatrick contended that the United States should remain supportive of friendly governments, even if they were right-wing dictatorships, and the Reagan administration indicated that it was more interested in "strategic alliances" than in the internal policies of friendly nations. A 1984 State

Department publication of key foreign policy statements of the Reagan administration was titled *Realism, Strength, Negotiation*. Later in the Reagan administration, however, a renewed emphasis was given to human rights as an important factor in American foreign policy. In the Bush administration, Secretary of State James Baker cited realism as one of the major principles of American foreign policy. However, Baker said, "The idea that American moral values and an engaged foreign policy are somehow in contradiction, I think, is clearly incorrect . . . Realism today means not the exclusion of values but their inclusion as the guiding light of our policy." [10]

LEGAL AND MORAL CONCEPTS

Nations often cite legal and moral justifications for their actions. For example, President Bush and leaders of allied nations cited such grounds for action against Saddam Hussein's Iraq in 1990–91. International law is, of course, associated with the framework of the international system as discussed in Chapter 2. The Charter of the United Nations (Article 2) prohibits the use of force by any state against the territorial integrity or political independence of another state. The United Nations Security Council authorized military action to liberate Kuwait if Iraq did not withdraw its occupying troops and release foreign hostages by a certain date. When it did not comply with the United Nations resolution, military action was taken against Iraq, and it could be said that the action had the international legal authority of the United Nations behind it.

International Law

International law can be considered as a concept of international order; or, to phrase it differently, international order is the aim of international law. International law is an instrument for achieving and maintaining order. It is supposed to regulate the conduct of states in their relations with each other. Treaties, which are discussed later in this chapter and in Chapter 5, are one form of international law. These bilateral and multilateral agreements among states may cover a variety of subjects and are binding on those states that are parties to them.

International law is based on the notion of sovereign equality of states and has developed in the modern state system since the Peace of Westphalia (1648). Hugo Grotius (1583–1645), the Dutch author of the celebrated treatise *De Jure Belli et Pacis* (*On the Law of War and Peace*), is often regarded as the father of international law. Grotius recognized that a sovereign state could not legally be controlled by another.

International law is usually more effective in dealing with functional issues in international relations, or what is sometimes referred to as "low politics"—trade, economic, social welfare, and communication issues, for example. Not surprisingly, international law has generally been less effective in managing the "high politics" issues of international security and armed conflict.

Because Saddam Hussein was widely viewed as having acted in a lawless manner and in violation of the United Nations Charter, there was widespread condemnation of his actions and, as noted earlier, United Nations authorization of military action against Iraq. Saddam Hussein attempted to argue that the invasion of Kuwait was an effort to reclaim areas that were rightfully part of Iraq. Even if there were any validity to his claims, Kuwait was internationally recognized as a sovereign nation, and Saddam Hussein could not justify his actions on the basis of international law. The United States and the other nations in the coalition had the principle of international law behind them. As indicated earlier, President Bush also cited moral grounds for the United States military action. (Indeed, in what was widely considered to be an overstatement, Bush said of Saddam Hussein's actions that there had been "nothing like this since World War II, nothing of this moral importance since World War II.")

"Just-War" Concept

Bush also spoke of the battle against Saddam Hussein and Iraq as a "just war." The *just-war* concept is one that is grounded in Western tradition and has often been the subject of debate, particularly in religious circles. Its origins can be traced to the ancient Greek states and to the Roman statesman, Cicero. Through the years, the just-war doctrine (sometimes referred to as *bellum justum*, the Latin term) has been refined by Christians, beginning with St. Augustine in the fourth century, who said that war should be waged only as a necessity. In the thirteenth century, St. Thomas Aquinas listed three elements of a just war: combat must be waged by competent government authority, the cause must be just, and there must be a "right intention" to promote good. Later, in 1625, in his famous work, Grotius wrote "no other just cause for undertaking war can there be excepting injury received."[11]

In the modern era, these are the criteria often cited for a just war:

■ It pursues a "just cause," such as self-defense of the conquest of evil.

■ It is directed by a "competent authority."

■ It is a "last resort" after peaceful means have failed.

■ It carries at least the "probability" of success.

■ It conforms to the standard of "proportionality"—the amount of force used is proportionate to the threat, and the good to be achieved outweighs the damage done.

■ It is "discriminate," avoiding harm to noncombatants where possible.

Although there is no precise Islamic equivalent to the just-war concept, the term *jihad* is often described in the West as meaning "holy war." The term means to strive or struggle to follow Islam, and is sometimes interpreted as including a holy war in the defense of Islam. Indeed, Saddam Hussein and others have sometimes referred to their actions as a jihad. Conversely, Saudi Arabia's Islamic rulers obtained a ruling from their ranking religious figure who declared that Saudi Arabia's self-defense justified a holy war against Saddam.

There will always be debates about moral justification for war and its conduct. While the United States has usually thought of itself as being morally justified in its military actions, this notion came to be hotly debated during the Vietnam War.

Blending Policies and Values

Most nations, regardless of their foreign policy goals, like to cloak them in moralistic or idealistic fashion. Andre Fontaine, a French commentator, has taken a somewhat critical view, particularly of the role of the superpowers. Writes Fontaine:

> No nation is free of pride, and one can even assert that the greater the nation, the greater the pride. Consider the incredible number of countries that have chosen as their national symbol predatory animals, such as the American eagle. But what the United States shares with only the USSR—and perhaps . . . the Ayatollah Khomeini's Iran and Colonel Khadaffi's Libya—is the conviction that its own moral code holds universal value and that it therefore has the right to make that code prevail.[12]

Fontaine notes that Europe "ceaselessly renounces the rules of real-politik inherited from the Romans, codified by Machiavelli, and exemplified in the writings of Shakespeare, but tends to do so with a quiet cynicism."[13]

The moralists maintain that foreign policies based on moral principles are more effective because they build cooperation among nations rather than conflict and competition. Realists see action and power as the keys to international relations and view moralists as utopian and ineffective and not recognizing the realities of national self-interest. The moralists, on the other hand, claim that the realists are sacrificing short-term gains for long-term achievements.

In practice, most policies are a mixture of realism and either moralism/idealism, ideology, or nationalism. The realist approach provides the means for achieving the ends or goals of policy while the moralist/idealist approach is often used to justify and win support for policies. The Marshall Plan, discussed in Chapter 2, was a classic case of a positive combination of realism and moralism/idealism.

GEOPOLITICS

Rather than human rights or other idealistic or moralistic considerations, American authorities have often spoken of *geopolitical* concerns when analyzing or formulating United States policy. Kissinger and Brzezinski are among those who have frequently invoked geopolitical concerns. Modern-day geopolitics is somewhat different from the more traditional concepts of geopolitics, which emphasize location, size, and geographic factors as primary influences in international relations. Various theories were advanced in the years before World War I relating to the importance of geographical factors in international affairs and as keys to security and power. Among the best known of these geopoliticians was Sir Halford Mackinder of Great Britain, who advanced the "heartland theory," arguing that control of the land mass of Eastern Europe and Western Asia was the key to world power. Another approach was the "sea power theory," developed by Alfred Mahan, an American admiral who maintained that the United States could become a major power through naval supremacy. Yet another geopolitical thesis was the "rimland theory," which contended that the rimlands of Europe, the Middle East, Africa, South Asia, and the Far East were the keys to United States security. This theory was advanced by American geographer Nicholas Spykman during World War II.

Although the geopolitical theories had their limitations, geopolitics remains an important factor in international relations. To some extent, of course, technological advances, including missiles and sophisticated weaponry, but also rapid transportation and satellites, used for both communications and intelligence, have rendered some traditional geopolitical considerations less important. In contemporary usage, geopolitics refers not so much to a particular theory about keys to power but to a broader concept involving locations, regional political and security balances, relationships with the great powers, presence of resources (for example, oil or vital minerals), and a variety of strategic factors, including location of military installations or accessibility to an area by the great powers. Such factors repeatedly lead to references to the geopolitical importance of the Middle East–Persian Gulf region. A related concept is *geostrategy* or the geostrategic approach, which emphasizes security aspects and strategic planning, based on a geopolitical assessment.

When the Soviet Union sent troops into Afghanistan in 1979, some Soviet strategists supported it as a necessary geostrategic move—to protect Soviet interests in a bordering country. Likewise, some American strategists argued that it was important for the United States, from a geostrategic standpoint, to counter the Soviet move, which was seen as a potential threat to Pakistan, a nation friendly to the United States. In cooperation with Pakistan and China, the United States provided assistance to the Afghan resistance.

Brzezinski, a professor of international relations who served as Carter's national security adviser, frequently invoked what he called "geopolitical imperatives."[14] During the late 1970s he spoke of a "crescent of crisis" which ran from Egypt through the Persian Gulf through Iran and to

Afghanistan. In the late 1980s he wrote of three regions of major geopolitical concern to the United States: Eastern Europe, the Persian Gulf/ Middle Eastern area, and Central America.

Geopolitics and the balance of power have often been cited as primary factors bearing on the United States's relations with China. American policymakers have emphasized China's geopolitical significance and stressed its importance as a counterbalance to the Soviet Union in Asia. Kissinger, in particular, has been associated with this view. Even in 1989 when the "prodemocracy" demonstrators in China were ruthlessly put down by the Chinese government, Kissinger warned that the United States must be very careful about entering into a diplomatic "antagonism" with China that could give the Soviet Union "a free ride" in influence in Asia.[15]

Kissinger was involved in the reopening of relations between China and the United States, which occurred while Richard Nixon was the United States president. The visit by Nixon to China in 1972 ended a period of more than two decades in which the United States and the People's Republic, which was established when the Communists came to power in 1949, had no diplomatic relations and very little contact. Later, writing about the Nixon initiative which he helped engineer, Kissinger said:

> China was not important to us because it was physically powerful: Chou-En-lai was surely right in his repeated protestations that his nation was not a superpower. In fact, had China been stronger it would not have pursued the improvement of relations with us with the same single-mindedness. Peking [Beijing] needed us to help break out of its isolation and as a counterweight to the potentially mortal threat along its northern border. We needed China to enhance the flexibility of our diplomacy . . . We had to take account of other power centers and strive for an equilibrium.[16]

As was discussed in Chapter 1, in the triangular relationship involving China, the Soviet Union, and the United States, each has at times tried to be the "balancer," or to use relations with one of the nations to influence behavior or policy of the third nation. This relationship has sometimes been referred to as an example of a *tripolar* system. However, in most respects, China, although the world's most populous nation, ranked well behind the United States and the former Soviet Union in superpower status. Thus, there was no real tripolar equilibrium. Still, China could be an important factor in the international power balance.

Another term used in international relations is *hegemony*, and it had particular resonance in the United States–Soviet–China relationship. In modern times, the term was popularized by China's Mao Zedong, who accused at times both the Soviets and Americans of seeking to exercise hegemony—preponderant influence or dominance over other nations or regions—just as Athens sought hegemony among the warring city-states of Greece. Wide discrepancies in power can result in hegemonic relationships between otherwise sovereign states.

The geopolitical reordering that contributed to and resulted from the end of the Cold War brought proclamations of "a new world order." However, the balance of power and geopolitics remain significant considerations in international relations in the view of some influential analysts and strategists. "The balance of power, a concept much maligned in American political writing—rarely used without being preceded by the perjorative 'outdated'—has in fact been the precondition of peace," Kissinger wrote.[17] However, Kissinger has recognized that the elements of power have changed somewhat.

He has written:

> . . . to the extent that balance of power means constant jockeying for marginal advantages over an opponent, it no longer applies. The reason is that the determination of national power has changed fundamentally in the nuclear age. Throughout history, the primary concern of most national leaders has been to accumulate geopolitical and military power. It would have seemed inconceivable even a generation ago that such power once gained could not be translated directly into advantage over one's opponent. But now both we and the Soviet Union have begun to find that each increment of power does not necessarily represent an increment of usable political strength.[18]

The next section of this chapter will consider how changing world circumstances have led to alternative ways of assessing power and of looking at world politics.

ALTERNATIVE PERSPECTIVES AND METHODS OF ANALYSIS

While the traditional and fundamental concepts which have been discussed thus far continue to have considerable significance in international relations theory, analysis, and policymaking, the changing global circumstances and growing complexities in world affairs have helped open up new perspectives and the development of a variety of other ways of analyzing and conceptualizing international relations. The first section of this chapter focused on such concepts as realism, the realist/idealist dichotomy, the balance of power, the role of history in analyzing international relations, and on strategic and geopolitical approaches. Other methodologies or frameworks are considered by some to be more suitable or at least to have important application for the world of today and tomorrow. Critics of more traditional theories have asserted that no general theory is relevant if it cannot take into account the rapidly changing technological, social, economic, and political environment.

Many analysts would agree that significant changes have occurred and that the rigid bipolarity which characterized the balance-of-power system that emerged after World War II has been significantly moderated as a result of a growing *polycentrism*, in which an increasing number of nations are able to exert influence on world affairs. A polycentric or *multipolar* system or world is one in which there are a number of power centers. George Shultz, the former American secretary of state, said, "The bipolar world which emerged in the postwar era has been steadily eroded by accelerating changes on a global scale—changes which have widely dispersed political, economic, and military power." [19]

It should be stated that the alternative approaches to analyzing international relations did not grow only from the dispersal of power and the broader range of actors and issues affecting world affairs. Some theorists believed that analysis of international relations required a more scientific approach. Known as *behavioralists*, this group moved beyond such traditional concerns as diplomatic history, current affairs, international organization, and international law, and concentrated on examining and interpreting behavior of states and policymakers through scientific analysis. Behavioralists rely on collection and analysis of quantitative data. Most serious students of international relations recognize that both the traditional and behavioral methods have a contribution to make and that there is some overlap between the various approaches.

Before discussing some of the newer paradigms, mention should be made of another valuable approach to analysis—the decision or *decision-making* approach, which is concerned with how and why decisions are made in international politics, and who makes them. This subject is dealt with in the following chapter, which looks at how national foreign policies are shaped and carried out. Throughout the book there are portraits of individual leaders and discussions of the role that key individuals can have in influencing national foreign policies and international affairs.

If the behavioralists were introducing a different approach to analyzing international relations, others were developing various perspectives or frameworks for viewing world affairs. As noted already, new trends and complexities in global affairs helped bring about these alternative approaches. Some of the most important of these approaches can be placed under the broad heading of *globalism* or the globalist school. Related to this is the concept of *transnationalism* or the transnationalist approach. Still another related approach is the *pluralist* approach. Not all writers and analysts will necessarily use these terms in the same way. However, all of these approaches recognize the importance of nonstate actors— meaning international or transnational actors other than governments. Realism emphasizes the state as the principal actor. These alternative approaches see nonstate actors as also being significant factors in international affairs. Examples of nonstate actors would be international organizations, multinational corporations, international financial institutions, mass communications media that operate internationally, even terrorist organizations.

A particularly useful contribution in this area has been made by Robert Keohane and Joseph Nye, beginning with their 1971 book, *Transnational Relations and World Politics*. The authors focused on the growing significance of nonstate actors in global politics and moved away from the realist emphasis on military security as always being the dominant goal of nations; instead, they suggested that national goals are more diverse and that a variety of issues come into play. This view of international relations centered on what is called *complex interdependence*. The concept of interdependence and its increasing significance as a factor in world affairs has already been discussed in this book and will be a recurring theme.

The perspective advanced by Keohane and Nye in their writings and by others with similar viewpoints begins with a recognition of the diffusion of global power that has occurred in recent years. This perspective is sometimes referred to as *neorealism*. Actually, Keohane and Nye argue that both realism and their alternative perspective are idealized versions and visions of political reality and that most situations in world politics fall somewhere in between. Realism provides a strong base for analyzing international relations because of its focus on the key elements of power and interests. But neorealism and the alternative perspectives such as globalism and transnationalism, recognizing the significance of interdependence and the diffusion and diversity of power, bring important added dimensions to analyzing and understanding international relations.

NATIONALISM AND INTERNATIONALISM

In studying and analyzing international relations, it is important to have an understanding of these analytical perspectives. An additional broad perspective is also useful and instructive. This perspective centers on the notion that much of what drives international relations today, and much of what characterizes the behavior of both state actors and transnational nonstate actors, is either nationalism or internationalism. Remember, these terms are being used broadly here. *Nationalism*, already discussed in this book, remains a powerful force in world affairs. In recent decades it was especially evident in the striving for independence by nations that were formerly under colonial control or other external domination. Nationalism is often a rallying point for nations or leaders who feel themselves threatened. Nationalism has often become entangled with and intensified by religious causes, as it was in Iran under Ayatollah Khomeini, who railed against outside influence.

In the 1950s, when a number of former colonies were obtaining national independence, the British writer Barbara Ward (Lady Jackson) said "The great paradox of the century is that we have reached an extreme pitch of national feeling all around the world just at the moment when, from every national point of view, we have to find ways of progressing beyond nationalism." Ward said that it was important "to rally all that we have of reason and clarity and common sense and look at our world not through a haze of national emotions but see it as it is, in cold, hard, reality." (Even this call for a more internationalist view is put in terms of realism.) She pointed out, "Mobility and accessibility are replacing the old rooted, isolated existence of mankind from one end of the globe to the other. We are also drawn together by the inter-connectedness of our world economy." [20]

Some would assert that nationalism is now fading as a primary factor in world affairs, and in certain important respects this is true, and it is expected to continue to become less important. Part of the reason that this is true is because of the increasing interdependence that has already been pointed out, and the benefits that can grow from cooperative efforts such as Europe's Common Market, and from the vast number of governmental and nongovernmental activities and ventures that cross national boundaries. This broad range of activities is what we refer to here as *internationalism*. In this sense the term is closely related to interdependence or to globalism or transnationalism, terms discussed previously. There are many factors that are pulling and pushing peoples of the world closer together, including technological as well as economic and political factors. Thus, both nationalism and internationalism can be seen as significant forces in world affairs, and many developments can be seen as being examples of one or the other. Some cases even involve both. It could be argued, for example, that Japan, a nation heavily dependent on trade, can be seen as strongly internationalist. On the other hand, Japan's economic policies, including import restrictions, have often been considered to be strongly nationalist, an example of economic nationalism, which is discussed in Chapter 8.

THE UNITED STATES, PANAMA, AND THE CANAL: SIGNIFICANT ISSUES

To demonstrate the usage and application of some of the key terms and concepts in international affairs, it is useful to look at some actual events and issues. The relations between the United States and Panama and the issues revolving around the Panama Canal provide some good examples.

There had long been interest in constructing a canal connecting the Atlantic and Pacific oceans so that ships would not have to make the long trip around South America. With the United States becoming more of a world power, with international trade increasing, the need for a shorter shipping route became more important by the beginning of the twentieth century. This need was dramatically underlined when, during the Spanish-American War, the United States dispatched the battleship *Oregon* from San Francisco to its Caribbean/Atlantic battle station after another battleship, the *Maine*, had been blown up in Havana harbor in 1898. It took the *Oregon* 67 days to complete the voyage, a trip of

12,000 miles—instead of 4,000 miles if there had been a canal across Central America linking the Atlantic and Pacific.

Panama's location at the narrowest point of the isthmus that connects North and South America made it an attractive site for the canal and gave it special *geopolitical* significance. Mention has already been made of American Admiral Alfred Mahan and his "sea power" theory of geopolitics, published in 1890. Mahan was a strong advocate of a canal across Central America. One of those strongly influenced by Mahan's theory was Theodore Roosevelt, who became president of the United States in 1901 and a key figure in development of the Canal.

The initial canal project was undertaken by a French company, and later reorganized with American support and completed by the United States. Panama was originally part of Colombia, but Colombia had turned down a United States treaty offer for rights to build a canal through Panama. With clear encouragement from the United States, Panama declared its independence from Colombia and formed a separate nation, the Republic of Panama, in 1903. Two weeks later a canal treaty was signed with the United States. To the dismay of the Panamanians, the treaty was written by a Frenchman (Philippe Bunau-Varilla) who had a financial stake in the outcome of the negotiations. His authority to act on behalf of Panama was questionable and the treaty was signed before any Panamanian had a chance to read it. The 1903 treaty immediately became a symbol to Panamanians of the external domination of their country and it continued to be a constant sore spot. The treaty was a source of constant irritation to Panamanian *nationalism*.

Why did Americans also have such strong nationalistic feelings about a canal in Panama? Construction of the canal was a remarkable engineering achievement and a source of great pride for the United States. The canal was opened in 1914 under United States operation, with the treaty granting the United States the rights to construct and operate the canal "in perpetuity" and to act as if it were sovereign in the area adjacent to the canal. Although the United States was never a *colonial* or *imperialist* power in the same sense as Britain or France, many would cite Panama as almost the equivalent of a colony, and the Canal Zone, the area adjacent to the canal where American employees and administrators lived, was akin to a colonial outpost. And the contrast between the prosperous lifestyle in the Canal Zone—off limits to most Panamanians—and Panama itself, where there was considerable poverty and underdevelopment, was striking.

Over the years some minor adjustments were made to the 1903 treaty, but there continued to be strong agitation within Panama against the United States and its control of the area's major economic resources. Criticism of the United States intensified over the establishment of American military bases and training camps for Latin American police and military in the area. In 1964, controversy about flying both the American and

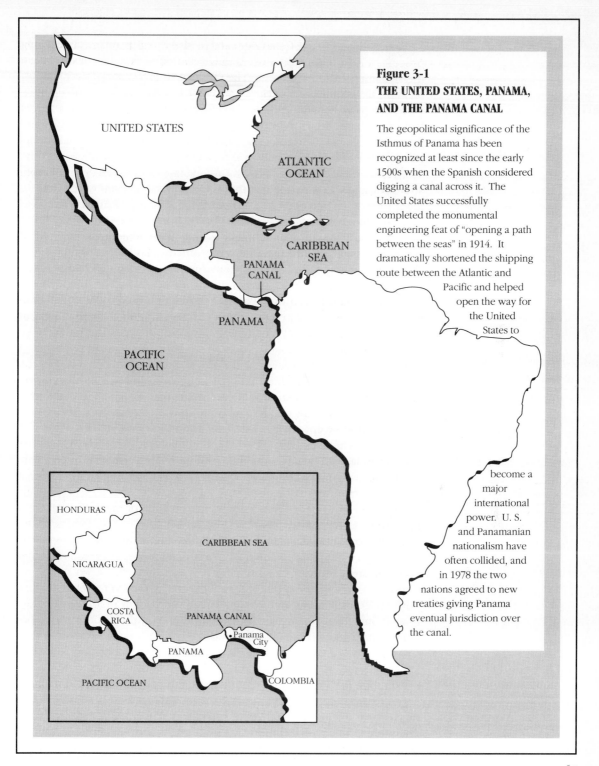

Figure 3-1
THE UNITED STATES, PANAMA, AND THE PANAMA CANAL

The geopolitical significance of the Isthmus of Panama has been recognized at least since the early 1500s when the Spanish considered digging a canal across it. The United States successfully completed the monumental engineering feat of "opening a path between the seas" in 1914. It dramatically shortened the shipping route between the Atlantic and Pacific and helped open the way for the United States to become a major international power. U. S. and Panamanian nationalism have often collided, and in 1978 the two nations agreed to new treaties giving Panama eventual jurisdiction over the canal.

UNITED STATES

ATLANTIC OCEAN

CARIBBEAN SEA

PANAMA CANAL

PANAMA

PACIFIC OCEAN

HONDURAS

NICARAGUA

CARIBBEAN SEA

COSTA RICA

PANAMA CANAL

Panama City

PANAMA

PACIFIC OCEAN

COLOMBIA

Panamanian flags in the Canal Zone led to bloody riots, and opened a long process of negotiations that eventually resulted in new treaties between the two countries in 1977–78. The fact that riots broke out over the display of flags is indicative of the importance of nationalism in the conflict, with the flags providing visual symbolism of national pride. Panama had finally earned the right to have its flag flown alongside the stars and stripes at some sites in the Canal Zone. In many ways it was a clash between United States nationalism and Panamanian nationalism. Before the 1964 crisis escalated to riots, both United States and Panamanian demonstrators "sang" their national anthems (in protest) at each other. Resentment over what was seen as a United States colony within its own borders stirred nationalism in Panama. On the other hand, the United States had an almost romantic attachment to the Canal, which was one of this country's first great international achievements and helped establish the United States as a world power. Construction of the Canal had been an epic event. It was Ronald Reagan, in his unsuccessful bid for the 1976 Republican presidential nomination, who made a statement which captured the sentiments of many Americans. Speaking of the Canal, Reagan repeatedly commented, "We bought it, we built it, we paid for it, and we intend to keep it."

The growing assertiveness of the Panamanians should be seen in the context of an important international trend that has been discussed previously—the anticolonial winds of change that began to be felt after World War II. Panama was not immune to the contagious nature of nationalism that swept Africa, Asia, and Latin America in the 1950s and 1960s and which largely ended the colonial era. In nearby Cuba, the revolution led by Fidel Castro was seen by many Panamanians as a successful slap at American power. It should be pointed out, however, that while Panamanian nationalism was strongly felt, not all Panamanians were really "anti-American." Actually, the attitude of many Panamanians toward the United States might best be described as a "love-hate relationship." Similar attitudes could be found in the Philippines, where the United States has also remained a powerful influence. There is much that Panamanians admire in the United States, but there has been strong resentment of the domination of their country by the United States. Thus, both the United States and Panama have been caught in a web of sometimes conflicting global trends. As a superpower, the United States has been concerned with geopolitics and the Canal's strategic value. In Panama there was anticolonial, reactive nationalism in opposition to United States hegemony.

Although the United States found itself subject to what could be compared to anticolonial pressures in Panama, there was some irony in this because the United States had, in broad terms, identified itself with and encouraged this global impulse. As George Moffett has written, "During World War II the United States had been openly critical of the overseas empires of its European allies, and afterward had acted as midwife to the United Nations, one of the most important forums for the expression of the anticolonialist persuasion."[21] Later, however, the United States, in a sense, replaced the French as the external power in Vietnam, and in Panama the principled anticolonial position previously taken by the United States was pictured by the Panamanians, who began to use the United Nations as a forum to gain support for their negotiating position against the United States, as hollow rhetoric. In 1973, the United Nations Security Council held a special meeting in Panama, only its second meeting away from the New York headquarters. The United States used its veto to block a Security Council resolution calling for a new treaty which would "guarantee full respect for Panama's effective sovereignty over all its territory." Although the United States killed the resolution, Panama scored important propaganda points in the United Nations meeting and demonstrated that it had wide support, especially in Latin America and the Third World.

As internal pressure for change continued to build in Panama, and as Panama successfully developed international support for its position, discussions and negotiations between the United States and Panama proceeded in fits and starts. American political leaders were reluctant to confront what had become an emotional and politically volatile issue. There was little public understanding of the position in which the United States found itself in Panama. Henry Kissinger and others recognized that the Canal, while becoming less vital to the United States from a military and economic standpoint, was becoming more vulnerable to sabotage or to political disruption. And the pressures of internationalism had to be taken into account. Venezuelan President Carlos Andres Perez stated that it was the unanimous opinion of all Latin America that Panama should have control over the Canal. If not, "Panama will become a keg of dynamite."[22] He and others actively pressed Panama's cause.

THE NEW TREATIES

It was a combination of *realism* and *idealism* that led the administration of President Jimmy Carter in 1977 to conclude negotiations on two treaties which would give Panama territorial jurisdiction over the canal in the year 2000 and increased revenues, while the United States retained the right to ensure the neutrality of the canal. Idealism was certainly an element that motivated the American decision to make the agreement—the conviction that, consistent with American principles and the ideals of the international political system, Panama should be able to exercise primary control over the canal and its territory. It was viewed as an example of American statesmanship and as an important gesture of goodwill toward Latin America, where United States control of the canal had been regarded as a remnant of imperialism. At the same time, however, there were compelling reasons that made the decision an example of realpolitik or political realism, based on a realistic assessment of the problems in Panama, international pressures, and United States *national interests*.

Ultimately, United States leaders determined that the nation's interests were best served by yielding complete control of the Canal rather than trying to hang on to it. In the era of giant oil tankers and container ships, the canal had become somewhat less important in global shipping, and, as noted earlier, the canal would be virtually impossible to defend effectively and efficiently, particularly against anti-American guerillas seeking to render it inoperable. It was said that the United States had to give up direct control over the canal in order to save it. Many American business leaders supported the treaties because they believed that United States economic interests would be hindered as long as the canal remained the center of bitter controversy.

In 1978, the United States Senate engaged in its longest treaty debate since the protracted consideration of the Treaty of Versailles in 1919–20. In that case, President Wilson, seeking approval for the treaty and United States participation in the League of Nations, was rebuffed by the Senate in a bitter fight. It was a triumph for isolationism and unilateralism and a rejection of Wilson's idealism and multilateralism/internationalism, although partisan politics entered into the decision as well. (Chapter 4 discusses national politics and their effects on foreign policies.) There was also a bitter fight over the Panama treaties, but this time the Senate gave its approval, although by the narrowest of margins. (A two-thirds vote is required in the Senate for treaty passage and both treaties passed with only one vote to spare.) This time there was no real question of American isolationism, and, as noted earlier, the rationale for the treaty was a blend of idealism, realism, and internationalism.

Of course, the new treaties did not end all problems between the United States and Panama or within Panama. Like many Latin American countries and many elsewhere in the Third World, Panama continued to be plagued by economic and political difficulties. General Omar Torrijos, who led Panama at the time that the new treaties were finalized, died in a 1981 plane crash. He was replaced by General Manuel Noriega, an autocratic ruler who controlled Panama's politics, and who was believed to have ties to international drug traffickers. Noriega blocked efforts by his political opponents to gain power through democratic elections and resisted pressure from the United States for him to step aside. He became an embarrassment to United States political leaders and an issue in United States politics. Ultimately, the United States intervened militarily in Panama, although on a limited basis. After other means, including diplomacy and economic pressure, failed to force Noriega out, the United States resorted to military power to topple him. The relationship between Panama and the United States is an ongoing saga, and is discussed further in Chapter 5.

Because of its geostrategic location, Panama will always be important to the United States. And there are strong and historic economic and political ties between the two countries. But the relationship, particularly the long controversy over the Canal and the differing perspectives of the two nations, is instructive, and illustrates many of the concepts and theories of international relations discussed earlier in this chapter.

POWER, POLITICS, AND NEW POSSIBILITIES

Remaining chapters will offer further examples of how these concepts and theories apply to world affairs, and will focus on the diffusion of international power and the changing nature and composition of power in international relations. The end of the Cold War period and some of the extraordinary political and economic changes that occurred as part of and as contributors to the demise of the old East-West rivalry opened up new possibilities for cooperation and compelled a new view of international politics—and of the importance that had been attached to the bipolar framework for analyzing international relations.

At a time of increasing integration and interdependence among nations, there are still powerful manifestations of independence and nationalism. Nor can we overlook the importance of domestic politics in shaping foreign policies, the significance of perceptions of national interests, and of the role of national leaders in influencing international affairs—topics that will be considered in the next chapter.

NOTES

1. Hans J. Morgenthau, *Politics Among Nations*, 6th ed., revised by Kenneth W. Thompson (New York: Alfred A. Knopf, 1985), p. 31.
2. Thucydides, *History of the Peloponnesian War*, trans. Rex Warner (New York: Penguin, 1982); also: *History of Peloponnesian War*, trans. R. Crowley (New York: Modern Library College Editions, 1985).
3. Henry Kissinger, (ed.), *Problems of National Strategy* (New York: Praeger, 1965), p. 3.
4. John Lewis Gaddis, "The Post-War International System: Elements of Stability and Instability" in Bruce Russett, Harvey Starr, and Richard Stall, *Choices in World Politics* (New York: W. H. Freeman, 1989), pp. 7–8.
5. Thucydides, *History of the Peloponnesian War*.
6. Ernest R. May, *"Lessons" of the Past* (New York: Oxford University Press, 1973).
7. Paul Kennedy, *The Rise and Fall of the Great Powers* (New York: Random House, 1987), p. 397.
8. George Kennan, "Morality and Foreign Policy," *Foreign Affairs*, vol. 64, no. 2, winter, 1985–86, pp. 217–18.

9. Jimmy Carter, *Keeping Faith* (New York: Bantam, 1982), p. 144, 151.

10. James Baker, (Secretary of State) "Power for Good: American Foreign Policy in the New Era," address before the American Society of Newspaper Editors, Washington, D.C., April 14, 1989.

11. Grotius, *De Jure Belli et Pacis*, Bk. II, Chap. I, sec. 1, par. 4, quoted in Hans Kelsen, *Principles of International Law* (2nd ed.), revised and edited by Robert W. Tucker (New York: Holt, Rinehart and Winston, 1967), p. 30.

12. Andre Fontaine, "Beyond Wilson and Rambo," *Foreign Policy* 65, winter, 1986–87, p. 33.

13. *Ibid.*

14. Zbigniew Brzezinski, "America's New Geostrategy," *Foreign Affairs*, vol. 66, no. 4, spring 1988.

15. Quoted in Thomas L. Friedman, "Bush Administration Ponders Response," *New York Times*, June 5, 1989.

16. Henry Kissinger, *White House Years* (Boston: Little, Brown and Company), 1979, p. 1049.

17. *Ibid.*, p. 195.

18. Henry Kissinger, *American Foreign Policy* (New York: Norton, 1974), p. 141.

19. George Shultz, "Managing the U.S.–Soviet Relationship," address before the Henry M. Jackson School of International Studies, Seattle, Washington, February 5, 1988.

20. Barbara Ward, *Five Ideas That Change the World* (New York: Norton, 1959), pp. 151–52.

21. George Moffett, *The Limits of Victory—The Ratification of the Panama Canal Treaties* (Ithaca: Cornell University Press, 1985), p. 26.

22. *Ibid.*, p. 39. See also: William J. Jorden, *Panama Odyssey* (Austin: University of Texas Press, 1984); William L. Furlong and Margaret E. Scranton, *The Dynamics of Foreign Policymaking* (Boulder: Westview, 1984); John Opperman, "The Panama Canal Treaties," in Hoyt Purvis and Steven J. Baker (eds.), *Legislating Foreign Policy* (Boulder: Westview, 1984); Walter La Feber, *The Panama Canal* (New York: Oxford University Press, 1978).

CHARLES DE GAULLE

Seldom has an individual leader better personified a nation or embodied national spirit than Charles de Gaulle of France.

De Gaulle was a towering figure, literally (6′4″ in height) and figuratively, who became a symbol of France's determination to uphold a proud national heritage and to set and maintain a course of national independence in the age of superpowers and bipolarism.

Twice De Gaulle rose up to revive France—first from defeat, then from internal division. He initially became an international figure during World War II. An obscure brigadier general, he escaped to London as his battered nation was about to capitulate to Nazi Germany. In London he broadcast back to France, urging his countrymen to resist the Nazis. He became the spokesman for the Free French cause. He took it upon himself to keep alive the independent spirit of France, to save the nation from total humiliation, and to assure it a place among the world powers after the war. Later, De Gaulle wrote, "What I was determined to save was the French Nation and the French State. What I had to bring back into the war was not just Frenchmen, but France."[1]

When Paris was liberated during the late stages of World War II, General Charles De Gaulle led a triumphal parade through the city, beginning at the Arc de Triomphe. De Gaulle was highly visible, standing out among the marchers who were cheered by 2 million people in an explosion of national fervor.

In August 1944, when Paris was liberated, De Gaulle led a triumphal march between two Parisian landmarks, the Arc de Triomphe and the Cathedral of Notre Dame. Although De Gaulle had not been involved in the actual liberation, he was the man in the spotlight. The picture of De Gaulle striding down the Champs-Elysées, resplendent in his military uniform, visible above all the rest, is one of history's memorable snapshots. When bursts of gunfire rang out from the rooftops at one point during the procession, the crowd scattered, and those in the march dove for cover. De Gaulle, however, appeared calm and unshaken amidst the confusion and panic, reinforcing his image as a hero, leader, and historic figure.

After the liberation, De Gaulle formed a provisional government. However, within a short time the French political factions were openly squabbling. Despite his opposition, a new constitution was approved, establishing a parliamentary system without the strong executive he believed essential for a renewed France. He resigned as prime minister in 1946. A year later he formed the Rally of the French People

(Rassemblement du Peuple Français), which he said was a party against parties. The RPF criticized the "weak" parliamentary system and inveighed against the Communists, who were a strong political force in France. After some early success, the RPF began to lose ground and eventually dissolved.

In 1955, nearing age 65, De Gaulle announced his retirement from public life, saying "We shall not meet again until the tempest again looses itself on France." As France stumbled through political instability, recurring bouts of inflation, and a disastrous colonial war in Vietnam, De Gaulle seemed left aside. But many more chapters were to be written in the De Gaulle story, and his greatest impact on the international scene was still ahead.

THE ALGERIAN CRISIS

By 1958 France was beset with deep internal divisions and on the brink of civil war. Again it was De Gaulle who pulled the nation together. Controversy over war in the French colony of Algeria was dividing the nation. The French

De Gaulle returned to power in France in 1958 to deal with the divisive and crippling crisis caused by the revolution for national independence in the French colony of Algeria. Seen here on a 1959 visit to Algeria, De Gaulle surprised many by agreeing to Algerian independence in 1962, a policy he believed to be consistent with France's long-term interests. The end of colonialism in Algeria helped speed the end of the colonial era.

government, already stung by the defeat at Dienbienphu in Vietnam and the loss of the Southeast Asian (Indochina) colonies, was bedeviled by the conflict over Algeria. Movements for national independence were sweeping the former colonial territories in much of the Third World. As the National Liberation Front, the Algerian nationalist organization, gained strength in its war to end colonial rule, French Army officers and some French residents of Algeria tried to seize administrative control of the country, openly defying the government in Paris. With the French government in disarray, De Gaulle emerged as the only figure who could again unite the country in time of crisis.

Although the push for national independence had already been successful in some former European colonies and was being strongly felt in others, Algeria was an especially intractable situation. Separated only by the Mediterranean Sea, Algeria was much closer to France than most colonies were to their colonial powers.

To the surprise of some, De Gaulle imposed an "Algerian Algeria" solution, moving to liquidate what he had previously sought to preserve—the French colonial system. There is reason to believe that De Gaulle concluded that the military and political cost of controlling the colonies would ultimately weaken France, a factor that other European powers, the United States, and the Soviets had to confront at various points in regard to their overseas involvement.

De Gaulle quickly gained approval for a new French constitution, giving the president wide powers. He was then elected president of the new system of government, known as the Fifth Republic. There was still a strong "French Algerian" movement which opposed independence for Algeria. Elements of the French Army and French settlers in Algeria sought to rebel against De Gaulle, and when that failed, a group known as the Secret Army Organization (OAS) undertook a terrorist campaign throughout France and Algeria in an effort to subvert De Gaulle and his plans for Algerian self-determination. De Gaulle was the target of assassination

attempts, and in one case a bullet missed his skull by an inch. Despite the intensity of the opposition, De Gaulle succeeded in ending the Algerian crisis and in 1962 Algeria became a sovereign independent nation. The end of colonialism in Algeria helped hasten the finish of the colonial era.

With the chaos over Algeria behind him, De Gaulle was finally free to pursue his visions and strategies in world affairs. De Gaulle was fiercely dedicated to establishing and maintaining an independent role for France and to upholding French prestige in the world. Some referred to De Gaulle's efforts as the politics of grandeur, and although De Gaulle achieved much, some of his aims and goals were probably unrealistic, more in keeping with an earlier age.

THE FRENCH NATION AND THE WORLD

Fundamental to De Gaulle's approach was his belief in the durability of the nation-state and in the sovereignty of France. He did not want France to be too dependent on or too closely tied to other nations.

One of his first steps was to try to gain a stronger role for France in the direction of the North Atlantic Treaty Organization (NATO). When the Americans and the British resisted this, De Gaulle began disengaging France from NATO, without formally withdrawing. Eventually, France did pull out of the alliance's high command. American military bases were removed from France and the NATO headquarters moved to Belgium. De Gaulle believed that France should have its own nuclear weapons capability, a *force de frappe* (striking force) which De Gaulle considered essential to France's independence and her status as an international power. He often asserted that American power would not necessarily come to the rescue of Europe if, at the same time, the United States was threatened with destruction.

His moves to assert France's independence sometimes brought him into conflict with the United States. (It was suggested by some that De Gaulle bore a grudge because he believed that he had been slighted by the Americans and British by being excluded from the final World War II allied summit meetings at Yalta and Potsdam, where the Americans, British, and Soviets agreed on the outlines of postwar Europe.) He resented what he saw as a threat of American dominance of Europe, aided at first by Britain and later by West Germany. He also resented America's cultural influence, and he saw part of his role as protecting France's cultural tradition and language. (He was strongly opposed to the incorporation of American words into French usage.) Much of what he did in world affairs was considered antagonistic to the United States, and many thought of him as anti-American. Nonetheless, he considered himself to be a man of the West and he sometimes emphasized the traditional ties between France and the United States. He was the first of the European allies to offer unreserved support to President Kennedy at the time of the Cuban missile crisis. When Kennedy was assassinated in 1963, De Gaulle was the first world leader to announce that he would attend the funeral.

FRANCE IN EUROPE

He preferred to keep Americans at a distance and he believed that a weak and divided Europe would remain subordinate and subservient to the United States. His strategy was that since European cooperation was desirable and probably inevitable as an historical process, he should do what he could to see that it developed in a way consistent with French interests. Contrary to early expectations, De Gaulle accepted the Treaty of Rome, setting up the European Common Market. But in some respects the Common Market would be a thorn in his side. He wanted France to benefit from European cooperation without sacrificing national identity or control. He believed in cooperative arrangements among nations to uphold the power and independence of the individual nations. As it eventually developed, and with Frenchmen playing a leading role, the Common Market went far beyond what De Gaulle might have imagined in terms of structure and integration, becoming something of a supranational grouping. De Gaulle had feared supranationalism, which involved transfer of some decision-making power from the individual nations to a central authority, and that has happened to an extent in the Common Market. On the other hand, De Gaulle thought it important for Europe to become more of a force in world affairs and a balance to Soviet and American power, and the Common Market has helped make that happen.

In 1963, De Gaulle opposed British entry into the Common Market and accused Britain of being a "trojan horse" for extending American influence into the Common Market. He believed that Britain's cultural, economic, and political traditions were too dissimilar from those of the six original Common Market countries. Not long afterward, he signed a treaty on Franco-German friendship, as De Gaulle, long critical and distrustful of the Germans, now saw France and West Germany as the cornerstone of the new Europe. De Gaulle sought to convert West Germany to a "European" rather than an "Atlantic" viewpoint. In effect, he was playing his "German card," just as some years later the United States would seek to play the "China card." Although De Gaulle and German Chancellor Konrad Adenauer institutionalized Franco-German cooperation, the two countries soon diverged on major issues, particularly after Adenauer left office late in 1963. The Germans favored British entry into the Common Market, and remained firmly committed to NATO. Later De Gaulle referred to West Germany as "America's Foreign Legion in Europe."

LOOKING TO THE FUTURE

If De Gaulle's European policy involved keeping the United States and Britain at a distance (although not too far), it also involved developing an *entente* or *rapprochement* with the Soviet Union. In 1966, De Gaulle made a dramatic trip to Moscow to meet Soviet leaders. He was

As president of France, De Gaulle wanted to establish his country as an international power with an independent foreign policy. He favored improved relations with Russia and in 1966 made a dramatic trip to Moscow to meet Soviet leaders. He is pictured at the Kremlin with Communist Party leader Leonid Brezhnev.

one of the first to envision a post–Cold War world and he believed that, regardless of ideology, it would eventually be in Russia's interest to join up with Europe. He spoke often and fondly of "a Europe from the Atlantic to the Urals." The Ural mountain range in Russia has traditionally been seen as the dividing point between Europe and Asia. De Gaulle said:

> Europe, the mother of modern civilization, must establish herself all the way from the Atlantic to the Urals, and live in a state of harmony and cooperation with a view to developing her immense resources, and so as to play, together with her daughter, America, her worthy role . . .[2]

De Gaulle also frequently referred to "Europe of the Fatherlands," making clear that he was not speaking of a federation, but of broad cooperation among independent nation-states—

Western Europe, Eastern Europe, and the Soviet Union. De Gaulle's grand design—an independent Europe largely free of ideological division and of American influence—suffered a major blow in 1968 when the Soviets invaded Czechoslovakia. However, two decades later echoes of De Gaulle's remarks could be heard in Mikhail Gorbachev's talk of a "common European home."

At the same time that De Gaulle was pursuing his European goals, he also sought to exert leadership in the Third World and among nonaligned nations by trying to create an alternative or balance to what he saw as the dual hegemonies of the United States and the Soviet Union. Polarization of the world into two opposing camps, he believed, tended to increase global tensions.

In 1964, De Gaulle stunned the world by extending diplomatic recognition to the People's Republic of China. Like the United States and most Western nations, France had not recognized the government in Beijing after the Communists took power in 1949. In making this move, De Gaulle was not only asserting France's independence but acting, as he saw it, as a realist. De Gaulle said that recognition did not imply "any kind of approval of the regime that at present dominates China." Instead, he said, "France only recognizes the world as it is."[3]

LEGEND AND LEGACY

While De Gaulle was pursuing his goal of international grandeur and his version of geopolitics, there were growing problems within France. Increasingly, in appearance and style, he was seen as representing an earlier age, a legendary figure in a time of rapid modernization. The younger generation in France was becoming restless with his failure to cope with growing social and economic problems. Grandeur—membership in the nuclear "club," foreign aid, stockpiling of gold reserves, development of supersonic passenger aircraft (the Concorde)—was costly.

The alienation of students and workers was dramatized in the Paris revolt of 1968, part of an international tide of protest. The Paris turmoil shook De Gaulle's government to its roots and forced new parliamentary elections. Although De Gaulle survived the events of 1968, his position had been seriously undermined. In 1969, French voters rejected De Gaulle's plan for a regional structure for France, which would have decentralized national administration. De Gaulle had warned that he would resign if the plan was not approved in a national referendum—a technique that he had used successfully in the past. This time it failed, and De Gaulle left the Elysée Palace and the presidency and again retired to his country home in Colombey-les-deux-Eglises. He died in 1970.

De Gaulle had succeeded in many respects, and he had made France once again an important force in world affairs. He was a powerful advocate for an independent France. He gave his country a new sense of direction and a stable system of government.

Unlike many contemporary national leaders, De Gaulle had a world view; even if it was a France-centered view, he nonetheless had a vision and a strategy to achieve his goals. He proved that the will of a great individual could still shape history.

There is, however, some paradox in the De Gaulle legacy. Although he was steeped in history and French tradition, he can be seen as a transitional figure, bridging different eras and concepts in international relations. He was a product of the colonial era, but he brought an end to a long period of French colonialism, even though his moves were probably based much more on realpolitik than on idealism. In a variety of important ways, the colonies were too costly for France to maintain. His efforts to establish France as a leader of a balancing force between the Soviets and Americans met with limited success. He emphasized the importance of the independent nation-state, which he saw as the foundation for international relations and

cooperation, but he also helped pave the way for a united Western Europe (which would include Britain) that headed far beyond what he had supported in terms of international integration. His actions to end French colonialism, his support for the European community, limited though it was, and his concept of a Europe "from the Atlantic to the Urals," can be seen as recognition of the need for an "independent" France to move into a more interdependent world of the twenty-first century.

It was often said that De Gaulle was a man out of the past, whose views of international relations were more attuned to the eighteenth or nineteenth century. He was also a man of vision, an ardent nationalist with a broad view of the world.

NOTES

1. Charles De Gaulle, *The War Memoirs of Charles De Gaulle*, vol. I, "The Call to Honor," (New York: Simon and Schuster, 1959); also, Alexander Werth, *De Gaulle: A Political Biography* (New York: Simon and Schuster, 1965), p. 103; Alden Whitman, "De Gaulle Rallied France in War and Strove to Lead Her to Greatness," *New York Times*, November 11, 1970.
2. Alexander Werth, *De Gaulle: A Political Biography* (London: Penguin, 1965), p. 348.
3. "Excerpts from President De Gaulle's News Conference," *New York Times*, February 1, 1964.

SUGGESTIONS FOR FURTHER READING

Cook, Don. *Charles De Gaulle: A Biography*. New York: Putnam, 1984.

De Gaulle, Charles. *Memoirs of Hope: Renewal and Endeavor*. Translated by Terence Kilmartin. New York: Simon and Schuster, 1971.

De Gaulle, Charles. *The War Memoirs of Charles De Gaulle*. 3 vols. Translated by Richard Hower. New York: Simon and Schuster, 1959.

LaCouture, Jean. *De Gaulle*. Translated by

Francis K. Price. New York: New American Library, 1966.

LaCouture, Jean. *De Gaulle: The Rebel, 1890–1944*. Translated by Patrick O'Brian. New York: Norton, 1990.

Macridis, Roy C. (ed.) *De Gaulle: Implacable Ally*. New York: Harper & Row, 1967.

Schoenbrun, David. *The Three Lives of Charles De Gaulle*. New York: Atheneum, 1966.

Werth, Alexander. *De Gaulle: A Political Biography*. New York: Simon and Schuster, 1965.

CHAPTER FOUR

National Perspectives, Politics, and Policies on the World Scene

Each nation has its own interests, policies, perceptions, and values. Nations define their interests and design their policies on the basis of their values, perceptions, and national experience. The world is a mosaic of nations, and although all fit together to form the global picture, each nation is a distinctive piece of the mosaic. Even in the era of growing interdependence, national policies and perceptions are important factors in international relations.

A variety of factors can affect a nation's perceptions of itself in regard to other nations. Among the factors bearing strongly on a nation's outlook are such considerations as its geographical location; economic conditions and needs; its sense of security and perceived threats; historical experiences, such as war and invasions; natural resources; political ideology; religious beliefs; and national character. The concept of *national character*, which may be shaped by all of the foregoing factors, is one that some international relations specialists shy away from because it can be rather vague, difficult to define, and may lead to or reinforce stereotypical or oversimplified views. National character refers to those qualities and characteristics associated with and valued by a particular nation. The national character is often reflected in the way a nation deals with foreign policy problems. Sometimes the term *national style* is used to describe the behavior patterns of a nation in international affairs. Normally, the national character or style is a function of the values, ideology, historical experiences, precedents, and traditions of a nation. While style or character may be a guide to national behavior, nations certainly do not always follow a predictable pattern. National style can often be an important consideration in diplomacy, which is discussed in Chapter 5.

Despite the difficulties associated with attempting to interpret and define national character, Hans Morgenthau, among others, has recognized the concrete significance that national character can have in international politics. Indeed, Morgenthau includes national character as one of the nine major elements of national power. The other components of national power he lists are geography, natural resources, industrial capacity, military preparedness, population, national morale, the quality of diplomacy, and the quality of government. According to Morgenthau, "The observer of the international scene who attempts to assess the relative strength of different nations must take national character into account," and the failure to do so will lead to errors in judgment and policies.[1]

National morale is another intangible factor but one that can be highly important. It refers to the support or commitment given by a nation's people to that nation's foreign policy, particularly in times of crisis or war. In a democratic system, such support is especially important. But almost any system of government requires a high level of support for international policies, particularly where sacrifice or sustained effort is involved. A notable example of national morale would be the British persistence through the dark hours of World War II. The nation faced great adversity, but spurred by the indomitable spirit of Prime Minister Winston Churchill, the British retained their morale. This passage from a famous Churchill speech during the early stages of the war helped rally the British people:

> Even though large tracts of Europe and many old and famous states have fallen or may fall into the grip of the Gestapo and all the odious apparatus of Nazi rule, we shall not flag or fail. We shall go on to the end. We shall fight in France, we shall fight on the seas and oceans, we shall fight with growing confidence and growing strength in the air, we shall defend our island, whatever the cost may be. We shall fight on the beaches, we shall fight on the landing grounds, we shall fight in the fields and on the streets, we shall fight in the hills. We shall never surrender![2]

There are other significant instances of sustained commitment under difficult circumstances. In more recent times, the citizens of Israel, who have often felt beleaguered, have provided such an example.

DOMESTIC AND GLOBAL POLITICS

National perceptions and values are reflected in and are a reflection of national character and morale and are part of a nation's politics and policies. Attempting to separate domestic politics and global politics can result in a very misleading and incomplete picture of international relations.

The impact of domestic factors on foreign policy and the interconnection between domestic and international affairs caused Bayless Manning to come up with the term "intermestic."[3] This term has particular applicability in the economic area because of the influence of international economics on domestic affairs.

Just as external factors can have significant impact on developments within a nation, so can attitudes or actions within a nation have significant external impact. Long ago, Thucydides noted that political conditions within a Greek city-state often had more to do with actions toward other city-states than anything that the other city-states might have done.

As was noted in Chapter 1, the war between Argentina and Britain over the Falkland or Malvinas Islands in 1982 is a prime example of a conflict in recent history that was largely driven by domestic factors within the two countries. The generals who were ruling Argentina at the time were facing an economic crisis and growing political opposition at home. Britain's control of the islands, 250 miles from the southeastern tip of Argentina, had long been a point of contention between the two nations. If the Argentine invasion had succeeded, the generals might have staved off their domestic problems. But nationalism in Argentina ran headlong into British nationalism. British Prime Minister Margaret Thatcher strengthened her position at home with a forceful response to the Argentine action, sending a large naval task force to the area, and ultimately regaining control of the islands after some heavy fighting.

Mikhail Gorbachev noted the "organic tie between each state's foreign and domestic policies," and said that this becomes particularly close and meaningful at crucial moments.[4] In his program of *perestroika* or restructuring, Gorbachev saw foreign policy as subject to change, just as was domestic policy. Some of the major changes in the foreign policy of the Soviet Union under Gorbachev in the late 1980s were undoubtedly impelled by domestic factors in the U.S.S.R. It should be understood, however, that the changes in international relations referred to in the previous chapter—the move from a bipolar to a multipolar system, and the dispersal of power—also contributed to the Soviet reassessment. Further, there was at least an implicit recognition by the Soviet leaders of the fact that military strength is only one measure of national power and one element of national security, and that the costs of an interventionist foreign policy are growing ever higher.

While the Soviets were spending heavily for a large military force and modern strategic weaponry, and were heavily involved in a number of other countries, there were serious problems at home, including a stagnant economy. Gorbachev sought to trim military spending through troop reductions and arms control agreements and by limiting foreign involvement without compromising Soviet security. The Soviet leader said, "We are saying openly for all to hear: We need lasting peace in order to concentrate on the development of our society and to cope with the tasks of improving the life of the Soviet people."[5]

NATIONAL/ INTERNATIONAL LEADERS

Gorbachev is one of those national leaders who has exceptional impact on international relations. (See Gorbachev Profile.) Although it is important not to overstate the influence or significance of particular individuals on international affairs, it would be equally wrong to dismiss or minimize the influence that key individuals can have at critical junctures in history. Their personalities, their vision, their ability, in some cases, to act decisively or dramatically or to articulate national or international goals can have considerable effect. Charles De Gaulle and Anwar Sadat are examples of individuals who at certain points had powerful effects on international affairs by revising their national policies. In some instances individuals come to personify a nation or a cause, sometimes a cause that we would view very negatively. Positively or negatively, we have to recognize that individuals can have a dramatic effect far beyond their borders.

Some indication of this can be seen by looking at the record of *Time* magazine's annual person (or persons) of the year. Each year since 1927 the magazine has chosen a person of the year, and frequently it has been someone who has had a major impact on world affairs. Some have been chosen for their positive contributions and leadership, others because of their unquestioned impact, even though it might be viewed unfavorably. Among the choices, several of whom are profiled in this book, have been Nazi Germany's Hitler, Soviet leader Joseph Stalin (twice), Ayatollah Khomeini of Iran, Chinese Nationalist leader Chiang Kai-shek*, Mohandas K. Gandhi of India, Britain's Churchill (twice), Konrad Adenauer and Willy Brandt of West Germany, De Gaulle, Sadat, Lech Walesa of Poland, Deng Xiaoping of the People's Republic of China (twice), Corazon Aquino of the Philippines, several American presidents and foreign policy officials, and Soviet leaders Nikita Khruschev, Yuri Andropov (selected with Ronald Reagan as Men of the Year in 1983), and Gorbachev, chosen in 1987 and also named "Man of the Decade" for the 1980s.

In Gorbachev's case, he earned an international reputation as an enlightened leader steering his nation away from a confrontational policy. However, he could not hold the Soviet Union together once he helped open the way to greater freedom.

---

*Henry Luce, long-time publisher of *Time* and one of its founders, was a strong supporter of Chiang Kai-shek and the Nationalist faction in China, and Luce was active in trying to influence American policy on behalf of Chiang and the Nationalists.

THE SOVIET/RUSSIAN EXPERIENCE AND VIEWPOINT

While the Soviet Union was clearly intent through much of the post–World War II period on becoming a military power equal to or, in the view of some, superior to the United States, that push must be seen not only as an effort to become a major power but as a reflection of Soviet history and experience. The Soviet view was shaped by a combination of communist ideology (Marxism/Leninism) with more traditional national goals, values, and political culture. Russian perceptions and policies are influenced by a variety of factors, including geography and the impact of history, not least the nation's experience during World War II. Geopolitical considerations have been important for Russia, which has been subjected to three major invasions from the West in the past 150 years, twice from Germany. Americans, particularly younger Americans, have relatively little awareness of what the Russians experienced in World War II, when the Soviet Union and the United States were allies. Of the 22 million lives lost by the winning nations in the war, an estimated 20 million were lost by the Soviet Union.

Many Russian villages and towns were destroyed. The city of Leningrad (St. Petersburg) was besieged. This experience, in particular, is believed to have conditioned the thinking of the post–World War II leadership of the U.S.S.R. World War II, still referred to in Russia as the Great Patriotic War, was clearly a deeply traumatic experience for the country. When foreign leaders visit Russia, they are frequently taken to war memorials such as the Monument to the Heroic Defenders of Leningrad and to the Piskarevskoye Cemetery, where thousands of Leningraders who died in the 900-day Nazi siege are buried in mass graves.

Although a variety of factors motivate Soviet foreign policy, there is little doubt that the Nazi invasion of 1941—despite a nonaggression pact the Soviets had earlier signed with Hitler—and the terrible losses suffered by the country had a significant impact on Soviet attitudes toward defense and national security. The experience probably contributed to sentiments among many Soviets that another major war must be avoided, and to the conviction that a powerful military tone might be necessary to assure the nation's defense. Some analysts believed, however, that the modern Soviet strategy was to be prepared to fight and win a nuclear war. Richard Pipes, a Harvard professor who served on the National Security Council staff during the Reagan administration, said in 1977 that the Soviet policy was "not deterrence, but victory, not sufficiency in weapons but superiority, not retaliation but offensive action."[6]

Freeman Dyson, an American arms control analyst, interpreted the Russian view and approach somewhat differently. The heritage of World War II, he believes, indicates that wars are fought by people, not weapons, and that morale is a highly important factor. Dyson wrote, "The central problem of the . . . military leadership is to preserve the heritage of the Second World War against oblivion, to transmit that heritage intact to future generations of soldiers, who never saw the invader's boot trampling Russian soil."[7]

Mikhail Gorbachev was the first Soviet leader of the post–World War II era who did not have vivid recollections of the war. He was only 10 when his country was invaded, and he lived in a rather remote area.

The Soviets and Afghanistan

One of the problems Gorbachev had to deal with in his early years in office was the Soviet military presence in Afghanistan, which had been invaded by Soviet forces late in 1979. There are some interesting parallels between the Soviet experience in Afghanistan and that of the United States in Vietnam not many years earlier. Among other things, the wars in Afghanistan and Vietnam provided evidence of the limits of power that could be exercised by even the most powerful nations. Similarly, both cases provided object lessons about the costliness—financially, in human terms, and in international standing—of such foreign involvement.

The Soviet invasion of Afghanistan, discussed in Chapter 1, sent relations with the United States, already shaky, plummeting to one of the lowest points of recent decades. Soviet forces were used in support of a weak communist government in Afghanistan, one of the countries on the Soviet Union's southern border, and a country of largely Islamic population. After nine years of occupation and a brutal struggle against the Afghan resistance, the Soviet forces were withdrawn by early 1989.

The 1979 move into Afghanistan, which took place while Leonid Brezhnev was the Soviet leader, could be looked upon as geostrategic— to assure a friendly, Communist government in a bordering country. However, as noted in Chapter 3, other nations, including the United States and China, looked at the action through their own geostrategic prisms and saw it as a possible move toward Soviet control or dominance of a region, and a possible threat to neighboring Pakistan.

Domestic Demands and Shifting Policy

As the war dragged on—and the resistance forces were aided by the United States, China, Pakistan, and others—and as casualties mounted, and as the Soviet population began to learn more about the costliness of the venture, there was growing dissatisfaction within the Soviet Union. Gorbachev, reflecting a new candor among Soviet leaders, called it a "bleeding wound." Though some in the West were skeptical when Gorbachev first indicated that Soviet troops would be withdrawn from Afghanistan, it seems clear that he had become convinced that it was in his nation's interest to pull out the troops. This bow to realpolitik was most certainly influenced by domestic imperatives and a recognition that if the Soviet Union was to sustain its superpower status, it had to move to significantly bolster its economy and modernize its industrial and technological base and infrastructure (transportation, communications, public services, and facilities). (It can be argued, as is noted elsewhere in this book, that the Soviet Union was a superpower only in military terms.) The linkage between domestic demands and foreign policy actions by Gorbachev was evident.

While the differing views of Soviet policy and the Soviet role in the world were not discussed and debated in the same open fashion as in the United States, where differing groups with differing perspectives compete to shape policy, there was growing, if quiet debate in Moscow over the future Soviet direction in the last years of Leonid Brezhnev's rule, even before Gorbachev came to power. Some of these topics were being discussed in government-affiliated institutes or "think tanks." In the United States such policy analysis and discussion occurs not only within government agencies but in privately funded think tanks and in universities, and in the media as well.

However, this shift in the Soviet approach to foreign policy, seen not only in Afghanistan but in other Gorbachev moves, such as proposals for arms control and troop reductions in Europe (discussed in Chapter 6), was still viewed with suspicion in some Western quarters. For years, Soviet analyses of world affairs had been full of references to the international *correlation of forces*. This was a means of calculating or assessing the relative strength of competing camps in world affairs, and referred not just to military capability. The assumption behind the concept of correlation of forces was that it would chart the movement of the world toward the socialist camp and socialism. In some respects, Gorbachev's policies were an acknowledgment that this had not happened and references to the correlation of forces came much less frequently.

THE AMERICAN PERSPECTIVE

During the Cold War period, the Soviet "threat" and anticommunism became major factors in American political life. Not only did American foreign policy revolve around concern about the Soviet Union and communism, it had a profound impact on domestic politics. The grip of anticommunism probably reached its strongest point in the early 1950s when Senator Joseph P. McCarthy generated widespread anticommunist hysteria with accusations—often unsupported and slanderous—of Communist infiltration of the United States government.

Beginning with the containment policy and the Truman Doctrine (1947) United States policy was aimed at thwarting the Soviets and communism. The anticommunist feeling became stronger and even more of a force in American politics after the success of the Chinese Communists in taking control in that country in 1949. That set off a wave of recrimination over the question, "Who lost China?" and helped set the stage for the McCarthy era. Even after the demagogic Wisconsin senator had been discredited and disgraced, American political figures generally continued to advocate a hard line toward the Soviets, and to support a "tough" foreign policy. There were occasional periods of improved relations between the United States and the Soviets, most notably the *détente* of the early 1970s engineered by Richard Nixon and Henry Kissinger in the United States and Leonid Brezhnev in the Soviet Union. (*Détente* is a French term meaning a relaxation of tension.) Thereafter, a gradual deterioration set in and both sides continued to build their nuclear arsenals. With the 1979 Soviet invasion of Afghanistan, the downward spiral was accelerated. When Ronald Reagan assumed the presidency in 1981, he was an especially harsh critic of the Soviet Union. He spoke of the Soviet Union as the "focus of evil in the modern world" and as the "evil empire." He said that the leaders in Moscow reserved "the right to commit any crime, to lie, to cheat." He described the Soviet-American conflict as a "struggle between right and wrong, good and evil."[8] Reagan and his advisors and some American analysts saw the hand of the Soviets in almost every international problem and, indeed, the two nations were often supporting opposing factions or forces in various regional conflicts. (See Chapter 7.) Reagan continued and added to a major defense buildup that had begun during the last year of Jimmy Carter's administration, and he found ample support for his position. Eventually, however, before he left the presidency, Reagan held a series of summit meetings with Gorbachev, including one in which he strolled through Moscow's Red Square with the Soviet leader. In 1987, Reagan and Gorbachev signed a treaty to abolish intermediate-range nuclear forces.

Historical Experiences

The United States and Russia have had significantly different historical experiences. Their geographical positions are dramatically distinctive. While the history of Russia and the Soviet Union is scarred with invasions by neighboring countries from all sides, the United States lived much of its history in relative isolation and has rarely known the threat of foreign attackers invading the country. It should not be surprising that the Soviets have an obsession with borders and buffer zones. Russia and the Soviet Union have experienced a much more tumultuous modern history than has the United States.

When the Bolsheviks (Communists) seized power on November 7, 1917, that culminated a long struggle for control in Russia, a lengthy period of rebellion and insurrection and attempts to end the rule of the czars. But the success of the revolution did not bring an end to the chaos, hunger, and suffering. There was a further struggle for power among the Communists. There was even a brief period of military intervention by the United States and other countries in limited opposition to the "red" Bolsheviks. The forces led by V. I. Lenin eventually prevailed in the struggle for power. It was Lenin who rallied the Russian people, following the long and disastrous fighting within the country, and it was Lenin who charted the broad course of socialism for the Soviet Union. However, Lenin died in 1924, and was succeeded by Joseph Stalin, who began an effort to consolidate power and ultimately set about to eliminate all opposition. He ushered in a reign of terror of massive proportions. It reached its peak between 1934 and 1939, when millions were killed or imprisoned.

From the beginning, the Communist revolution had a rather hostile reception in the United States, where many found the atheism, radical rallying cries, and militantly anticapitalist attitudes repugnant and threatening, although in some cases the images presented in the United States were badly distorted and far from reality. The United States did not give diplomatic recognition to the Soviet Union until 1933.

Although there were certainly those in the United States who were sympathetic to the revolution and there were a small number of Communist adherents in this country, support for the Soviets diminished significantly even among these groups when word of Stalin's terror began to reach the West. Still, there were some who doubted the extent of Stalin's bloody purge.

DIFFERENT AND SIMILAR EXPERIENCES

While the Soviets experienced repeated periods of devastation and turmoil and made limited economic headway, despite all of the socialist planning, the United States, with the notable exception of the worldwide depression of the 1930s, enjoyed long periods of economic growth and technological development. The economic disparity became even more apparent in the 1970s and 80s when the Soviet Union not only lagged far behind the United States but behind a number of other countries as well. By the time Gorbachev attained power, the economic difficulties could no longer be ignored by the Soviet leadership. The U.S.S.R. had paid a high price for the long-term military build-up and international activism. However, to suggest that the United States did not also pay a high price would be very misleading. And, of course, a major reason why the United States expended billions on defense and international security, including military bases in far-flung areas of the world, was to counter what was seen as the Soviet/communist threat.

Costs and Limits of Power

The major rationale for the American involvement in Vietnam, which was costly to the United States in a number of respects, was to checkmate communism. The conventional view within the American government during the initial stages of involvement in Vietnam was that the United States had to take a stand in Vietnam to stop China, which literally and/or geopolitically was seen as threatening to control all of Southeast Asia. In this view, the Chinese were the agents of the Soviets and, in turn, North Vietnam and the Vietnamese Communists were subagents of China. Both the Soviets and Chinese did lend support to Ho Chi Minh in North Vietnam, but the United States analysis was terribly misguided and mistaken. In fact, by the early 1960s, the split between China and the Soviet Union had already occurred. Further, China and Vietnam had a long history of antagonism, and, in 1979, after the communists had triumphed in Vietnam, China attacked its smaller neighbor. In the 1950s and 1960s United States policymakers were so intent on seeing the international dimensions of the conflict in Vietnam that they tended to overlook the extent to which it was a Vietnamese civil war. Before United States involvement in Vietnam ended, it had become a highly controversial and extremely costly venture, with 57,000 American lives lost and at least $120 billion expended by the American government directly and much more indirectly, with serious damage to the United States economy. There were, of course, huge casualties among Vietnamese, with combined civilian and military deaths (North and South) estimated at more than one million.

Both the American experience in Vietnam and the Soviet experience in Afghanistan made clear, as was pointed out previously, that even the military superpowers face limitations in their ability to successfully undertake unilateral action. Both of them misjudged and misperceived the significance, the threats, and, particularly, the cultural dynamics of the conflicts and societies into which they interjected themselves. They also overestimated the effectiveness of their superior military firepower. Both superpowers learned that the costs of unilateral projection of power could be high, and that it was difficult to maintain necessary support at home for prolonged and costly military involvement in situations that did not seem vital to national security in the eyes of the citizenry at home. Earlier in this chapter the importance of national morale was discussed. A nation needs the support of its citizenry for its international policies, particularly where a long-term effort is involved. Unless national morale remains high, it is difficult to sustain foreign military operations.

ENEMIES AND THE ENEMY IMAGE

Although Americans and Soviets had somewhat similar experiences in Vietnam and Afghanistan and although there has been some recognition of the common ground and overlapping interests shared by the United States and Soviet Union, the two had become accustomed to thinking of each other as the enemy.

Throughout history, the enemy image has been a significant factor in contributing to international tensions and conflicts. In some cases there may, of course, be valid reasons for a nation or people to view another as the enemy. However, there is a tendency for such images to become distorted, overblown, and self-serving and to stand in the way of conflict resolution. In the United States and the Soviet Union, as the Cold War continued, the hostile and negative views of each other became ingrained in each society. Exaggeration and oversimplification frequently characterized the views held by Russians and Americans of each other.

A Soviet specialist on international relations has written:

> If the other state is seen as an "absolute enemy," as an "evil empire," as "the most inhuman system in human history," as an embodiment and receptacle of everything that is hateful, then the policy towards that state is based on these preconceptions, and in its turn leads to greater enmity.[9]

The same writer, Andrei Mellville, said such misconceptions and stereotypes hamper the search for mutually acceptable solutions and compromises. In the nuclear age, when stakes are so high, deep-rooted prejudices could undermine rational action. As Mellville says, "It is therefore particularly dangerous to dehumanize one's opponent, to turn the other side into an 'absolute evil' or an 'absolute enemy' devoid of any human traits." In his view, widespread anti-Soviet prejudices and biased information about the U.S.S.R. fixed in American minds the idea "that the Soviet Union is a country whose entire system of economy, politics, and ideology is completely hostile to the American one and poses a 'deadly challenge' to America."[10] Another Soviet analyst, Georgi Arbatov, said, "Somewhere deep in the American political conscience there still lives the thought that we are something illegitimate, created not by God but by the Devil, and that our existence in its present form should be ended somehow."[11]

When Gorbachev began to bring about changes in Soviet policy, and United States—Soviet relations improved, it was suggested that he was depriving Americans of an enemy and destroying many of the old stereotypes.

Psychologists note that having a common enemy, a common object of loathing, can be a significant factor in promoting the cohesion of ethnic or national groups. In the early stages of the Cold War, George Kennan suggested that the Soviet leadership of the time was so insecure and so unimaginative that it felt obliged to cultivate external enemies in order to maintain itself in power.

Particularly as the Soviet Union faded from its position as the "evil empire," the United States has often focused on an individual as the "enemy." This was certainly true in 1990–91 when Saddam Hussein was pictured as the personification of evil and became a focal point for American fury. President Bush referred to Saddam as "another Hitler." Despite the opprobrium directed toward Saddam, the Hitler analogy was widely considered to be a gross exaggeration, since Hitler had worldwide, not regional, ambitions and because Hitler is generally regarded as the benchmark of modern villains. Before Saddam Hussein, Manuel Noriega, the Panamanian strongman discussed in Chapter 3, was seen as a United States enemy. Earlier, Libya's Moammar Khadaffi and Iran's Ayatollah Khomeini were in the limelight of contempt; Khadaffi because of his association with terrorism and Khomeini as the leader of the Islamic fundamentalist revolution in Iran which was strongly antagonistic to the United States. Indeed, the United States and President Carter filled the enemy role in Khomeini's Iran and were seen as "The Great Satan."

Japan: Views and Counterviews

In the period before Iraq's Saddam Hussein came to be considered a major international villain, he was relatively little known outside the Middle East. At the same time, if asked to name a country that was a "threat" to the United States, many Americans would probably have cited Japan because of its growing economic power, which was seen by many as undermining United States economic strength. Some Western Europeans might have also put Japan at the top of their enemies lists. (See Chapter 9 for discussion of Japan's role in international economics.)

A number of United States politicians and commentators have been accused of "Japan bashing"—blaming American problems on Japan, and suggesting that Japanese businesses have unfair advantages. Likewise, some Japanese have engaged in "American bashing"—castigating the United States for blaming its problems on Japan. While praising United States achievements, various Japanese officials have criticized the United States for national complacency and resting on past laurels. These criticisms of each other have become part of the fabric of each nation's domestic politics, which, in turn, can influence foreign policies.

Some leading Europeans have also been critical of Japan. Edith Cresson, the first woman to serve as prime minister of France, was frequently scornful of the Japanese and their policies. Japanese publications labeled her as Japan's public enemy number one in Europe while she served as France's agriculture and trade minister and minister of European affairs. Cresson said, "Japan is an adversary that doesn't play by the rules and has an absolute desire to conquer the world." Cresson said that her priority is to keep France competitive. "My only concern is to be heard on what I believe is in the interests of France." [12]

NEIGHBORING POSITIONS AND PERSPECTIVES

A perception of external threat can often serve as a rallying point within a nation and will stir strong nationalist sentiment. Fidel Castro in Cuba was only one of many who used the threat of attack from another nation to consolidate power within his own country. As Hugh Thomas has pointed out, the very thing Castro needed to consolidate his regime "was an unsuccessful attack from without, backed, though not to the hilt, by the U.S." [13] Thomas noted that both the French and the Russian revolutions had been consolidated by invasions by exiles, and when American-supported exiles invaded the Bay of Pigs in 1961, an invasion that Castro's forces repelled, it greatly strengthened Castro's position within Cuba.

Like Cuba, Mexico often sees itself or is seen as being in the shadow of its large and powerful neighbor, the United States. A popular saying in

Mexico is the lapidary comment, "Poor Mexico! So far from God and so near to the United States."

The disparities in size and military and economic power are only part of the differences between Mexico and the United States. There are also differences in history, religion, culture, and language. Mexico sees the United States as having little understanding of its problems. As Alan Riding wrote in his aptly titled book, *Distant Neighbors*:

> Contiguity with the United States has proved a permanent psychological trauma. Mexico cannot come to terms with having lost half of its territory to the United States, with Washington's frequent meddling in its political affairs, with the U.S. hold on its economy and with growing cultural penetration by the American way of life.[14]

This feeling among Mexicans toward the United States doesn't necessarily result in an "enemy image" of their northern neighbor, but it does contribute to an ambivalence toward the United States, comparable in some ways to the "love-hate" attitude toward the United States, which, as was previously noted, is also found in such countries as Panama and the Philippines, where the United States is both resented and respected.

Mexico is, of course, dependent upon the United States in many ways, and its interests are closely tied to those of the United States, with the economies of the two nations consistently growing closer. At the same time, Mexican nationalism runs strong and, in words, if not always in deeds, Mexico has attempted to chart a more independent course in foreign policy, particularly in regard to United States policies toward Central and South America. Mexican political leaders often find it important to assert their independence of the United States on these matters. In practice, however, that nationalism and independence is tempered by political and economic realism, based on recognition of the vital links between Mexico and the United States as well as the power of the United States.

Carlos Salinas de Gotari, who became president of Mexico in 1988, said "The time has come to build a new relationship free of myths and mistrust, abuses and recriminations. It is the spirit of a new friendship that does not attribute the cause of problems to others."[15]

By and large, the relationship between the two countries is a friendly and cooperative one—unlike some cases where neighboring nations have long-standing and in some instances extremely bitter rivalries.

GREECE VERSUS TURKEY

Greece and Turkey, for example, have a long-standing and bitter feud that is rooted in history. In recent years this hostility has focused on the island nation of Cyprus and on control of the Aegean Sea. Cyprus is only 40 miles south of Turkey and about 600 miles southeast of Greece. Cyprus' population of 630,000 is largely of Greek origin, but with a substantial Turkish minority. Cyprus became an independent republic in 1960, after 82 years of British rule, and following a civil war between the Greek and Turkish communities. When the civil war was settled, there was agreement that Cyprus would not participate in any political or economic union with another state. However, there has been a continuing movement among elements of the Greek community for *enosis*, or union with Greece. In 1974, Turkey invaded Cyprus, claiming that extremists among the Greek-Cypriot majority were trying to put the island republic under Greek control.

This hostile relationship figures prominently in the domestic politics and foreign policies of both nations, even though both are among the allied members of NATO. The "Turkish threat" is seen as a significant factor in the Greek view of international affairs, while Turkey has viewed itself as caught between the ambitions of Greece on one side and the power of the Soviet Union, of which the Turks have long been fearful, on another. Turkey's location also exposes it to the turmoil of adjacent Middle East nations. Political leaders in both Greece and Turkey have frequently played up tensions with the other in order to distract attention from internal problems.

The Greek-Turkish hostility also affects United States policies. Trying to maintain a balance between the two has often been a complicated exercise, and the Turks have felt at a disadvantage because of the influence that Greek-Americans have on United States policy. From 1975 to 1978 the United States Congress imposed an arms embargo on Turkey in response to the invasion of Cyprus and with strong prodding from the Greek community in the United States. Turkey believed that its actions had been fully justified and saw itself as a trustworthy ally of the United States. Turkey had allowed the United States the use of important military installations in the country. The arms embargo seriously strained relations between Turkey and the United States. When American aid to Turkey was restored, Congress developed a formula under which for every $10 of security assistance provided to Turkey, Greece must receive at least $7. This 7:10 ratio, imposed by Congress over the objection of several American presidents, is an example of a compromise forged to balance competing domestic and foreign policy concerns.

DOMESTIC AND FOREIGN FACTORS

In addition to the Greek-Turkish enmity, there are a number of other cases of hostile relations between neighboring countries which have significant impact on domestic policies and international relations of those nations. Pakistan-India and Iraq-Iran are two cases of sometimes-bitter relations, with religious factors having significant bearing on the troubled relationships. (Regional conflicts and flashpoints are discussed further in Chapter 7.)

India and Pakistan fought a series of wars following the establishment of the two as independent nations after the end of British control of what had been colonial India. Once Britain withdrew, major fighting, generated by religious hatred, occurred between the two partitioned nations, India being predominantly Hindu and Pakistan primarily Muslim. In its foreign policy, Pakistan eventually developed close relations with China, another antagonist of India. Although officially neutral, India built a relatively close relationship with the Soviet Union, which Pakistan has regarded as hostile.

Iran and Iraq clashed in efforts to establish regional dominance and bolster their identities. It was also a clash of the populist Islamic movement (Iran) against the establishment Islamic regime of Iraq, and this was a driving factor in the policies of the two nations. Iraq felt itself threatened by Iran's revolution, Iran by Iraq's expansionism. The location of the two nations in the oil-rich Persian Gulf region, which much of the world depends upon for petroleum supplies, added an important international dimension to the conflict.

The Middle and Near East regions have been the scene of considerable tension and hostility. It has already been pointed out that Israel has often seen itself as a beleaguered nation, surrounded by hostile elements. The horrible history of the Holocaust, when the Nazis systematically eliminated six million Jews in Germany, gives the Jewish nation a special concern about security.

In the United States there is strong domestic support for Israel. That support has significantly influenced American policy in the Middle East, although the United States has attempted to maintain good relations with the "moderate" Arab states, particularly Saudi Arabia and Jordan, as well as Egypt, which under Anwar Sadat, and with American encouragement, signed a peace agreement with Israel. The concern of Israel about its security is reflected in the fact that military and related expenditures account for a substantial portion of its national budget.

A major factor in the Middle East conflict has been the claims of two peoples to the same land. In this tense situation there has been a tendency on the part of some on each side of the Palestinian/Arab-Israeli conflict to cast each other in stereotypical terms, or, as Professor Charles D. Smith has written, there has been "the denial of the other in human as well as political terms." [16] The divisions in the Middle East have been further complicated by being intertwined with the great power rivalries.

MUTUAL PREOCCUPATION AND DISTORTED VIEWS

This leads back to the rivalry between the United States and the Soviet Union, a rivalry that often dominated the policy outlooks of the two most militarily powerful nations, but also frequently had significant bearing on the policies of nations in the Middle East and elsewhere. From the beginning of the post–World War II period, neither the Americans nor the Soviets demonstrated much sympathy for the goals and interests of the other. Nor did they demonstrate much empathy for each other. Empathy refers to the ability to understand the feelings of someone else—the ability to put yourself in the position of another. It is frequently lacking in situations where nations are at odds.

Despite all of their mutual preoccupation, the United States and the Soviet Union had difficulty understanding each other and frequently resorted to stereotypical views of one another. Americans watched cold warriors from James Bond to Rambo taking on ruthless and inhuman Soviet agents, while the Soviet people often received a distorted view of American life and harsh portrayals of American officials.

In the early stages of World War II, Britain's Winston Churchill referred to Russia as "a riddle wrapped in a mystery inside an enigma." That classic description has characterized the difficulty that the West had in understanding the Soviets. However, Churchill added that if there was a key to forecasting Russian action, it was the Russian national interest. The real key, of course, is understanding how the Russians (or Soviets) see their national interest, understanding *their* perspective. Such understanding, as discussed earlier in this chapter, requires knowledge of their historical experience, culture, and political environment. Such a vast gap separated the world views of the Soviet and American leaders that not only did they tend to expect the worst of each other but this suspicion often stood in the way of fully understanding the rationale for the other's actions. At the same time, preoccupation with the enemy can preclude rational decisions.

The danger, as John Stoessinger has stated, is that a self-fulfilling prophecy can be set in motion. "When leaders attribute evil designs to their adversaries, and they nurture those beliefs for long enough, they will be proved right." [17]

Interestingly, George Kennan, who, as previously noted, was closely associated with the origins of the United States containment policy toward the Soviet Union, said years later, "I have never thought of the Soviet Union as a military threat to this country—except during the time of the Berlin blockade. Even then, Soviet motives were primarily defensive. Otherwise, since the Second World War, I have seen no evidence of Soviet desire or intention to attack us or our allies." [18]

Nonetheless, as was pointed out earlier in this chapter, the Soviet "threat" was for many years a primary factor in American politics and policy.

NATIONAL PERSPECTIVES AND DOMESTIC CONTEXT

Different nations and individuals and groups within those nations can define or interpret the same situation very differently, depending on their perspective and their view of the national interest. An example of this was seen in the case of Panama and the United States, discussed in Chapter 3.

The Philippines, which has also had a close and complex relationship with the United States, offers another interesting example. The country was long the site of two major United States military installations. The bases generated considerable economic benefit for the Philippines, which needed the economic boost. However, the bases were highly controversial in the Philippines and drew criticism from Filipinio politicians on a variety of grounds. A big part of the problem was resentment over foreign control of the bases, which some saw as an infringement of the nation's sovereignty. Others argued that the United States did not pay enough for the right to operate the bases. In the United States some maintained that changing world conditions reduced the strategic importance of the bases. One of the installations, Clark Air Base, was eventually closed as a result of the effects of the volcanic eruption from nearby Mount Pinatubo in 1991. Although the United States negotiated to retain use of Subic Bay Naval Base, the Philippines Senate failed to approve the agreement.

Each country operates within its own domestic context and on the basis of the world view prevalent in that country. The Japanese national outlook, for example, is very much conditioned by the view that, as a small island nation lacking in natural resources, Japan must rely on international trade to survive.

The decision-making process in each of those countries involves a number of domestic and international influences. In democratic and pluralist societies, a variety of forces can bear on foreign policy decisions. Political campaigns and elections can be important factors affecting the internal setting for foreign policy. Pressure groups can also exert significant influence on foreign policy, and such groups have influence in all societies, whether democratic or authoritarian. This is perhaps even more the case in the United States, because Congress, the representative body in the democratic system, has a strong role in the foreign policy process. The American system, with the possibilities for a potent legislative voice in foreign relations, is unusual in that respect.

There is a tendency for the United States and other nations not only to want to see other nations through their own eyes but to judge other nations by their own values and standards. Westerners have frequently had difficulty comprehending China, in part because of the tendency to see China from a Western perspective, filtering their observations through the spectacles of their own experiences and backgrounds. As a result, Westerners have often been confounded by China's actions.

Images and the International Fabric

An anthropologist has written of the American tendency to see everything in American terms and of how foreigners sometimes react to Americans:

> . . . [H]arsh as it may seem to the ordinary citizen, filled as he is with good intentions and natural generosity, much of the for-

eigners' animosity has been generated by the way Americans be-
have . . . We insist that everyone else do things our way. Consequently, we manage to convey the impression that we simply
regard foreign nationals as "underdeveloped Americans" . . . We
are not only almost totally ignorant of what is expected in other
countries, we are equally ignorant of what we are communicat-
ing to other people by our own normal behavior.[19]

Certainly there have been significant exceptions to this pattern and
there are many examples of Americans in both official and unofficial roles
who have developed sophisticated and empathetic views of other cultures. Nonetheless, it remains a problem. An example of this occurred
when President Carter, a man not lacking in sensitivity to other cultures,
still committed an undiplomatic blunder and offended his hosts on a visit
to Mexico when he said that on a previous visit he had experienced an
attack of "Montezuma's revenge" (diarrhea).

Images and how a nation is perceived or how it perceives others become interwoven into the fabric of international relations. The image
projected by the United States is multidimensional, with elements ranging from massive military power to humane generosity. On the individual
level, this is also true, and clearly there are still cases in which individual
Americans are seen as personifying the "ugly American" stereotype, ignorant of local culture and customs when abroad.

In many ways the power of American culture, the vitality of American
society, conveys its own image, and that image can have significant international impact. A comment from Regis Debray, a French social critic
who has often criticized the United States, signaled this. Said Debray,
"There is more power in rock music, videos, blue jeans, fast foods, news
networks, and TV satellites than in the entire Red Army."[20] Obviously,
power must be viewed in a variety of ways, and there is no denying the
real power of the Red Army. Nonetheless, images and perceptions can be
extremely important. Intangible factors do matter in international relations. The importance that the "enemy image" can have in international
affairs has already been discussed, and future chapters will note how
factors such as diplomacy, propaganda, and communications can affect
images.

Images and perceptions can change rather quickly. This can be seen in
the changing American view of the People's Republic of China, which
was viewed in an extremely negative manner until after President
Nixon's visit in 1972. By the early 1980s China was generally well-
regarded in the United States, many American businesses developed interests in China, and it became a popular destination for tourists. There
was even talk of a "strategic relationship" between the United States and
China for a time. However, when the Chinese government engaged in a
brutal crackdown and repression of the "prodemocracy" movement in
1989, the image of China suffered dramatically in the United States.

A Japanese prime minister said of the problems Japan has internationally with its image that this is due to a "perception gap," which "meant that sometimes Japan's efforts have not been understood and appreciated." [21]

The distinguished psychiatrist, Erich Fromm, has cited the lack of objectivity in the way in which nations view each other. Dr. Fromm wrote:

> The lack of objectivity, as far as foreign nations are concerned, is notorious. From one day to another, another nation is made out to be utterly depraved and fiendish, while one's own nation stands for everything that is good and noble. Every action of the enemy is judged by one standard—every action of oneself by another. Even good deeds by the enemy are considered a sign of particular devilishness, meant to deceive us and the world, while our bad deeds are necessary and justified by our noble goals, which they serve. [22]

While power, particularly military and economic power, undoubtedly constitutes a primary factor in foreign policies and international relations, a key to using power effectively is in understanding other nations. A nation's international actions can't be seen in isolation from the domestic context. Domestic factors, often reflecting national perceptions, politics, and values—as this chapter has emphasized—have a significant impact on a nation's foreign policy and international role. Furthermore, a key foreign policy interest of any nation is the creation and maintenance of favorable conditions for domestic stability and progress.

NOTES

1. Hans J. Morgenthau, *Politics Among Nations*, 6th ed., revised by Kenneth W. Thompson (New York: Alfred A. Knopf, 1985), p. 152.
2. Winston Churchill, address to the House of Commons, June 4, 1940; quoted in *Churchill—The Life Triumphant* (New York: American Heritage Publishing, 1965), p. 92.
3. Bayless Manning, "The Congress, the Executive and Intermestic Affairs," *Foreign Affairs* 57, 1979, pp. 308–24.
4. Mikhail Gorbachev, *Perestroika* (New York: Harper and Row, 1987), p. 132.
5. *Ibid.*
6. Richard Pipes, "Why the Soviet Union Thinks It Could Fight and Win a Nuclear War," *Commentary* 64, July 1977, pp. 21–34.
7. Freeman Dyson, *Weapons and Hope* (New York: Harper and Row, 1984).
8. Ronald Reagan, White House Press Conference, January 29, 1981; address to the National Association of Evangelicals, Orlando, Florida, March 8, 1983. See *Realism, Strength, Negotiation: Key Foreign Pol-*

icy Statements of the Reagan Administration (Washington: U.S. Department of State, 1984); also, "Focus of Evil," chapter 13 in Lou Cannon, *President Reagan: The Role of a Lifetime* (New York: Simon and Schuster, 1991).

9. Andrei Mellville, *How We View Each Other: The Enemy Image and New Political Thinking* (Moscow: Novosti Press Agency Publishing House, 1988), p. 5.

10. *Ibid.*, p. 21.

11. Georgi Arbatov and William Oltmans, *The Soviet Viewpoint* (New York: Dodd, Mead and Company, 1983), p. 148.

12. Steven Greenhouse, "The Fighter of France," *New York Times*, May 16, 1991.

13. Hugh Thomas, *The Cuban Revolution* (New York: Harper and Row, 1977), p. 534.

14. Alan Riding, *Distant Neighbors* (New York: Alfred A. Knopf, 1985), p. 316.

15. Carlos Salinas de Gotari, address to Joint Session, United States Congress, October 4, 1989.

16. Charles D. Smith, *Palestine and the Arab-Israeli Conflict* (New York: St. Martin's, 1988), p. 291.

17. John G. Stoessinger, *Why Nations Go to War*, 4th ed. (New York: St. Martin's, 1985), p. 209.

18. George Kennan, "Obituary for the Cold War," *New Perspectives Quarterly*, 5, Summer 1988, p. 48.

19. Edward T. Hall, *The Silent Language* (Garden City, New York: Doubleday, 1959).

20. Regis Debray, "From Kalashnikovs to God and Computers," *New Perspectives Quarterly*, Fall 1988, p. 42; *New Perspectives Quarterly*, Summer 1988, p. 3.

21. Prime Minister Toshiki Kaifu quoted in James Fallows, "Is Japan the Enemy?", *New York Review of Books*, vol. 38, no. 10, May 30, 1991, p. 31.

22. Erich Fromm, *The Art of Loving* (New York: Harper and Row, 1956), p. 20.

PROFILE

RONALD REAGAN

Before becoming president of the United States in 1981, Ronald Reagan had little experience in international relations. Like his predecessor, Jimmy Carter, his primary experience in public affairs was as a state governor. Unlike his successor, George Bush, and most other recent presidents, Reagan had not served in Congress. Many members of Congress do become involved with international affairs, particularly if they serve on committees regularly dealing with such matters. (The United States Congress is unusual because most national legislative bodies do not play a major role in foreign policy.)

Even though Reagan lacked experience, he entered office with some clear, if broad, concepts of international relations and of the proper role of the United States within the world. He tended to see the world as divided into good guys and bad guys and did not have much time for or interest in the more subtle aspects of diplomacy and negotiations. The reality is that many international issues are not clear-cut and can't be seen in simple black or white terms, but instead are complex matters with many shadings of gray in their texture.

Despite Reagan's preconceptions, during his

eight years in office he was a part of some significant changes in international relations, particularly in regard to relations between the United States and the Soviet Union. Reagan began his presidential tenure as a hardliner against the Soviet Union, disdaining any agreements with the Soviets and favoring a major United States military buildup to overcome what he saw as a growing Soviet threat. By the end of his tenure, Reagan had signed an arms control agreement with the Soviets (the intermediate-range nuclear forces of INF treaty) and spoke highly of Soviet leader Mikhail Gorbachev, with whom he held a series of summit meetings.

While Reagan appeared to change his attitude toward the Soviets during his presidency, some would argue that most of the change occurred on the Soviet side and that it was influenced by Soviet recognition of the futility and the costliness of continuing an all-out military competition with the United States. That topic and some of the forces impelling both of the superpowers are explored in later chapters. However, it is probable that both Reagan and the Soviets were driven by a combination of

President Ronald Reagan worked closely with British prime minister Margaret Thatcher. The two leaders conferred frequently, and their similar views on many international issues gave added meaning to the "special relationship" that has characterized British-American ties.

94

realpolitik (or realism) and idealism. The realism was based on the growing recognition that the national interest of each of the countries required some limitations on the military buildups because of the enormous cost involved. The idealism was motivated by the desire of Reagan and the Soviet leader to be remembered for contributions to the prospects for world peace by improving superpower relations and limiting the arms race.

Reagan's approach has been described by Robert Tucker as "a combination of the ideologue and the realist," referring to the president's conservative, anticommunist ideology. When confronted with reality that contradicted his vision of the world, according to Tucker, Reagan usually adjusted his vision to take account of the circumstances conditioning and limiting the conduct of the nation's foreign policy. Yet Reagan would say, and apparently believe, that he had remained faithful to his vision.[1]

UNILATERAL ASSERTIVENESS AND REALITY

Reagan promised a more assertive America. In doing so, he appealed effectively to elements in the American national character, and his actions helped lift national morale. In addition to countering what he described as the growing Soviet "threat," Reagan promised that he would not allow smaller nations "to push the United States around." This pledge struck a resonant chord with an American population weary of the complexities and frustrations of United States involvement in such areas as Southeast Asia, Latin America, and Iran. It was the Iranian hostage crisis, in which the United States was made to appear virtually helpless, that especially affected the American political psyche. In contrast, Reagan offered the prospect of a more confident United States, "standing tall" in the world.

The balance sheet on the Reagan administration's international policies and their results will long be debated. Reagan supporters give the administration credit for strongly influencing the move toward democracy that occurred in many parts of the world by the late 1980s and believe that the Reagan policies forced the Soviet Union to reassess its foreign and defense policies and step back from a confrontational posture. Reagan's critics maintain that the dramatic changes that occurred around the world were largely the result of other forces and that, particularly in the international economic realm, the United States lost significant ground during the Reagan years.

The reality is that the Reagan period was one of contradictions, just as there were contradictions between his view of the world and the real world with which he had to deal. Inherent in Reagan's approach, especially in his rhetoric, was the notion that the United States could essentially act on a *unilateral* basis in world affairs—that is, the United States could act on its own and could base its policies solely on its perceived national interests, with little regard for or attention to the interests and priorities of other nations. While some would argue that the Reagan administration did, in fact, have some success in acting unilaterally, at nearly every turn matters proved to be more complicated and to involve other nations and a variety of forces and factors not always within Reagan's control. Reality impinged upon Reagan's world view.

The Reagan administration was seen by most observers as more nationalist than other United States administrations of the post–World War II period. It entered office with a more hostile view of the world, reflected in attitudes toward both Third World nations and some of the international institutions they were often dominating (the United Nations and some of its agencies, such as the United Nations Educational, Scientific, and Cultural Organization [UNESCO]) and some of the industrialized allies. This view reinforced the tendency toward a unilateral approach in foreign policy.

THE REAGAN DOCTRINE

Reagan intended to counter the Soviet Union and communism not only by engaging in a buildup of nuclear arms and overall military capability but in directly challenging leftist regimes and Soviet involvement in the Third World. This became known as the Reagan Doctrine (discussed in Chapter 7): American support for anticommunist revolution as the centerpiece of a revived and revised policy of containment.[2] Reagan liked to use the term "freedom fighters" to describe those being supported by the United States in such countries as Nicaragua, Angola, and Afghanistan.

The Reagan Doctrine proclaimed a new international order in which the legitimacy of governments no longer rested simply on their effectiveness, but on conformity with the democratic process. It held that the United States had a moral responsibility to support insurgencies against communist domination and that such support was consistent with American vital interests.

A pure realist view would see some of these ventures as marginal to United States interests and likely to overextend United States resources. In other words, the costs would outweigh the benefits. This view would also contend that the doctrine promised more than it could deliver.

Although in the final analysis Reagan did blend realism with his broad ideology and idealism, Charles Krauthammer, a strong advocate of the Reagan Doctrine, saw the Reagan policies as very much the opposite of realism. In Krauthammer's view, realism had become a combination of multilateralism (reliance on international institutions) and "a new and ill-disguised form of isolationism." The Reagan policies were best described, according to Krauthammer, as *neo-internationalism*. The Reagan Doctrine was at the heart of neo-internationalism, which was based on the concept that the goal of American foreign policy was not just United States security, but democracy

around the world. Such a goal required "an assertive activist, interventionist: U.S. foreign policy."[3] Although disdaining realism, Krauthammer would undoubtedly argue that the neo-internationalist approach was, in fact, based on a realistic reading of the world as it was and not as it might exist in some utopian sense. "The international arena is not a community, but a state of nature," he argued.[4]

Jeane Kirkpatrick, who served as Reagan's ambassador to the United Nations, had her own notion of Reagan policy and purpose. In Kirkpatrick's world view there was a significant difference between "authoritarian" governments (which Reagan initially supported in South Africa, the Philippines, and Argentina, among others) and "totalitarian" regimes on the order of China, the Soviet Union, and nations aligned with them. Kirkpatrick contended that the authoritarian regimes were acceptable, even though nondemocratic. Such governments had a chance of evolving into more democratic regimes, while totalitarian governments would not, she maintained. Critics of this view argued that this was simply a way of rationalizing support for repressive right-wing governments that were friendly toward the United States.

Kirkpatrick insisted that if Jimmy Carter had adhered to the guidelines she proposed and had not been so concerned with "human rights," then the Shah of Iran and the Somoza government in Nicaragua, both authoritarian and both friendly to the United States, would have remained in power. Kirkpatrick seemed to give little significance to powerful indigenous factors that impelled the revolutions in those two countries.

DEALING WITH REALITY

While Kirkpatrick's views enjoyed some initial popularity in Reagan circles, they eventually ran headlong into competing foreign policy considerations, international linkage, and the "democratic" emphasis of the Reagan Doctrine.

By 1983, for instance, Reagan was emphasizing cooperation with China, a move which could be considered a clear case of realist and balance-of-power policy.

Despite his sweeping condemnations of communism and his long-standing antagonism toward the government of Beijing, Reagan deemed cooperative relations with China to be in the economic, political, and security interests of the United States and thought it useful to use a Sino-American relationship to help balance off the Soviets. (The United States and China were both supporting the opponents of the Soviet-backed regime in Afghanistan.)

Reagan's changed policy toward China was only one of a number of cases where his broad aims and sweeping rhetoric bumped up against international realities and/or domestic constraints.

In the Middle East, the Reagan administration proposed a "strategic consensus," but it was a concept that never got off the ground and seemed to fly in the face of regional realities at the time. The policy was to be built around shared opposition to the Soviet Union, but other issues in the region, particularly the Arab-Israeli conflict, overshadowed concerns about the Soviets.

CENTRAL AMERICA AND INTERNATIONAL INVOLVEMENT

It was to Central America—Nicaragua, in particular—that Reagan gave special emphasis. From the beginning of his administration there was a preoccupation, even an obsession, with the tiny Central American country, which was governed by the leftist Sandinista regime. Reagan strongly supported the *contra* forces seeking to overthrow the Sandinistas and backed a number of other steps designed to squeeze the Sandinistas. (See Chapter 7.)

By the mid-1980s it was clear that the *contras* could not defeat the Sandinistas militarily. Instead, the Reagan administration encouraged them to carry on a low-intensity war aimed at disrupting the Nicaraguan society and economy. As part of this plan, the United States Central Intelligence Agency mined Nicaraguan harbors, and covertly supported other actions to undermine the government. The United States found little international support for its policies. In 1984, Nicaragua filed a case with the International Court of Justice (World Court), the principal judicial organ of the United Nations, charging that United States support of the *contra* rebels and mining of the harbors violated international law. (The concept and role of international law was discussed in Chapter 3.) The United States argued that the Nicaraguan charges were political and were, therefore, not within the court's jurisdiction. When the court decided to hear the case anyway, the United States withdrew its previous agreement to submit to the court's jurisdiction. Thus, when the court ruled for Nicaragua, it had no direct legal effect on the United States, but it did damage the American image.

Although Reagan enjoyed broad popularity at home, he found it difficult to get public and congressional backing for his Nicaraguan policies, especially military aid for the *contras*. Reagan insisted that United States "vital interests" were at stake. Appealing for support for aid to implement his policies in Central America, Reagan said in 1984, "The issue is our effort to promote democracy and economic well-being in the face of Cuban and Nicaraguan aggression, aided and abetted by the Soviet Union." He added, "It's in our national interest to do so; and, morally, it's the only right thing to do."[5]

Reagan repeatedly stated that he had no intention of sending American troops into combat in Central America, but part of the opposition to Reagan's policies stemmed from public concern that Central America might prove to be "another Vietnam," with American forces becoming bogged down in another prolonged struggle. Reagan seemed to find domestic support for the quick United States invasion of Grenada (1983) to oust a radical leftist government that cooperated with Fidel Castro and, it was said, to protect United States medical students who were supposedly endangered there. The action came just two days after 241 United States troops had been killed by terrorists in Lebanon, and Reagan critics said the Grenada action was an unnecessary flexing of United States muscles. There were also several bombing raids on Libya during the Reagan years, in response to what Reagan said was Libyan leader Moammar Khadaffi's support for terrorism. Khadaffi was a target in the raids, but escaped injury. The actions against Libya and Grenada, while drawing some domestic and considerable international criticism, were apparently acceptable to many Americans, as long as they were quick and did not involve lengthy and costly United States commitments.

To counter the lack of domestic support for its Central American policy, the Reagan administration turned to other means of providing aid to the *contras*. Among the tactics employed was the secret diversion of some of the profits from the illegal sale of arms to Iran to the *contra* leadership in Central America. The Iran arms deal became known in 1986 and quickly mushroomed into the "Iran-Contra" affair. This venture was related to Reagan's preoccupation with freeing United States hostages in the Middle East. (See the discussion of terrorism in Chapter 8.) The deals were also said to be aimed at bolstering "moderates" in Iran and leading to improved United States relations with that country. The sales were in violation of Reagan's stated policy of prohibiting negotiations with terrorists. The administration had branded Iran as "the leading supporter of terrorism." The deals also violated the United States arms embargo against Iran, imposed after the taking of hostages at the United States Embassy in Tehran in 1989.

Critics maintain that Reagan gave too much attention to Central America and had little to show for the effort and cost involved. They note that the hostility to the Nicaraguan regime grew into the single most divisive issue in United States international relations since the Vietnam War, and that it distorted United States relations with Latin America and regions as distant as the Middle East as the Reagan White House searched for the means to justify and act on this obsession. For example, because he provided some assistance in the anti-Sandinista effort, the Reagan administration long overlooked some of the transgressions of Panama's double-dealing Manuel Noriega, whose involvement in drug trafficking, corruption, and human-rights abuses eventually became a major embarrassment for the United States.

Reagan supporters say that the Reagan policy kept the Sandinistas on the defensive and prevented them from carrying their revolution into surrounding countries. In 1990 the election of an anti-Sandinista candidate in Nicaragua was pictured by some as a vindication of the Reagan policy.

CONFLICTS AND CHANGE

As some of the steam went out of the Reagan drive against the Sandinistas, more and more attention was focused on weightier issues—arms control and the changing relationship with the Soviet Union. Reagan's unabashed hostility toward the Soviets in his early years and his seeming lack of interest in arms limitations had stirred concern among Western Europeans, who saw themselves as having a major stake in arms control and improved East-West relations. Europeans were also troubled by what they saw as United States hypocrisy in giving priority to domestic economic and political considerations over the principles of stated United States policies. A notable example of this was when Reagan, under strong pressure from domestic agricultural interests, championed the sale of United States grain to the Soviets, ending an embargo established by Carter following the Soviet invasion of Afghanistan. This happened at a time when Reagan was harshly condemning the Soviets. And, during the same period, Reagan roundly criticized and sought to block construction of a pipeline that would carry natural gas from the Soviet Union to Western Europe, a project that the Europeans deemed beneficial to their interests (and which would also benefit the Soviets economically). Reagan's unilateral, nationalist approach brought a strong negative reaction from Europeans.

There was also concern in Europe and elsewhere when Reagan announced his planned Strategic Defense Initiative (SDI), which was to be a space-based defense system. (See Chapter 6.) Many feared the so-called "Star Wars" scheme would be destabilizing and actually result in an escalation of the arms race, or in any case, divert billions of dollars to what numerous experts considered to be a dubious project. Reagan argued that SDI would make nuclear weapons obsolete. Though widely criticized as unworkable, the proposal found some support. "The idea of unleashing American technological genius to provide a total defense appealed to a nostalgic, anachronistic . . . deep desire to see America again invulnerable, independent, and self-reliant, freed from the shackles of interdependence, with its fate no longer tied to mutual vulnerability through mutual deterrence."[6]

It appeared that Reagan's insistence on keeping the SDI option alive (even though it was far from a reality) might be an impediment to United States–Soviet arms negotiations. However, a variety of forces and factors were leading the superpowers toward a changed relationship, and it was in this area that Reagan had his most notable impact.

The changes did not begin to take hold until after the Reagan administration played a key role in the move by the North Atlantic Treaty Organization (NATO) to deploy intermediate-range missiles in Europe in response to the SS-20 missiles deployed earlier by the Soviets.

Reagan was aided in this effort by the election of a more conservative government in West Germany (headed by Helmut Kohl) and by Margaret Thatcher's conservative government in Britain. (See Thatcher Profile.) Reagan partisans insist that this firmness on missile deployment and the SDI proposal were major factors in convincing the Soviets that they couldn't gain an upper hand in the arms race and that this recognition led to the 1987 Intermediate-Range Nuclear Forces (INF) Treaty, which is discussed in Chapter 6. In effect, it is argued that Reagan's tough policies drove the Soviets to the negotiating table.

Others see matters differently, and an obvious factor in changing the direction of world affairs was Mikhail Gorbachev's rise to power in Moscow and his acknowledgement that the Soviet Union had to concentrate much greater attention and resources on its growing domestic problems. (See Gorbachev Profile.)

As Gorbachev had to be attentive to internal difficulties, so did Reagan. Under Reagan, the United States budget deficit soared, and his detractors claim that the massive Reagan military expenditures contributed significantly to the budgetary problems. Yes, they would say, Reagan left the United States "standing tall"— on a mountain of debt.

Although Reagan continued to enjoy popular support at home, he became increasingly sensitive to the impression that he was uninterested in arms control, while Gorbachev was managing, through intensive public diplomacy, to identify himself with the cause of peace. Thus, the man who earlier disdained arms control and accused the Soviet Union of multiple violations of previous treaties wound up championing an arms control agreement with the Soviets and holding four increasingly friendly meetings with the leader of what he had described as the "evil empire."

How much Reagan's policies influenced the changes that occurred in the world near the

Reagan began his presidency as a strong critic of the Soviet Union. However, later in his presidential tenure he found he could work with Mikhail Gorbachev, and the two leaders held a series of increasingly friendly meetings and con- cluded several important agreements. Here the two leaders are seen in the White House oval office along with interpreters, who play an important part in many meetings between international leaders.

end of and shortly after his presidency will remain a point of contention. His backers will recall that in Berlin in 1987 Reagan called for Gorbachev to "tear down the wall" to prove his commitment to change. And, of course, Gorbachev did set in motion developments that brought down the wall.

Whatever effect Reagan's pressure on and challenges to the Soviets may have had, he was a major figure in an era marked by dramatic international change, including the end of the period of bipolar domination of world affairs. Although he would deny that he changed much, Reagan's own policies also underwent significant change, as realism and idealism tempered his ideological convictions.

NOTES

1. Robert W. Tucker, "Reagan's Foreign Policy," *Foreign Affairs: America and the World 1988/89*, vol. 68, no. 1, 1989, p. 13.
2. See Charles Krauthammer, "In Defense of In-

terventionism," in Steven L. Spiegel (ed.), *At Issue: Politics in the World Arena*, 5th ed. (New York: St. Martin's, 1988), pp. 27–28.

3. *Ibid.*, p. 25.

4. *Ibid.*

5. President Ronald Reagan, "U.S. Interests in Central America," televised address to the nation, May 9, 1984, in *Realism, Strength, Negotiation: Key Foreign Policy Statements of the Reagan Administration*, Washington: U.S. Department of State, Bureau of Public Affairs, 1984.

6. Raymond L. Garthoff, "Security, Arms, and Arms Control," in Steven L. Spiegel (ed.), *At Issue: Politics in the World Arena*, 6th ed. (New York: St. Martin's, 1991), p. 66.

CHAPTER FIVE

Diplomacy and Negotiations

Nations conduct their official relations with each other through diplomacy. Broadly speaking, diplomacy can refer to the full range of actions taken by a nation to represent and pursue its interests. Traditionally, diplomacy has been thought of as a formal process, consisting mostly of negotiations and discussions by austere gentlemen in a stuffy atmosphere where protocol and ceremony always prevail. That hardly constitutes a full or accurate image of diplomacy, especially today. Nations engage in a variety of diplomatic activities as they seek to foster and implement their foreign policies, to transmit information, and to collect political and economic information and intelligence.

At the center of diplomacy are communications by and between governments. These communications are carried out in various ways, the most common of which are through formal or informal discussions or negotiations, sometimes in the form of "summit" meetings between national leaders. Often such diplomacy is aimed at resolving or avoiding conflicts between or among nations, or at reaching agreements on matters of mutual interest. However, diplomatic communications are by no means restricted to such meetings and negotiations. Nations can express themselves and seek to advance or protect their interests through pronouncements or by *signaling*—statements or actions designed to establish a nation's position and, in some cases, to influence others.

A related component of diplomacy is what is sometimes referred to as public diplomacy, which includes what might be called international public relations or image-building. An element of such efforts may be *propaganda*, which essentially refers to communications designed to influence public opinion. (These topics are discussed further in Chapter 11.) Soviet leader Mikhail Gorbachev was especially effective in mounting a public relations offensive in Europe, helping to present a new image of the Soviet Union and reducing concern about the Soviets as a potential threat to Western Europe.

Although we think of diplomacy as involving tactful and polite behavior, what is really involved in much of diplomacy is the effort by a nation to get its way. Raymond Aron, the noted French political scientist, suggested that diplomacy might be called an act of convincing without using force.[1]

The elements of national power, as delineated by Hans Morgenthau, have been discussed earlier in this book. It is interesting and important to note that along with geography, natural resources, industrial capacity, military preparedness, population, national character, national morale, and the quality of government, Morgenthau lists the quality of diplomacy. Indeed, he said, "Of all the factors that make for the power of a nation, the most important, however unstable, is the quality of diplomacy."[2] As Morgenthau noted, diplomacy combines all of the other factors into an integrated whole. Diplomacy has been called the brains of national power, the means through which a nation seeks to give direction to its efforts to assert its national interests.

In recent times some of the best-known examples of diplomacy have included the Nixon-Kissinger opening to China in the early 1970s; the United States—Soviet summit meetings and arms control negotiations; the Camp David accords involving Israel, Egypt, and the United States; and the Panama Canal treaties. In the aftermath of Iraq's 1990 invasion of Kuwait and its unwillingness to withdraw, President Bush and United States officials undertook an intense diplomatic effort to coordinate opposition to Iraq. All of these cases are discussed at various points in this book. They are examples of a practice and process that has been developed and refined over the centuries.

THE ART AND PRACTICE OF DIPLOMACY

A *diplomat* is an officially accredited agent or representative of a government who serves as a medium for the conduct of international relations. Diplomacy has been practiced or attempted as long as there have been relations among people. Clearly, diplomacy was practiced during the time of the Greek city states, in the Roman and Byzantine Empires, and later among the royal courts of Europe. Monarchs dispatched envoys to other courts so that there could be systematic communication, with messages sent back and forth concerning the relations between governments.

The Byzantines, who reached their zenith after the Romans, and Niccoló Machiavelli, the Florentine scholar and diplomat (1469–1529), have become associated with a particular approach to diplomacy. (Machiavelli was discussed in Chapter 3.) The Byzantines were known both for their scheming and the use of deceit and espionage in their dealings with others, as well as for elaborate protocol. Fraudulent military parades were staged by the Byzantines, with the same troops entering one gate and marching to another, only to return in different uniforms.

The maneuvering associated with the Byzantine rule was as complex as the architecture developed in fifth-century Byzantium, famed for its intricate spires and minarets and extensive use of mosaic. Machiavelli, similarly, was known for his crafty, unscrupulous, win-at-all-costs approach. Today, when such tactics are employed, they are often referred to as Byzantine or Machiavellian.

More positive contributions to and refinements of diplomacy were made within Europe in the sixteenth and seventeenth centuries. The Italian states and various European powers began to appoint permanent ambassadors. By the late sixteenth century, permanent embassies were being established, instead of the temporary missions that had previously been the norm.

In the seventeenth century, the French statesman Richelieu introduced new concepts in the organization and conduct of diplomacy which remain visible in today's diplomacy. Among his most important contributions was his recognition that the art of negotiation is a permanent, long-term, continuing process rather than a short-term expediency. Diplomacy, he said, should seek to create solid and durable relations, not incidental opportunistic arrangements.

The diplomacy of the time was, however, often "Machiavellian," consistent with the principles set forth in *The Prince* and *The Discourses*, written by Machiavelli, in which he advocates realism, power politics, and the notion that the end justifies the means—whatever means necessary. Machiavelli said that it was necessary to be part fox and part lion—a fox to recognize traps, and a lion to frighten wolves. He wrote:

> Therefore, a prudent ruler ought not to keep faith when by so doing it would be against his interest, and when the reasons which made him bind himself no longer exist. If men were all good, this precept would not be a good one; but as they are bad, and would not observe their faith with you, so you are not bound to keep faith with them.[3]

Not surprisingly, perhaps, ambassadors were often looked upon as "honorable spies," and in the early seventeenth century, Sir Henry Wotton, then British Ambassador to Venice, said, in a statement that has often been cited, "An ambassador is an honest man sent to lie abroad for the good of his country."[4]

After serving as national security adviser to President Carter, Zbigniew Brzezinski said, "At some times when you are pursuing an objective . . . you cannot state openly what your objective is." For example, he said,

"We may seek to improve relations with country A as a means of putting pressure on country B," but it would be impossible to acknowledge that openly.[5]

MODERN DIPLOMACY

The foundations for the modern era of diplomacy were laid at the Congresses of Vienna (1815) and Aix-la-Chapelle (Aachen, 1818), when diplomatic titles and orders of rank were codified. Four classifications of diplomats were established: (1) ambassador extraordinary and plenipotentiary [invested with full power], and papal legates and nuncios [representatives of the popes]; (2) envoys extraordinary and ministers plenipotentiary; (3) resident ministers; (4) *chargé d'affairs*. These titles remain in use today. Normally an ambassador heads up his or her nation's representation, serving as "chief of mission," although a minister may also serve in that capacity. The official quarters of a mission are called an embassy when the mission is headed by an ambassador, a legation if headed by a minister. A *chargé d'affairs* is a diplomat who heads a mission in the absence of an ambassador or minister serving as chief of mission. Sometimes nations withdraw or delay in appointing ambassadors in order to make a diplomatic point, often to express displeasure. In such case, a *chargé* might be left as the senior official.

At the time of the Vienna and Aix-la-Chapelle agreements, European royalty still dominated diplomacy, but the American and French revolutions had begun to change that pattern. The years after World War I brought an end to the old European diplomacy and marked the beginning of the modern diplomatic era.

Previously, diplomacy had been the domain of the elites, normally royalty and nobility, usually operating in secrecy. There were some important diplomatic achievements in what have been referred to as the great periods of European cabinet diplomacy—between the Treaty of Westphalia (1648), which ended the Thirty Years War, and the French Revolution (1789) and between the Congress of Vienna (1815) and World War I (1914). As Henry Kissinger has noted, during these periods, "wars were limited because there existed a political framework which led to a general acceptance of a policy of limited risks."[6]

It was Karl von Clausewitz who wrote, in a statement that has frequently been cited: "War is not merely a political act, but also a real political instrument, a continuation of political commerce, a carrying out of the same by other means." Clausewitz was a Prussian general and writer on military strategy whose famous *On War*, originally published in 1832, has been a guidebook for military strategists and has had significant impact on thinking among international relations theorists. In effect, war or military action could be viewed as part of what might be called a nation's diplomatic arsenal, although we normally think of diplomacy as having the goal of avoiding war.

The failure by the European diplomats to prevent World War I gave impetus to a new turn in diplomatic relations, with calls for "open diplomacy." This was exemplified in President Woodrow Wilson's call at the end of World War I for "open covenants, openly arrived at," as part of his Fourteen Point peace program.

Diplomatic Development and Trends

Although diplomacy has not always been "open" in the modern era, it has been more open than previously. Further, diplomacy has changed in a number of other ways, with some of these changes reflecting the increase in the numbers of independent nations, the growth of international organizations, and the complexity of issues. Advances in communications and transportation, as well as the increasing interconnections among nations, have also contributed to changes in diplomatic operations and in the conduct of international relations. The modern era has been characterized by such trends and practices as

- negotiations conducted in private followed by public declarations;
- regularized international gatherings and the growth of international organizations and multilateral diplomacy;
- the expansion of diplomacy to cover areas such as trade and economic relations;
- summit meetings, with national leaders playing leading roles in diplomacy;
- crisis diplomacy, as exemplified by the 1962 Cuban missile crisis;
- public debate in democracies and open societies about diplomatic issues;
- the development and further refinement of national negotiating styles;
- the continued use of "coercive diplomacy," with some recognition of the limits of such an approach;
- broadening of the diplomatic agenda to cover a range of matters as diverse as regulation of telecommunications and civil aviation, and a growing number of economic issues;
- the increasing importance of public diplomacy, referred to earlier as international public relations or image-building.

To understand modern diplomacy and some of the changes that are occurring in the modern era, it is appropriate to look at how current-day diplomats function, examining the roles of embassies, ambassadors, and diplomatic staff.

AMBASSADORS AND EMBASSIES

Members of the modern-day diplomatic corps can find themselves dealing with a broad range of issues and problems. While diplomats serve as representatives abroad of their governments, they may be involved not only with political/diplomatic and military/security relations between nations, but consular and emigration issues, as well as business, economic, and trade questions. They also have to deal with problems encountered by citizens from their home countries traveling or living in the host country—problems such as lost passports, medical emergencies, or individuals who find themselves in difficulty with host-country authorities.

An ambassador and others on an embassy staff spend considerable time developing contacts with government officials and other leaders of the nation where they are stationed. Ambassadors and other top-ranking diplomats have the responsibility of conveying the views and representing the interests of their governments. At the same time, they are expected to keep informed about relevant developments within the host nation. Ambassadors and other embassy officials are usually active on the social circuit, hosting and attending a variety of events at which they will come into contact with key figures from the host nation and, in some cases, diplomats from other countries. In the years before President Richard Nixon made his trip to China in 1972, ending the long period of official isolation between the United States and China, some of the initial contacts concerning a possible rapprochement were in conversations between the American ambassador to Poland and his Chinese counterpart in Warsaw when they met at diplomatic functions.

A Diplomatic Example: The United States and Britain

The United States ambassador to a nation with which America has extensive relations will have regular and frequent contact with officials of the host nation, and, where appropriate, embassy personnel may also have regular contacts with opposition leaders and other opinion leaders in the host nation. For example, the close and wide-ranging relations between the United States and Britain (known officially as the United Kingdom of Great Britain and Northern Ireland) mean that each maintains a large and active diplomatic staff in the other's capitol. The United States ambassador to London (officially referred to as the ambassador to the Court of Saint James, the formal name for the royal court of the British sovereign) will normally be in regular contact with the British foreign minister or other representatives of the Foreign Office. Likewise, the top British diplomats in Washington will talk or meet with the secretary of state or officials of the United States State Department. Some of the contacts will occur at social functions or on ceremonial occasions, as well as at actual meetings. If there are important developments or issues between the two nations, the American ambassador in London might call upon top British officials to discuss them. This could happen, for example, if a prominent American government official made critical remarks about British policies or actions. The ambassador would explain the reasons for the criticism. Or, if the United States planned a major foreign initiative—even if it were in another region of the world—it might be considered important to keep the British informed. Thus, the ambassador would be asked by

Washington to inform London of the planned action. Similarly, if the president, secretary of state, or another high-ranking United States official were considering a trip that might include a London stop, the ambassador would meet with British officials to discuss the possible visit.

The State Department and most foreign ministries maintain "desks" for each major country. Desk officers are given specific responsibility for closely following developments within the assigned country. For example, the British desk in the United States State Department would monitor events and trends in Britain and would keep in regular contact with British diplomats in Washington, as well as the United States Embassy in London.

In London and in other major capitals, the United States maintains a large embassy staff, with sections for economic and commercial affairs, political affairs, public affairs, administration, consular affairs, agriculture, and military attachés.

Embassy Staffs and Facilities

Staffs of several hundred or more in American embassies abroad are not uncommon. In Iran, before the revolution of 1978–79, the United States maintained a diplomatic staff of about 1,100. At the time of the seizure of the embassy in Teheran by Iranian militants in November 1979, the number had been reduced to less than 75, although that was hardly the "skeleton" force that had been called for.

Many of the American embassies are located in large, landmark buildings. Some of them are noted for their distinctive architecture. The modernistic United States Embassy in New Delhi, India, was designed by Edward Durrell Stone, who also designed the John F. Kennedy Center for the Performing Arts in Washington. The handsome American Embassy in Grosvenor Square in London was designed by another leading architect, Eero Saarinen, an American of Finnish extraction. On the other hand, Washington is the location of many large, and, in some cases, architecturally distinctive embassies. Canada and Australia, for example, have recently constructed new and large embassy facilities in Washington.

For years there was controversy over the American embassy in Moscow and reports of Soviet "bugging" of the facility. Both sides were known to closely monitor activities of each other's embassy. Although not diplomats in the normal sense of the word, intelligence agents and others concerned with intelligence have operated out of embassies, sometimes using "diplomatic cover."

The Iranian Case

In Teheran, when the militants took over the American embassy, they claimed that it had been "a net of spies." After seizing the embassy, the Iranians discovered a stockpile of classified documents which the Americans had inexplicably failed to destroy or dispose of. Some of the documents had been shredded, but the Iranians laboriously pieced them back together. Of course, an embassy is supposed to be inviolable. In effect, it is to be considered a tiny piece of one nation located within another. This is sometimes referred to as *extraterritoriality*, although that term has broader connotations. Extraterritoriality was often imposed by a powerful state on a weaker state during the era of imperialism and colonialism, giving the dominant state jurisdiction within the territory of the weaker state. Extraterritoriality protected the citizens of the more powerful state from prosecution outside their own country, and it sometimes served to heighten cultural conflicts. Although extraterritoriality usually resulted from a treaty signed by two countries, it normally benefitted only the stronger country and was often resented as an imposition on the sovereignty of the weaker nation. Even though the broader concept of extraterritoriality has largely disappeared, it remained a particularly sensitive issue in Iran. Few Americans understood that United States' insistence on a status-of-forces agreement that exempted American military personnel (or civilian employees of the Defense Department) serving in Iran, and their families, from Iranian law was deeply resented in Iran. The law, which went into effect in 1964, was referred to in Iran as the Capitulations Agreement.

One of those most critical of the immunity law was Ayatollah Ruhollah Khomeini, a religious leader. He attacked the Shah and the United States for attempting to destroy the dignity, integrity, and autonomy of Iran. As James Bill, a leading authority on Iran, has written, "The issue of immunity and extraterritoriality had long been a sensitive issue for Iranians, who considered their country the victim of capitulations to the British and Russians from 1828 to 1928."[7] Khomeini was already in trouble with the Shah's government, and his 1964 attack on the immunity agreement resulted in his being exiled from the country. He maintained his criticism of the Shah and Americans from outside the country, and 15 years later he returned to Iran in triumph after the Shah had fled.

Although the 1964 Iranian law had extended immunity beyond the diplomatic community, diplomats around the world are supposed to enjoy full immunity under provisions of the Vienna Convention on Diplomatic Relations. As was noted earlier, embassies are also supposed to be immune; of course, that did not prevent the Iranian followers of Ayatollah Khomeini from taking control of the United States embassy and holding hostages for 444 days, clearly violating principles of diplomatic immunity and privilege.

Sanctuary, Subversion, and Diplomatic Status

Embassies have, on occasion, provided refuge for individuals seeking political *asylum* or protection. By remaining in an embassy, these individuals are beyond the reach of national authorities. However, even though the local government cannot enter the embassy to seize those who have been given asylum, it is not obligated to allow those persons to leave the country. Usually these are individuals who would be subject to some form of persecution if they did not take refuge. Notable examples have included Josef Cardinal Mindszenty, Hungarian Catholic leader, who took refuge in the United States embassy in Budapest during the unsuccessful revolt against communist rule in Hungary in 1956. Mindszenty had been a champion of freedom and had been imprisoned on trumped-up treason charges. He was freed by the revolutionaries, but when the revolution failed, he fled to the United States embassy, where he remained for 15 years. (During part of that time, when the United States and Hungary had limited diplomatic relations, the embassy was referred to as a legation, the title used for a diplomatic mission with limited status.) In 1989, after the Chinese government put down the "prodemocracy" movement in China, Fang Lizhi, a leading dissident, and his wife took temporary sanctuary in the United States embassy in Beijing. They were charged by the Chinese government with "committing crimes of counterrevolutionary propaganda and mitigation."

Occasionally a diplomat will be declared *persona non grata* (unacceptable person) by a host government. This usually occurs when a diplomat does something to grossly offend the host country. Although the individuals might have violated a law, they would not be arrested but would be asked to leave the country. This has happened when individuals with diplomatic status have been caught or are suspected of engaging in spying or improper intelligence gathering or subversive activities. During the Cold War period, if one nation—the United States or one of its allies—ordered someone from the Soviet Union or another communist country to leave the country, it was almost certain that there would be reciprocal action by the country of the accused diplomat.

EMBASSIES AS SYMBOLS

Embassies can take on symbolic significance, constituting visible and tangible representation of a nation. In some cases, this marks an embassy for protests and demonstrations. The South African embassy in Washington, for example, was the scene of numerous protests against the nation's apartheid policies. In the mid-1980s, regular protests, which drew a number of prominent personalities from American politics, the civil rights movement, and the entertainment world, generated considerable attention and helped bring pressure in Congress for limited economic sanctions against South Africa.

At various times, other embassies in Washington, such as those of Iran, the Soviet Union, and China, have been the target of demonstrations. Following the 1989 crackdown by the Chinese government on the prodemocracy movement in that country, large numbers of protestors gathered in front of the Chinese embassy.

United States embassies and other United States government facilities, such as United States Information Agency centers, have sometimes been the targets of protestors in various countries. One of the most serious occurrences was in 1979 when the American embassy in Islamabad, Pakistan, was burned by a rampaging mob which had been stirred up by an erroneous radio report that Americans had been involved in an attack on the sacred Islamic religious sites in Mecca.

EMBASSY ACTIVITIES

A primary function of any embassy is to report back to the home government. Among major countries there is a great volume of cable or telegram traffic back and forth between government officials at home and the embassy. Many of these communications are rather routine, consisting of reports, updates, and analyses on economic or political conditions, or dealing with embassy administrative matters. Most cables are sent out in the name of the ambassador, even though they may represent the efforts of an embassy staff member. Some of the reports and communications are classified, dealing with confidential, secret, top secret, or extremely secret ("eyes only" or specially coded) information.

The vast majority of diplomats are civil servants, belonging to their nation's foreign service. Often they follow a career path that may begin with consular positions, where duties include dealing with citizenship, passports, and visas, and assisting with problems encountered by their country's nationals traveling abroad. A successful career may lead to the level of chief of mission or ambassador. The ability to speak one or more foreign languages is, of course, an important qualification for diplomats, and some specialize in certain regions or subject areas. Foreign service officers may rotate between assignments abroad and in the State Department or foreign ministry in their home capitals.

Some ambassadorial posts are filled by "political" appointees, individuals from outside the diplomatic service. Sometimes these appointees are eminent persons or individuals with special experience. In the United States it has become common for presidents to appoint large campaign contributors as ambassadors. Although some of these appointees may be prominent persons or individuals whose close ties to a president give them special access, some of them are poorly qualified. In his first year in office, more than half of the ambassadors nominated by President Bush were friends and supporters rather than career foreign service officers.

Some have suggested that because of the rapidity of transportation and communications today, embassy personnel might be less important than they once were and that ambassadors have a lesser role in dealing with a foreign government, serving more as messengers than as negotiators. Home governments now have a variety of sources of information which they can draw upon, making them less dependent on embassies. Further, as will be discussed later in this chapter, high-ranking national officials increasingly have tended to undertake their own travels and diplomatic missions. Summit meetings and international organizations bring national leaders together with regularity.

The Role of Major Embassies

Nonetheless, the trend is for larger, more diversified embassies, particularly among the economically and politically powerful nations. The growing volume of international business and the increasingly intricate interconnections among nations give impetus to this trend. For example, Japan and Saudi Arabia each have more than 100 accredited diplomats in their Washington embassies. These numbers do not include support personnel. Germany and the United Kingdom also have large embassy staffs in Washington.

The German embassy, in addition to the ambassador and deputy chief of mission, has staff assigned to political affairs, consular affairs, economics and commercial matters, transportation, postal and telecommunications, agriculture, labor, science and technology, press and public affairs, and administration, plus there are military and defense attachés.

Japan's embassy in Washington, which is that nation's largest, is the hub of Japanese efforts to monitor American economic and political developments. The Japanese are noted for their attention to details and to the nitty-gritty of Washington politics, closely following developments in both the legislative and executive branches. Like Germany and other nations which have a major stake in what happens in Washington, the Japanese embassy assigns several staff members to concentrate on Congress. They regularly visit congressional offices and lunch with key congressional staff members. Others are keeping tabs on developments in various departments within the executive branch, particularly matters that may affect trade and economic relations between the United States and Japan. Many of the Japanese diplomats in Washington have done graduate study in the United States and have served previous tours in the American capital.

Much of the effort of the Japanese diplomats is, of course, aimed at influencing attitudes and actions on matters relating to Japan. In addition to the official activities of the embassy, a number of American law firms, lobbies, and public relations groups work on behalf of the Japanese government or major Japanese companies, who often coordinate their activities with those of the government.

DIPLOMATIC AND NEGOTIATING STYLES

The Japanese have a style of their own, one that they have refined as they have become an increasingly potent force in contemporary global affairs. In dealing with Washington, for example, the Japanese, as has been discussed, work assiduously to compile detailed information about matters bearing on United States–Japanese relations. Formally or informally, Japan and the United States have been engaged in discussion and negotiation—often on controversial issues—over trade and economic questions for some years. Japanese representatives emphasize proper form and process, like to avoid conflict, and can deftly sidestep confrontation. A recurring pattern in meetings and negotiations between Japan and the United States over trade issues is that American participants leave the sessions proclaiming that the Japanese have made concessions or promised steps that will reduce problems between the two countries. However, while the problems may change in form, there is often little difference in substance, and the American side is often frustrated about the failure to achieve meaningful change. Americans see implementation of a negotiated solution as a natural step while the Japanese tend to view implementation as a subject for further negotiation.

As was noted in Chapter 4, there are dangers in generalizing about national character and style. Nonetheless, there are some characteristics which can be associated with the approaches that various nations take to international negotiations. As indicated in Chapter 4, national styles are influenced by such factors as a nation's history, culture, political system, and world view.

Chinese Style and Issues

The Chinese, for example, like to orchestrate matters in such a way as to emphasize the country's importance, independence, and great tradition and history, even though modern-day China has often been relatively weak politically and economically. When foreign officials visit China, their hosts usually try to encourage tours to the major historic sites such as the Great Wall or the Forbidden City, mixed with banquets in the Great Hall of the People. Leaders of the People's Republic have also had a tendency to lecture foreign officials about China's view of the world.

In their approach to negotiations, the Chinese, reflecting, perhaps, their many centuries of history, are unusually patient, not necessarily expecting matters to be resolved quickly. Their approach has been described as "linear," often proceeding in sequential and relatively discrete stages. The Chinese attach great importance to personal relationships, attempting to identify foreign officials who are sympathetic, build friendships with them, and then depend heavily upon these relationships.[8] An indication of this Chinese tendency can be seen in the way in which top officials of the PRC continued to give Richard Nixon red-carpet treatment on visits to China long after the former president had left office under a cloud. Nixon, however, had established himself as a friend of China because of his role in reopening relations between the United States and China.

Negotiating Techniques—The Shanghai Communiqué

The handling of the Shanghai Communiqué, negotiated between China and the United States in 1972, offers some interesting insights into the diplomatic process and the styles of the participants. The communiqué— the joint statement issued at the conclusion of the historic visit by President Nixon to China, the first high-level, formal meetings since relations had been ruptured in 1949—was the result of some skillful, careful diplomatic draftsmanship. The communiqué was unusual in format because it stated conflicting points of view, as the two sides knew from the beginning that there were points on which they would not agree and on which each felt it important, in some cases for domestic political reasons, to set forth their positions.

A particularly thorny problem was how to handle the question of Taiwan. The Chinese leaders insisted that Taiwan, to which the defeated Chinese Nationalists had fled in 1949 when the Communists took over the mainland, was a part of China. The United States had, of course, recognized Taiwan as the legitimate government of China, rather than the Communist government based in Beijing, with which Nixon and Henry Kissinger were now negotiating.

On the issue of Taiwan, the two positions had been so dramatically opposed that even the unusual technique of separate statements within the joint communiqué still required carefully calculated compromise and long negotiating sessions. In effect, what the negotiators achieved was for each side to maintain its basic principles while putting the Taiwan issue in abeyance, a problem to be managed over time rather than something that could be solved immediately. Some in the United States believed that Nixon and Kissinger had "sold out" Taiwan, yielding too much to China's position. However, as Kissinger later wrote:

> The Taiwan paragraph of the communiqué was not a "victory" by one side or the other; no constructive relationship can be built on that basis. In a joint enterprise of sovereign states only those agreements endure which both sides have an interest in maintaining. Rather, it put the Taiwan issue in abeyance, with each side maintaining its basic principles. Despite the continuing difference over Taiwan our rapprochement with China accelerated because we shared a central concern about threats to the global balance of power.[9]

Not only does Kissinger describe the reality of United States—China negotiations over Taiwan, but also he makes a larger and more important point about international negotiations: Agreements must merit the support of both (or all) of the involved parties if they are to endure.

THE TREATY PROCESS

Agreements that are perceived as one-sided can create new problems or exacerbate old ones. Most international agreements or treaties involve compromise: that is the essence of negotiations. Each side seeks to obtain the most advantageous position, one that is favorable from its perspective. However, unless there is compromise, unless each side yields some, there will probably be no agreement. Symbolic gestures can sometimes be extremely important in such negotiations, giving the appearance of compromise and agreement with neither side "losing face." Sometimes this only delays dealing with complex or controversial issues, but it can serve to defuse them, and to make them more manageable. To some extent this was what happened, or at least what the negotiators attempted, in the Shanghai Communiqué.

As noted in Chapter 3, American critics of the Panama Canal Treaties of 1977–78 argued that the United States was giving up too much. But any treaty would have required some concessions by the United States. The *status quo*, which kept the Canal as a festering controversy in Panama, was not politically realistic, and a new agreement seemed imperative. As the former American ambassador to Panama said, "If the treaties had not been negotiated—or had been rejected by the Senate—what almost certainly would have happened would have made current events in neighboring Central America look like a Sunday School picnic." [10] He was of course referring to the turmoil in El Salvador and Nicaragua.

Ellsworth Bunker, who was one of the American negotiators with Panama and who had participated in a number of important international negotiations, said that the most important element in such negotiations is integrity and trust, and that it is vital "to nurture the other side's trust in your intentions and your sincerity." Some other factors critical to successful negotiations according to Bunker are: putting yourself in the other person's position, seeing what is important to him; finding out what is important to the other side; recognizing the bounds of the possible; patience and perseverance; and being attuned to political realities. [11]

In formulating the Shanghai Communiqué, the negotiators utilized the technique of separate statements within a single document. In the Panama Canal negotiations, the negotiators determined that it would be useful and would make matters more politically and diplomatically manageable if the issues were divided into two treaties, one dealing with security and neutrality issues, the other with the administration of the Canal. A participant recalled,

> The treaty, after all, was being developed in an anything-but-harmonious atmosphere, and both sides had to be able to explain the treaty to two populations which approached it from entirely different angles. Therefore, in the minds of the negotiators, a certain amount of ambiguity was convenient.

He also pointed out that negotiating such treaties is a dynamic process.

> The U.S. government does not lock in its negotiating position with absolutely fixed parameters for the entire negotiation. There is considerable give and take. In fact, the negotiations between the negotiating team and its own bureaucracy was one of the more exciting aspects of the whole process. [12]

The Panama treaties and the Versailles Treaty after World War I are classic examples of the points discussed in Chapter 4—that international relations and diplomacy can't be separated from domestic and intra-governmental politics, particularly in more open societies such as the United States. The Versailles Treaty, in which President Woodrow Wilson had played such an important part, found a formidable array of critics in the United States. Ultimately the treaty, which established the League of Nations, failed to receive the necessary two-thirds approval in the Senate. Democrat Wilson had refused to compromise with the Senate and its Republican Chairman of the Foreign Relations Committee, Henry Cabot Lodge, who wanted to add certain reservations to ratification of the treaty.

As was discussed in Chapter 3, the Panama Canal treaties narrowly gained Senate approval, but only after a long and bitter fight, and after key Senators engaged in some diplomatic activity of their own. Because the United States Constitution provides that two-thirds of the Senate must concur in any treaty agreed to by the president, the legislative body becomes somewhat more directly involved in the diplomatic process than is the case in most governmental systems. This is particularly true during periods when the Senate is in an assertive mood, as was the case at the time of the Versailles and Panama Canal treaties. For the Panama treaties, not only was there consultation by the executive branch with the legislative during the negotiations process, but also there was some "renegotiation" in direct discussions between Senate leaders and Panamanian officials after the treaties had been submitted to the Senate. Indeed, without the refinements of the treaties worked out by senators, it is unlikely that they would have gained approval.

Negotiating Arms Control

The American Congress also kept a wary eye on negotiations between the United States and the Soviet Union on arms control issues.

Arms control was at the center of the United States—Soviet agenda for much of the 1970s and 80s. Although there were other important topics in discussions and negotiations between the military superpowers, arms control issues often dominated the dialogue between the two. (Arms control issues are examined in detail in the following chapter.) Beginning with the 1967 summit in Glassboro, New Jersey, the issue of strategic arms limitations was a primary subject when Soviet and American leaders met. In more recent years, especially, United States—Soviet or Russian summit meetings have become a somewhat regular occurrence. The early conferences involving the United States and the Soviets also included European powers, but beginning with the 1961 Kennedy-Khrushchev meeting in Vienna, there have been a series of sessions confined to the two military superpowers. That these meetings were often concerned with strategic arms and international security issues should not be surprising in view of the dominant role of the United States and the Soviet Union in that domain.

ECONOMIC SUMMITS

There are also regular economic summit meetings, attended by leaders of the major economic powers. These annual sessions began in 1975 and each year they bring together the leaders of the United States, Canada, Japan, West Germany, France, the United Kingdom, and Italy (sometimes referred to as the Group of Seven or G-7). Recently, a representative of the European Community has also been included. These summits, held on a rotational basis within the participating countries, chart broad guidelines on subjects of common interest. The topics center around economic issues but vary from year to year and reflect international concerns of the time. Such subjects as Third World debt, energy, agricultural subsidies, terrorism, and East-West relations have all occupied prominent positions on summit agendas. These meetings of what has been called "the world's most private club" not only consist of formal sessions among the governmental leaders, but they are also opportunities for the leaders to get to know each other better through smaller informal discussions, which can help build mutual confidence and develop important personal relationships.

In fact, however, these summits are in many ways "media events," a series of photo opportunities. The economic summits, like the United States–Soviet/Russian summits, draw thousands of journalists from around the world and receive extensive television coverage. Such coverage keeps government leaders in the spotlight and can strengthen their standing at home.

SHERPAS AND PRELIMINARIES

The economic summits produce a final communiqué, setting forth a united position on major issues of the day. The final communiqué, while reflecting the interests of the individual national leaders, is largely the product of some intensive work by their aides, referred to as *sherpas*. The name comes from the Sherpas of Tibet and Nepal who are known for their work as guides for climbers of the highest mountain summits. The sherpas of the economic summits perform a similar service, working as guides for their respective national leaders. These sherpas usually work out well in advance the terms of the final communiqués, negotiating the details among themselves. The chiefs of state, of course, have the final word, but in most cases they have limited time to negotiate on the finer points of such statements. Such preparation is made all the more necessary by language differences which necessitate translation into several languages. The meetings themselves have simultaneous translation as at the United Nations and other major international meetings.

Extensive preparations have usually—but not always—gone before United States–Soviet summits too. This has been particularly true because of the frequent emphasis on arms control topics, which in some cases have been negotiated for many months before summit sessions. But even the 1989 Bush-Gorbachev shipboard summit in Malta, which did not feature arms control, was preceded by meetings between Secretary of State James Baker and Soviet Foreign Minister Eduard Schevernadze. For the 1990 Bush-Gorbachev summit in Washington, Baker and Schevernadze again did much of the acutal negotiating in a series of ministerial meetings beforehand. On the American side, as many as 15 different working groups were involved in resolving United States positions on issues ranging from nuclear weapons reductions to housing for United States embassy staff in Moscow.

Late in 1991 Baker found himself dealing not with one foreign minister but a number of them as he visited five former Soviet Republics. The breakup of the old Soviet Union presented new logistical and communications challenges for the diplomatic staff.

For ministerial meetings and presidential summits, the United States State Department prepares briefing books on key issues for officials involved in the negotiations and press kits for journalists covering the event.

Then, there is the special role of the interpreters. A slip-up by an interpreter can be very costly and lead to misunderstandings. They may be interpreting toasts at state dinners or documents related to diplomatic agreements, but they must be precise. They have to compare, for example, the Russian and English versions of all treaties and agreements before they can be finalized, making sure that the two versions don't convey different meanings.

SOVIET DIPLOMACY

Gorbachev brought some changes to the Soviet approach to diplomacy and negotiations and to some of the characteristics which traditionally marked Soviet tactics. For many years the Soviets were considered to be brusque, overbearing, and relatively inflexible in negotiating sessions. An experienced American diplomat said that traditionally the Soviets were not as much concerned about concluding an agreement in negotiations as in using the process "to promote their own interests." Americans often feel uneasy if a negotiation does not conclude with a "success"—a completed document, signed, sealed, and delivered. Not so the Russians, according to this view.[13]

Although the Soviet reputation for bluster was not without basis, the Soviet diplomatic corps long had a strong professional element, with experienced, skillful diplomats such as Andrei Gromyko, who was a key figure in foreign affairs for 40 years, almost 30 as foreign minister, and Anatoly Dobrynin, who learned his way around Washington very well in his nearly 25 years as ambassador to the United States. Gromyko could be bellicose and harsh but he was a clever tactician with great aplomb.

At the 1982 United States–Soviet negotiations in Geneva, with the arms discussions going nowhere, the two chief negotiators, Paul Nitze and Yuli Kvitsinsky, would occasionally meet privately to discuss possible compromises and seek common ground. On one occasion they took a "walk in the woods" of Switzerland and agreed on a joint exploratory package for the consideration of their respective governments. It became known as the "walk in the woods" formula. This proposal was rejected in both capitals, but the informal diplomacy helped keep channels of communications open and did provide some basis for the eventual 1987 treaty on intermediate-range nuclear forces, which was agreed to when the political climate was much more favorable.

Under Gorbachev the Soviets became less predictable, more likely to seize the initiative. The Soviets also became increasingly sophisticated in their understanding of the United States. This was at least partially due to the work of the Institute of the United States of America and Canada Studies of the Academy of Sciences, usually referred to as the U.S.A. Institute. This government think tank, working along with other bodies such as the Institute of World Economy and International Relations and the Diplomatic Institute, gave officials a much better reading of world affairs and of the United States in particular. For example, the U.S.A. Institute closely monitored the work of the American Congress and analyzed domestic influences on American foreign policy. Altogether, this led to a better-informed view of the United States and of other Western nations. The Soviets also developed a more sophisticated understanding of and approach to international public relations or public diplomacy. Following the dissolution of the Soviet Union, Russia assumed many of the assets and much of the diplomatic role of the former union.

SUMMITRY AND PERSONAL DIPLOMACY

Scheduled summit meetings are only one type of summit diplomacy, as Gorbachev demonstrated in his travels to numerous capital cities around the world. And, of course, heads of government take part in diplomacy in a variety of ways, beginning with their statements on and formalization of foreign policy. They may communicate with each other in various direct and indirect channels. They may send special envoys or emissaries to other countries to convey messages or deal with specific problems.

President Bush has been a frequent practitioner of personal diplomacy. Within his first year in office he visited 15 countries and held more than 100 separate one-on-one meetings with presidents, prime ministers, and kings. Bush also phoned foreign leaders with some regularity. When he traveled to Japan for the funeral of Japanese Emperor Hirohito, he took the opportunity to meet not only with Japanese officials but with leaders of other nations who were attending the funeral. He also visited China and South Korea while he was in the region.

American presidents frequently have foreign leaders as guests. Most visits are a combination of serious diplomatic discussions and ceremonial or public events. Although there are formal occasions such as state dinners at the White House, foreign leaders are sometimes given a chance to see other aspects of American life. Bush took Egyptian President Hosni Mubarak to see a Baltimore Orioles baseball game. When Nikita Khrushchev visited the United States in 1959, the Soviet leader wanted to visit an American farm. He made a well-publicized romp through an Iowa corn field with the media recording it all. With his international barnstorming, Khrushchev, though he could be belligerent, stubborn, and boisterous, nonetheless enjoyed the public spotlight and represented a sharp change from the grim visage of Soviet foreign policy under Stalin and Vyacheslav Molotov, foreign minister from 1939 to 1949 and from 1953 to 1956.

In some cases American presidents invite their guests to the presidential retreat at Camp David, Maryland, where discussions can be held in a more relaxed and isolated atmosphere. Khrushchev met President Dwight Eisenhower there. One of the first breakthroughs in Soviet-American relations occurred at the time, leading to talk of the "Spirit of Camp David," although it was rather short-lived. Soviet leader Leonid Brezhnev spent part of his 1973 visit to the United States at Camp David with President Nixon, during a period of détente between the two countries.

President Carter used Camp David as the location in 1978 for his efforts to help forge a peace agreement between Israel and Egypt. In marathon negotiating sessions over 13 days, Carter served as a mediator between Egyptian President Anwar Sadat and Israeli Prime Minister Menachem Begin. At times, Carter, patient and persistent, shuttled back and forth between the lodges where the Egyptian and Israeli delegations were quartered, trying to work out the agreement which eventually resulted in the 1979 treaty between Egypt and Israel. It was an extraordinary example of personal diplomacy.

Sadat had already engaged in a bold personal diplomatic venture of his own, flying to Jerusalem in 1977. After announcing his intention to visit Israel and address the Israeli Knesset (Parliament), he was formally invited to do so by Begin. It was under Sadat's leadership that Egypt had attacked Israel in 1973 and for decades the two nations had not recognized each other diplomatically. The only contact had been through intermediaries. Sadat's trip to Jerusalem revolutionized the diplomatic context and political landscape of the Middle East. His address to the Knesset was seen on television in many countries, as were pictures of Sadat shaking hands with Israeli leaders and visiting Yad Vashem, Israel's monument to the victims of the Holocaust. Sadat and Begin granted joint interviews to the American media. Seldom had there been a more dramatic and unexpected move to seize the diplomatic initiative and alter international perceptions.

High-Profile Diplomacy   In addition to these examples of personal diplomacy, the notion of *shuttle diplomacy* came to be associated with the Middle East. As mentioned earlier, President Carter engaged in a form of shuttle diplomacy within the confines of Camp David, serving as a kind of mediator between Israel and Egypt. Later he traveled to the two countries to help further the peace process. Secretary of State James Baker shuttled through the region in the weeks before and after the 1991 Persian Gulf War, first trying to coordinate policy in opposition to Saddam Hussein and later trying to convince the Israelis and disparate Arab nations that they should agree to negotiate with each other. These later efforts led to the 1991 Middle East peace conference in Madrid.

There was a flurry of diplomatic activity in the days and weeks before war began in the Persian Gulf area, even though this activity did not include actual negotiations. Mention was made earlier of the effective diplomacy, some of it within the United Nations, by the United States in assembling the diverse coalition of nations aligned against Iraq. In announcing the launching of the multinational military action to force Iraq out of Kuwait, President Bush said that the action came only after "months of constant and virtually endless diplomatic activity on the part of the United Nations, the United States and many, many other countries."[14]

Secretary of State Baker alone, in the period between Iraq's invasion of Kuwait in August 1990 and the beginning of the war in January 1991, held more than 250 meetings with foreign heads of state, foreign ministers, and other high foreign officials. He traveled more than 125,000 miles in the course of these contacts.

Just days before the war, Baker met in Geneva with Tariq Aziz, Iraq's foreign minister. Bush said that Baker was "totally rebuffed" at the meeting. However, no real attempt at negotiations occurred. Neither side put anything on the table. For negotiations to occur, there has to be some offer, some starting point. Baker presented Aziz with a letter that the Iraqi foreign minister did not consider to be in language appropriate for communication between heads of state, and Aziz said he would not pass it on to Saddam Hussein. Bush's letter said, "There can be no reward for aggression. Nor will there be any negotiation. Principle cannot be compromised . . ."[15]

There were several other last-ditch efforts to avoid war, with attempts by the European Community, France, and Algeria to find some basis for discussion. United Nations Secretary General Javier Perez de Cuellar also made a final trip to Baghdad to try to persuade Saddam Hussein that it was in his best interests to leave Kuwait. Although he said that he was well received, Perez de Cuellar found Iraq to be intransigent.

Kissinger and Personal Diplomacy

Probably the best-known examples of shuttle diplomacy were undertaken by Henry Kissinger when he was secretary of state. Kissinger shuttled by jet between Middle East capitals in the aftermath of the 1973 Arab-Israeli war, negotiating withdrawal and disengagement agreements. (See Kissinger Profile.)

George Ball, an experienced American diplomat, questioned what he called Kissinger's "one-man diplomacy" and said that the shuttle efforts were part of a pattern of "virtuoso diplomacy" which Kissinger attempted to practice. Ball wrote:

> The government of a power with worldwide interests is like a juggler who must keep many balls in the air, but Kissinger, the virtuoso always center-stage under the spotlight, . . . specialized in trying to throw one or two balls at a time to record heights, while letting the rest ricochet aimlessly around the stage. By attempting to be both foreign minister and his own diplomatic corps, he has necessarily limited the scope of his attention, and the result has been a narrowly conceived polity—a policy that ignores relations with nations that happen for the moment to be out of the spotlight, and, in the long run, encourages a practice of haphazard improvisation.[16]

Opinions may differ about Kissinger's performance and strategy, but Ball's comments illustrate a genuine problem in today's international relations. National leaders and top foreign-policy officials of major nations have so many different matters to contend with that there is a tendency to concentrate on a few high-profile issues which capture media attention.

Kissinger himself has been critical of "personal negotiation." According to Kissinger, "Some of the debacles of our diplomatic history have been perpetrated by presidents who fancied themselves negotiators. As a general rule the requirements of the office preclude the follow-through and attention to detail negotiation requires." At the 1972 Moscow summit, prior to the signing of the SALT I agreement, Kissinger said that it was evident that neither Brezhnev nor Nixon had mastered the technical issues involved, and he said that the meetings "demonstrated that heads of government should not negotiate complex issues."[17] An added problem, Kissinger believes, is that when heads of government become negotiators, no escape routes are left for diplomacy.

CRISIS DIPLOMACY

Summit diplomacy, international conferences, and visits by national leaders are important components of international relations. However, this set-piece diplomacy is only part of the picture. Diplomatic mettle is truly tested in times of crisis or high tension.

In modern times probably the best example of high diplomatic drama occurred during the 1962 Cuban missile crisis. In this case, the heads of the United States and Soviet governments played leading roles and were actively involved. However, many channels and forms of diplomacy, conventional and unconventional, were used during the period, which many believe was the closest that the United States and the Soviet Union came to a direct military confrontation in the nuclear era. Fortunately, it was basically a diplomatic rather than a military confrontation.

The crisis began when American reconnaissance photos, taken from a U-2 aircraft, confirmed that the Soviets were building a medium-range missile base in Cuba. On October 16, 1962, President John F. Kennedy was informed of the evidence and a period of 13 critical days of confrontation, crisis, and negotiation had begun.

Decision-Making in an International Crisis

Kennedy assembled a group of trusted advisors, which came to be referred to as the Executive Committee or ExComm, to analyze the situation and recommend options for the president. The group deliberated intensely for the next five days, examining the problem from almost every conceivable perspective. Options debated ranged from launching a full-scale invasion to applying various forms of diplomatic pressure on Castro and Khrushchev, setting up a naval blockade, or launching a "surgical strike" on the missile installations.

There was fear that prolonged diplomacy would give the Soviets time to make the missiles operational. The officials debated over whether the missiles would significantly alter the balance of power, with military leaders contending that they would. After lengthy deliberation, the ExComm members finally decided upon a naval blockade or "quarantine" of Soviet arms shipments to Cuba. (There was concern among some that the action might draw a retaliatory Soviet blockade in Berlin. As is discussed elsewhere in the book, Berlin had been the scene of some previous Soviet-American or East-West showdowns.) The quarantine was considered to be a compromise, short of more direct military action and leaving some flexibility for further moves.

A significant factor, particularly during the initial phase of the crisis, was that the American ExComm was able to operate in secrecy. As one of the participants later said, "Nothing could be worse than to alert the Russians before the United States had decided its own course."[18] Another key player on the American side, former General Maxwell Taylor, looking back after 20 years, said that the "secrecy maintained during the planning phase" was extremely important to the American success in dealing with the crisis. Taylor commented that, "Today it would be next to impossible to count on the secrecy which contributed so much to the success in the Cuba crisis," referring to the tendency to "leak" secret information to the media and to a more assertive Congress.[19]

Although a crisis atmosphere was building, little was known publicly before President Kennedy made a dramatic television speech on October 22, capturing world attention with his revelation about the missile installations and his demand for their removal. Kennedy warned that if any of the weapons were launched against the United States, he would fully respond against the Soviet Union. Tension-packed days followed, as some feared that the world was on the brink of nuclear war. Within 48 hours the western European allies endorsed Kennedy's action and the Organization of American States unanimously supported the blockade.

At the United Nations, the United States scored important diplomatic points. Using photographs to refute Soviet claims, Ambassador Adlai Stevenson's dramatic revelation of Soviet deception about the missiles had an electrifying effect on mobilizing international support for the American position.

Military and Diplomatic Maneuvers

Meanwhile, the United States Strategic Air Command (SAC) was placed on full alert, with part of the force of B-52 bombers, loaded with nuclear bombs, in the air at all times. American ships patrolled the Caribbean and ground forces were positioned for possible action. Soviet vessels were sailing toward Cuba, but on October 24 some of them changed course to return home and others stopped. Meanwhile, Khrushchev and Kennedy were exchanging letters and statements and there were other formal and informal contacts between the two countries. On October 26, a diplomat in the Soviet Embassy in Washington, known to be a senior intelligence (KGB) officer, contacted newsman John Scali of the American Broadcasting Company (ABC) and requested an urgent meeting. Using Scali, with whom he had occasionally lunched, as an unofficial diplomatic channel, the Soviet agent floated a proposal: the Soviets would disengage the missiles if the United States promised not to invade Cuba in the future. He asked Scali if he could find out what American officials would think of the proposal. This use of Scali is an example of what is sometimes referred to as *back-channel diplomacy*. Back-channel communications can be governmental; the point is that they are normally unofficial or not intended to represent an official diplomatic position. Such approaches can also be called *track-two diplomacy*. Track-one diplomacy refers to formal government-to-government interaction. Track-two, on the other hand, involves nongovernmental, informal, and unofficial activity. Having used Scali to probe the American negotiating position, Khrushchev followed with a letter stating much the same offer, although still insisting that the missiles were not offensive but defensive.

Resolution and Results

What seemed to be a hopeful development was, however, followed the next day by a Khrushchev note with a different tone, demanding that in return for withdrawing the Cuban missiles, the United States remove its missiles from Turkey, which borders the Soviet Union. Kennedy had, months before, planned to remove the missiles from Turkey, but accepting Khrushchev's demand now would appear to give the Soviets a major public victory. In Cuba, meanwhile, work on the Cuban missile installations continued; they appeared to be nearing the operational stage. An American U-2 plane filming the missile sites was shot down over Cuba. In what turned out to be a key move, President Kennedy accepted a suggestion from his brother Robert, the attorney general. Robert Kennedy suggested that the president ignore the last Khrushchev letter and, instead, respond to the Khrushchev suggestion of October 26, accepting that proposal. Kennedy included a demand that Moscow stop work immediately on the missiles. At the same time, however, he had Robert Kennedy inform a Soviet diplomat that the American missiles had been ordered out of Turkey, although the United States would make no public announcement. On October 28, Khrushchev accepted the deal: the missiles would be removed from Cuba in return for a no-invasion pledge from Kennedy. The crisis had ended.

Afterwards, it was often said that the Americans and the Soviets had been eyeball to eyeball and that the Soviets had blinked first. War was avoided, and the United States succeeded in getting the missiles withdrawn from Cuba. However, the results and longer-term effects of the missile crisis were complex, not entirely favorable to the United States.

The United States's approach to the crisis has been referred to as an example of "total diplomacy," using all available channels and negotiating by action as well. President Kennedy and his advisors were praised for their handling of the crisis. A later assessment of Kennedy's role lauded his disciplined restraint and said that he demonstrated qualities long regarded as essential for a successful negotiator.[20] Among the qualities cited were: wisdom to grasp the essential national interests from the perspective of both sides; a sense of resolution combined with flexibility; strong nerves and moral toughness; effective use of consultative capacity; a desire to reach an agreement; understanding of the correlation between power and the negotiating process; and a determination not to humiliate the adversary or to gloat over the outcome.

Positive outcomes included Kennedy's increased concern about avoiding crises and pursuing arms control. This led to the 1963 Test Ban Treaty, the first United States-Soviet arms control agreement, and to the installation of the "hot line," a direct link between the White House and the Kremlin to be used in potential crisis situations.

On the other hand, some of the fallout from the crisis was less positive. The Soviets, who referred to the affair as the "Caribbean crisis" rather than the Cuban missile crisis, are widely believed to have undertaken the massive military buildup which became evident in the 1970s as a result of the Cuban experience. They had been shown to be an inferior nuclear power and in some sense felt humiliated before the world. Quite possibly the missile crisis led to an intensification of the arms race.

The missile crisis, while giving impetus to the need for crisis or conflict avoidance and the means to deal with and resolve such situations, served to glorify boldness, toughness, and action diplomacy, perhaps even encouraging military solutions to diplomatic problems. There was a tendency for other national leaders to want to prove their "toughness under pressure" and to create or suggest a crisis atmosphere in order to demonstrate their ability to act boldly in such circumstances.

Regardless of whether such a legacy was actually justified by the Cuban missile crisis, some critics felt that Kennedy had disdained diplomatic opportunities and private negotiations in favor of public confrontation. Some believed that Kennedy had engaged in "brinkmanship" and that he could have headed off or defused the crisis by confronting the Soviets privately rather than publicly.

COERCIVE DIPLOMACY

The 1962 blockade of Cuba could be considered an example of *coercive diplomacy*. As noted in the beginning of this chapter, diplomacy can involve a full range of actions taken by a nation to represent and pursue or protect its interests. Coercive strategy, in contrast to the traditional military strategy, aims at affecting the adversary's will rather than upon negating the adversary's capabilities. If threats do not suffice and force is actually used, it is employed in a limited, selective manner. As Alexander George has written, force is used "in an exemplary, demonstrative manner, in discrete and controlled increments, to induce the opponent to revise his calculations and agree to a mutually acceptable termination of the conflict." [21] In such cases, force and the threats of force may become part of a carrot and stick approach to getting the adversary to take a certain course of action. Force is subordinated to what is essentially not a military strategy at all, but rather a political-diplomatic strategy for resolving or reconciling a conflict of interests with the adversary.

Coercive diplomacy of this type will be applicable only in certain situations, and there are liabilities involved, among them the dangers of escalation into prolonged military conflict. One of the themes emphasized in this book is that nations, particularly the military superpowers, have had to come to terms with the limits of military power as an instrument of foreign policy.

There are occasions when the major powers can use limited military force, a form of coercive diplomacy, to deal with conflicts. As was discussed in Chapter 3, the United States has had an especially close and complicated relationship with Panama, particularly because of United States involvement with the Panama Canal. In the late 1980s the United States found itself increasingly at odds with the military government in Panama headed by General Manuel Noriega. When various diplomatic and political efforts to push Noriega out of power were unsuccessful, the United States intervened militarily in Panama. The United States action allowed a democratically elected government to take office, which Noriega had previously prevented. The United States declared that the coercive move was necessary for a variety of reasons, including allowing the elected government to take power. Noriega had been indicted in the United States for involvement in the drug trade. The Panamanian dictator had also declared that a "state of war" existed between the United States and Panama and there had been several incidents in which Americans in Panama had been killed or wounded by Panamanian forces. After the United States invasion, Noriega sought refuge in the papal nunciate in Panama (the Vatican's diplomatic mission) and remained there for several days until surrendering to United States authorities.

The United States intervention in Panama drew criticism from some in Latin America who said it was a return to the days of *gunboat diplomacy*. The term actually refers to the iron fist of threatened force inside the velvet glove of diplomatic relations, and was first associated with Western domination of China early in this century, which United States and British interests maintained by gunboats on the main rivers and harbors. In essence, gunboat diplomacy is associated with imperialism or domination by external powers.

The Organization of American States, the regional organization of American republics, voted 20-1 to deplore the United States action in Panama. Latin American nations are particularly sensitive to United States intervention. There were a series of military interventions, especially in Central America, early in the twentieth century and these incursions had a strong influence on Latin American perceptions of the United States. (See Chapter 7.)

CHANGING PATTERN

There are, as the Panama case indicates, contemporary examples of coercive diplomacy and of more traditional uses of political and diplomatic power. However, as discussed earlier in this chapter, a significant change in international relations in recent years has been the increasing emphasis on public diplomacy, on international public relations, and on efforts by governments and national leaders to influence other nations and world affairs through public diplomacy channels. In an era of global telecommunications links, this pattern seems likely to grow even stronger in the future as nations and national leaders can communicate more easily across borders, and as the diplomatic agenda broadens to deal with a range of issues resulting from the increased interdependence among nations.

NOTES

1. Raymond Aron, *Peace and War: A Theory of International Relations*, translation by Richard Howard and Annette Baker Fox (New York: Praeger, 1968), p. 24.

2. Hans J. Morgenthau, *Politics Among Nations* (New York: Alfred A. Knopf. 3rd ed., 1960), pp. 139, 540–52.

3. Niccoló Machiavelli, *The Prince and the Discourses*, translation by Luigi Ricci (New York: Modern Library, 1950), Ch. XVIII, p. 64. (Original publication in 1513.)

4. See Logan Pearsall Smith, *Life and Letters of Sir Henry Wotton* (Oxford: Oxford University Press, 1907).

5. Murrey Marder, "Duplicity Called Useful in Diplomacy," *Washington Post*, August 1, 1984.

6. Henry Kissinger, *Nuclear Weapons and Foreign Policy* (New York: Doubleday/Council on Foreign Relations, 1957), p. 139.

7. James A. Bill, *The Eagle and the Lion: The Tragedy of American-Iranian Relations* (New Haven: Yale University Press, 1988), p. 158.

8. See Richard H. Solomon, "China: Friendship and Obligation in Chinese Negotiating Style" in Hans Binnendijk (ed.), *National Negotiating Styles* (Washington: U.S. Department of State, Foreign Service Institute, 1987).

9. Henry Kissinger, *White House Years* (Boston: Little, Brown, 1979), p. 1080.

10. Comments by William J. Jorden in Diane B. Bendahmane and John W. McDonald, Jr. (eds.), *Perspectives on Negotiation* (Washington: U.S. Department of State, Foreign Service Institute, 1986), p. 5. See also William J. Jorden, *Panama Odyssey* (Austin: University of Texas Press, 1984).

11. See comments by Ellsworth Bunker in *Perspectives on Negotiation*, p. 14.

12. Comments by Ambler H. Moss in *Perspectives on Negotiation*, pp. 23–24.

13. Comments by Helmut Sonnefeldt in U.S. Congress, House, Committee on Foreign Affairs, *Soviet Diplomacy and Negotiating Behavior: Emerging New Context for U.S. Diplomacy*, vol. 1. (Washington: U.S. Government Printing Office, 1979), p. 506.

14. President George Bush, address to the nation, January 16, 1991. Text printed in *New York Times*, January 17, 1991 and *Congressional Quarterly*, January 19, 1991, pp. 197–98.

15. "Bush Informs Congress: Diplomacy Has Failed," *Congressional Quarterly*. January 19, 1991, pp. 198–99; "Text of Refused Letter from Bush to Saddam," (Associated Press), *Arkansas Democrat*, January 16, 1991.

16. George W. Ball, *Diplomacy for a Crowded World* (Boston: Atlantic/ Little, Brown, 1976), p. 15.

17. Kissinger, *White House Years*, pp. 142, 1220.

18. Arthur M. Schlesinger, Jr. *A Thousand Days: John F. Kennedy in the White House* (New York: Houghton Mifflin, 1965), p. 802.

19. Maxwell D. Taylor, "Reflections on a Grim October," *Washington Post*, October 5, 1982.

20. "The Cuban Missile Crisis 1962: Negotiations by Action" in *Soviet Diplomacy and Negotiating Behavior: Emerging New Context for U.S. Diplomacy*, vol. 1. (Washington: U.S. Government Printing Office, 1979), pp. 332–60.

21. Alexander L. George, David K. Hall, and William R. Simons, *The Limits of Coercive Diplomacy: Laos, Cuba, Vietnam* (Boston: Little, Brown, 1971), p. 18.

PROFILE
HENRY A. KISSINGER

During his tenure as a top-ranking government official and a longer career as an analyst and commentator on world affairs, Henry Kissinger has been associated with some of the classic traditions and concepts in diplomacy and international relations. In particular, Kissinger has been identified with realism and the balance-of-power concept.

Kissinger gained international prominence while serving as President Richard Nixon's national security assistant (1969–73). He became Nixon's secretary of state in 1973 and continued in that position under Gerald Ford through 1977, after Nixon's 1974 resignation. He was a powerful, if sometimes controversial, practitioner of diplomacy.

Born in Germany, at age 15 he emigrated to the United States with his family in 1938, fleeing Nazi persecution of Jews. After service in the United States Army, Kissinger attended Harvard, receiving his Ph.D. in 1954. He specialized in the study of diplomacy and wrote his dissertation on the Congress of Vienna (1815), the heyday of balance-of-power politics. He displayed an appreciation for power politics and a disdain for the moralistic assumptions that, in his view, frequently block long-term solutions to international problems. As a diplomat, he sought to employ in the modern age some of the classic diplomatic concepts and theories that he had studied. Kissinger was often said to be especially influenced by Prince Klemens Metternich, a key figure in the period that Kissinger studied. (Metternich and the Congress of Vienna were discussed in Chapter 2.)

Henry Kissinger played a role in one of the most dramatic and significant diplomatic developments of modern time, helping to engineer renewed contacts between the United States and China in the early 1970s after the two countries had been isolated from each other for more than 20 years. He is seen here with Mao Zedong, Chinese Communist leader.

While teaching at Harvard during the 1950s and early 1960s, Kissinger became interested in "nuclear strategy," taking the position that nuclear weapons were a reality and had to be coordinated into a realistic defense policy. After some experience in both the Kennedy and Johnson administrations as a consultant on arms control and foreign policy, Kissinger was named to the national security position by Nixon when he was elected president. During his years in Washington, Kissinger was involved with a number of major international issues, including Vietnam, the Middle East, United States relations

130

with China and the Soviet Union, and arms control.

KISSINGER'S DIPLOMACY
AND THE VIETNAM DILEMMA

The primary problem facing the Nixon administration at the beginning was how to "honorably" end United States involvement in Vietnam, which had become a quagmire for the United States under Johnson. Kissinger became a central figure in the policy and diplomacy related to the Vietnam dilemma. Nixon and Kissinger realized that to try to achieve a clear military victory would involve a sustained commitment at a level which the American public would not support. On the other hand, they opposed unilateral United States withdrawal because it would be unworthy of a great power and would undermine United States credibility in world affairs. Instead, they attempted a policy of "Vietnamization," which would gradually transfer responsibility for conducting the war to South Vietnam as United States forces were withdrawn. Kissinger wanted to leave behind a stable balance of power within Vietnam and in the region, one that would protect the overall geopolitical balance. However, Kissinger came to realize that South Vietnam was incapable of successfully carrying out this policy within a reasonable period of time.

Two major problems foiled Kissinger's vision. One was the corruption and ineffectiveness in the South Vietnam government; it was not truly a democratic government either, which undermined the principles that the United States purported to uphold. Another factor was that the North Vietnamese knew that time was on their side and that they could simply outwait the Americans.

Kissinger tried to combine personal diplomacy with periodic military escalations in an attempt to pressure North Vietnam into a settlement. In addition to the formal negotiating sessions he conducted with North Vietnam,

Kissinger showed his penchant for secret diplomacy by engaging in furtive talks with officials from North Vietnam and other countries. Despite Kissinger's intense efforts, the North Vietnamese were unyielding in the negotiations, particularly on the subject of mutual withdrawal from South Vietnam. The North would not agree to remove its troops. Meanwhile, United States domestic pressure to end the war was becoming overwhelming. Kissinger and Nixon were aware that prolongation of the Vietnam problem was hindering their pursuit of broader diplomatic goals, including dealings with China and the Soviet Union.

When the peace talks finally began to produce results in 1972, it was only because of significant modifications in the United States negotiating position. However, when the talks still remained deadlocked on some key points, Nixon, with Kissinger's backing, ordered massive bombing of the north late in 1972 in yet another futile attempt to force concessions. The bombing, which came just after Nixon's reelection in the 1972 presidential race, provoked still another storm of domestic protest. Finally, in January 1973, Kissinger and Le Duc Tho, the chief negotiator for North Vietnam, settled on a plan little different from what had been agreed the previous year. For their efforts, Kissinger and Le Duc Tho were awarded the Nobel Prize later in 1973.

THE POLITICS OF
INTERNATIONAL POWER

If the morass of Southeast Asia and the limitations on the power that a great nation could exercise were frustrating for Kissinger, he found other diplomatic tracks much more amenable to his skills and interests. Kissinger's approach seemed more suited for power politics, and he was intent on exploiting the differences between the two communist powers, the Soviet Union and China. In one of the most dramatic diplomatic maneuvers of modern times, he made a secret trip to China in 1971 to engineer the subsequent visit by Nixon. During the Nixon visit, Kissinger was involved in negotiating the Shanghai Communiqué, the joint declaration discussed in Chapter 5, which served as the basis for relations between the two nations. It was a significant diplomatic breakthrough. As Kissinger described it, "Leaders of two powerful nations had taken the measure of each other and judged that they could conduct compatible foreign policies, revolutionizing world diplomacy." From the Chinese perspective, as Kissinger explained, in order to help balance off Soviet strength, China "correctly judged that the visible presence of American power was crucial for maintaining a balance of power in Asia and Europe." [1]

In turn, Kissinger wanted to use the opening to China to pressure Moscow to be more forthcoming in its dealings with Washington; otherwise, the Soviets would find themselves isolated within the strategic triangle. This all fit well within Kissinger's notions about the balance of power. And, indeed, the United States–China entente probably contributed to the period of United States–Soviet détente which followed. However, a variety of practical reasons, including the costliness of the continued arms rivalry, as well as pressure from Europe—some of the same factors that helped drive United States–Soviet détente in the late 1980s—also influenced improved relations. Kissinger played a major role in working out the first strategic arms limitations agreement (SALT I) and helped launch the SALT II negotiations. He also visited Moscow to break a deadlock on expanding bilateral trade.

VIRTUOSO DIPLOMACY?

It was his diplomacy in the Middle East, however, that probably earned Kissinger the most attention as a peripatetic negotiator and a virtuoso of diplomacy, even though some questioned Kissinger's "lone ranger" approach. Despite his liking for secret negotiations, Kissinger seemed to enjoy the limelight and had a knack for political theater. In the aftermath of the 1973 war, Kissinger became the mediator between Israelis and Arabs. His plane was nicknamed the "Yo-Yo-Express" because it was up and down so often on his flights between the countries in the region as he engaged in shuttle diplomacy. The rapidity and relative ease of transportation and communications—Kissinger could stay in regular, secure contact with Washington even on the plane, which was one of the United States presidential fleet—made possible this kind of diplomatic full-court press. It was referred to as "step-by-step" diplomacy, as Kissinger painstakingly constructed an agreement on the disengagement of the opposing forces. A key breakthrough was Egypt's agreement to back down from its antagonism toward Israel. In broader geopolitical terms, Kissinger helped draw Egypt closer to the United States and away from its dependency upon the Soviets. Of course, it was Anwar Sadat, the Egyptian leader, who took the decisive steps, seeing it in Egypt's interest to do so. For all Kissinger's efforts, the peace was a fragile one, with many complex problems left unresolved.

A group of journalists traveled with Kissinger on his shuttle plane, and he received immense media attention. *Newsweek* featured him on its cover as "Super K," even while President Nixon was entering the final days of his troubled presidency, the Watergate scandal having finally overwhelmed him. As Kissinger continued his role in the Ford administration, he still faced a full agenda of critical international problems. At one point in the early months of the Ford administration, for example, Kissinger flew back to the Middle East on a "salvage" mission for his step-by-step approach. Only a week after returning to Washington, he was airborne again—first, to Moscow, to try to revive the stalled arms talks; next, to South Asia, to attempt to repair United States relations with India and to

Much of Kissinger's diplomacy involved the Middle East, where he shuttled between countries to negotiate agreements. A major figure in this process was Egypt's president Anwar Sadat, who met frequently with Kissinger and whose actions helped lead to an eventual Egyptian-Israeli peace treaty.

massage United States relations with Pakistan; then, to almost half-a-dozen other countries before addressing the World Food Conference on how to meet the crisis of food shortages; finally, to the Middle East again, where he made his usual stops in Egypt, Saudi Arabia, Jordan, Syria, and Israel.[2]

THIRD-WORLD LIMITATIONS

In 1975, President Ford and Kissinger failed to obtain congressional approval for funds to support one of the factions fighting for control in newly independent Angola. Instead of attempting to negotiate a diplomatic solution, the United States was providing covert aid to one of the Angolan groups—until Congress stopped the funding. For Kissinger, who often disdained the bureaucracy and the government's international relations apparatus in conducting his diplomacy, it was a frustrating lesson in the constraints of domestic politics on foreign policy. He argued that United States interests were at stake because if the United States didn't act, a group aided by the Soviets and Cubans would control Angola. As is discussed in Chapter 7, the Soviets had positioned themselves to be influential in an independent Angola by long support of one of the nationalist groups fighting to end Portuguese colonial rule. Kissinger and the United States, in the meantime, had been locked in a close relationship with the dictatorial regime in Portugal, which was a member of NATO. It seemed to be a terribly short-sighted approach. When the Portuguese dictatorship collapsed and Angola became independent, the United States found itself with little influence in Angola. As historian Walter LaFeber wrote, Nixon and Kissinger, "bet on the wrong horse."[3]

Congress showed little inclination, in the immediate aftermath of Vietnam, to provide the military assistance Kissinger wanted, and there was fear of becoming involved in another Third World civil war. Kissinger considered this a major setback to United States interests and condemned the congressional action. However, had Kissinger distanced the United States from Portuguese colonialism, the United States might have been in a much more influential position. That pro-Portugal policy, according to John Lewis Gaddis, reflected "all the prescience of a Marie Antoinette in 1789."[4] In other words, it went against the tide of history.

The reality was that Kissinger had previously shown little interest in Angola and generally paid little attention to Africa. The Third World was not a major concern for him, and even when he did focus on Third-World issues it was usually in relation to the superpower rivalry. Angola became a priority matter only when it became a factor in the superpower quest for power and influence. It was, as noted earlier, when what he considered to be the international equilibrium was at stake that Kissinger became most effectively engaged.

EQUILIBRIUM OF STRENGTH

Kissinger persistently returned to the principles of power balancing as the way to maintain an acceptable international order, based on a certain equilibrium of strength. At the same time, it was Kissinger's view that the United States needed to have the realism to accept the world as it was, together with the ingenuity to make the best of it, this later challenge being one that called for skilled diplomacy and prudent exercise of power.

Kissinger foresaw the end of the Cold War and helped hasten its end, even though he sometimes seemed trapped in the Cold War power game. He also recognized the coming transition from a bipolar to a multipolar world and, as early as 1973, said, "It is wrong to speak of only one balance of power, for there are several which have to be related to each other." He said that in the military sphere there were two superpowers, but in economic and political terms there were other groupings that had to be considered centers of power.[5]

At various points after Kissinger left office following Ford's defeat by Jimmy Carter in 1976, there was speculation about a possible return to public life. That did not happen, but during the Reagan administration Kissinger chaired a presidential commission on Central America. The commission called for more economic and military aid to the region but had little real impact on the continuing controversy about the United States role in Central America.

New Power Balance

Kissinger continued to be a regular commentator on international relations. During the 1991 Gulf War, his views reflected his steadfast commitment to realism and balance-of-power politics. Kissinger wrote, "Over the long run, our biggest challenge will be to preserve the new balance of power that will emerge from this conflict." This new balance, according to Kissinger, "will see many centers of power, both within regions and between them." He added, "These power centers reflect different histories and perceptions. In such a world, peace can be maintained in only one of two ways: by domination or by equilibrium." Since the United States neither wants to dominate, nor is it any longer able to do so, "we need to rely on a balance of power, globally as well as regionally."[6]

According to Kissinger, if "radical countries are tempted by some vacuum every few years," the same crises will be played over and over again, albeit with different actors. In his view, this is why "the so-called diplomatic options" would have only made matters worse in the Gulf crisis. Although Kissinger supported Bush's choice of the military option, Kissinger was troubled by the idealism expressed in Bush's new world order concept. (See Chapter 13.) Kissinger likened the approach to Woodrow Wilson's attempt to impose a community of interests on a balance-of-power system after World War I, and to aspects of the United Nations vision at the end of World War II. He cautioned against repeating these experiences, arguing that instead there should be acceptance of the reality of conflicting interests in the international system and the necessity for a balance-of-power strategy. Kissinger acknowledged that a balance-of-power strategy sits uncomfortably with Americans because of its "apparent moral neutrality" and the fact that it "knows few permanent enemies and few permanent friends." And he notes that the United States cannot by itself play the role of "balancer," but instead requires the assistance of others and the ability to distinguish between situations where critical United States interests are involved and those where they are not.[7] In short, amidst all of the talk of a new world order, Kissinger continued to rely on the basic concepts associated with the balance-of-power diplomacy that he studied and practiced.

NOTES

1. Henry Kissinger, *White House Years* (Boston: Little, Brown, 1979), pp. 1090, 1096.
2. A description of some of Kissinger's travels is found in Marvin Kalb and Bernard Kalb,

Kissinger (Boston: Little, Brown, 1974 and New York: Dell, 1975, paper).
3. Walter LaFeber, *The American Age* (New York: Norton, 1989), p. 628.
4. John Lewis Gaddis, *Strategies of Containment* (New York: Oxford University Press, 1982), p. 330.
5. Henry Kissinger, address to *Pacem in Terris III* Conference, Washington, October 3, 1973, in Henry Kissinger, *American Foreign Policy* (3rd. ed.), (New York: Norton, 1977), pp. 128–29.
6. Henry Kissinger, "A Postwar Agenda," *Newsweek*, January 28, 1991, p. 44.
7. Henry Kissinger, "False Dreams of a New World Order," *Washington Post*, February 26, 1991, p. 21. See the analysis by Stanley R. Sloan, *The US Role in a New World Order: Prospects for George Bush's Global Vision*, Congressional Research Service, Library of Congress, Washington, March 28, 1991.

SUGGESTIONS FOR FURTHER READING

Ball, George. *Diplomacy for a Crowded World.* Boston: Little, Brown, 1976.

Hersh, Seymour M. *The Price of Power: Kissinger in the Nixon White House.* New York: Simon & Schuster, 1983.

Isaak, Robert. *Individuals and World Politics.* (2nd. ed.) Monterey, California: Duxbury Press/Wadsworth, 1981.

Kalb, Marvin and Bernard Kalb. *Kissinger.* Boston: Little, Brown, 1974 and New York: Dell, 1975 (paper).

Karnow, Stanley. *Vietnam: A History.* New York: Viking, 1983.

Kissinger, Henry. *American Foreign Policy.* (3rd. ed.) New York: Norton, 1977.

Kissinger, Henry. *The Necessity for Choice: Prospects of American Foreign Policy.* New York: Harper & Row, 1961.

Kissinger, Henry. *Nuclear Weapons and Foreign Policy.* New York: Harper & Row, 1957.

Kissinger, Henry. *White House Years.* Boston: Little, Brown, 1979.

Kissinger, Henry. *A World Restored: Metternich, Castlereagh, and the Problems of Peace, 1812–1822*. New York: Houghton Mifflin, 1957; also, *A World Restored: The Politics of Conservatism in a Revolutionary Age*. New York: Grosset & Dunlap, 1964 (paper).

Kissinger, Henry. *Years of Upheaval*. Boston: Little, Brown, 1982.

Kissinger, Henry. (ed.) *Problems of National Strategy*. New York: Praeger, 1965.

Roskin, Michael. "An American Metternich: Henry A. Kissinger and the Global Balance of Power," in Frank J. Merli and Theodore A. Wilson (eds.) *Makers of American Diplomacy*. New York: Scribner's, 1974.

Shawcross, William. *Sideshow: Kissinger, Nixon and the Destruction of Cambodia*. New York: Simon & Schuster, 1979.

PART II

Global Issues and Concerns

CHAPTER SIX

Arms, Arms Control, and Security in the Nuclear World

Security issues have often been at the forefront of international relations. Safeguarding the security of their citizens is a primary function of national governments. To this end, they raise and support military forces and develop and manufacture weapons or obtain them from other nations. Through the ages, as weaponry has become ever-more sophisticated, the costs of developing and maintaining military forces and weaponry have risen steadily, as have the potential costs of war in terms of human loss and physical destruction.

World War II ended with the dropping of the most destructive weapons mankind had produced up to that time—the atomic bomb. In the period since, the world has witnessed numerous military conflicts; threats of many others; the spread of advanced weaponry around the globe; and the development, refinement, and proliferation of nuclear weapons with awesome destructive capability. Fortunately, despite all of the conflicts and adversarial action that the world has seen in recent decades, there has been no use of nuclear weapons. Indeed, while the United States and the Soviet Union built up their nuclear stockpiles, and other nations joined the nuclear club, there have also been steady, if not always very successful or ambitious efforts to impose limitations on the nuclear arsenals.

There has been dramatic growth in "conventional" weapons as well. Conventional weapons refer to those weapons other than nuclear, chemical, or biological. Some of these weapons can, of course, be highly destructive, even though conventional warfare is sometimes referred to as "limited" war. Generally, conventional warfare might be thought of as the more traditional type of armed conflict in which opposing forces, usually ground troops or foot soldiers, are amassed against each other. But technology has greatly augmented the lethal and destructive potential of all military operations, large and small, regardless of whether they involve the great powers.

Much of the warfare and military action that has been conducted in recent decades has actually been *"unconventional"* warfare. This term can be applied to guerilla warfare, certain terrorist activities, and paramilitary operations, and can include sabotage or various forms of covert or clandestine (secret) action. Most examples of unconventional fighting have occurred in the Third World. Sometimes the term *"low-intensity conflict"* is applied to these actions, which are described as confrontations short of full-scale war, but beyond the limits of peaceful competition. (Chapter 7 takes a closer look at such conflicts and regional rivalries.) It has been calculated that some 127 wars were fought between the end of World War II and the beginning of the 1990s, most of them in developing or Third-World countries. (In this calculation, to be counted as a war, there must have been at least 1,000 casualties.) Altogether, more than 10 million lives have been lost in these conflicts.

Wars are fought for a variety of reasons. Many of the factors that have led or could lead to war are discussed elsewhere in this book. Among those causes or sources that have played or can play an important part in leading to international conflict are territorial disputes or expansionist or imperialist aims, which may be ideologically driven. Nationalism, economic considerations, religious or ethnic factors, threats to a perceived balance of power, geopolitical concerns, or a combination of some of these may be contributors to moves toward war. Often, conflicts within one nation can spill across national boundaries and involve other nations. And, as has also been noted earlier, domestic political considerations can strongly influence foreign policies, and national leaders have on occasion exploited foreign wars to achieve unity or political power at home.

VITAL INTERESTS AND NATIONAL SECURITY

Nations almost always cite "vital national interests" as being at stake when they go to war. Vital interests are sometimes said to be those which a nation is willing to fight for to preserve. A most obvious example of a vital national interest is the sovereignty and territorial integrity of the nation itself.

As Bernard Brodie, an authority on strategy and national security, said, vital interests are those for which "we are prepared to take or threaten some kind of military action, including if necessary—and, one would hope, if sufficiently 'vital'—full-scale war. Or, at any rate . . . war in the prenuclear style."[1] There was much debate in the United States over whether Vietnam was vital to American interests; ultimately, there was little to support the case that it was.

A variety of psychological and cultural factors can come into play, influencing leaders and affecting perceptions of national interests. Such considerations as maintaining credibility—the credibility of a nation's commitments, for example—can become a justification or rationale for war or military action. This factor was often cited as a reason for American military moves in recent decades, including the prolonged United States presence in Vietnam.

The concept of *national security*, referred to in earlier chapters, can be interpreted in a number of ways. The clearest component of national security is the protection of a nation's sovereignty. In physical terms this means protection of a nation's boundaries from encroachment by other nations; it also can involve the protection of a nation's political and cultural identity. National security can thus refer to both physical and psychological security.

Fundamentally, national security involves the survival, welfare, and protection of a nation-state and the well-being of the people. A nation is secure, according to Walter Lippmann, to the extent to which it is not in danger of having to sacrifice core values, if it wishes to avoid war, and is able, if threatened, to maintain those values by winning a war.

Traditional realists emphasize the relationship between power and national security, although one of the important lessons in contemporary international relations is that national security does not only involve military power but that a variety of other considerations, including economic strength, bear on national security. Indeed, one of the most prominent realists, Hans Morgenthau, cited the multifaceted nature of national power. As noted in Chapter 4, Morgenthau lists military preparedness as only one of the nine major elements of national power.

When national interests or national security interests of nations come into conflict, or are perceived as being in conflict, the result may be war, particularly if diplomacy fails to resolve the differences. As Kenneth Waltz has written, "with each state judging its grievances and ambitions according to the dictates of its own reason or desire—conflict, sometimes leading to war, is bound to occur." [2]

What one nation may consider to be steps to protect itself, another may see as threatening to its interests. This leads to what Robert Jervis has called "the spiral of international insecurity." Of course, one of the ways in which nations seek to strengthen their capacity for security is by increasing their armaments. However, Sir Edward Grey, who was British Foreign Secretary when World War I broke out, offered this opinion:

> The increase of armaments that is intended in each nation to produce consciousness of strength, and a sense of security, does

not produce these effects. On the contrary, it produces a consciousness of the strength of other nations and a sense of fear.[3]

WAR AND ITS CAUSES

History is, of course, replete with stories of war. People have warred against each other throughout the ages, using the instruments and weapons technology available to them, whether axes or arrows or fighter aircraft, whether cannon or chemical explosives or atomic chain reactions.

The question of what causes war has long confounded political thinkers and philosophers. As noted earlier, causes can range from clashing economic interests or conflicts between political factions to struggles between antagonistic ideologies, ethnic groups or neighboring rivals. There may be a combination of several of these factors or a variety of other causes. (The concept of "just war" was discussed in Chapter 3.)

Thomas Hobbes, the seventeenth-century English philosopher, believed that the state of nature is anarchic, and that without government there would be nothing to prevent war. Lacking what he called a Leviathan—a giant authority, or, in contemporary international relations terminology, a hegemonic power, a dominant force, or world government—Hobbes saw mankind engaged in constant conflict and war. Many theorists over the years have at least implicitly accepted Hobbes's premise about the potential for global anarchy if there is not strong government/authority. His position can be considered as a precursor of the realist view of world affairs, suggesting that not only would people war against each other in the absence of government/authority but so would nations war against each other in the absence of international authority or dominant powers.

Sigmund Freud, the highly influential founder of psychoanalysis, also asserted that the causes of war are within human nature. Not only did Freud see war as inevitable, he envisioned that it would become more severe and intense as civilization became more complex. Freud was, of course, known for his view that individuals are torn between a life instinct (*eros*) and a death instinct (*Thanatos*), and one way of resolving the tension between these two instincts is through aggression. Writing at the time of World War I, Freud noted that it had been hoped that a community of interest among nations, established by commerce among them, would produce a compulsion toward morality and peace. However, he commented, that "it would seem that nations still obey their immediate passions far more readily than their interests."[4]

Human Aggressiveness

Others have approached the issues of aggression and war from a biological standpoint. Konrad Lorenz, Robert Ardrey, and Desmond Morris are among those who have been associated with the notion that man is innately aggressive. Aggressiveness, writes Ardrey, is "natural to all living beings . . . the determined pursuit of one's interests."[5] In his 1966 book, *The Territorial Imperative*, Ardrey argued that the drive to gain, maintain, and defend territory is a basic instinct. These ideas about innate aggressiveness and the territorial drive are reflected in such well-known novels/fims as *Lord of the Flies* and *A Clockwork Orange*.

Not everyone accepts these assertions that aggressiveness and war are inherent in human nature. Anthropologist Margaret Mead, for example, saw war as a learned custom that does not have a biological basis. A contrary view is also taken by Ashley Montagu, another anthropologist, who, arguing that behavior is the result of interaction between genetic and environmental factors, disputes the view of instinctive or natural aggressiveness and violence.

Montagu emphasizes the importance of individual leaders in causing conflicts and wars:

> Modern wars are not made by nations or peoples, nor are they made by men in a state of aggression welling over with an instinct of territory. Wars are usually made by a few individuals in positions of great power, "great leaders," "thoughtful" and "respected" statesmen generally advised by "the best and the brightest," almost always with calm and deliberation, and the pretense if not the conviction of complete moral rectitude.[6]

Individual and National Influences

Throughout this book, the significance and impact of individual leaders has been noted. Various analysts of international relations give greater or lesser importance to the role of individuals. John Stoessinger, for example, contends that a leader's personality is a decisive element in the making of foreign policy. According to Stoessinger, "Whether a leader uses his power for good or evil is secondary to the fact that this power exists as an objective reality . . . Differences in leaders' personalities . . . may make or break a nation's foreign policy. It matters very much, in short, *who* is there at a given moment."

Noting that the conventional wisdom has been that war is "an ineradicable part of human nature," Stoessinger says that this missed the human essence of the problem. "After all," writes Stoessinger, "wars were begun by people. Yet this personality dimension was seldom given its due weight."[7] Stoessinger believes that in no war did personalities play a greater role than in Vietnam, and he maintains that five American presidents based their policies in Indochina "not on Asian realities but on their own fears and, ultimately, on their hopes." Each president, according to this view, made a concrete policy decision that escalated the war and left it in worse shape than before.[8]

Most observers and analysts agree that whatever the factors—individual, national, international—that may lead to conflict and warfare, the nuclear age brings different dimensions to international relations and new constraints on individuals and nations and on the way in which conflicts are resolved. As Robert Ardrey points out, "warfare and the triumph of arms have through all our history been the final arbiter of the arguments of peoples." However, he says, nuclear cataclysm is not warfare "since among the dead one finds no differences."[9]

THE NUCLEAR RIVALRY

As has been noted earlier in this book, nuclear weapons have constituted a powerful new factor in world affairs. A central element in international relations in the nuclear age has been the United States–Soviet rivalry, particularly the arms race. Since World War II, major international security issues have often revolved around the United States–Soviet or East-West rivalries, which frequently permeated other nations and regions around the world.

For a brief time following World War II, the United States was the only nuclear power. As was mentioned in Chapter 2, the United States made a proposal in 1946 to internationalize control of the atom through the United Nations. It was known as the Baruch Plan, and it came during a period when the United States and its Western allies still, at least publicly, looked to the United Nations to serve as protector of the world's collective security. Under the Baruch Plan, the United States said that it was willing to give up its monopoly and place its fissionable materials under international control. Other nations would have been prevented from developing nuclear weapons. The Baruch Plan would have given a United Nations agency ownership and management of all atomic materials in the world. Peaceful use of the atom and related research could have been carried out only under the United Nations agency's licensing and inspection. It was in many ways a bold move that would have established a powerful precedent of international cooperation.

However, there was probably not ever much likelihood that the Baruch Plan would be accepted by all nations. For one thing, generous as the plan may have been, it would, nonetheless, have maintained at least an indirect United States monopoly on atomic bomb technology. As Richard Smoke has written, "Knowledge of that technology, once held by the United States, could not be eliminated or forgotten," and any other country would be prevented from conducting the research that could reproduce it. "Although the United States would not retain any actual weapons, if the system broke down it could build new ones quickly and no one else would be able to."[10]

Some have suggested that the United States never expected the plan to be adopted. In any case, the Soviet Union rejected the proposal and moved ahead with development of its own atomic bomb. The arms race was on.

In 1949, the Soviet Union successfully carried out a test of an atomic device. It was a period of heightened world tensions. The Soviets had strengthened their hold on Eastern Europe and imposed the Berlin blockade (although, as is discussed in Chapter 2 and in the Berlin City Portrait, the West overcame the blockade with the Berlin Airlift). In 1950, the Korean War broke out.

These developments undoubtedly contributed to the decision by the United States to push ahead with a still more destructive weapon, and in 1950 President Harry Truman authorized production of the hydrogen bomb (H-bomb). In 1952, the first hydrogen device was exploded in Eniwetok Atoll in the Pacific.

The Soviets, in a pattern that would become characteristic of the nuclear age, soon proceeded with development and testing of a hydrogen or thermonuclear weapon of their own. These fusion weapons were immensely more powerful than the fission (atomic) bombs, such as those dropped on Japan.

Fusion involves the joining, rather than the splitting, of the atom. Fission weapons like the atomic bomb were measured in thousands of tons of TNT or *kilotons*. The hydrogen weapons, using the fusion process, are measured in millions of tons of TNT, or *megatons*.

Increased Destructive Capability

Thus, within only a few years after World War II, the world had seen the development of weapons that were far more destructive—potentially thousands of times more damaging—than those which had devastated Hiroshima and Nagasaki, bombs which had been far more potent than any weapons used before that time. The great leap in destructive capability could be seen, for example, in the fact that one of the early generation of nuclear-age bombers, the B-52, could carry 25 megatons of explosive power, which is 1.5 times the total explosive power of all the bombs dropped during World War II, including the two atomic bombs. Most modern nuclear weapons are 3 to 50 times as powerful as those bombs used in 1945. In the nuclear era, major cities and surrounding areas could be completely destroyed by a single bomb. Estimates indicate that a one-megaton bomb exploded over the center of the American industrial city of Detroit would kill nearly 500,000 people and injure up to 600,000 others. A surface burst in the same city would cause 70 square miles of property destruction and additional damage from widespread fires. A one-megaton explosion over the Russian city of Leningrad (St. Petersburg), a major industrial and transportation center, would result in about 900,000 deaths and nearly 1.3 million injuries. The use of several hundred such weapons on major population centers could put an end to a nation as a functioning society.

In the event of a major nuclear attack, according to a study by the United States Office of Technology Assessment (OTA), in addition to tens of millions of deaths during the days and weeks after the attack, there would probably be further millions (perhaps further tens of millions) of deaths in the ensuing months or years. The OTA study stated:

> In addition to the enormous economic destruction caused by the actual nuclear explosions, there would be some years during which the residual economy would decline further, as stocks were consumed and machines wore out faster than recovered production could replace them. Nobody knows how to estimate the likelihood that industrial civilization might collapse in the areas attacked; additionally, the possibility of significant long-term ecological damage cannot be excluded.[11]

The same study reported that even a "small" or "limited" nuclear attack would be enormous. OTA examined the impact of a small attack on economic targets (an attack on oil refineries limited to 10 missiles), and found that while economic recovery would be possible, the economic damage and social dislocation would be immense. While the consequences might in some sense be endurable, the number of deaths could be as high as 20 million. Moreover, the uncertainties are such that no government could predict with any confidence what the results of a limited attack or counterattack would be, even if there was no further escalation.

Clearly, the nations possessing large nuclear stockpiles had the capacity to obliterate each other, and over the decades the Soviets and Americans accumulated vast nuclear arsenals, while other nations—Britain, France, China, and India—developed their own capability, and became confirmed members of the nuclear club.

NUCLEAR DOCTRINE AND DETERRENCE

Although the Soviet Union possessed nuclear weapons, in the 1950s it still lacked effective means for delivering them against the United States, which meant that there was still American nuclear superiority. In 1954, the American Secretary of State, John Foster Dulles, warned the Soviets that if they threatened Western Europe, the United States would respond forcefully. He announced that it was American policy "to depend primarily on a great capacity to retaliate by means and at places of our choosing." This became known as the "*massive retaliation*" doctrine, holding out the possibility of a nuclear response to virtually any aggressive action that called for a military reaction. Nuclear arms were thus viewed not only as a deterrent but as a substitute for costly conventional arms and troops that otherwise might have been needed to balance Soviet conventional forces.

Key aspects of the military balance were beginning to change by the late 1950s. It was also in this period (1957) that the Soviet Union launched *Sputnik*, the first earth satellite, demonstrating that the Soviets were making rapid advances in science and technology and stirring great concern in the United States. By the early 1960s, the Soviets had a force of intercontinental ballistic missiles (ICBMs) capable of reaching and destroying American cities. Massive retaliation was no longer viable—if it ever had been—as an American policy.

In 1960, when he ran for president, John F. Kennedy charged that United States missile production was lagging behind Soviet production and said that a "missile gap" was being created. In fact, the United States still had a preponderance of nuclear strength, as was evident at the time of the Cuban missile crisis in 1962 (discussed in Chapter 5), when the Soviets tried to neutralize the United States strategic advantage by placing missiles in Cuba. Having to withdraw the missiles from Cuba and, in effect, to acknowledge the United States's nuclear superiority, it is widely believed that the Soviet leadership determined never to let a humiliation like the Cuban missile crisis happen again. In any case, Moscow undertook a rapid and massive buildup of nuclear arms. An indication of the Soviet buildup was in the number of ICBMs it possessed. From 1966 to 1970 the number grew from 292 to 1,300, with 300 more under construction, and the Soviets had passed the United States in this category. By the early 1970s the United States had lost its unquestioned lead in strategic missiles.

Assured Destruction As Deterrence?

During the 1960s, American nuclear doctrine underwent a change. In the midsixties, Defense Secretary Robert S. McNamara began speaking of an *assured destruction* strategy. McNamara believed that since the Soviets were on their way to matching United States strategic capability, American policy should no longer be based on the premise of nuclear superiority; indeed, it was dangerous to retain that policy. Instead, McNamara and others saw a sort of strategic standoff developing and believed that with each side maintaining an assured destruction capability, there would be stable *deterrence*—the threat of a counterattack would deter an opponent from launching an attack.

The concept of assured destruction, which became more widely known as *mutual assured destruction* or MAD, refers to the capability to inflict a high level of damage on an aggressor (or aggressors) even after absorbing a *first strike*. MAD is the condition in which an assured destruction capability is possessed by opposing sides. A first strike is the first offensive move in a war, and in a nuclear war it would be aimed at knocking out the opponent's ability to retaliate.

Under the assured destruction strategy, it was assumed that the United States could destroy in a massive retaliatory strike one-third to one-fourth of the Soviet population and 50 to 75 percent of Soviet industry. McNamara estimated that the United States needed only 1,000 ICBMs to be able to accomplish this, and when this number was reached in 1967, the United States stopped adding to its arsenal of Minutemen missiles.

The Strategic Equation

Of course, United States nuclear capability was not confined to the land-based missiles. The United States relied on what is known as the strategic *triad*, a tripartite mix of weapons utilizing land-based, sea-based, and aircraft-based delivery systems.

McNamara and others hoped that the arms race would be stabilized as the Soviets drew even with the United States in land-based ICBMs. However, both nations continued to develop new weapon systems. The Soviets further built up their ICBM force, and developed an arsenal of submarine-launched ballistic missiles (SLBMs). They also began developing an antiballistic missile (ABM) system. The ABMs were designed to intercept and destroy incoming missiles, thus having the possibility of throwing the strategic equation off balance. If the system worked, it could provide a sharp advantage. By countering a first strike, an ABM system could destroy the stability of mutual deterrence.

The United States moved to build an ABM system of its own and also began developing MIRVs—multiple independently targetable re-entry vehicles. The MIRVs would greatly increase the threat from each missile, carrying several warheads, each capable of striking a different target.

These new developments and the pace of the arms race heightened the pressure for arms control. The only significant arms control agreement between the military superpowers had been the 1963 limited test ban treaty, in which the Soviets and Americans agreed to end all nuclear tests except those conducted underground. It was eventually signed by 116 nations under the auspices of the United Nations, although France and China did not accede to the treaty. Another multilateral treaty was the 1968 Treaty on the Non-Proliferation of Nuclear Weapons (NPT), in which non-nuclear nations agreed to forego the acquisition of nuclear weapons. (Nuclear proliferation is discussed in Chapter 8.)

STRATEGIC ARMS LIMITATIONS

Negotiations on arms limitation between the United States and the Soviet Union were scheduled to begin in the fall of 1968 but were put off by President Lyndon Johnson after the Soviets sent troops into Czechoslovakia in August 1968. Talks, called the Strategic Arms Limitation Talks (SALT), did not begin until 1969 under the administration of President Richard Nixon. The American decision to build an ABM system hastened Soviet willingness to agree to talks to limit both ABM systems and strategic arms.

Agreement was not reached until 1972 in what became known as the SALT I negotiations. It is likely that one of the factors that stimulated the Soviets to come to terms was concern about the budding relationship between the United States and China. What resulted from SALT I was (1) an "interim agreement" on the limitation of strategic offensive arms, designed to expire in five years, by which time a permanent treaty was expected to replace it, and (2) the ABM treaty—a treaty "on the limitation of antiballistic missile systems."

The ABM treaty restricted each side to two antiballistic missile sites and that was later reduced to one site each. An agreed statement appended to the treaty provided for further discussions in the event that new "ABM systems based on other physical principles" were developed. The treaty was of unlimited duration.

The ABM treaty was seen by some as recognition of the concept of mutual assured destruction or MAD by both Americans and Soviets. In effect, the treaty limited what either side could do defensively, acknowledging that both were vulnerable to the other's offensive strength and retaliatory capacity.

SALT I also established a unique institution, the Standing Consultative Commission (SCC), to deal with questions of treaty implementation and compliance. The SCC met at least twice yearly and provided a forum for discussion of SALT-related matters outside the negotiating framework. It proved to be an important example of cooperation between the superpowers on technical matters related to arms control. However, some American critics, especially during the Reagan administration, contended that the SCC failed to resolve any significant treaty compliance issues.

A period of United States–Soviet détente that had begun under Nixon and Soviet leader Leonid Brezhnev helped give impetus to the opening of negotiations for a SALT II Treaty. However, Nixon left office in disgrace in 1974 and the arms negotiations lost some momentum. Gerald Ford, Nixon's successor, did meet with Brezhnev in the Russian port city of Vladivostok in 1974 and agreed on principles for a SALT II agreement. But Ford was soon involved in competition for the 1976 Republican presidential nomination with Ronald Reagan, who was a critic of détente and arms agreements, and Ford put SALT on the back burner. At the same time, the atmosphere for arms control was being clouded by other issues, including Soviet/Cuban involvement in Southern Africa. Meanwhile, weapons developments sparked growing concern over the stability of the nuclear balance. Both superpowers "MIRVed" their strategic forces, the Soviets concentrating on ICBM warheads, while the United States concentrated on submarine-launched ballistic missiles (SLBMs). "MIRVing" involved multiple independently targetable warheads—several warheads mounted on a single ballistic missile and capable of being aimed at separate targets. As noted earlier, MIRVing meant that a single missile could carry a number of warheads which could seek out different targets.

NEGOTIATING SALT II

When Jimmy Carter became president in 1977, his administration resumed efforts to negotiate a SALT II treaty. In his inaugural address he pledged to seek "the elimination of all nuclear weapons from this earth," a lofty goal that remains far beyond the reality of today's world. Carter's first move in arms control was to propose going beyond the Vladivostok framework by making "deep cuts" in the level of United States and Soviet nuclear forces. The Soviets, caught off guard by Carter's proposal and unaccustomed to dealing with surprise, sweeping propositions, quickly rebuffed the plan. The failure to accurately gauge the mood and intention of the Soviet leaders was costly, indicative of the problems that can result when one nation misreads another. (Later, Mikhail Gorbachev would become a master at making the unexpected proposal, but before Gorbachev the Soviets moved at a very deliberate pace in arms negotiations.) The Carter proposal was also seen by the Soviets as working to the advantage of the United States.

From the Western viewpoint, it seemed like a rational approach and one that would involve actual reductions in nuclear arms rather than just the imposition of higher and higher ceilings on numbers of arms. From the Soviet perspective, however, the proposal put virtually all of the burden for reductions on Moscow because it was aimed at reducing "heavy" missiles, which were the central element in Soviet nuclear strength.

When the Soviets made clear that they would not accept Carter's proposals, his administration regrouped and went back to the Vladivostok accords as the basis for negotiations. A number of delays slowed progress on the SALT II agreement. Negotiations often bogged down over what seemed to be extremely minor points—where to place a comma or the phrasing of a footnote. United States foreign policy officials had to take into account two important considerations which also had bearing on the pace and direction of the negotiations: other developments in international relations and the sometimes related-factor of domestic public opinion and politics (as discussed in Chapter 4). The Carter administration gave much of its attention to the problems in the Middle East (see Chapter 7) and to the Panama Canal treaties (discussed in Chapter 4). Increasing attention was also given to what appeared to be expanding Soviet influence and military power in the Persian Gulf, Horn of Africa, Angola, the Caribbean, and Central America. The administration had to recognize that the American public and Congress linked their attitudes toward arms control agreements to Soviet global behavior.

Agreement on SALT II seemed within close reach in late 1978, However, the Soviets stalled the treaty when the United States announced that it was normalizing diplomatic relations with China. In 1972, the United States opening to China had helped spur the Soviets to agree to SALT I. Now, formalization of those relations was holding up SALT II. Once again the triangular relationship had come into play.

Controversy and Compliance

The SALT II treaty was finally signed by President Carter and General Secretary Brezhnev at a summit meeting in Vienna in June 1979. By the time the treaty was finally signed, however, and during the months immediately thereafter, the momentum for arms control lessened. Relations between the superpowers worsened and a variety of developments helped sidetrack the treaty from consideration by the United States Senate. Meanwhile, there was growing concern about the military balance between the superpowers, with some American analysts and political leaders arguing that the Soviets had attained a position of military superiority over the United States.

The SALT II treaty was controversial in the United States, but its provisions were largely observed by the Soviets and Americans, even though it was never formally ratified. It was, in fact, a rather modest achievement in arms limitations. It set aggregate ceilings on a number of strategic nuclear systems, with each side to be limited to a total of 2,250 strategic delivery vehicles—still a massive nuclear capability. (Delivery vehicle or delivery system refers to a device such as a missile silo, submarine tube, or strategic bomber, from which a strategic weapon can be launched. Sometimes these vehicles are referred to as launchers.) SALT II also placed restrictions on MIRVing. And it permitted each side to build only one new type of ICBM, although that would still allow the United States to go ahead with planned development of the MX missile.

SIDETRACKING SALT II: POLITICS AND GEOPOLITICS

A mix of geopolitical and security concerns and domestic politics contributed to the climate that prevented SALT II from being approved by the United States Senate. Initially, there appeared to be a reasonable prospect for Senate approval, though not without contentious debate. But the treaty's chances suffered a series of blows. The first of these resulted from a flap surrounding the "discovery" of a Soviet "combat brigade" in Cuba.

The Cuban Complication

Few issues in American foreign policy carried more political and emotional charge than those relating to Cuba. Further, as noted in Chapter 5, the Cuban missile crisis left a strong legacy. One aspect of the legacy has been the tendency to view subsequent developments relating to Cuba through the prism of the missile crisis. All American presidents since John F. Kennedy have been determined to appear as skillful and courageous as Kennedy was portrayed as being in the 1962 crisis. Thus the revelation about the combat brigade had significant repercussions in the United States. The Carter administration was sensitive to suggestions that it was not being sufficiently vigilant in regard to Soviet activities in Cuba and feared that SALT II opponents might use this to undercut prospects for the treaty. Ironically, the handling of the issue by the administration did just that. Apparently afraid that treaty opponents might break the news of the combat brigade first—not an unlikely development in leak-prone Washington—the administration decided that it should seize the initiative. Key members of Congress were informed about the brigade.

Senator Frank Church, then chairman of the Senate Foreign Relations Committee, was among those informed, and within a short time he held a news conference calling for "the immediate removal of all Russian combat troops from Cuba." This was a clear example of domestic politics coming to bear upon international relations. Church said that the Senate would not approve SALT II while the combat troops remained in Cuba. Church's statements were followed by similar sweeping statements from Carter administration officials, even though the full facts of the situation in Cuba had not yet been established. Church was actually a supporter of SALT II, but he was facing a tough re-election campaign (which he subsequently lost), and it was widely believed that Church seized upon the "Soviet troops" issue to prove his toughness on foreign policy. (He was under attack for his support of the Panama Canal treaties, discussed in Chapter 3.) Church denied any political motivation for his action, but, whatever his reason or intent, the effect was to seriously damage chances for SALT II approval.

Upon closer examination it appeared that there was nothing particularly unusual about the Soviet activities; that the troops had been in Cuba some years; that there was no violation of any United States–Soviet agreements; and that the whole issue had been badly overblown. As David D. Newsom, former State Department official, has written, "The bizarre episode of the Soviet brigade in Cuba had an impact out of all proportion to the circumstances. It seems clear that the unit that created the uproar was the successor to the one present in 1962, which had remained with at least the tacit consent of the Kennedy administration." [12] Newsom notes that it was equally clear that the unit "posed no military threat to the United States." Gradually, the controversy died down, but it had caused a costly delay in the SALT II schedule, and the treaty was going to run afoul of other events and problems. The episode of the Soviet brigade was indicative of the unpredictable nature of international relations and how arms control and security issues become entangled with domestic politics and could not be kept separate from other problems in United States–Soviet relations.

Deteriorating Atmosphere

Before the SALT II treaty could get back on the Senate track, the international atmosphere became increasingly sour, further diminishing chances for approval of the SALT II treaty. In November 1979, a group of Iranian militants seized hostages in the United States Embassy in Teheran. This development contributed to a growing sense of frustration and weakness in the United States, a superpower unable to use its might to prevent such actions. For the United States it was a painful, even humiliating example of the limits of power, and military might was of little importance in this case. Initially, there was a tendency on the part of some to suspect that the Soviets were involved in the events in Iran, but that was not the case.

In late December 1979, the prospects for SALT II approval were finished off when the Soviets invaded neighboring Afghanistan. There was no chance that the United States Senate would approve the treaty after the Afghanistan invasion, and President Carter asked the Senate to suspend action. The treaty was never formally acted upon by the Senate.

NUCLEAR COMPETITION AND STRATEGIC CONCEPTS

The early 1980s brought a different climate for arms control, particularly in the United States. And there was some heated international controversy and debate about arms issues and policies.

In his successful campaign for the presidency in 1980, Ronald Reagan emphasized as one of his key themes the need for the United States to strengthen its national defense. Arms control was not a high priority with Reagan; indeed, he expressed skepticism about arms agreements. (See Reagan Profile.)

Already in the late 1970s, as was reflected in some of the debate surrounding SALT II, there had been expressions of concern in some American quarters about the trends in nuclear arms competition. Some Americans, including Reagan at times, argued that the Soviets had gained or were gaining an advantage in strategic capability. The Soviets had begun deploying a new and versatile generation of intermediate-range missiles, the SS-20, with ranges of 300 to 3,400 miles. It could be used for striking Western Europe from the countries of Eastern Europe, which were then aligned with the U.S.S.R. in the Warsaw Pact. The Soviets also continued deployment of more of their "heavy" intercontinental missiles. With improvements in accuracy, the Soviets developed the theoretical capacity to destroy much of the United States land-based missile capability in a first strike. These and other developments, such as the expansion of the Soviet air-defense system and the MIRVing of Soviet ICBMs, contributed to the concerns about the trends in the strategic balance.

Modernization and Strategy

To help counter concerns about the Soviet capability, the United States had taken steps to strengthen its nuclear arsenal. In the late seventies the United States improved the capabilities of 300 of its 550 Minutemen II missiles, doubling their explosive power and improving their guidance systems. By 1980, the United States was deploying a new Trident I missile on submarines. The Trident I was more accurate and had twice the explosive force of the weapons it replaced. However, the total number of

United States warheads was not significantly increasing, and the total number of United States launchers decreased slightly as some older bombers and submarines were retired from service.

The Carter administration put forth in 1979–80 a new version of American strategic doctrine, which it called the *countervailing strategy*, and which could be considered as a refinement of the earlier strategic concepts which had been seen as based on the notion of mutual assured destruction (MAD). In fact, despite all of the talk about MAD, American policy had consistently emphasized targeting military and military-related targets rather than population centers. The countervailing strategy was aimed at making clear to the enemy that it could not hope to gain any rational objective—that any enemy gain would entail offsetting losses. The policy stressed the central importance of secure facilities, while placing greater emphasis on targeting enemy command and control centers for command, control, communications, and intelligence.

A key concept in this strategy was called *escalation dominance*, aimed at deterring a range of possible Soviet actions by making clear that escalating to a higher level of nuclear exchange would not bring victory. As part of this strategy, the United States would modernize all three components of its strategic *triad*. As was mentioned earlier in this chapter, the triad concept had been fundamental to American strategic policy, the basic structure of the United States deterrent force. The triad refers to the three elements of that force—(1) land-based ICBMs; (2) the sea-based nuclear submarine force with its submarine-launched ballistic missiles (SLBMs); and (3) the long-range bomber force. The triad theory maintains that since each element of the triad relies on somewhat different means for survival, an enemy's potential for a successful first-strike attack is severely complicated. The Soviets might develop a defense against one component, or destroy it in a first strike; it was highly unlikely that they could successfully defend against or destroy all three forces.

As part of the modernization effort, the Carter administration gave the green light to development of the 10-warhead MX missile, which was supposed to be mobile, thus reducing the potential vulnerability of the American land-based missile force. However, deploying the MX proved to be a complex challenge, particularly because of the difficulty of finding a strategically and politically acceptable and practical basing mode for the missile. All sorts of schemes—ranging from what was called the shell game or race track mode to dense pack to a rail-based plan—were proposed, but all had drawbacks. One justification for keeping the MX on the strategic drawing boards, according to some, was so that it could be used as a "bargaining chip" in negotiations with the Soviets.

Strobe Talbott, who has written extensively about nuclear weapons and arms control negotiations, has commented that the utility of nuclear weapons is not so much military as political. They are symbols of power or bargaining chips that "exist to be talked about, not to be used."[13] As

Talbott has said, the terms for the nonuse of these weapons are always on the agenda of the superpower relationship.

However, when Reagan entered office in 1981 he was pledged to close what he had called a "window of vulnerability," referring to the potential vulnerability of American land-based missiles. Rapid deployment of the MX in a survivable basing mode would help close that window, Reagan claimed, and that was just one of a number of steps he proposed to strengthen American national defense. (As noted earlier, however, finding a satisfactory basing mode for the MX proved extremely difficult. The Reagan administration never really resolved the issue and the concerns about the "window of vulnerability" faded.)

REAGAN—LIMITED WAR AND THE NUCLEAR BALANCE

Charging that SALT II was fatally flawed, Reagan concentrated not on arms control but on expanding American military strength and building up the United States nuclear arsenal so that there would be no chance of United States strategic "inferiority" in the competition with the Soviets. Reagan mistrusted existing treaties and did not want to consider additional agreements until the United States had new ICBMs, new SLBMs, new cruise missiles, and new bombers in its strategic arsenal. The United States also wanted to proceed with deployment of intermediate-range nuclear forces (INF) in Europe. In 1982, he said that the "truth of the matter is that on balance the Soviet Union does have a 'definite margin of superiority.'" The Soviets were said to have "engaged in the greatest buildup of military power seen in modern times."[14] Never before had an American president expressed such a pessimistic view of the military balance, and concern with that balance was a major factor influencing Reagan's world view and policies.

In addition to launching a major military buildup of its own, the Reagan administration also outlined strategies for actually fighting a nuclear war. While previous policy had emphasized the importance of mutual deterrence, the Reagan administration seemed to give much greater credence than its predecessors to the notion of "winning" a prolonged nuclear war. Much more attention was being given to the development of a nuclear-war fighting and war-winning capability than had been the case in previous administrations. Part of the assumption in a scenario for a prolonged nuclear war was that it could be largely limited to strategic/military targets. There was discussion and analysis in the government of "post-exchange recovery scenarios," referring to a period after nuclear exchanges. Some of these scenarios covered periods as long as five years and assumed as many as 100 million dead on each side.

Some prominent nuclear strategists and policy analysts challenged the Reagan administration's gloomy assessment of the nuclear balance. Likewise, the administration was challenged on its apparent belief that a nuclear war could be "won." Earlier in this chapter there was discussion of estimates of the damage that would be caused by nuclear weapons. Many experts have expressed doubt that any nuclear exchange could remain limited—that a "limited" nuclear war was a contradiction in terms. The International Institute for Strategic Studies (IISS) in London concluded: "Limited nuclear conflict . . . would be a miracle; it is not an assumable probability." [15] One of the problems with carrying on a limited nuclear war is that it would be extremely difficult to sustain command, control, communications, and intelligence (C^3I) systems. These electronic systems, vital to the conduct and coordination of warfare, would be highly unlikely to survive a nuclear exchange.

Comparing Nuclear Arsenals

On the subject of the military balance, the IISS, a highly respected research center, pointed out the difficulty of comparing the strategic capabilities of the two military superpowers. As the IISS noted, no single measurement can give a full representation of the strategic nuclear balance. There is considerable debate among analysts as to which measures should be given greatest weight in assessing the overall balance. A central complication in assessing the relative strength of the United States and the Soviet Union was that their strategic systems were structured very differently. The most straightforward means of measuring the strategic balance would seem to be by counting the total number of delivery systems—ICBMs, SLBMs, and long-range bombers—possessed by the two sides. However, this measure alone is of limited relevance, for it neglects the fact that almost all delivery systems now can carry several (and, in some cases, a varying number of) warheads which can be directed against separate targets.

At a time when the Reagan administration was emphasizing that the Soviets had gained "superiority," the IISS said that, subject to all the qualifications and uncertainties implicit in assessing the strategic balance (an exercise that is sometimes referred to as nuclear bean counting), there was "approximate equality between the strategic forces" in terms of ICBM and SLBM warheads. [16] The United States had an advantage when bomber-delivered weapons were factored in (due to the much smaller size of the Soviet strategic bomber force). On the other hand, the Soviets had an advantage in "equivalent megatonnage" (EMT), which refers to the total potential explosive capability of weapons. EMT is acknowledged to be a very crude measurement, because, for example, it does not consider the accuracy of the weapons involved. Because so much of the Soviet strategic arsenal consisted of "heavy" weapons, the Soviets long exceeded the United States in megatonnage.

THE ROUNDABOUT RETURN TO ARMS CONTROL

Although Reagan and his administration came into office determined to concentrate on strengthening the United States military posture and not really interested in pursuing arms control, two key constituencies did want to see efforts towards arms control. The push toward arms control came from the United States Congress, speaking for the American public, and from the Western Europeans. As Strobe Talbott noted, both of these constituencies had leverage. The Europeans could block the deployment of new missiles in Europe, and Congress could thwart the Reagan administration's ambitious plans for building up the nation's strategic capabilities.

The administration's belligerent rhetoric tended to heighten the fear of war in Europe. All of the talk about "limited" nuclear war contributed to growing international unease about the arms race and the threat of nuclear conflict. Both domestic and international public opinion had an effect on Reagan's policies, and the administration was compelled to give some attention to arms control.

Long before, Albert Einstein, the physicist whose theories helped make possible the development of the atomic bomb, said that its development "may intimidate the human race to bring order into its international affairs, which, without the pressure of fear, it undoubtedly would not do." [17]

Despite Reagan's doubts, the arms control process simply would not die, although there was little movement during the first half of the 1980s.

In June 1982, with both sides feeling domestic and international pressure for action on arms control, formal negotiations on long-range nuclear weapons were reopened in Geneva. These discussions were referred to as START (Strategic Arms Reduction Talks) to emphasize a shift in emphasis from arms limitations to arms reductions and to signify a break from the SALT negotiations. At the same time, negotiations were underway on intermediate-range nuclear forces (INF) in Europe. It is likely that neither the White House nor the Kremlin really expected serious progress to be made on either front. However, each side was sensitive to the political importance of being at the negotiating table and giving the appearance of seriousness about arms control. (The "walk in the woods" by United States and Soviet negotiators in Geneva, discussed in Chapter 5, occurred during the early stages of the INF talks.)

INF AND SDI

Having inherited the 1979 "two track" NATO decision—a commitment to modernize American/NATO INF in Europe while negotiating with the Soviets on possible INF limitations—the Reagan administration had to establish that it was really willing to negotiate. Nonetheless, there was no progress in INF talks, and a Soviet "peace campaign" in Europe failed to cause European NATO members to back away from the INF modernization decision. New missile deployment began late in 1983. Europe was the stage upon which the nuclear debate was carried out, and both Americans and Soviets conducted intense public relations campaigns aimed at winning support among Europeans. Each side attempted to convince the Europeans that it was committed to arms limitations/reductions and to improving international relations.

When the INF talks failed to achieve agreement, and the deployment of

American missiles in Europe proceeded as scheduled, the Soviets, as they had threatened, walked out of both the INF and START negotiations. No date was set for the resumption of talks. The outlook for arms control was dismal.

Other important developments of 1983 also affected the arms control environment. In March 1983, President Reagan surprised the world by announcing plans for development of a ballistic-missile defense system. Reagan envisioned a space-based defense system that would provide a high-tech defensive shield against incoming missiles. Reagan called the program to develop this system the Strategic Defense Initiative (SDI). Such a system, Reagan said, would render nuclear weapons "impotent and obsolete." Although this grandiose scheme found some supporters, there were critics and skeptics at home and abroad. The Soviets said that the system would violate the 1972 ABM treaty and would be destabilizing. It was argued, for example, that SDI might even cause a nuclear war if the side possessing the defense system thought it could launch a nuclear attack, destroy most of the attacked nation's nuclear weapons, and then rely on the defensive shield as protection against any retaliation that the attacked country might be able to attempt. It was the same type of contention that had led to the signing of the ABM treaty. Others maintained that if one side had the defensive shield, the other side would simply plan to overwhelm it with vast quantities of missiles—a plan that could set off an unlimited arms race.

Critics also focused on the extremely high cost (as much as $1 trillion), and many scientific experts doubted that such a system could be perfected. A variety of scientific and strategic arguments were made against the proposal. Nonetheless, Reagan stuck by his plan, which was, to his dismay, labeled "Star Wars," a name drawn from a popular futuristic film which featured spectacular battles in space. In later years emphasis on the project was gradually downgraded.

Another development which contributed to strained superpower relations in 1983 was the Soviet downing of a Korean civilian aircraft, killing 269 people. Reagan labeled the action a "crime against humanity." There were some indications that the Soviets thought they were intercepting a military spy plane which was flying over some of their most sensitive military installations. The complete story may never be known. In any case, the period probably marked the lowest point in United States–Soviet relations since the early days of the Cold War.

A new era in United States–Soviet relations and of progress in arms control was on the horizon, however, even though it was barely discernible in 1984–85. President Reagan was re-elected in November 1984 and Mikhail Gorbachev ascended to the top position in the Soviet Union in March 1985. Reagan's re-election meant that the Soviets would either have to deal with him or leave relations in deep freeze for four more years. Gorbachev gave signs of moving Soviet policy in new directions, helping to open the way for improved relations.

As is discussed in Chapter 4, Gorbachev's policy changes were undoubtedly influenced by domestic concerns, with the Soviet economy in great difficulty, partially due to the heavy imbalance toward military spending. Of course, some argued, as discussed in the Reagan Profile, that the changes in Soviet policies resulted from Reagan administration policies—that the $2-trillion United States defense buildup, the Strategic Defense Initiative, and the "Reagan Doctrine" of support for anticommunist revolution or opposition in such areas as Afghanistan forced Gorbachev's hand.

In any case, nuclear arms talks resumed in Geneva in the spring of 1985 and the international climate improved enough that, in November 1985, Reagan and Gorbachev held their first summit meeting. With Gorbachev beginning to score important public relations victories in Europe, the United States was under increasing pressure to pursue arms control negotiations more purposefully and to help reduce international tensions. The Geneva summit did not achieve any breakthroughs in arms control, but there was agreement to accelerate negotiations. Gorbachev displayed a tendency, unlike previous Soviet leaders, to seize the initiative and make bold proposals. In January 1986, he made a dramatic statement proposing a program for the phased reduction and ultimate elimination of all nuclear weapons by the year 2000.

Both sides were showing signs of flexibility on some key issues, including INF. The second Reagan-Gorbachev summit, at Reykjavik, Iceland, in October 1986, unexpectedly became very wide ranging, with Gorbachev injecting his notion of a nuclear-free world by 2000, and Reagan apparently suggesting that both sides eliminate all ballistic missiles within 10 years. The two leaders did agree in principle to reduce strategic offensive nuclear forces by 50 percent within five years, but ultimately the talks foundered over disagreement on SDI. Nonetheless, the groundwork had been laid for an INF treaty, which was signed when Gorbachev visited Washington in December 1987.

In a major breakthrough, the two nations actually agreed to destroy thousands of nuclear weapons, eliminating an entire category of weapons. Never before had two world powers agreed to take such action. Some indication of the complexity of the issues involved and of the agreement is seen in the length of the treaty text: 125 pages of single-spaced text. Accompanying the treaty is an Inspection Protocol, outlining the procedures for inspection/verification; an Elimination Protocol, detailing how each item covered by the treaty will be eliminated; and a Memorandum of Understanding, declaring type, number, location of each item to be eliminated, and diagrams of the sites to be inspected.

The approach taken by the United States and its allies in negotiating the INF treaty included these four major principles:

■ equal rights and limits between the United States and the Soviet Union (even if one side had to make more reductions, which the Soviets did);

- limitations on Soviet and United States systems only (the Soviets originally wanted to cover British and French systems too);

- global application of limitations (the Soviets initially sought to limit any INF agreement to Europe, while the United States said it should also apply to Asia);

- effective verification of the treaty (the problem was simplified by the agreement to eliminate all United States and Soviet intermediate-range missiles worldwide).

Verification had been a sticking point in some previous negotiations, and it is a keystone of arms control. Verification is the process of determining whether the other party to an arms control agreement is complying with its provisions. Ronald Reagan cited what he said was an old Russian proverb, "Doveryai, no Proveryai,"—trust, but verify, and he made these watchwords for the United States in arms control agreements. Reagan said that the INF agreement "contains the most stringent verification regime in history."

The INF treaty was the first arms control agreement in eight years, the unratified SALT II treaty having been signed in 1979. The improved climate in East-West relations opened the way for possible action on other military and security issues. In particular, there appeared to be an opportunity for reductions in the massive strategic arsenals of the superpowers. These arsenals had continued to grow during the interim between arms agreements.

The INF treaty did not by any means bring an end to the nuclear era in Europe. But it was one of a series of steps that could lead to significant reduction in the concentration of forces and weaponry in Europe and in the overall dependence on nuclear weapons.

FORCE REDUCTION, START, AND CONTINUING ISSUES

Even though the nuclear stockpiles of the superpowers and nuclear weapons in Europe have been at the heart of international security concerns, there are, of course, other highly important questions and problems in international security. Reducing conventional forces in Europe was the subject of long negotiations between East and West, sometimes in the forum of the MBFR (mutual and balanced force reduction) talks in Vienna. A combination of factors, including the budget problems facing the United States and the Soviet Union plus the changing political climate in Europe, gave added impetus to efforts for reduction of forces. In 1990, leaders of the 22 nations that were members of NATO and the moribund Warsaw Pact, helped codify the end of the Cold War by signing the Conventional Forces in Europe (CFE) Treaty. The CFE agreement limits many categories of non-nuclear weapons in Europe and effectively dismantled the massive Soviet army in Europe that had long been a dominant factor in the continent's East-West division.

Shortly before the signing of the CFE agreement, British Foreign Secretary Douglas Hurd said, "I regard NATO as the key to all this." He commented, "NATO was devised to protect us . . . against the threat which was very real, created by a communist empire, which clearly had from time to time expansionist notions. We built up NATO to prevent war and it did so." Hurd said that this was the "biggest success story of the Atlantic Community" since World War II. The result, he said, was "that the threat has, in its old form, disappeared. The dangers of a massive attack from the Soviet Union have receded." [18]

In 1991, after nine years of sporadic negotiations, the Strategic Arms Reduction Treaty (START) was finally signed in Moscow by Presidents Gorbachev and Bush. The 700-page treaty is the first to actually reduce American and Soviet long-range (strategic) nuclear arsenals, although both retained massive nuclear capability.

"It is important that there is a growing realization of the absurdity of armament," said Gorbachev, "now that the world has started to move toward an era of economic interdependence and that the information revolution is making the indivisibility of the world ever more evident." [19]

Bush said that the reduction of international tensions and ending of the Cold War changed the atmosphere at the negotiating table and paved the way for the START agreement. "By reducing arms, we reverse a half-century of steadily growing strategic arsenals. But more than that, we take a significant step forward in dispelling a half-century of mistrust," Bush said. [20]

Later in 1991, President Bush took the American strategic bomber force off its "alert" status, which had been in effect for 34 years. He also initiated further reductions in the United States arsenal, primarily by withdrawing and disposing of land-based, short-range (tactical) nuclear weapons (artillery shells and missile warheads) from bases in Europe and Asia.

Gorbachev responded with a pledge to make significant additional cuts. However, he soon relinquished control of the nuclear arsenal, which was placed under a "unified command" headed by the Russian president (Yeltsin), who was to act in consultation with leaders of other "nuclear" states of the former Soviet Union. Despite the agreement to keep the nuclear weapons under a single command, international concern grew, as will be discussed in Chapter 8, about security of the strategic and tactical nuclear weapons dispersed in various areas within the states that formerly made up the Soviet Union. Decentralization and the increasing independence of the states raised questions about ultimate control of the nuclear weapons.

Although the easing of East-West tensions encouraged troop reductions in Europe by the major powers and signing of the START agreement, there will still be strong pressure for them to maintain significant military forces and arsenals. Military capability remains an important element of power politics, even though, as is emphasized in this book, national security involves much more than military strength. The diffusion and potential diffusion of destructive capability among other nations, discussed in detail in Chapter 8, is another factor weighing against the likelihood of massive force reductions by the great powers. Arms control and international security issues are, it should be apparent, closely connected to political issues. A worsening of the political atmosphere in Europe, and/or the former Soviet Republics could halt the momentum for military reductions among the major powers.

CHRONOLOGY OF THE ARMS RACE AND ARMS CONTROL

1817   *Rush-Bagot Treaty* between the United States and Britain limited naval forces on the Great Lakes and Lake Champlain. This was one of the first and most successful arms-control agreements of modern times.

1899 and 1907   *Peace Conferences at the Hague* resulted in agreements to ban certain weapons (poisonous gas and dum-dum bullets) and on the regulation of war, but World War I participants disregarded some of these agreements.

1921, 1930, and 1935   *Washington and London Naval Conferences* led to naval treaties regulating the ratio of tonnage limits for ships of major sea powers.

1925   *Geneva Protocol* ("Prohibition of the Use in War of Asphyxiating, Poisonous, or Other Gases, and of Bacteriological Methods of Warfare"). Most nations have ratified this protocol, although the United States did not do so until 1975.

1928   *Kellog-Briand Pact* was initiated by the United States and France and signed by 63 nations, renouncing war as an instrument of national policy. There were no provisions for ensuring compliance and many signatories attached qualifications that made the agreement meaningless.

1932   *Geneva Disarmament Conference* (League of Nations) considered a variety of measures to limit armed forces and weapons but no agreement was achieved, and after Hitler came to power Germany withdrew.

1945   *United Nations Charter* was signed in San Francisco in June. Among the goals of the United Nations is reducing the level of global armaments.

Atomic bombs were dropped by the United States, devastating the cities of Hiroshima and Nagasaki, Japan, in August.

1946   *Baruch Plan* offered by the United States for international arms control and disarmament. Although the atom would have been under international control, the United States would have retained the capability to make atomic weapons. The Soviet Union rejected the plan.

1949   *Soviet Union* successfully tested an atomic device. Britain (1952), France (1960), China (1964), and India (1974), followed, and at least three other nations are believed to have developed nuclear capability.

1950   *United States* announced plans to develop the hydrogen bomb.

1959   *Antarctic Treaty* demilitarized the Antarctic continent, an example of nations working together to prevent conflict before it developed.

1963   *Limited Test Ban Treaty* banned nuclear weapons tests in the atmosphere, in outer space, and under water. (Underground tests were not covered.) More than 110 nations have agreed to the treaty.

   Hot-Line Agreement (United States–Soviet Direct Communications Link) established an emergency communications channel between the superpowers after the Cuban missile crisis.

1967   *Outer Space Treaty* banned nuclear or other mass-destruction weapons from outer space and prohibited military installations on the moon or other celestial bodies.

   Latin American Nuclear-Free Zone Treaty (Treaty of Tlatelolco) prohibited the testing, use, manufacture, or acquisition of nuclear weapons in Latin America. Signed by 22 nations.

1968   *Non-Proliferation Treaty* (NPT) prohibited the transfer of nuclear weapons by nations that have them and the acquisition of such weapons by other nations. Nations agreeing to the treaty also pledged to work for the cessation of the nuclear arms race and for disarmament. More than 120 nations have signed, but not all of the nuclear powers are among them.

1969   *Chemical and Biological Weapons* were restricted under United States policy announced by President Nixon. First use of lethal chemical weapons was renounced, and production of chemical weapons halted, although it was later resumed.

1971   *Seabed Treaty* banned the placement of weapons of mass destruction on the seabed beyond a 12-mile zone outside a nation's territory.

   Accidents Measures Agreement between the United States and the Soviet Union pledged each party to guard against accidental or unauthorized use of nuclear weapons and provided for immediate notification of any accidental, unauthorized incident involving possible detonation of a nuclear bomb.

1972   *Biological Weapons Convention* prohibited the development, production, stockpiling, or acquisition of biological agents and any weapons designed to use such agents.

Strategic Arms Limitation Talks (SALT I) resulted in two agreements:

    Anti-Ballistic Missile (ABM) Treaty, limiting United States and Soviet ABM sites;

    Interim Agreement on Offensive Arms, freezing the number of United States and Soviet ballistic missile launchers for five years.

1973   *Prevention of Nuclear War Agreement* pledged the Soviets and Americans to make the removal of the danger of nuclear war and the use of nuclear weapons an objective of their policies.

1974   *Threshold Test Ban Treaty (TTBT)* established a nuclear "threshold" by prohibiting underground tests having a yield exceeding 150 kilotons.

    Vladivostok Accords established a framework for United States–Soviet negotiations in SALT II on offensive nuclear arms.

1975   *Confidence-Building Measures,* involving cooperative arrangements for communications among nations about military activities and maneuvers, were provided in the Final Act of the Conference on Security and Cooperation in Europe (CSCE) at Helsinki.

1976   *Peaceful Nuclear Explosions (PNE) Treaty* limited United States and Soviet underground nuclear explosions for peaceful purposes to 150 kilotons. Signed but not ratified by the United States.

1979   *Strategic Arms Limitation Treaty (SALT II)* set equal aggregate ceilings on United States and Soviet missile launchers and heavy bombers. Never approved by the United States Senate.

1981   *"Zero Option"* plan was proposed by President Reagan under which the United States would cancel new missile deployment in Western Europe in return for dismantling of comparable Soviet missiles.

1982   *Strategic Arms Reduction Talks* (START) between the United States and the Soviet Union begin.

1983   *Strategic Defense Initiative* (SDI or "Star Wars"), a plan announced by Reagan for developing a space-based defense system "to render nuclear weapons impotent and obsolete." It was a major stumbling block in arms control negotiations for several years.

1985   *Geneva Summit* brought Reagan and Soviet leader Mikhail Gorbachev together for the first time and opened the way for progress in arms control.

    South Pacific Nuclear-Free Zone (Treaty of Raratonga) agreement prohibits the manufacture or acquisition of weapons in the region.

1986   *Stockholm Document* extended provisions of the 1975 CSCE Final Act, involving a set of politically binding confidence- and security-building measures. These were designed to increase openness and predictability about military activities in Europe, with the aim of reducing the risk of armed conflict in Europe.

1987   *Nuclear Risk Reduction Centers* (NRRCs) agreement committed both the United States and Soviet Union to work toward improving constant communication between Washington and Moscow.

Intermediate-Range Nuclear Forces (INF) Treaty signed in Washington by Gorbachev and Reagan, eliminating all United States and Soviet nuclear missiles with ranges between 300 and 3,400 miles, the first agreement to eliminate an entire class of United States and Soviet nuclear arms.

Missile Technology Control Regime was established by a group of Western industrialized nations to restrain the proliferation of ballistic missiles.

1990   *Chemical Weapons* accord was signed by the United States and the Soviet Union, pledging the two nations to drastic cuts in their chemical weapons stockpiles, and to work for a worldwide ban.

Nuclear Testing protocols were signed by the Soviet Union and the United States establishing verification procedures for earlier agreements restricting nuclear testing.

Conventional Forces in Europe (CFE) Treaty was signed in Paris by leaders of 22 NATO and Warsaw Pact nations, agreeing to limit or destroy many categories of non-nuclear weapons in Europe.

1991   *Strategic Arms Reduction Treaty* (START) signed in Moscow by the Soviet Union and the United States, providing for reductions in long-range (strategic) nuclear weapons of both countries, the first treaty to actually reduce their arsenals of strategic weapons.

Unilateral Cuts, primarily in tactical nuclear weapons, and further arms reductions were announced first by President Bush and then by Soviet leader Gorbachev.

Unified Command of nuclear weapons was agreed to by leaders of the independent states of the former Soviet Union, who pledged to honor arms-control agreements.

NOTES

1. Bernard Brodie, *War and Politics* (New York: Macmillan, 1973), p. 342.
2. Kenneth Waltz, *Man, the State and War* (New York: Columbia University Press, 1959), p. 159.
3. See Viscount Grey, *Twenty-Five Years, 1892–1916,* vol. 2, 1925,

quoted in Lewis F. Richardson, *Arms and Insecurity* (Pacific Grove, California: Boxwood Press, 1960), p. 17.

4. *The Collected Papers of Sigmund Freud*, vol. 4 (New York: Basic Books, 1959), p. 300.

5. Robert Ardrey, *The Social Contract* (New York: Atheneum, 1970), p. 319.

6. Ashley Montagu, *The Nature of Human Aggression* (New York: Oxford University Press, 1976), p. 271.

7. John G. Stoessinger, *Why Nations Go to War* (5th ed.) (New York: St. Martin's, 1990), p. ix.

8. *Ibid.*, pp. x–xi.

9. Ardery, *The Social Contract*, p. 301.

10. Richard Smoke, *National Security and the Nuclear Dilemma* (Reading, Mass.: Addison-Wesley, 1984), p. 130.

11. *The Effects of Nuclear War*, (Washington: Office of Technology Assessment, U.S. Congress, 1979), p. 4.

12. David D. Newsom, *The Soviet Brigade in Cuba* (Bloomington, Indiana: Indiana University Press, 1987), p. 51.

13. Strobe Talbott, *Deadly Gambits* (New York: Alfred A. Knopf, 1984), p. 5.

14. Ronald Reagan, White House Press Conference, March 31, 1982; see "President's News Conference on Foreign and Domestic Matters" *New York Times*, April 1, 1982; *see also* Ronald Reagan, White House Press Conference, May 13, 1982; Ronald Reagan, "Reducing the Danger of Nuclear Weapons," address to the World Affairs Council, Los Angeles, March 31, 1983; Lou Cannon, "Reagan: 'Peace Through Strength'," *Washington Post*, August 19, 1980; Lou Cannon, *President Reagan: The Role of a Lifetime* (New York: Simon and Schuster, 1991), pp. 162–63; Barry R. Posen and Stephen W. Van Evera, "Reagan Administration Defense Policy," in Kenneth Oye, Robert Lieber, and Donald Rothchild, *Eagle Defiant: United States Foreign Policy in the 1980s* (Boston: Little, Brown, 1983), pp. 67–104; Talbott, *Deadly Gambits*, p. 6.

15. *Strategic Survey* (London: International Institute for Strategic Studies, 1982), p. 1.

16. *The Military Balance* (London: International Institute for Strategic Studies, 1982), pp. 138–39.

17. Albert Einstein, *Ideas and Opinions* (New York: Bonanza, 1954), p. 122.

18. Douglas Hurd, "Europe and the Atlantic," October 9, 1990, *Arms Control and Disarmament Quarterly Review*, Foreign and Commonwealth Office, London, January 1991, p. 3.

19. "Bush, Gorbachev Salute Treaty As New Foundation of Peace," *Congressional Quarterly*, August 3, 1991, p. 2192.

20. *Ibid.*

MIKHAIL GORBACHEV

When Mikhail Gorbachev emerged as the new leader of the Soviet Union in 1985, it was a development that received relatively little international attention. He was generally viewed as simply a part of a continuum in Soviet leadership, unlikely to dramatically alter Soviet policies.

In the preceding period the Soviet Union had been ruled by a series of aging and often infirm leaders. This period began with Leonid Brezhnev's later years. The increasingly stagnant Brezhnev regime came to an end in 1982, when the man who had been the Soviet leader for 18 years died. Brezhnev's successors, Yuri Andropov and Konstantin Chernenko, both died within a short time after taking office and neither held power long enough to establish an international presence.

Many experts didn't believe that real change was possible, especially in Soviet foreign policy. For example, Adam Ulam, a leading authority on Soviet affairs, wrote in 1983 that it was possible that a new Soviet leader might emerge who would try to "shake up the ossified state and party bureaucracy" and attempt to bolster the Soviet economy, particularly the perennially ailing agricultural sector. However, changing the basic pattern of Soviet foreign policy "looms as a much more difficult and complex problem." Ulam wrote, "It is tempting but unrealistic to postulate that the next generation of Russia's leaders would want or could afford to change drastically the traditional pattern of Soviet foreign policies and/or seek genuine co-operation with the West."[1]

It was against this background that Gorbachev came to power. Many viewed him as just another in the line of gray, stolid Soviet leaders likely to remain trapped in and by the very bureaucracy and Communist party hierarchy from which he had emerged.

The deterioration in superpower relations that had become so pronounced in the early 1980s and the implications of that deterioration for world affairs are discussed elsewhere in this book. Ronald Reagan, beginning his second term as the American president when Gorbachev assumed power, had been noted for his hard-line anti-Soviet posture. (See Reagan Profile.) United States–Soviet détente, which had briefly flowered in the 1970s, was moribund.

Soviet leader Mikhail Gorbachev's international impact was demonstrated by the reception he received on his first trip to the United States in 1987. En route to a White House meeting with President Reagan, Gorbachev halted his motorcade and plunged into the welcoming Washington crowd.

167

Reagan said that he was prepared to deal with Gorbachev with an open mind, but he doubted that Moscow's policies would change much.

Gorbachev did, however, represent a new generation of Soviet leadership. He was the first Soviet general-secretary to have been born after the 1917 revolution. And while the trauma of the Soviet experience in World War II had left an enduring mark on the Soviet leadership for more than 40 years, Gorbachev had been only a young boy during the war. He was also the first Soviet party leader since Lenin to have earned a university degree, graduating from the law faculty of Moscow State University.

CHANGE AT HOME AND ABROAD

Within a short time after his election as general-secretary of the Communist Party, it began to be apparent that Gorbachev, if for no reasons other than his health and relative youth (age 54), was a different type of Soviet leader. The differences were, of course, to go well beyond appearance, although it took some time for that to become clear.

There were some early hints that Gorbachev might attempt real change. Late in 1984, Gorbachev had made a little-noticed speech in which he foreshadowed many of the policy changes he would eventually seek to implement. Shortly before becoming general-secretary, Gorbachev visited Britain and was labeled by British Prime Minister Margaret Thatcher as the kind of leader with whom the West could "do business." The initial tendency, however, was to conclude that while Gorbachev represented a change in style, substance was another matter. His early international efforts were referred to, somewhat derisively, as a "charm offensive."

International Attention

But Gorbachev didn't confine himself to image building. He plunged ahead vigorously, and when he began acknowledging Soviet problems and acting to try to correct them, he began to be taken more seriously abroad. What had been seen as a "charm offensive" became a "diplomatic offensive" and a "peace offensive." Gorbachev proved very adept in the international public-relations competition which has become an important part of world politics. A tide of "Gorbymania" began to sweep across Europe, with many Europeans responding favorably to the Soviet leader's image and initiatives. Within two years after coming to power, some European polls indicated that the leader in the Kremlin was more popular than the leader in the White House. Before the end of the 1980s, United States polls showed that Gorbachev ranked as the world's second most admired man, just behind Reagan. In what was then West Germany, Gorbachev at one point ranked higher in public esteem than Chancellor Helmut Kohl.[2] He was named as the "man of the decade" for the 1980s by *Time* magazine.

Gorbachev's foreign policy reflected his recognition that the Soviet Union needed to step back from its all-out competition with the West in order to be able to devote more of its energy and resources to critical domestic problems. As part of his strategy, Gorbachev was determined to engage in personal diplomacy with Reagan. As discussed in Chapter 5, Gorbachev introduced a more dynamic brand of diplomacy, unlike the glacierlike approach usually associated with the Soviets. In particular, Gorbachev wanted to see movement on arms control as, eventually, did Reagan.

He made a major effort to gain worldwide identification with the cause of arms reduction. He was concerned about the dangers of the arms race, but he was also concerned about the costs. There was, as suggested, a direct correlation between Gorbachev's foreign and domestic policies. Change in domestic policy, he said, "inevitably leads to changes in the attitude in international issues." Although he insisted that it was an oversimplification to suggest that So-

Gorbachev helped bring about important achievements in arms control and reductions. Meeting at the Kremlin in 1991, Presidents Gorbachev and Bush announced agreement on the START treaty. Although he helped bring about major changes in international relations, Gorbachev could not hold the Soviet Union together.

viet arms control efforts were primarily motivated by the need to focus on domestic problems, he stated, "We are saying openly for all to hear: we need lasting peace in order to concentrate on the development of our society and to cope with the tasks of improving the life of the Soviet people."[5]

At home the bywords were *perestroika* (restructuring) and *glasnost* (openness), as Gorbachev sought to end Soviet economic stagnation and create a more open society. He recognized the need for his country to be more a part of the international economy and understood that it risked falling still further behind because it was cut off from many of the technological advances that were benefiting the West. (See Chapter 11.)

Gorbachev's lifting of many of the controls in the Soviet Union through his *glasnost* policies heightened awareness of Soviet problems and shortcomings, and of some of the sordid aspects of Soviet history. And the *glasnost* of international communications helped carry Gorbachev's message and reshape the international image of the Soviet Union.

Late in 1985, Gorbachev held his first summit meeting with Reagan. Although the two leaders focused on arms control, there were no major breakthroughs. However, there was clearly a sharp change in the atmosphere of superpower relations and there was agreement to accelerate arms negotiations.

Steadily, Gorbachev was gaining in international stature and helping to open the way for major changes in international affairs. His frequent travels and public appearances and his accessibility to the international media made him one of the world's most recognized figures, even while within the Soviet Union there were growing signs of turmoil and discontent. In the ongoing domestic political struggle, he dismantled some of the power held by the Communist Party while the national legislature was given more freedom and power. He was elected president of the restructured government, but he was often under attack from those demanding even broader change.

In 1987, Gorbachev made his first trip to the United States, and he and Reagan signed the Intermediate-Range Nuclear Forces (INF) Treaty (discussed in Chapter 6). The visit demonstrated Gorbachev's international popularity. In downtown Washington he halted his motorcade and plunged into the crowd, shaking hands like the most practiced United States politician, with the TV cameras capturing it all.

Remarkable as those scenes were, especially considering the disastrous state of United States—Soviet relations just a few years earlier, even more remarkable sights were seen on television sets around the world in 1988 when Gorbachev and Reagan held a summit meeting in Moscow and strolled amicably through Red Square.

GORBACHEV AND A TIME OF CHANGE

The year of 1989 will be remembered as one of the most dramatic and significant in modern international relations, and Gorbachev figured prominently in the events that made it such an extraordinary time. Even though Gorbachev had already made major changes in Soviet policies, many in the United States and elsewhere remained skeptical about how far Gorbachev would take changes or allow them to go. There were, for example, those who doubted that Gorbachev would adhere to his promise to withdraw Soviet troops from Afghanistan. For

nine years the Soviets had been bogged down in a costly effort there, trying to bolster successive Marxist regimes that were locked in a civil war. Gorbachev pledged to pull out Soviet forces early in 1989, but skeptics pointed out that since World War II the Soviet Union had not relinquished territory that it had sought to dominate. However, Gorbachev lived up to his promise and the Soviet troops went home.

In May 1989, Gorbachev made a visit to China to meet Chinese leaders. The purpose of the trip was to restore normal relations between the two communist nations, which had been alienated from each other for most of 30 years. The visit, which had been planned well in advance, happened to coincide with the growing "prodemocracy" demonstrations in China, and upon his arrival in Beijing, Gorbachev found himself cast in the unusual role of champion of democracy. As on a number of occasions, Gorbachev served as a catalyst. He was looked to as someone who pointed the way out of a fossilized system, as he had been welcomed on earlier trips to such countries as Czechoslovakia and Hungary.

The support for Gorbachev in Beijing was an embarrassment to China's Deng Xiaoping (see Profile), for whom the summit should have been a personal triumph. Before leaving Beijing, Gorbachev portrayed the protests in China as a part of a painful but healthy worldwide upheaval in communist countries. Later, following Gorbachev's departure, the Chinese leadership cracked down brutally on the demonstrators.

Although the Chinese movement was squelched, it helped inspire the citizens of Eastern Europe to begin or continue efforts to change their societies. Gorbachev's actions and statements had indicated that he might accept some change in Eastern Europe, which had been part of the Soviet bloc for more than 40 years, but few expected that he would become a patron of change.

With Communist power rapidly eroding in

Hungary, Poland, and Czechoslovakia, the clamor for change spread to East Germany, which had been the bulwark of the Soviet bloc. Gorbachev had visited West Germany during the summer of 1989, scoring another public relations triumph while there. He had made it clear that he wanted to build economic relations with West Germany and saw that as a key to his notion of a "common European home," of which the Soviet Union would be very much a part.[4] Visiting East Berlin in early October 1989 for the fortieth anniversary of the communist state, Gorbachev refused to join in the traditional attacks on the West. Further, he cautioned the East German leaders not to expect Soviet support if they used force to crack down on the growing protests by their own citizens. He advised them to launch their own *perestroika*. Within days, the veteran East German leader, Erich Honecker, was forced out of office and the process of change was underway.

Gorbachev had repeatedly pledged a policy of nonintervention in the East bloc, and on a visit to Finland later in October he stated that the Soviet Union had no moral or political right to interfere in the affairs of its East European neighbors. This was seen as a repudiation of what some had called the Brezhnev Doctrine— which implied a Soviet policy of armed intervention to prevent changes in the Communist government of the Warsaw Pact nations.

These statements by Gorbachev were widely taken as a signal that not only would he not oppose change but that he supported it. In East Germany, in particular, the antigovernment movement seemed to take its cue from Gorbachev's implied disassociation from the government. Ultimately, this growing pressure led to the demise of the Berlin Wall in November 1989. Gorbachev had played a major part in unleashing the forces of democracy and he had served as a catalyst for the development of a new, undivided Europe.

In 1990 Gorbachev was named winner of the Nobel Prize in recognition of his initiatives in promotion of international peace, including the championing of political change in Eastern Europe and helping to end the Cold War.

At the time the award was announced, Gorbachev was embroiled in controversy at home over economic problems and ethnic or nationalities issues, with various republics seeking to break away from the union, or at least gain greater autonomy. Indeed, because of the domestic turmoil, Gorbachev was unable to attend the original awards ceremony and had to deliver his Nobel acceptance speech much later.

Transforming International Relations

The Nobel Committee said Gorbachev was honored because of "his leading role in the peace process which today characterizes important parts of the international community."[5]

In just a few years Gorbachev had played a major part in transforming international relations. He brought sweeping change to his own country and revolutionized its foreign policy. He altered superpower relations, engaging in a series of successful summit meetings with United States presidents. He pursued arms control; withdrew Soviet troops from Afghanistan; and allowed popular revolutions to topple old-line Communist governments in Eastern Europe, which helped pave the way for further significant developments, including German unification. Gorbachev also helped repair Soviet relations with China and broke new diplomatic ground by developing ties with such nations as South Korea and Saudi Arabia, bridging a huge divide which had previously kept those countries alienated from the Soviet Union.

In 1990–91 he joined the United States and others in the condemnation of Iraq, formerly a close Soviet ally, for its invasion of Kuwait, although his efforts to broker a diplomatic solution to the crisis were unsuccessful.

Gorbachev's priorities were undoubtedly

driven to a considerable extent by recognition that if the Soviet Union hoped to keep pace in the modern world, it had to become a part of the global economy. In many respects it was simply a realistic assessment of national interests, but other Soviet leaders had been unable to recognize this reality or unable to act to deal with it.

Achievements and Challenges

Analyzing Gorbachev's record, author Robert Kaiser wrote, "Mikhail Gorbachev transformed the world. He turned his own country upside down. He woke a sleeping giant, the people of the Soviet Union, and gave them freedoms they had never dreamed of." In foreign policy, "he tossed away the Soviet empire in Eastern Europe with no more than a fare-thee-well. He ended the Cold War that had dominated world politics and consumed the wealth of nations for nearly half a century."[6] However, Kaiser points out, then Gorbachev discovered that he "had started a revolution he could not control," referring to the rising expectations of the people of the Soviet Union.[7] He tried to balance competing forces and hold the union together, but the powerful nationalist impulses, beginning in the Baltic republics, were simply too strong. He was increasingly powerless as leaders of other republics moved to form a Commonwealth of Independent States.

A group of Communist hardliners attempted to seize power in August 1991, and for three days Gorbachev was under house arrest at his vacation home in the Crimea while the leaders of the *coup* or *putsch*, sought to establish control. The group was composed of some Communist, KGB (Committee on State Security/secret police), and military officials who were opposed to the Gorbachev reform efforts and to the increasing independence of the republics that had made up the Soviet Union. The hardliners opposed the weakening of the once-powerful central government. They apparently expected most citizens to go along with their

"state of emergency," hoping to capitalize on dissatisfaction with economic conditions and on the fears and passivity of a population long cowed by the ruthless control of the government and party. However, change had gone too far to allow a return to the stifling, rigid rule of the pre-Gorbachev period. The conspirators behind the coup proved rather inept and encountered strong opposition. Particularly significant was the role played by Boris Yeltsin, president of the Russian Republic, largest and most important of the 15 republics that had made up the U.S.S.R. Yeltsin and Gorbachev were often at odds, particularly on the relationship between the republics and the central government and on the pace of reform. Some saw Yeltsin as anxious to grab power, but at the time of the coup

Russian president Boris Yeltsin urged resistance to the attempted takeover by hardliners in Moscow in 1991. When Soviet military vehicles massed in front of the Russian Parliament building, Yeltsin climbed atop an armed personnel carrier and called for a nationwide strike to protest the *coup* or *putsch* and called for the return of Mikhail Gorbachev, who was being held incommunicado at his vacation residence. While Yeltsin spoke, a Soviet soldier covered his face. Yeltsin's international stature was bolstered when television beamed this scene and his defiant call around the world.

One of the major issues confronting Mikhail Gorbachev in the post-Communist era was the push for independence or greater autonomy among the republics that had made up the Soviet Union. Russian leader Boris Yeltsin became a key figure, and at a meeting of the Russian parliament he and Gorbachev debated the future of the Soviet government and the republics.

it was Yeltsin's heroic defiance that rallied the public, thwarted the attempted takeover, and captured the world's imagination. The Russian Parliament building in Moscow (also, of course, the capital city of the Soviet Union) became the nerve center of the broad resistance to the coup.

Internationally, the takeover attempt was widely condemned. As the lack of domestic support became increasingly apparent, the coup collapsed. While there was considerable relief in many corners of the world that Gorbachev had survived, he returned to Moscow to find that the abortive coup had actually hastened a broader revolution. It was a turning point in history. The institutions of the old order and the Communist Party, which Gorbachev had attempted to modernize but retain, were thoroughly discredited. Within a short time Gorbachev resigned as Communist general secretary and effectively brought an end to the party's official status. Although Gorbachev survived the coup, the old Soviet Union was soon dissolved, and Gorbachev was without power in a structure of independent republics.

Despite Gorbachev's difficulties and limitations in dealing with the problems involved in transforming the Soviet Union, he was the key figure in opening the way for change there and in world affairs. His actions helped rearrange the geopolitical map, altering the basic outline of world politics and introducing a new era in international relations.

NOTES

1. Adam B. Ulam, *Dangerous Relations: The Soviet Union in World Politics, 1970–1982* (New York: Oxford University Press, 1983), p. 312.
2. See, for example, John Dillin, "Soviet-Bashing Loses Luster in US," *Christian Science Monitor*, July 25, 1989.
3. Mikhail Gorbachev, *Perestroika* (New York: Harper & Row, 1987), p. 132.
4. *Ibid.*, pp. 194–205. For further discussion of Gorbachev and the "common European home," see Jerry F. Hough, *"Perestroika* and Soviet Relations With the West," in Donald R. Kelley and Hoyt Purvis (eds.), *Old Myths and New Realities in United States-Soviet Relations* (New York: Praeger, 1990), pp. 27–28.
5. Sheila Rule, "Gorbachev Gets Nobel Peace Prize For Foreign Policy Achievements," *New York Times*, October 16, 1990.
6. Robert G. Kaiser, "Gorbachev: Triumph and Failure," *Foreign Affairs* 70, no. 2, spring 1991, p. 160.
7. *Ibid.*

SUGGESTIONS FOR FURTHER READING

Clark, Susan L. *Gorbachev's Agenda.* Boulder, Colorado: Westview, 1989.

Gorbachev, Mikhail. *The August Coup: The Truth and the Lessons.* New York: Harper Collins, 1991.

Gorbachev, Mikhail. *Perestroika.* New York: Harper & Row, 1987.

Gwertzman, Bernard and Michael T. Kaufman (eds.). *The Collapse of Communism.* New York: Random House/Times Books, 1990.

Hough, Jerry F. *Russia and the West: Gorbachev and the Politics of Reform.* New York: Simon and Schuster, 1988.

Kaiser, Robert G. *Why Gorbachev Happened.* New York: Simon and Schuster, 1991.

Kelley, Donald R. and Hoyt Purvis (eds.) *Old Myths and New Realities in United States–Soviet Relations.* New York: Praeger, 1990.

Walker, Martin. *The Waking Giant: Gorbachev's Russia.* New York: Pantheon, 1986.

CITY PORTRAIT: BERLIN

Berlin was the capital of Germany under the Nazi Third Reich, and before that it had been the capital of the Kingdom of Prussia and of the German Empire. Once a cosmopolitan city and an intellectual and cultural center, under Hitler it was the headquarters for a brutal, fascist government.

After the defeat of the Nazis and the end of World War II, Berlin became the symbol of East-West division. Indeed, Berlin was more than a symbol. Not only did it sit on Europe's east-west divide, the city itself was divided by a wall constructed in 1961 by East Germany with Soviet backing.

More recently, when the wall began to disappear in late 1989, its fall was a dramatic and clearly visible symbol for the end of the Cold War and the rigid division that had separated East and West into two distinct international camps.

At the end of World War II, the victors had agreed to divide Germany into four zones of occupation. Berlin, much of which lay in ruin, became a separate area under four-power control, with the French, British, Soviets, and Americans each occupying a sector. The city was an island situated within the Soviet-occupied Eastern zone of Germany.

As the Cold War became a reality, Berlin became a stage on which the drama of East-West conflict was played out. In March 1948, the Soviet Union withdrew from the Inter-Allied Governing Authority (Kommandatura), which was responsible for coordinating the administration of the city. The Soviets did not want the existence of a Western enclave within their occupation zone and tried to pressure the Western powers out of Berlin. It was in June 1948 that the Soviets imposed the blockade on land-access routes to West Berlin, effectively cutting it off from the outside world. The West responded with the Berlin Airlift, discussed in Chapter 2, one of the most remarkable supply operations ever undertaken.

Through the airlift, the Western powers demonstrated their commitment to the maintenance of a free Berlin. Recognizing the failure of the blockade and having experienced a considerable international public-relations setback, the Soviets entered into negotiations with the West, which led to an

The opening of the Berlin Wall in November 1989 symbolized the end of the Cold War and of the East-West division of Germany and Europe. Jubilant crowds danced on the wall in celebration of the dramatic fall of the Communist-imposed barrier.

175

end of the blockade in May 1948. Actually, the blockade probably resulted in a firmer resolve by the Western powers to remain in Berlin, but it was only one in a series of many dramatic events, crises, and showdowns in Berlin.

When the Federal Republic of Germany (West) and the German Democratic Republic (East) were officially established in 1949, the two parts of Berlin were affiliated with the respective German states, although West Berlin formally remained a separate entity, not fully integrated into West Germany. The East took a number of steps to isolate West Berlin. Communications and transportation between the two sections of the city were restricted or cut off by the Eastern authorities. Meanwhile, West Berlin became an outpost for democracy and capitalism and, in many ways, a Western showcase. With strong economic support from West Germany and the Western powers, a major reconstruction effort was undertaken, restoring and modernizing West Berlin. The difference between East and West Berlin became increasingly evident, and this dramatic distinction heightened tension within the divided city. In 1953, Soviet troops were used to put down an antigovernment uprising in East Berlin.

The stream of refugees from East to West was steadily increasing, despite Eastern efforts to impede the flow. This loss of population was a matter of growing concern to the Eastern authorities. Between 1949 and 1961, more than 2.6 million people left East Germany for the West. Soviet Premier Nikita Khrushchev was insisting that the Western powers should leave Berlin. The tension over the divided city reached a boiling point during the summer of 1961. An average of 1,000 refugees a day were heading West. It was one of the most dramatic periods of the nuclear era. At the Vienna summit in June 1961 and in the following weeks Khruschev and the young American president, John F. Kennedy, engaged in a verbal battle over Berlin, backed up by military buildups on both

sides. Responding to Soviet demands that Western troops be withdrawn, Kennedy said, "We cannot and will not permit the Communists to drive us out of Berlin either gradually or by force."

Before dawn on August 13, 1961, in a shocking turn of events, the Soviets and East Germans moved to halt the flow of refugees and assert total control over East Berlin. East German troops began tearing up the streets at crossing points on the East Berlin side and setting up barbed-wire barricades. Within a few days workmen sealed off buildings and began constructing a wall to close off the Soviet sector.

In the early days of the wall there were many valiant and not always successful efforts to es-

For more than 28 years the Berlin Wall stood as an outrageous symbol of the division of Europe and the world and of Communist suppression. For Berliners it was very real, and over the years the East Germans strengthened and fortified the wall, making escape virtually impossible and creating a "no-man's land" in the adjacent area on the eastern side. In the background is the historic Reichstag (parliament) building.

cape to the West. People leaped from windows of apartment buildings, and there were those who swam across the Spree River or tunneled their way under the wall. Gradually, however, the wall became more permanent and more difficult to penetrate. Although the United States and its allies denounced the wall and made clear their commitment to the freedom of West Berlin and their determination to maintain Western access to the city, the wall was in the Soviet sector and soon became a fact of life. In 1963, President Kennedy visited Berlin and the wall. He addressed a huge throng in West Berlin and spoke the famous words, "Ich bin ein Berliner." (I am a Berliner). Kennedy's words became a rallying cry and an expression of international solidarity with the Berliners.

At first the wall was crudely built, and in some cases the boundary simply consisted of a patchwork of boarded-up buildings. Behind the barrier, East Berlin was bleak and barren. Ruins from World War II were still in evidence. East Berlin, with its nearly deserted streets, was a sharp contrast to the thriving West side. Berlin became the favorite setting for spy novels and films, a city of intrigue, where East and West confronted each other. *The Spy Who Came in From the Cold*, *Funeral in Berlin*, and *Berlin Game* were among many novels and films which had a Berlin setting. Checkpoint Charlie, a crossing point between East and West for foreigners and officials, became a visual representation of East-West tension.

In the years after the wall was constructed, East Berlin gradually was modernized, and, indeed, became something of an East European showcase, though it still paled in comparison with the vibrant West Berlin. The wall became part of the physical and political landscape. From East Berlin, the wall was omnipresent, but antiseptic in appearance. On the west side, however, the wall became covered with graffiti, a somewhat perverse tribute to freedom of expression.

As East Germany and East Berlin became more prosperous, the wall ranked as an embarrassment, and little was said about it in official publications or statements, although East German school books referred to it as the "anti-fascist protection wall." While the wall had political and psychological costs for the East, the West paid a high price in real terms in order to help sustain West Berlin. In addition to the military costs to the West associated with the security of West Berlin, West Germany subsidized West Berlin in a variety of ways, including tax advantages and incentives.

Gradually, as East-West tension reduced, movement between the two Berlins and the two Germanys became more common.

The Wall Comes Down

In 1989, 40 years after the establishment of East Germany, large numbers of East Germans took advantage of the liberalization in the Soviet bloc and began fleeing to the West in the largest exodus since the wall was built in 1961. In October 1989, Soviet leader Mikhail Gorbachev was in East Berlin for the ceremonies marking the fortieth anniversary of the German Democratic Republic. However, Gorbachev declined to join in the attack launched by East German officials on the Bonn government. Instead, he used the occasion to call for Soviet-style reforms in East Germany and for continuation of "mutually advantageous and satisfactory arrangements" between Bonn and Moscow. In effect, Gorbachev sent a signal that the Soviet Union would not take special steps to back the increasingly shaky East German regime.

Large-scale protests began to occur in East Berlin, with demonstrators calling for freedom and reform. Western leaders again challenged the East German and Soviet officials to tear down the wall and end the division of Berlin.

The East German government became virtually powerless in the face of the growing popular protests. Finally, the East German govern-

With Berlin and Germany united once again, Checkpoint Charlie, which served as the Berlin Wall crossing point for the Western allies, was removed in 1990. Located in the American sector, the checkpoint was used by non-Germans traveling between Berlin's two halves. No entry restrictions were imposed on the western side, but the East Germans maintained rigid controls on those seeking to enter or depart the eastern side. In 1961 Soviet and American tanks massed on each side of the checkpoint, but no armed action occurred. American secretary of state James Baker and other allied officials took part in ceremonies marking the removal of the checkpoint.

ment announced that it would open its borders and allow citizens to travel to the West. On November 8–9, 1989, citizens from both East and West flocked to the wall and began a joyous celebration. Young people danced atop the wall, and began chipping away pieces of the barrier that symbolized the Cold War division. In the following weeks, East Germany began to dismantle sections of the wall.

Although the wall stood for 28 years, ultimately it could not hold back the tide of freedom. Those living behind the wall were increasingly aware, particularly because of their ability to watch television from the West, of the stagnation of their own society. Although East Germany was relatively prosperous by most international standards, those in the East could see that it lacked the economic vitality of the West, and they longed for the freedom of movement that Westerners enjoyed. Berlin again became an open city. In 1991, with East and West Germany united, the German Bundestag (parliament) voted to make Berlin the nation's capital once more.

CHAPTER SEVEN

International Flashpoints and Conditions for Conflict

Much of the conflict and turmoil in the late twentieth century has been centered in what is generally referred to as the Third World. There are, of course, rivalries, conflicts, and contentious issues among the more developed nations, and some of the conflicts in the Third World, as noted in previous chapters, have been directly tied to the superpower rivalry. Nonetheless, even though the outside powers have often been directly or indirectly involved in the conflicts within the Third World, it has been in Africa, Asia, Latin America, and the Middle East where conflict has usually broken out. This was vividly demonstrated in the 1990–91 events in the Persian Gulf. Iraq's invasion of Kuwait and the threat to attack other countries was a conflict that not only involved countries in the region but eventually involved a coalition of forces from 30 nations aligned against Iraq. A number of other countries provided various forms of assistance to the coalition effort.

A variety of factors contribute to the creation of international flashpoints—situations that could ignite and which are potentially volatile. In addition to the fact that the East-West rivalry during the Cold War period often became a factor in or was related to what are often referred to as "regional problems," many of these problems have to be seen within a broader historical context. As was pointed out earlier, a number of Third-World nations are former colonies, having in most cases been controlled by one of the European colonial powers. Nationalism (discussed in previous chapters) was often a rallying point for those struggling to obtain independence—probably a natural response to colonialism. In some cases the colonies revolted against the colonial powers, seeking and eventually gaining their independence. Some of these revolutions have been prolonged affairs, and in certain cases competing groups, often with outside backing—sometimes with the Americans supporting one side and the Soviets the other—have continued to struggle for national control even after independence. These conflicts tend to spill over into or involve neighboring nations.

Nationalism, ideology, and religious, ethnic, and racial factors have been among the forces that have contributed to conflict and volatility. When we call the roll of conflicts and flashpoints of recent and current times, most of the nations involved—Vietnam, Afghanistan, Nicaragua, Lebanon, Angola, Iraq, and Cuba for example—are in the Third World. However, it should be remembered that World War I and much of World War II were fought in Europe, and that Europe was also the original theater for the Cold War. There were points of high tension in Europe in recent decades—Berlin being a notable example (see Berlin City Portrait). Eventually, however, a standoff developed in Europe (while the Western nations pulled further and further ahead economically). Gradually much of the East-West conflict began to shift to the Third World, even though the very notion of a "Third World" was supposed to distinguish those countries within it from the countries associated with the two major power blocs. The term *Third World* has important economic connotations too, and those will be dealt with more in the following chapter.

THIRD-WORLD DEPENDENCE AND INDEPENDENCE

The original use of the term *Third World* was in French (*tiers monde*). Probably the first to use it was the French demographer, Alfred Sauvy. He used the term in 1952, although it did not come into widespread usage until the late 1960s. It has always been a term that has limitations, and applying it too broadly can be misleading, particularly if it seems to imply that the Third World is monolithic.

For purposes of discussion in this chapter, Third World applies to most of the nations of Africa, Asia, and Latin America, many of which were emerging from external domination in the post–World War II period, or were at least seeking to become more independent, even though some of them already were in a technical sense, if not always in a practical sense.

Some of the early leaders of newly independent nations sought to take a neutral or nonaligned posture in international affairs (or at least claimed such a position) and tried to avoid the entanglements of the two power blocs in the Cold War. (Certain Third-World leaders became rather adept at playing the two blocs off against each other in an interesting twist on the traditional balance-of-power scenario.) Leading early advocates of the nonalignment posture were Nehru of India, Nasser of Egypt, Sukarno of Indonesia, and Nkrumah of Ghana. At the Afro-Asian Conference in Bandung, Indonesia, in 1955 and the 1961 Belgrade Conference, these nations began to coalesce into what was called a "third force" or "third party," and was eventually referred to as Third World. Collectively, however, although they sometimes sought to exercise influence in a more purely political sense, most of their common concerns and efforts were economically oriented and at various points they generated major activity and attention to development issues within the United Nations and various international fora.

One of those given credit for popularizing the concept of the Third World was Frantz Fanon, a psychiatrist from Martinique (which was a French colony in the Caribbean) who became an important figure in the Algerian rebellion against France. Fanon wrote an anticolonial polemic, *The Wretched of the Earth* (first published in France in 1961 as *Les Damnes de la Terre*). He advocated peasant-based or grassroots revolution and believed that the colonized nations must reject the European model. "Europe," he wrote, "undertook the leadership of the world with ardor, cynicism, and violence." He called for a "Third World starting a new history of man," one that would draw upon the authentic roots of the peoples in the Third World.[1]

VOLATILE REGIONS

Individual nations and regions within the Third World increasingly became focal points for revolution and for the United States—Soviet rivalry. Nationalism and regional rivalries often became entangled in broader international divisions and difficulties, or, in some cases, it might be more correct to say that the external powers sometimes became caught up in or contributed to the revolutionary conflicts and regional rivalries.

As was mentioned in the previous chapter, it has been calculated that 127 wars were fought between the end of World War II and the beginning of the 1990s, and most of those were in Third-World nations.

It must be pointed out that as the Cold War subsided, not all of the points of tension around the world did likewise, making it obvious that such problems did not revolve solely around the rivalry between the Soviets and Americans.

A closer look at some of those areas that have been and may again be international flashpoints can provide a better understanding of some of the factors contributing to and causing tension and conflict and how these problems affect international relations.

Those areas to be examined are as follows:

■ The Middle East and Persian Gulf regions, including Iran. (This region is sometimes referred to as the Near East.)

■ Central America

■ Southern Africa

THE MIDDLE EAST AND PERSIAN GULF

The Middle East is usually considered to be the most volatile and unstable region. (Here *Middle East* is being used in the broadest sense, taking in the area from North Africa, through the Arabian Peninsula, Israel, Jordan, Lebanon, Syria, Turkey, Iraq, and east to Iran.) Two major factors significantly complicate the politics of the region and its international importance: religion and resources. (See Figure 7-1.)

As the historic center of several of the world's major religions—Christianity, Islam, and Judaism—there is a powerful attachment to the region and a long history of religious conflict among peoples of the area. Further complicating relations within the region and its place in international affairs is the history of external involvement in the area, first by the European imperial powers, primarily the British and French, and later by the leaders of the East-West blocs, the Americans and the Soviets. The tragic case of Lebanon, torn apart by religious and regional rivalries, has already been discussed in Chapter 1.

The region, particularly the Persian Gulf area, has a substantial portion of the world's oil reserves, with well over half of the estimated reserves found in the area. Among individual nations, Saudi Arabia is by far the world's largest single source of oil.

Japan and Europe have been heavily dependent on oil from the Middle East, as has the United States to a lesser extent. The region's importance as a supplier of oil and gas adds to its geopolitical significance as an international crossroads between Europe, Africa, and Asia, located alongside some key waterways.

A Tumultuous Period

Until after World War II, the Middle East had for a long period been primarily dominated by Britain, with France controlling much of nearby North Africa. Involvement of the United States and the Soviet Union did not begin to become very significant until the 1950s.

The process of withdrawal of the British and French was in some cases prolonged and difficult. France fought against a nationalist rebellion in Algeria for nearly a decade before France's Charles de Gaulle helped bring an end to the conflict. Algeria received its independence in 1962. (See De Gaulle Profile.)

A key development in the region was the establishment of the independent nation of Israel in 1948. After World War I the area that later became Israel had become part of the British-administered League of Nations Palestine-mandate territory. However, the following years brought increasingly serious conflict between Jews and Arabs. When Jewish emigration from Europe grew sharply, following the rise of Hitler in Germany, tensions in the area increased. After World War II and the holocaust of European Jewry, the Jewish demand that the survivors be allowed to

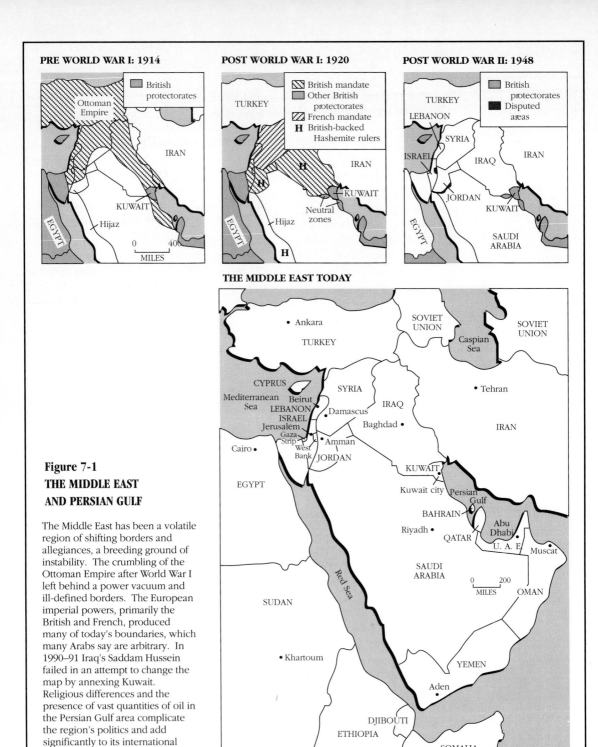

PRE WORLD WAR I: 1914

British protectorates

Ottoman Empire

IRAN

KUWAIT

EGYPT

Hijaz

0   400
MILES

POST WORLD WAR I: 1920

British mandate
Other British protectorates
French mandate
H British-backed Hashemite rulers

TURKEY

IRAN

H

H

KUWAIT

EGYPT

Hijaz

Neutral zones

H

POST WORLD WAR II: 1948

British protectorates
Disputed areas

TURKEY

LEBANON

SYRIA

ISRAEL

IRAQ

IRAN

JORDAN

KUWAIT

EGYPT

SAUDI ARABIA

THE MIDDLE EAST TODAY

• Ankara

SOVIET UNION

SOVIET UNION

TURKEY

Caspian Sea

CYPRUS

SYRIA

IRAQ

• Tehran

Mediterranean Sea

Beirut
LEBANON
ISRAEL
Jerusalem
Gaza Strip
West Bank

• Damascus

Baghdad •

IRAN

• Amman

JORDAN

Cairo •

KUWAIT

Kuwait city

Persian Gulf

EGYPT

BAHRAIN

Abu Dhabi

Riyadh •

QATAR

U. A. E.

Muscat

Red Sea

SUDAN

SAUDI ARABIA

0   200
MILES

OMAN

• Khartoum

YEMEN

Aden

DJIBOUTI

ETHIOPIA

SOMALIA

Figure 7-1
THE MIDDLE EAST AND PERSIAN GULF

The Middle East has been a volatile region of shifting borders and allegiances, a breeding ground of instability. The crumbling of the Ottoman Empire after World War I left behind a power vacuum and ill-defined borders. The European imperial powers, primarily the British and French, produced many of today's boundaries, which many Arabs say are arbitrary. In 1990–91 Iraq's Saddam Hussein failed in an attempt to change the map by annexing Kuwait. Religious differences and the presence of vast quantities of oil in the Persian Gulf area complicate the region's politics and add significantly to its international importance.

immigrate to the area, American pressure in support of this immigration, and Arab opposition, led the British government to announce its intention of withdrawing. A United Nations Special Committee on Palestine recommended partitioning Palestine into Jewish and Arab states, with the city of Jerusalem under international control. The United Nations approved the plan, but it was rejected by the Arabs. On the day the British withdrew in 1948, the state of Israel was proclaimed. Arab forces attacked, and war between the newly independent Israel and its Arab neighbors continued until early 1949. However, the hostility did not really end, and the stage had been set for years of Arab-Israeli conflicts, which were to include three more wars, plus invasions, armed strikes and counterstrikes, and insurgencies.

The Suez crisis of 1956 saw the last attempt by Britain and France to assert their power in the region. The Egyptian leader, Gamal Abdel Nasser, had depended upon American and British support for his dream of building the Aswan Dam on the Nile river, which he believed would be a great boon to his nation. However, the United States and Britain decided not to finance construction, and in response Nasser seized and nationalized the Suez Canal to obtain his own funds and to defy the West. (The 101-mile canal connects the Mediterranean and Red Seas. Opened in 1869, it was largely controlled by British and French interests and was scheduled to revert to Egyptian government control in 1968.) With French and British backing, Israel attacked Egypt in October 1956, but the United States opposed the action, and the three nations eventually withdrew. For the British it was a serious setback; some said that it marked the end of Britain's status as a great power. Nasser's stock within the Arab world was bolstered, and, as the United States had feared, Egypt began looking to the Soviet Union for support.

This opened a period of acute tension between the United States and the Soviet Union over the Middle East, as the two became major factors in the region, each developing its own "clients."

In 1967, with both sides preparing for conflict, Nasser provoked another war by forcing the withdrawal of United Nations forces from the region, sending Egyptian troops into Sinai, and cutting off access to the Israeli port of Eilat. But what became known as the Six-Day War ended in a stunning victory for Israel. After the war, Israel occupied some of the territories it had captured, taking the West Bank of the Jordan River and East Jerusalem from Jordan; the Sinai Peninsula and Gaza Strip from Egypt; and the Golan Heights from Syria.

From that point the United States became more heavily involved in the region and has been a major arms supplier and aid donor for Israel. The United States also provided assistance to Jordan and sold large amounts of arms to Saudi Arabia and later aided Egypt. The Soviets were primary suppliers to Syria and Iraq, and the Middle East became a major target for Soviet aid. Soviet influence was probably at its zenith in the late 1960s and early 1970s, with friendly governments in North Yemen, Algeria, and Egypt, in addition to Syria and Iraq. Later, South Yemen joined the list, and North Yemen became more nonaligned. (Libya was also a sometimes friend of the Soviets.)

In October 1973 on Yom Kippur, the holiest day in the Jewish calendar, the Egyptians and Syrians launched a sudden attack against Israel. Israel recovered and prevailed militarily, eventually surrounding the Egyptian Army in the Sinai, and threatened to invade Egypt. Anwar Sadat of Egypt appealed to the Soviets for help, and Soviet troops were mobilized for an airlift into the Middle East. However, the United States warned Soviet leader Leonid Brezhnev to stay out of the region, and United States nuclear forces were put on alert. At the same time, though, the United States demanded and got an Israeli cease-fire (threatening to hold back Israeli supplies) and allowed resupplying of the surrounded Egyptian forces. The crisis was defused. Although not victorious, the Egyptian Army under Sadat had performed creditably and Egypt regained some self-respect. Sadat then turned the tables on the Soviets and expelled all the Soviet military advisers from his country. Sadat had established himself as an important international figure and began turning to the United States and the West for help.

It was at this stage that American Secretary of State Henry Kissinger became more actively involved in the Middle East, engaging in the shuttle diplomacy that was mentioned in Chapter 5. Kissinger managed to get troop disengagement agreements, but a full settlement eluded him. Efforts to find a solution to the ongoing conflict generally centered around United Nations Resolution 242 of 1967, which called for Israel to withdraw from the territories occupied in 1967 in return for acceptance by Israel's neighbors of Israel's right to live in peace within secure and recognized borders.

One of Kissinger's diplomatic aims was to keep the Soviets from expanding their influence in the area and from playing a role in negotiations. However, in the early 1990s, the United States welcomed Soviet cooperation in the Middle East, no longer fearing the Soviets as a disruptive force in the area.

Oil Power

After the 1973 Middle East war, the United States and the West were faced with a significant problem, one that underlined the international importance of this volatile region. The Arab nations decided to use their "oil weapon." Oil resources gave these nations considerable political as well as economic leverage. Because of United States support for Israel and the use of NATO bases in Western Europe as transport points, the Organization of Petroleum Exporting Countries (OPEC), dominated by the Arab nations, imposed an oil embargo on the industrialized nations.

The embargo threatened to strangle the Western and Japanese economies. (The United States and the Netherlands were the primary targets of the embargo.)

As was noted earlier in this chapter, the Middle East is the source of much of the world's oil, and that is a major reason for interest and involvement in the region by external powers. Political withdrawal from the area by the European nations did not lead to economic disengagement. Oil became an even greater prize as the industrialized nations came to depend upon it more and more. Earlier, the Europeans had relied heavily on coal for their primary energy supply.

The Soviets had failed in an attempt to secure an oil concession from Iran in 1946, but Western companies, primarily British and American, continued to hold concessions obtained earlier and to get new ones. As the governments of the nations in the region became stronger, some of them tried to change the terms of the concessions or to end them. In 1951, a nationalist government under Mohammed Mossadeq nationalized Iran's oil industry, precipitating a major dispute with the British. In 1953, the British and Americans succeeded in subverting Mossadeq's government, leading to the return to power of the Shah (Muhammad Reza Shah Pahlavi). A new agreement was negotiated between the Shah's government and the oil companies, and thereafter all of the concessions were gradually modified so as to give the nations with the oil resources larger royalties and greater control.

To gain more strength in dealing with the major international oil companies (mainly American, British, and Dutch), a group of 13 nations, including Iran plus Saudi Arabia and several other Arab nations, formed OPEC, which carried out the 1973 oil embargo.

The Soviet Union was not, at the time of the embargo, dependent upon oil from the Middle East. (Later, in 1977, a controversial American CIA report projected that the Soviets would suffer an oil shortage by the early 1980s and would become more covetous of the oil fields in the Persian Gulf region.) Portions of the former Soviet Union border with the Middle East, and some of these areas have large Islamic populations.

After the disengagement of the combatants from the 1973 war, the embargo began to fade, but the oil shock had damaged the economies of the industrialized nations, and, as will be related in the following chapter, it did serious harm to some of the non-oil-producing countries of the Third World. The embargo also succeeded in driving something of a political wedge between the industrialized nations. Some of the European countries and Japan sought to distance themselves from American support for Israel and to arrange their own agreements with oil-producing nations.

By 1974–75, a significant slowdown in the international economy caused a reduction in world oil demand. Meanwhile, the increased oil prices had resulted in greater conservation and energy efficiency in many countries. Although oil power had limited and uneven impact, the embargo demonstrated that power can be exercised in a variety of ways and by nations other than the established military and industrial powers. Later, events involving Iran, Iraq, and the Persian Gulf area would again focus world attention on oil power.

Arabs and Israel

Egypt is not a major oil producer (even though it helped organize the oil embargo), and to some extent it was dependent on financial support from its oil-rich Arab neighbors. However, when Anwar Sadat stunned the world with his trip to Jerusalem in 1977, he jeopardized Egypt's standing among Arab nations. Indeed, because of Egypt's eventual diplomatic recognition of Israel, Egypt was ostracized by almost the entire Arab world.

Before his trip to Israel, Sadat had already expelled the Soviets from his country and turned to the West for aid. Sadat believed that he could obtain more assistance from the West, and had come to regard the Soviets as unreliable and considered their technology and products to be inferior. He also thought that a period of détente in United States–Soviet relations might lead to relaxation of tensions in the Middle East as well, making it an auspicious time to make a peace move. Finally, he believed that good relations with the United States would help bring American mediation of a settlement with Israel.

The United States, under President Jimmy Carter, did mediate between Egypt and Israel. (Carter's Camp David diplomacy is described in Chapter 5.) Earlier it had appeared that the United States might accept Soviet involvement in constructing a Middle East peace. However, under strong pressure at home and from Egypt and Israel, Carter decided to leave the Soviets out of the process. While the Camp David accords and the Egyptian-Israeli treaty of 1979 were significant achievements, they did not, as had been hoped, provide the framework for a comprehensive settlement. Indeed, in some respects, problems in the region grew both broader and deeper.

The United States continued to provide large-scale aid to both Israel and Egypt, but each, in its own way, remained isolated in the region. In 1981, Sadat was assassinated in Cairo by Islamic fundamentalists, but his successor, Hosni Mubarak, maintained close relations with the United States. The Arab-Israeli dispute continued, exploding violently in Lebanon in the 1980s, as is discussed in Chapter 1, and the problem of the Palestinians grew in intensity. Although the Camp David accords envisioned progress toward Palestinian autonomy, the future of the five million Palestinians, many of whom insisted that they have their own nation, remained unresolved.

In 1964, Arab leaders had founded the Palestine Liberation Organization (PLO), an umbrella organization for Palestinian groups, claiming to be the "sole legitimate representative" of Palestinian people and aiming to see a Palestinian nation established. Israel regarded the PLO as a terrorist organization. A number of acts of terrorism were associated with the Palestinian cause, and although most of them were attributed to break-away factions and extremist groups at odds with the PLO, Israel still held the PLO and its leader, Yasser Arafat, responsible. In the late 1980s, Palestinians began what was known as the *intifada*, an uprising directed against the Israeli occupation of the West Bank and Gaza Strip, which further heightened tensions in the area.

The Iranian Clash

As noted earlier, the Arab-Israeli conflict was only part of the turbulence in the region and of the reason for the focus of international attention on the area. Much of the turmoil has revolved around the nation of Iran, which experienced a dramatic revolution in the late 1970s. The government of the Shah was replaced by an Islamic Republic initially led by Ayatollah Ruhollah Khomeini, who had been in exile from 1964 until he made a triumphant return in 1979. As was discussed in Chapter 5, one of the reasons that the Shah had forced Khomeini into exile in 1964 was because of Khomeini's fiery opposition to what he considered to be capitulation by the Shah's government in agreeing to immunity and extraterritoriality for American military and civilian government personnel in Iran. Khomeini saw this as a great affront to Iran's sovereignty and national dignity, removing Iranian jurisdiction over foreigners within Iran. Khomeini's position was a classic nationalist viewpoint.

Khomeini was strongly critical of the Shah and his government for policies and actions that he believed were inconsistent with Islamic religious principles and were corrupting traditional values and culture. In particular, Khomeini and his followers were critical of the Shah's close relations with the United States, resulting, in their view, in too much American influence in Iran. Part of what was involved in Iran was, as described in Chapter 1, a fundamental conflict in contemporary international relations: traditionalism vs. modernization.

Cyrus Vance, who was the American secretary of state at the time of the fall of the Shah in 1979, said that it was "a textbook example of a clash between Western modernization and traditional religious, economic, and social structures."[2]

The oil-rich regime of the Shah did undertake to modernize Iran, to move it more into the Western orbit. The Shah's programs were responsible for progress in areas such as literacy and land tenure. Women were allowed greater social freedom. There were some important material advances and economic growth. However, widespread poverty remained and corruption was abundant. The Shah's regime was often repressive and failed to allow broad participation in political affairs.

Nonetheless, Iran's oil and strategic location caused it to be considered of special importance by a succession of American administrations. For example, there were American intelligence installations ("listening posts") in Iran. Using sophisticated electronic equipment, the United States monitored Soviet missile and space activities. Iran began to figure increasingly prominently in American foreign policy. In the early 1970s, the Nixon administration "opened the store" to the Shah, giving the Iranian ruler *carte blanche* to purchase almost any non-nuclear weapons in the American inventory. With all of Iran's oil revenues, the Shah went on a buying spree, acquiring some of the most advanced American military equipment, including the highly sophisticated F-14 and F-15 aircraft. Just in the period from 1972 through 1978, Iran purchased more than $18 billion in military hardware from the United States.[3] Although Iran was relatively well off, particularly with the increase in oil prices, it was spending a substantial portion—an estimated 40 percent of the national budget—for military and security purposes.

The justification for the Nixon administration's special treatment of Iran was the "Nixon Doctrine." This policy was a reaction to the American experience in Vietnam. Rather than direct involvement by American forces in areas where American interests might be threatened, the United States would rely on the nation or nations which were in a threatened region and would provide them appropriate military and economic assistance. In effect, under this concept, the United States would depend on "surrogate" nations to protect American interests in key regions. Iran was to be the trusted local power in the Persian Gulf.

When Jimmy Carter became president, despite his emphasis on human rights, his administration continued to place a high premium on relations with Iran. Arms sales proceeded apace, and, although there was some criticism of the Shah's human rights policies, Carter remained committed to the "special relationship" between the two countries. On a visit to Iran on New Year's Eve 1977, Carter made a statement that would later haunt him: "Iran under the great leadership of the Shah is an island of stability in one of the more troubled areas of the world."

Within a short time, Iran was to become one of the most troubled spots in this troubled region. Carter's visit was interpreted by the Pahlavi regime to mean that it could continue to pursue its course. The Shah's opponents interpreted it as a signal that the United States was inconsistent in its commitment to human rights and unconcerned about the narrowly based, corrupt government in Iran. Shortly after Carter's visit, the protests and demonstrations, which culminated in the Shah's downfall a year later, began. Instead of recognizing the growing opposition to the Shah and the serious problems within Iran, the United States continued its ardent pro-Pahlavi policy, although some criticized Carter for not being sufficiently forceful in backing the Shah and said Carter's human rights policy undermined the Shah. Some United States analysts and policymakers tended to see the troubles in Iran as Soviet-generated, reflecting a "Sovietcentric" view of the world, rather than recognizing the religious/nationalist origins of the burgeoning revolution.

The Shah's opponents took advantage of growing discontent within the country over the ostentatious lifestyle of the Shah and his coterie and resentment of the Shah's international orientation at a time when many in Iran felt that they were reaping no benefit from the nation's wealth. Ayatollah Khomeini and his Islamic revolution struck a deep chord of national pride in a country that had long felt itself exploited by foreigners. In 1872, Baron von Reuter, an Englishman, had been granted control over much of the country's natural resources, establishing a pattern that would continue for many years. Later in the nineteenth century, the British shared influence over Iranian territory with Russia. In 1907, they effectively divided Iran into zones of influence—Russians in the north, British in the southeast, with a neutral zone in between. In 1919, the secret Anglo-Persian Agreement gave Britain enormous political, military, and economic control over Iran. During World War II, the British helped put the Shah on the throne. In 1951, the forces of nationalism and anti-colonialism, which were beginning to be felt in many parts of the world, made their mark in Iran. Mohammed Mossadeq, an opponent of the Shah, was elected prime minister and, as was discussed earlier in this chapter, proceeded to nationalize the oil industry, placing it entirely under Iranian control. In 1953, with Iran's economy in disarray because of a boycott by the international oil companies, the British and Americans, as noted previously, helped engineer Mossadeq's overthrow and the restoration of the Shah to power. The United States was motivated not only by the desire for direct access to Iranian oil but also by the preoccupation with communism and the fear that Iran under Mossadeq was ripe for a communist takeover. James Bill, a leading specialist on Iran, wrote that the American intervention of 1953 "left a running wound that bled for 25 years and contaminated America's relations with the Islamic Republic of Iran following the revolution of 1978–79."[4]

The Shah's *megalomania* (delusions of grandeur and an exaggerated belief in his own power and omnipotence) was replaced by the *xenophobia* (fear or distrust of foreigners) of the religious autocracy. Xenophobia may be seen as a kind of extreme nationalism, particularly observable among peoples who see themselves as having suffered from exploitation by others.

Iran, like many other nations that experienced direct or indirect colonialism and external domination, harbored powerful resentment. As was discussed in Chapter 4, such national experiences often have significant influence on a nation's foreign policy. Dramatic evidence of the anti-American feelings stirred up by the Islamic Revolution was provided by the 1979 takeover of the American Embassy in Tehran by Iranian militants, holding members of the embassy staff hostage for 444 days. The embassy takeover was said to be in response to an American decision to allow the Shah (who had gone first to Egypt and Morocco after fleeing Iran in January 1979) to enter the United States for medical treatment. The Shah was, in fact, seriously ill, but the revolutionaries in Iran saw his presence in the United States as a threatening and defiant gesture by the Americans. (The Shah later spent time in Panama before returning to Egypt, where he died in July 1980.)

The "hostage crisis," as it came to be known in the United States, was a humiliating experience for Americans, another lesson in the limits of power. The United States government attempted by a variety of diplomatic means to gain release of the hostages, and even launched an ill-fated military rescue attempt that never reached Tehran. The hostage crisis frustrated Americans and greatly influenced the United States political atmosphere, contributing to the defeat of Jimmy Carter by Ronald Reagan.

The Iran-Iraq and Gulf Wars

Iran considered itself to be at war with the United States, which it referred to as the "great Satan." While Iran did not actually fight the United States on the battlefield, it did engage in a long and costly war against Iraq. Both sides acquired and used large quantities of sophisticated weapons in the Iran-Iraq War, as is discussed in the following chapter.

Iraq attacked Iran in September 1980, hoping for a quick victory, intending to assert its power in the region and to claim sovereignty over the Shatt al Arab waterway, rather than accepting the old boundary which had divided the waterway between the two nations. Iraq also objected to what it saw as efforts by Iran's Shiite Muslims to extend their revolution into Iraq. However, Iraq's expectation that the new Iranian regime and Iran's military would be disorganized proved to be incorrect. Although Iraq did gain an early advantage, the war soon became stalemated. It was marked by large-scale infantry battles, reminiscent of World War I. At times, Iran utilized "human wave" attacks, which were of limited success and resulted in enormous Iranian losses. As was discussed in Chapter 6, Iraq began using chemical weapons, and both sides used ballistic missiles against enemy cities.

The war threatened the security of oil supplies from the Persian Gulf. Both Iran and Iraq mined and attacked neutral tankers in the Gulf. At the urging of Kuwait, also located on the Persian Gulf, the United States agreed to allow the tiny oil nation to place some of its oil tankers under United States protection by "reflagging" them. As a result, the United States sent a large naval task force into the Gulf region in 1987. Several other NATO member nations eventually joined the United States in attempting to protect Gulf shipping. Although the "tanker war" between Iran and Iraq continued, there was no major disruption of all traffic in the Gulf.

In 1988, Iran and Iraq finally accepted a United Nations–sponsored cease-fire, bringing the devastating war to an end. More than 1 million were believed to have been killed. Iran's Khomeini thought the war effort and the revolution would sustain each other, but it had become obvious that continuing the war could threaten the revolution. He died in 1989 and was buried in the "cemetery of martyrs," alongside many of those who died on behalf of the revolution.

Meanwhile, in 1990, Iraq turned on its tiny neighbor, Kuwait, and was seen as threatening other neighbors in a bid to exercise more political dominance, as well as more control over oil production and prices. After Iraq failed to comply with United Nations resolutions and withdraw from Kuwait, the United States—led coalition of nations launched a devastating attack against Iraq in 1991. Iran remained on the sidelines, as its neighbor offered little effective resistance to the six weeks of powerful air bombardment on targets in Iraq or to the liberation of Kuwait by coalition forces. Iraq did wreak considerable destruction during its invasion of Kuwait and left behind burning oilfields resulting in major financial and environmental damage.

A Regional Balance?

The Middle East remains a tinderbox, with the dangerous cross-currents of conflict and antagonism keeping tensions high. As journalist Karen Elliott House has written, "In the Mid-east there is no concept of balance of power; the only shared value is search for advantage." [5] When one side has a perceived advantage, it shows little interest in a negotiated settlement.

Terrorism has been endemic and 7 of the 20 largest military establishments in the world are concentrated in the region. As will be discussed further in Chapter 8, the nations in the area are prime customers for the world's arms merchants, creating a kind of regional balance of terror. The increasing scale and sophistication of the weapons in the area adds an ominous dimension to the complex and explosive equation.

CENTRAL AMERICA

The United States has loomed large in the affairs of the Central American region, even though at times the region has been a very minor concern for United States policymakers. The region's proximity to the United States almost inevitably draws it into the United States sphere of influence. Some would say that rather than a sphere of influence, it might be more properly called the United States domain of domination.

There is a long history of United States involvement in Central America, with frequent intervention in the region's economic and political affairs. The pervasive United States influence has caused many Central Americans to view their northern neighbors with a combination of resentment and respect. There is much about the United States culture, political system, and standard of living which they admire. But, not surprisingly, many of them resent the political and economic power exercised over their countries by the United States. This is a theme which recurs throughout this book: nations resent being dominated by others, and such resentment often stirs nationalistic fervor and revolutionary tendencies.

Periodically, there would be political turmoil in Central America, occasional outbursts of violence, revolution, or efforts for reform, and the United States, once it began to emerge as a global actor, looked unfavorably on such signs of instability in the region. As early as 1823, United States President James Monroe had declared that "the American continents . . . are henceforth not to be considered subjects for future colonization by any European powers." The Monroe Doctrine, as the policy came to be known, was intended to keep the European powers out of the Western hemisphere. (The doctrine was not an international agreement, but a unilateral declaration by the United States, asserting its power and interests.) In 1904, the Monroe Doctrine was given added meaning by President Theodore Roosevelt in what became known as the Roosevelt Corollary. Roosevelt asserted that the United States had the right to take on the role of an "international police power" in order to prevent European governments from exploiting the region's instability. This led to the period of what was referred to as "gunboat diplomacy" or "dollar diplomacy" in the region, in which it might be said that the United States exercised hegemony or hegemonic power over the Central American nations. As was noted in Chapter 5, some critics of the United States claimed that the 1989 invasion of Panama represented a return to the days of gunboat diplomacy, when the United States frequently sent troops into the region.

Franklin D. Roosevelt's "Good Neighbor Policy" marked the beginning of a period when the United States backed away from direct intervention in Central American affairs. However, the Cold War brought a revival of United States fears about external involvement and influences in Central America and instability in the region. This concern was heightened after the success of the Cuban revolution in 1959, which brought Fidel Castro to power in the island nation near Central America.

The United States became identified in the minds of many with the *status quo* in the region, being content to work with the military oligarchy that generally ruled. In 1954, the United States Central Intelligence Agency (CIA) intervened in Guatemala, supporting the overthrow of Jacobo Arbenz, the popularly elected president, by a group of exiles who invaded the country. United States officials maintained that Arbenz represented a Communist threat. He did have the support of Guatemala's relatively small Communist party, but Arbenz was a nationalist, not a Communist, and what really put him at odds with the United States was his insistence on major changes in a country where much of the population lived in extreme poverty. These changes included a land redistribution program, which would have expropriated unused land from the United States–based United Fruit Company, which had long been a major factor in Guatemalan economics and politics. United Fruit said that the compensation offered was inadequate, and there was a bitter dispute. Arbenz also prohibited the entry of foreign oil prospectors. The issues were not dissimilar from those involving Mossadeq in Iran, discussed earlier. When Arbenz was overthrown, it inaugurated a generation of political turmoil in Guatemala, including a prolonged guerrilla war. The United States provided substantial aid to Guatemala, but much of it went to build a strong military apparatus that usually dominated the country's political life.

In 1961, the United States again supported an effort to overthrow a government, this time in nearby Cuba. (See Fidel Castro Profile.) However, the Bay of Pigs invasion was unsuccessful. Fidel Castro remained in power, and Cuba became a symbol of revolution in the hemisphere and evolved into a Communist regime allied with the Soviet Union. A major United States policy aim—some would argue that it became an obsession—was to prevent "another Cuba" in the region, and Central America was a particular concern in this regard.

While much of the world tended to think of Central America as a collection of sleepy banana republics, by the late 1970s conditions in the region had become increasingly explosive. To the historic mixture of social injustice, poverty, and oligarchical political systems (in which a small elite rules, usually based on wealth, military power, or social standing), were added the problems caused by a worldwide economic recession and mounting insurgencies which drew communist support. The region's dependence on oil imports, which had zoomed in cost, and the drop in the value of the region's exports, meant that Central American economies were increasingly squeezed.

At this point, it is important to note that Central America is not an entity of identical nations but a group of nations. These nations, while similar in some respects, are quite different in others. The narrow isthmus bridging North and South America links these small nations, which share some commonalities of language, culture, and religion, but also have their distinctive histories. For example, Costa Rica, though it has had serious economic difficulties, has maintained a democratic government and has no national military force, obviously putting it in a different category than the other nations. Panama's history centers around the Canal and is discussed in Chapter 4. Guatemala has a large Indian population, and, with a total population of more than 8 million, is considerably larger than most of the others. (See Figure 7-2.)

In 1960, the Central American Common Market (CACM) was established, and it helped bolster the region's economies for a time. After two decades, however, most of the countries were losing ground economically, a condition which both contributed to and was influenced by the growing political turmoil in the area. Rapid urbanization and population growth exacerbated the region's problems.

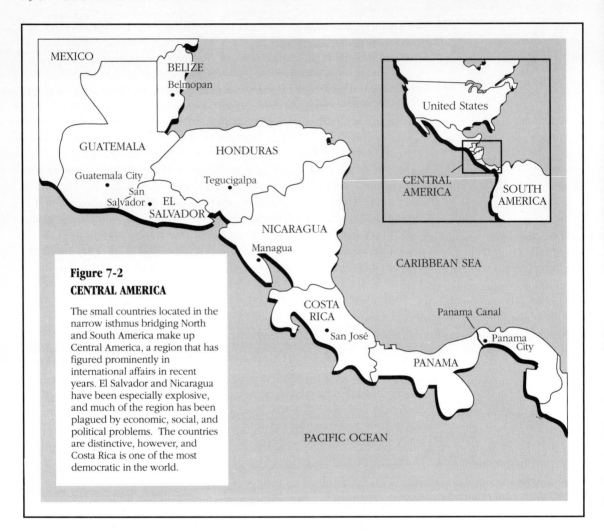

Figure 7-2
CENTRAL AMERICA

The small countries located in the narrow isthmus bridging North and South America make up Central America, a region that has figured prominently in international affairs in recent years. El Salvador and Nicaragua have been especially explosive, and much of the region has been plagued by economic, social, and political problems. The countries are distinctive, however, and Costa Rica is one of the most democratic in the world.

War and Proxy War

El Salvador and Nicaragua have been the scenes of the greatest turmoil, each torn by revolution/civil war with significant international implications.

In 1979, the 46-year-old Somoza dictatorship was brought to an end in Nicaragua. During their decades in power, the Somoza family members had acquired huge fortunes at the expense of their countrymen. Despite gross corruption and brutality, the Somoza dictatorship generally enjoyed United States support, presumably because it maintained order and stability and backed the United States policy of isolating Cuba and opposing further communist inroads in Latin America. Only in the final stages of Anastasio Somoza's rule did the United States begin to back away from the dictatorship.

At the same time that the anti-Somoza revolutionaries were taking control in Nicaragua, armed rebellion was breaking out in El Salvador, the most densely populated of the Central American countries and probably the poorest, with an estimated 80 percent of the 5-million population living in extreme poverty, even after a period of industrialization in the early 190s which generated substantial foreign investment. The nation had become increasingly polarized between Marxist guerillas and right-wing paramilitary groups known as "death squads." El Salvador's beleaguered government became a major beneficiary of American aid, but it was constantly under siege from the left or right or both, and the war further devastated the nation's economy.

Meanwhile, in Nicaragua the turmoil did not end with the downfall of Somoza. The dictator was replaced by a government that was increasingly dominated by the Sandinist National Liberation Front, or Sandinistas, who had led the offensive against the Somoza government. (The Sandinistas took their name from Augusto Cesar Sandino, a guerilla leader who fought against the government and United States Marines in the 1920s and 1930s.) Initially, the new government had considerable international support, including aid from the Carter administration in the United States. By 1981, however, several significant developments thrust Nicaragua into a prolonged war, into the center of American foreign policy, and into a controversial role in United States–Soviet relations.

Among the factors that pushed Nicaragua into the international spotlight were the following:

■ Actions by the Sandinistas to transform the nation's political and military structures along Marxist-Leninist lines

■ Formation of an opposition guerilla force that became known as the *contras*, largely composed of former Somoza National Guardsmen and dissatisfied revolutionaries, intent on overthrowing the Sandinistas

■ Evidence that the Sandinistas were aiding the rebels in nearby El Salvador

■ Determination by the Reagan administration to drive the Sandinistas from power

What developed out of this was what some referred to as a superpower "proxy war," with the *contras* representing American interests and the Sandinistas having the support of the Soviets, Cubans, and some East European nations. Throughout much of the 1980s, there was military fighting in Nicaragua between the Sandinistas and *contras*; political battling in the United States over the extent to which there should be American involvement in Nicaragua and backing of the *contras*; and diplomatic skirmishing between the United States and the Soviet Union over their respective positions on the Nicaraguan conflict.

The Reagan administration viewed the Central American conflicts as a classic East-West confrontation and laid most of the blame on Cuba and the Soviet Union. (See Reagan Profile.) In 1983, President Reagan told Congress, "The national security of all the Americas is at stake in Central America." He said, "If we cannot defend ourselves there, we cannot expect to prevail elsewhere. Our credibility would collapse, our alliances would crumble, and the safety of our homeland would be put in jeopardy."[6]

Major concerns for Reagan in Central America were the consolidation of power by the Sandinistas in Nicaragua and the growing strength of the Marxist rebels in El Salvador. A document issued by the State and Defense Departments in 1985 (titled *The Soviet-Cuban Connection in Central America and the Caribbean*) said that a major purpose of United States policy in Central America was "to provide security assistance to enable the countries to defend themselves against Soviet-bloc, Cuban, and Nicaraguan supported insurgents and terrorists intent on establishing Marxist-Leninist dictatorships."[7]

Vital Interests?

Reagan repeatedly insisted that American national interests, indeed *vital* interests, were at stake in Central America. As is discussed in earlier chapters, these can be rather elusive terms and what actually is a national interest can be the subject of internal debate. Protecting and upholding its interests, as pointed out in Chapter 4, is a primary foreign policy goal of a nation, those interests being the principles, beliefs, and economic interests of a nation, as well as its sovereignty and territorial integrity. Vital interests (see Chapter 6) are usually those considered to be of critical importance and worth a major commitment of political, economic, and military resources to uphold. Reagan's United Nations ambassador, Jeane Kirkpatrick, claimed in 1982 that Central America was "the most important place in the world for the United States," and Reagan said Central America and the Caribbean represented a "vital strategic and commercial artery for the United States." Reagan said, "Make no mistake: The well-being and security of our neighbors in this region are in our own vital interest."[8] Although within Latin America the Central American nations were among the smallest—certainly in comparison with giants such as Brazil—their proximity to the United States, and what the Reagan administration considered to be a vital strategic location, gave them special importance.

Since the Vietnam war there had been a lack of consensus about the definition of American vital interests, and this lack of consensus was still evident in the debate over United States policy on Central America. If, on the one hand, the United States wanted to avoid "another Cuba," it also wanted to avoid "another Vietnam."

Although the Reagan administration gave great emphasis to Central America and what it saw as a critical effort to combat communism in the hemisphere, the American Congress and public were less enthusiastic about this crusade, and there was a constant struggle over funding to carry out the Reagan policies. The *contras* were unable to defeat the Sandinistas militarily, but, with United States support, they carried on a low-intensity war which kept the Nicaraguan society in turmoil and played havoc with the economy.

Change and Constancy

Meanwhile, as the fighting continued, other nations in the region became increasingly concerned about its effects and the danger of being drawn more directly into the conflict. (Honduras, situated between Nicaragua and El Salvador, had been indirectly involved in both civil wars and at the behest of the United States had allowed the *contras* to use camps in Honduras as staging areas. Honduras received substantial United States military aid.) Several attempts were made to devise regional peace plans, but the most successful was the effort led by President Oscar Arias of Costa Rica. The Arias Plan, as it became known, finally helped bring an end to the fighting in Nicaragua. Arias was awarded the 1987 Nobel Peace Prize for his efforts.

With changes that were occurring in the Soviet Union and its foreign policy under the leadership of Mikhail Gorbachev, there was reduced emphasis on Soviet support for Third-World allies, and, indeed, Moscow indicated that it planned to significantly reduce military and economic aid in Central America. The Soviets encouraged the Sandinistas to improve relations with the United States and work out a solution with the internal opposition. This, and the overall improvement in United States–Soviet relations, helped defuse the international aspects of the conflict in Nicaragua.

This diminution of the United States–Soviet rivalry had an important impact on Central America and in some other areas of the Third World. In Nicaragua, the picture brightened, at least temporarily. With the fighting stopped and Nicaragua no longer a major point of contention in United States–Soviet relations, there were significant political developments within the country. As part of the agreement that brought an end to the fighting in Nicaragua, the Sandinistas agreed to hold internationally supervised elections by early 1990. Some were surprised that the Sandinistas permitted the elections, although there was considerable international pressure for them to do so, not just from the United States but from European countries, which conditioned future aid on the holding of free and fair elections. Even more surprising to many was the outcome of the voting. The candidate of the opposition (called UNO—Unified Nicaraguan Opposition), Violeta Chamorro, was elected by a wide margin over the Sandinista candidate, President Daniel Ortega. Chamorro took over as leader of a country ravaged by war and facing serious economic problems.

Not only does Nicaragua still face major problems but much of the Central American region remains gripped by poverty and subject to political upheaval. The repressive, oligarchical governments that historically dominated most of the countries in Central America and the social and economic inequities experienced by many of the people made the region ripe for revolution. While the end of the Cold War rivalry diminished the prospects of further superpower proxy wars, the potential for polarization in the region between the elites and those with little stake in the existing order remains strong.

SOUTHERN AFRICA

Many of the issues discussed in this chapter, and many of the factors that can create conditions for or contribute to tension and conflict, have existed in Southern Africa. Colonialism, nationalism, involvement by the superpowers and other external forces, racial division, international pressure and sanctions have all been factors within Southern Africa and in relations of nations in the region with the rest of the world. The region has been a focal point for attention by the United Nations, as is discussed in Chapter 2. (See Figure 7-3, p. 202.)

Southern Africa's rich mineral resources have long made it an area of particular interest for Europeans and, for a shorter period, for the United States. In more recent decades, it also became not only the subject of great international controversy but was caught up in the rivalries and interests of the great powers.

Among those countries in Southern Africa that had been colonized, the transition to independence was often more complicated and violent than elsewhere. Then there is the special case of South Africa, an independent nation, but one with a tangled and complex history, and a nation long ruled by its white minority.

European colonization of Southern Africa began in the late fifteenth century with Portuguese merchants in search of slaves and a route to India. In 1652, the Dutch East India Company established the first white settlement in what was to become South Africa, and Britain captured the Cape of Good Hope at the end of the eighteenth century. Competition and conflict between the British and the Afrikaners (descendants of the Dutch) for land, resources, and political control eventually led to the Boer War (1899–1902). Britain was the victor, but at great cost, and the Afrikaners gained much of what they had sought, and ultimately they came to dominate South African politics and government.

South Africa was granted independence from Britain in 1934. The neighboring British colonies of Northern Rhodesia, which became Zambia, and Southern Rhodesia, which became Zimbabwe, did not become independent until much later. Zambia achieved its independence in 1964.

In Zimbabwe there was a prolonged struggle for control and the new nation did not gain its full independence until 1980. In 1965, a government headed by Ian Smith had declared itself independent from Britain, but this unilateral declaration of independence (UDI) was not recognized by Britain or by most other countries, and it was fiercely opposed by the majority black population of the country. A long period of political conflict and guerrilla warfare followed, and the minority government headed by Smith was subjected to economic sanctions by most nations. By 1979, the long civil war and world condemnation, which left the country increasingly isolated, forced the Smith government to step down. Elections were held and a government was formed which was dominated by the Zimbabwe African National Union (ZANU), one of the groups which had fought against the white minority government. ZANU and a rival group, the Zimbabwe African People's Union (ZAPU), had both received external assistance in their struggle, ZANU primarily from China and ZAPU from the Soviet Union.

Among the last territories under colonial rule were two other Southern African nations, both of which had been colonized by Portugal: Angola and Mozambique. Angola, in particular, was the scene of a long and bitter conflict, as rival liberation movements fought first to overthrow the Portuguese, and then, after gaining independence in 1975, battled for control of the nation, each side aided by outside powers.

Yet another Southern African territory which became the subject of intense international controversy was the area formerly known as South West Africa, now Namibia. As is discussed in Chapter 2, South West Africa was for many years the subject of debate and resolutions in the United Nations, where there was strong international objection to South Africa's control of the neighboring territory. Indeed, it was South Africa's policy toward Namibia, not South Africa's own apartheid policies, that first drew international attention in the early years of the United Nations after World War II.

Before World War I, South West Africa was a German colony. After the war it was assigned by the League of Nations to South Africa to be administered as a mandated territory. After World War II, South Africa did not recognize United Nations authority over the territory, and continued to occupy it. In the first of several similar rulings, the International Court of Justice held in 1950 that the area was still under an international mandate and that it was subject to United Nations supervision and control. However, South Africa remained defiant for many years. In 1966, the United Nations officially revoked the South African mandate when South Africa began to implement its policies of racial separation in Namibia. Also in 1966, the South West Africa People's Organization (SWAPO), began a war of independence.

Why did South Africa hang so tenaciously to this seemingly barren territory with a population of only 1.1 million?

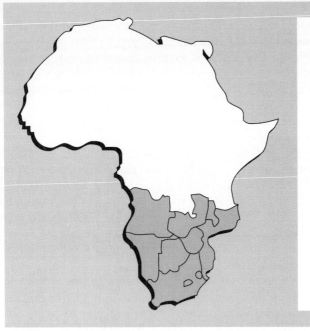

Figure 7-3
SOUTHERN AFRICA

Southern Africa has experienced considerable tension and conflict. Involvement by outside powers, including a long period of colonial rule for much of the area, and sharp racial divisions have characteried the region, which has been the subject of major international controversy. The 1914 map indicates colonial control in the area at that time. Portuguese colonialism lasted until the 1970s; in Angola a long war for political control followed. South Africa gained its independence in 1931 but its racial policies and its long domination of South West Africa (Namibia) were long condemned by other nations. Recent changes in South Africa, the region's most powerful country, have marked the beginning of a new era in an area that is rich in resources.

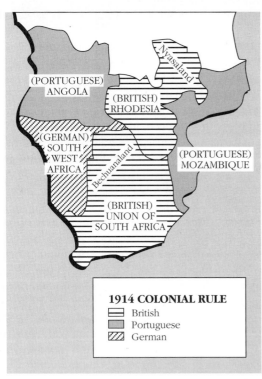

1914 COLONIAL RULE
- British
- Portuguese
- German

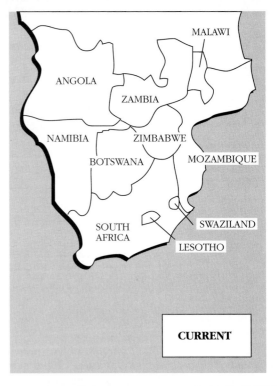

CURRENT

Although much of the country is desert, Namibia is actually rather rich in minerals—not comparable to South Africa, but there are substantial deposits of diamonds and uranium. That mineral wealth made the area attractive to South Africa, but it was really the location of Namibia that made it important to South Africa. The countries share a long border, and, particularly as other countries in the region gained their independence and became ruled by black majorities, Namibia served as a buffer between South Africa and unfriendly governments.

For years South Africa ignored United Nations resolutions calling for withdrawal of South African troops from Namibia and for actions leading to Namibian independence. The conflict over Namibia eventually became linked to other problems in the region, especially the conflict in Angola, with all of its international dimensions.

An International Battleground

Angola, as was noted earlier, experienced a long struggle for independence from Portugal, and, after independence in 1975, rival groups, backed by outside powers, continued to battle for control within the country. The liberation struggle against the Portuguese lasted 13 years, with several groups involved in leading the effort. The strongest of these nationalist groups was the Popular Movement for the Liberation of Angola (known by its Portuguese initials: MPLA), which had significant support from the Soviet Union. When a popular revolution occurred in Portugal in 1974, ending a dictatorship that had long governed that European country, it hastened the end to Portugal's colonial empire. It also marked the beginning of an intensification of the effort to win control in Angola and of increased external support for the rival groups. The Soviets were anxious to insure that the MPLA gained control, and provided massive arms shipments and other aid to that faction. Cuba, which saw itself as a champion of Third-World revolution, also became heavily involved in support of the MPLA. Cuban troops arrived in Angola in 1975 and joined in fighting against the National Union for the Total Independence of Angola (UNITA), which was contesting the MPLA for control of the country. South Africa intervened on behalf of UNITA and UNITA also drew some support from China and later from the United States, as Angola truly became an international battleground, with the outside powers contending for influence.

The joint efforts of the Soviets and Cubans (with some East German involvement as well) helped maintain MPLA in power, but UNITA applied relentless pressure. The United States Congress had rejected a request from President Gerald Ford in 1975 for funds to provide direct aid to oppose the MPLA-Soviet-Cuban alliance. Once again, Congress was strongly influenced by the Vietnam experience. However, it also is important to note that the Soviets had a long record of strong support for MPLA and public commitment to the liberation of Angola.

Indeed, the Soviets engaged in a long-term effort to encourage liberation movements in Southern Africa, and to identify communism with nationalism and antiracism, positioning themselves to exercise considerable influence in the area. On the other hand, Portugal, the colonial power, was an ally of the United States, and the United States government had done little to identify itself with the anticolonial, liberation cause in the area. (See Kissinger Profile.)

Later, during the Reagan administration, the American government did provide substantial support for the UNITA forces, led by Jonas Savimbi, fighting the MPLA. This action was consistent with what became known as the Reagan Doctrine—providing backing for anticommunist revolution or resistance. (See Reagan Profile.)

Charles Krauthammer, one of the first to refer to the Reagan Doctrine, described it as "American support for anticommunist revolution," and he said that this was "the centerpiece of a revived and revised policy of containment . . . the return of active American intervention."[9]

The war in Angola continued, bloody and inconclusive. The MPLA maintained control of the government but was unable to establish its authority throughout the entire country. The war created some anomalous situations, such as the ironic spectacle of Cuban troops guarding the facilities of American oil companies. Angola has significant oil resources, and American companies have been among those active in the country, dating back to the Portuguese era. Angola's new government made clear that it wanted to continue to do business with the West. With its oil and other resources, Angola is potentially one of the richer countries in Africa. However, both the colonial experience and the lengthy civil war after independence hindered Angola from developing that potential.

The Angola-Namibia Link

Increasingly, the situation in Angola became tied to that in neighboring Namibia. Finally, in 1988, South Africa agreed to give up control of Namibia as part of a United States-brokered accord (based on United Nations Security Council Resolution 435 of 1978) that hinged on the phased withdrawal of Cuban forces from Angola. There had been as many as 50,000 Cuban troops in Angola.

The reduction in Soviet involvement in the Third World under Gorbachev obviously contributed to the environment which helped make the agreement on Namibia and the Cuban withdrawal from Angola possible. Over the years the Soviets provided billions of dollars worth of military assistance to Angola. According to Professor Peter Vanneman, it was a case of Moscow conducting "coercive diplomacy far from its periphery." He wrote, "The magnitude of communist involvement for a decade-and-a-half constitutes an unparalleled projection of power into a distant area."[10] In this view, Soviet involvement in Southern Africa was seen as part of a larger strategy to engage the United States in "marginal areas" where the risks of significant confrontation were perceived to be relatively minimal, "thereby distracting its superpower adversary, in a cost-effective way, from devoting full attention to areas of vital interest." [11] Another analyst, Raymond Garthoff, contends that the initial Soviet role in independent Angola related to what the Soviets perceived to be evidence of collusion by China and the United States against the Soviets in the Third World. [12] Both China and the United States were supporting UNITA, and Savimbi, the UNITA leader, had been aided by China in the fight against Portugal. Moscow had seen the Chinese Communists as a threat to efforts to establish the Soviet Union as the chief patron of liberation and revolutionary movements in Africa. (Later, in another Third World conflict in Afghanistan in the 1980s, the United States and China both aided the opposition fighting against the Soviet-backed government forces. See Chapter 4.)

One of the reasons why Angola was linked to the Namibia settlement in the minds of the South Africans was because the Namibian independence movement, SWAPO (South West African People's Organization) had military bases across the border in Angola. In March 1990, with the withdrawal of Cuban forces from Angola underway, Namibia finally became an independent nation after 75 often restive years under South African rule.

The Angola/Namibia arrangements were heralded as possibly opening the way for a new age of pragmatism—"enlightened self-interest"—within regional relationships and among the international powers.

South Africa's Shadow

A long shadow has been cast over the entire Southern Africa region by the economic and military power of South Africa. International politics in the region are deeply affected by the tensions surrounding South Africa's domestic policies.

Although not happy about it, the other nations of Southern Africa are closely linked to the economy of South Africa and subject to its power. Despite South Africa's dominance of the regional economy, however, Ronald Libby has pointed out that the nations of Southern Africa are economically interdependent with, rather than simply dependent upon, South Africa. [13] In any case, South Africa is the most economically developed country in Africa, and with its great resources is potentially a major factor in the international economy. In the period following the collapse of Portuguese colonialism in 1975, South Africa had sought to remake the regional political landscape to its own advantage. "Military force and economic leverage were used by South Africa in order to obtain from its neighbors recognition of the hegemonic power in the region." [14]

Because of its racial policies, South Africa was long the target of international criticism and of actions aimed at bringing about change in those policies. Chapter 2 relates the role of the United Nations in drawing attention to the problems there. The policy of apartheid or racial separation, which was the centerpiece of comprehensive segregation in South Africa, was routinely condemned by international organizations. In 1963, the United States unilaterally embargoed arms sales to South Africa, and the United Nations Security Council imposed an international arms embargo in 1977. South Africa had responded to the embargo by building a sizable arms industry of its own and, threatened with economic sanctions, developed and expanded key industries in order to strengthen its economic self-sufficiency. Earlier chapters have pointed out that South Africa is widely believed to have developed nuclear weapons capability.

United States Policy

Although the United States had kept something of an arm's length relationship with South Africa, there were, nonetheless, substantial economic ties between the two countries. In the late 1970s, the Carter administration, with its emphasis on human rights, sought to promote change in South Africa through strong public condemnation and the threat of economic sanctions. As a presidential candidate in 1980, Ronald Reagan called this approach unrealistic and counterproductive. When it took office in 1981, the Reagan administration introduced a policy of "constructive engagement" toward South Africa. The policy was based on the belief that quiet persuasion would more effectively encourage change in South African racial policies and resolution of regional issues, such as the future of Namibia, while at the same time protecting American interests and influence. The Carter administration was criticized for being insensitive to the need to protect United States interests and America's position of power within the global system. The Carter policy was pictured as having placed African interests above American interests and consequently having failed to check the potential spread of Soviet power into Southern Africa. As one analyst described it, the basic intent of the Reagan policy in Southern Africa as elsewhere, was "to break with the accomodationist policy pursued by President Carter and return to the traditional postwar American strategy of containing the Soviet Union worldwide."[15] Within the Southern Africa context, the Carter administration was seen as accomodationist because it was said to have tried to adapt its positions to meet the concerns of the so-called Front Line States (Zambia, Tanzania, Angola, Mozambique, and Botswana), the nearby nations which wanted change in South Africa.

Reagan administration policymakers believed theirs was more of a realist approach, based on the notion that South Africa's military strength and high degree of economic self-sufficiency made it relatively invulnerable to pressure. Some saw the Reagan policy as a return to the Nixon-Ford (and Kissinger) policy, which had been more sympathetic to the South African view of regional issues, and "which had been perceived in sub-Saharan Africa as relatively friendly toward the white regime in South Africa."[16]

The "constructive engagement" policy did not appear to produce much change in South Africa; indeed, violence was growing and there was little evidence of meaningful progress toward resolving problems. Meanwhile, there was mounting opposition within the United States to South Africa's continued failure to implement significant change. Beginning in late 1984, there was a strong push in the United States for the imposition of economic sanctions against South Africa, with much of the impetus coming from American black leaders. In the Reagan view, Southern Africa was seen within the context of East-West relations, and South Africa was looked upon as an anticommunist bastion. Reagan condemned apartheid but resisted sanctions, insisting that constructive engagement was the best way to influence change. However, public pressure for sanctions increased, particularly as the South African story received heavy coverage in the United States media. American businesses were also under pressure to withdraw from South Africa. Eventually Congress overrode Reagan's objections and voted limited economic sanctions against South Africa.

SANCTIONS

Many of the world's nations were intent on applying pressure on South Africa to end its abhorrent racial practices, but most had relatively little leverage. South Africa's government had proven itself to be relatively immune to the opprobrium heaped upon it by other nations. Thus, sanctions received increasing attention as a means of attempting to compel change in South Africa.

Sanctions in international relations usually involve a collective effort of the international community to force a nation to comply with international law. Sanctions can also be unilateral, that is, applied by one nation against another. Normally, however, to be effective a collective effort is necessary. Usually sanctions are imposed only after diplomatic and legal techniques of settling disputes have failed. As has been mentioned, various efforts through the United Nations in the 1960s and 1970s had relatively little effect on South Africa.

Indeed, there was considerable basis for doubt and cynicism about the effectiveness of sanctions because of the historical record. In the 1930s, the League of Nations voted sanctions against Italy after it invaded Ethiopia, but the sanctions were not seriously applied and had limited effect. After the unilateral declaration of independence in Rhodesia (Zimbabwe) in the 1960s, a variety of national and international sanctions were imposed on what was considered by the United Nations and most of the world to be an illegal government. Although ultimately the sanctions did have some effect in bringing about change, the impact was diminished by South Africa's support for and cooperation with the Rhodesians.

It should be noted that there is a distinction, though it may not always be readily apparent, between sanctions and embargoes. An embargo, such as the Arab oil embargo referred to earlier in this chapter, is a weapon of national economic policy, intended to achieve strategic or political objectives. Sanctions have more of a legal connotation, usually resulting from a formal act by a national or international body.

The United Nations Security Council voted to apply sanctions against Iraq following its 1990 invasion of Kuwait. Some maintained that the cut-off of trade and financial dealings with Iraq was having a strong impact. After all, Iraq is a country that depends heavily on oil exports for its foreign exchange earnings, and those were being shut off; and it is also heavily dependent on the import of food and industrial goods, which were being severely limited. However, President Bush and his supporters insisted that sanctions would take too long to have the desired effect and that military action could not be put off. There was also concern that some nations would not remain steadfast participants in the economic blockade.

On a number of occasions since World War II, the United States has employed sanctions as a foreign-policy weapon. Countries as diverse as Vietnam, Libya, Iran, and North Korea, as well as Iraq and South Africa, have been among the targets. In most cases the sanctions had limited effect. When the United States halted trade with Cuba in the early 1960s, Havana simply moved closer to the Soviet Union, and the East bloc —along with Japan, Spain, and Canada—became Cuba's largest trading partners. When President Carter embargoed American grain sales to the Soviet Union after the Soviets invaded Afghanistan in 1979, the loss of American grain was quickly made up by sales from Argentina, Canada, and Australia.

Although intended to have a real effect, the enactment of sanctions by the United States Congress against South Africa can be seen as a symbolic political move. As is noted elsewhere in this book, politics, diplomacy, and international relations often revolve around symbolic acts. Sentiment in the United States against South Africa's racial policies was sufficiently strong that Congress believed that some action had to be taken, and economic sanctions were chosen as the best available means of conveying the United States opposition to South African policies.

The sanctions were part of a larger effort to isolate South Africa. Over the years not only were there campaigns to end foreign investment in South Africa but there were international campaigns for cultural and sports boycotts against South Africa. For example, South Africa was banned from the Olympic Games, beginning in 1968, and was not readmitted until the 1992 Games, after considerable internal change in South Africa. International politics often infringe on international sports competitions.

OPPOSITION AND CHANGE IN SOUTH AFRICA

Whites make up only about 14 percent of the South African population, blacks around 70 percent, and other "nonwhite" groups the remainder. Some maintained that the economic sanctions did little to hurt the South African government and that black workers in the country would be the ones who suffered most. However, leaders of the African National Congress (ANC), the oldest and largest opposition group in South Africa (and officially outlawed by the government in 1961), encouraged sanctions, as did other black leaders, such as Bishop Desmond Tutu, the Anglican Church official who won the Nobel Prize in 1984 for his campaign for social justice in South Africa. The award to Tutu helped focus international attention on his nation.

The effects of the sanctions imposed by the United States and by the European Community were debated, but they were almost certainly among the factors, along with the growing unrest in the country, that led to the beginning of significant change in South Africa by the late 1980s. When F. W. De Klerk became president in 1989, although he was a member of the National Party, which had long upheld apartheid, he initiated a series of changes which began to dismantle the apartheid system. One of the most dramatic steps taken by De Klerk was the release of Nelson Mandela from prison in 1990. Mandela had been imprisoned on charges of treason since 1962 and had become a living martyr for the opponents of apartheid. Mandela was a lawyer and a leader of the ANC. Originally an advocate of nonviolence, he and the ANC in the early 1960s turned to sabotage and an armed struggle against the intransigent white government. The ANC, founded in 1912, became increasingly radicalized, particularly after the 1960 Sharpeville massacre, when police opened fire on a peaceful demonstration, killing about 70 and wounding 180. For many years thereafter, the ANC operated underground and from outside South Africa. The ANC was one of a number of groups, some much more radical, that were banned by the government until 1990. Although the ANC has had widespread support among blacks, there have been differences and rivalries within the South African black community, some along tribal lines.

The ANC has long included some Communist elements within its ranks, and the concern about Communist influence was one of the reasons the United States government kept its distance from the organization for many years. However, the United States had for a lengthy period urged the release of Mandela, who repeatedly described himself as a nationalist, not a Communist. Not long after his release from prison,

Mandela made a triumphal tour of the United States, receiving a hero's welcome.

In many ways, South Africa remains the key to stability and development in the region. Resolution of the problems in South Africa would significantly lessen the tensions in the region. As long as there is turmoil and racial strife in South Africa, there are serious limits on prospects for peace and progress in the area.

INGREDIENTS FOR CONFLICT

The three regions which have been examined in this chapter—the Middle East–Persian Gulf, Central America, and Southern Africa—have all experienced major upheavals in recent decades, and external powers, particularly the United States and the Soviet Union, have been at least indirectly involved. Although the East-West rivalry has been a definite factor in these troubled regions, the point has already been made that an improvement in superpower relations does not necessarily portend a significant reduction of tensions in any of these areas.

Nationalism remains a potent force throughout the world, and there are additional ingredients in each of these three regions that could continue to spark violence and conflict within individual countries and broader areas—and with international implications. In the heavily armed Middle East, besides nationalism, there are religious conflicts, traditionalism versus modernization, and the presence of coveted oil resources. In Central America there are hopeful signs, but years of social injustice and deprivation have helped polarize politics, and prolonged conflict in some countries has wreaked economic havoc. In Southern Africa the colonial legacy and civil war have seriously hindered political and economic development, and the racial factor in South Africa constitutes a dangerous dimension.

Ethnic Factors and Escalation

It should be emphasized once again that conflict and the prospects for conflict are not confined to these regions, nor to Third-World countries. Northern Ireland, for example, has seen many years of violent religious and political conflict. This book's concluding chapter considers the seemingly contradictory trends of integration and disintegration that are affecting the world. While economic imperatives are pulling nations together, many ethnic and nationalist or subnationalist groups are seeking more autonomy. The end of the Cold War opened the way for some of these groups to be more assertive, as occurred in the Soviet Union and Yugoslavia. The resulting tensions have added a new dimension to global security concerns.

Within the Third World, Asia also has its share of religious, ethnic, and nationalist conflicts, which have often taken violent turns. Ethnic identity has been an important factor in contributing to political tensions in South Asia. Ethnic groups are culturally distinct groups within a nation, or they may be spread across several nations, or even more widely dispersed. Ethnic groups are usually held together by one or more of these factors: racial or cultural heritage, tribal affiliation, religion, language, kinship, or residential ties. As was noted earlier in this book, national boundaries were often drawn without giving these factors much consideration. In some cases, ethnic groups that are in a minority within a nation-state believe they are being discriminated against, and they may turn to violence or attempt to disrupt a nation's political system in order to express their grievances or seek change. Since some of these ethnic communities may extend across national borders, that can complicate relations between nations. Also, as is the case in some of the examples discussed earlier, rival ethnic groups may be situated in adjacent nations or within the same region, thus setting the stage for possible conflict.

As was pointed out in Chapter 1, throughout the colonial era Pakistan was part of British India. In 1947, Pakistan became a separate, predominantly Muslim or Islamic nation. In India, which is composed of numerous ethnic groups, Hindus are the largest religious group. A third nation, Bangladesh, was formed in 1971 when the Bengalis of East Pakistan broke away, with Indian aid, from Pakistan.

India and Pakistan have frequently been at odds. One of the sources of conflict has been the area of Kashmir, the mountainous northern India state nestled between Pakistan and China. India and Pakistan have gone to war over Kashmir and been on the brink of war on other occasions. Separatists within Kashmir have argued that the state should either be independent or attached to Pakistan. (A portion of the old principality of Kashmir is part of Pakistan.) The debate over Kashmir has many of the ingredients that are typically found in international quarrels:

1. *A border dispute.* This debate goes back to the 1947 partition of India, mentioned earlier.

2. *Ethnic and religious rivalry.* Although Kashmir is mostly Muslim, one part of the Indian state, Jammu, is mostly Hindu, and about 130,000 Buddhists live in the northeast section.

3. *Conflicting principles.* While the separatists invoke the principle of self-determination, those who want to stay within India point to the sanctity of the union, as does the government in New Delhi.

Both India and Pakistan are believed to have the capability to prduce nuclear weapons, as well as possessing large inventories of conventional weapons. Analysts in both nations have discussed scenarios in which the other might either attempt to engage in "nuclear blackmail" or feel compelled to actually use nuclear weapons in order to avoid a defeat.

OLD AND NEW SOURCES OF CONFLICT

Part of the danger in today's world is that terrorists or renegade groups could come into possession, if not of nuclear weapons, then of other highly sophisticated and lethal weapons. The problems and dangers of terrorism and weapons proliferation, including the spread of biological and chemical weapons and ballistic missiles, which risk turning regional conflicts into global catastrophes, are discussed in the next chapter.

The Cold War rivalry and tensions between the superpowers have often dominated the world's attention in recent decades. However, the real conflicts, the actual battles, have occurred, as has been pointed out, primarily in Third-World countries. The superpowers extended their rivalry into the turbulent politics of the Third World. In some cases they found themselves in a quagmire, as when the United States became bogged down in Vietnam or the Soviets in Afghanistan. In many respects, the struggle with the United States for influence in the Third World proved highly unrewarding for the Soviets. And several American presidents met their Waterloo in the Third World. As Charles William Maynes has written, "In even minor skirmishes with Third World states America has not fared well." He noted that several recent administrations "have suffered a humiliating setback at the hands of a second-class or even a third-class developing country."[17] William Pfaff has noted that a series of American presidents were "damaged or wrecked" by ill-conceived attempts to dislodge or dominate "radical nationalism" in a non-Western country.[18]

As has been indicated in this chapter, both sides in the Cold War developed a roster of "clients" in the Third World. As the United States assembled a global network of military bases and of nations to which it had security ties, it became increasingly costly to maintain. Some domestic critics of United States foreign policy said that the clients too often called the tune. The need to uphold its credibility as the protector of anticommunist regimes sometimes led the United States into acts inconsistent with its interests and identified it with some repressive and reactionary governments. Both the Soviet Union and United States diverted enormous resources away from domestic needs into the Cold War, which in some respects was damaging to their national security in the long run. The Soviets, as has been suggested, had their own problems in their relations with Third-World nations, finding it difficult to sustain influence over long periods. The Soviet problems were further complicated by the increasing evidence that its economic system was not an effective model.

The relaxation of Cold War tensions may help deemphasize ideology in international relations (although often its importance was exaggerated as a factor in Third-World conflicts) and reduce the significance of some Third-World conflicts, which were seen as part of the larger global power struggle. However, many of these conflicts are deeply ingrained, as has been indicated earlier in the chapter. With the superpower rivalry attenuated, regional conflicts can be seen to be more clearly driven by local/internal causes.

Professor John J. Mearsheimer argues that the Cold War kept nationalism at bay in Europe and that the end of the Cold War may unleash long-contained "hypernationalism," especially in Eastern Europe. He sees a paradoxical situation in which Europe may witness more conflict under a multipolar, post–Cold War system than it did during the Cold War with its bipolar power division. The prospect of conflict in Europe increases as the Cold War recedes, according to this view.[19]

Cooperation and Conflict

There is hope that the United Nations can play an increasingly effective role in helping to mediate regional disputes, in monitoring and verifying agreements, and in employing peacekeeping forces where needed. There have been signs, as was pointed out earlier, that the United Nations is more and more capable of assuming such assignments, and has performed creditably in some areas. With support from the major powers, the United Nations would be much better positioned to exercise such responsibilities.

As this chapter has indicated, potential flashpoints remain, and there are bound to be continuing conflicts and disputes, many of them based on ethnic, nationalist, racial, or religious differences and rivalries, some of which are age-old. Undoubtedly, as some nations seek to assert themselves or exercise greater power within their regions, new conflicts will occur.

However, there is strong reason to believe that economic-related matters will assume greater importance in relations among nations. Economic factors have, of course, often contributed to instability and disruption, especially in Third-World nations. Economic problems were among the compelling reasons for change in Eastern Europe in the late 1980s. Economic issues and economic relations, combined with an agenda of emerging international issues, some of which are economically based, offer prospects for both conflict and cooperation in international relations, and will be discussed in later chapters.

NOTES

1. Frantz Fanon, *The Wretched of the Earth* (New York: Grove Press, 1968), translation by Constance Farrington, pp. 311–15.
2. Cyrus Vance, *Hard Choices: Critical Years in America's Foreign Policy* (New York: Simon and Schuster, 1983), p. 346.
3. Robert C. Byrd, "The Senate and Arms Sales," *Congressional Record*, p. S16620, October 7, 1977, 95th Congress, 1st Session.
4. James A. Bill, *The Eagle and the Lion: The Tragedy of American-Iranian Relations* (New Haven: Yale University Press, 1988), p. 86.

5. Karen Elliott House, "See-Saw of Power: Peace vs. War in the Middle East," *Wall Street Journal*, July 12, 1990.

6. President Ronald Reagan, "Central America: Defending Our Vital Interests," address to Joint Session of Congress, Washington, April 27, 1983, in *Realism, Strength, Negotiation: Key Foreign Policy Statements of the Reagan Administration*, U.S. Department of State, Bureau of Public Affairs, 1984.

7. *The Soviet-Cuban Connection in Central America and the Caribbean*, U.S. Departments of State and Defense, Washington, March 1985, p. 1.

8. Reagan, address to Congress, April 27, 1983; also, Ann McDaniel, "In El Salvador, a war by proxy," *Dallas Times Herald*, February 28, 1982.

9. Charles Krauthammer, "In Defense of Interventionism," in Steven L. Spiegel (ed.), *At Issue: Politics in the World Arena*, 5th ed. (New York: St. Martin's, 1988), p. 27; Charles Waterman, "Controversial Reagan policy leaves its mark," *Christian Science Monitor*, October 17, 1988.

10. Peter Vanneman, *Soviet Strategy in Southern Africa: Gorbachev's Pragmatic Approach* (Stanford, California: Hoover Institution Press, 1990), p. 45.

11. *Ibid.*, p. 106.

12. Raymond Garthoff, *Detente and Confrontation* (Washington: Brookings, 1985), pp. 527–28.

13. Ronald T. Libby, *The Politics of Economic Power in Southern Africa* (Princeton: Princeton University Press, 1987).

14. Robert M. Price, "Creating New Political Realities: Pretoria's Drive for Regional Hegemony," in Gerald J. Bender, James S. Coleman, and Richard L. Sklar (eds.), *African Crisis Areas and U.S. Foreign Policy* (Berkeley: University of California Press, 1985), p. 87.

15. Robert M. Price, "U.S. Policy Toward Southern Africa" in Gwendolen M. Carter and Patrick O'Mera (eds.), *International Politics in Southern Africa* (Bloomington, Indiana: University of Indiana Press, 1982), p. 53; also, Richard Burt, "Reagan Aides Diagnose 'Regionalists' in U.S.–Africa Policy," *New York Times*, December 7, 1980.

16. Price in Carter and O'Mera, p. 51.

17. Charles William Maynes, "America's Third World Hang-ups," *Foreign Policy* 71, summer 1988, p. 122.

18. William Pfaff, *Barbarian Sentiments: How the American Century Ends* (New York: Hill & Wang/Noonday, 1989), p. 131.

19. John J. Mearsheimer, "Why We Will Soon Miss The Cold War," *The Atlantic*, August 1990, pp. 35–50.

FIDEL CASTRO

Early in 1959 a tall, bearded man wearing rumpled khaki fatigues triumphantly entered the city of Havana, Cuba. Fidel Castro, at age 33, had led a revolution which overthrew the corrupt dictatorship of General Fulgencio Batista. It marked the beginning of an extraordinary period in which Castro and Cuba became a focal point in United States–Soviet relations and figured in a number of major international events and controversies.

Cuba, located just 90 miles off the coast of the United States, had long been dominated by its powerful neighbor. The Cuban economy was closely tied to that of the United States.

Cuba had been a Spanish colony, but gained its "independence" after the Spanish-American War at the end of the nineteenth century. When the *U.S.S. Maine*, anchored in Havana harbor to protect United States citizens, sank in 1898, President William McKinley sent United States troops to fight alongside the Cuban rebels. The Spanish were quickly defeated, but the American troops remained in Cuba for three years. Even when Cuba proclaimed its indepen-

dence in 1902, it included in its constitution, at the United States's insistence, an amendment that gave the United States the right to intervene in Cuba when Washington deemed it necessary for the preservation of Cuban independence and the maintenance of a stable government. Over the following 20 years, the United States responded to political upheavals in Cuba with a series of military interventions.

In the 1930s, Batista emerged as the key political figure in Cuba. Although he was out of power from 1944 to 1952, he seized power once again in a bloodless coup. Castro later said that it was the 1952 coup that convinced him that change in Cuba was not possible through the political process. The young law-school graduate began his revolutionary activity against Batista on July 26, 1953, when he led an attack against the Moncada Barracks, a weapons storehouse. The attack was unsuccessful, with all the 165 youthful raiders either being killed or jailed. But the resulting publicity made Castro a national figure and gave his crusade a name— the 26th of July Movement.

In 1955, Castro was released in an amnesty

Within a few months after the success of the revolution in Cuba in 1959, Fidel Castro made his first trip as Cuban leader to the United States and the United Nations. Clad in his familiar fatigues, Castro attracted considerable attention as the world tried to size up this charismatic figure. On this visit to the United Nations, photographers turned out to record the occasion.

for political prisoners. After a brief stay in Mexico, Castro returned to Cuba to resume his revolutionary role. Based in the Sierra Maestra mountains, the rebels led by Castro launched guerrilla attacks against the Batista forces. There was also a campaign of sabotage by anti-Batista elements in Havana. As Batista's government was threatened, it became more repressive. Castro's rebels found growing support, not only among the poor people in the countryside but among the middle class in Havana. (A similar pattern contributed to successful revolutions elsewhere, including Iran and Nicaragua. A key to success for a revolutionary movement is its ability to win support of broader segments of the population.)

With Castro receiving increasing attention in the American press, much of it favorable, the United States suspended arms shipments to Batista in 1958. Later, the United States tried to get Batista to resign in favor of a caretaker government to help forestall a Castro takeover. Batista refused to step aside, but with Castro's forces nearing Havana, Batista finally fled the country in 1959. Within a few days a new government headed by Castro had taken over.

CASTRO TAKES CONTROL

The United States quickly recognized the new government, but the Eisenhower Administration was wary of Castro. Overtly, both the United States and Cuba initially acted as if they were interested in developing good relations, but, covertly, each country was pursuing plans that would bring them into conflict. At first, Castro appointed a moderate cabinet to lead the country and spoke of free elections, democratic government, and civil liberties. However, within short order, show trials and public executions were being conducted. Even some of those who had supported Castro were imprisoned. Property was expropriated from many, and large numbers of Cubans began to flee the island.

The Cuban revolution hadn't ended when Castro came to power in 1959; in a sense, it was just beginning. Once Batista had been overthrown, Castro set out to destroy the old social order in Cuba. He established a "hidden government," concealed from his "official" cabinet, to develop revolutionary planning. Author Ted Szulc, a long-time Castro-watcher, has described how in the first months Castro and a small group carried on a secret effort to consolidate power and pave the way for the establishment of a Marxist-Leninist government that would control all facets of Cuban life.

Although Castro was identified with nationalism and anti-imperialism, at some point he determined to commit Cuba to a communist course. The transition to communism in Cuba was completed rather quickly. Historians debate as to when Castro became a communist. But by late 1961, Castro said, "I am a Marxist-Leninist and will be one until the day I die."[1]

The official United States position was that it had looked upon the Castro regime with sympathy. The State Department said, "We made clear our willingness to discuss Cuba's economic needs. Despite our concern at the Cuban regime's mounting hostility toward the United States and its growing communist tendencies, we attempted patiently and consistently from early 1959 until well into 1960 to negotiate differences with the regime."[2]

However, when the American Society of Newspaper Editors had invited Castro to the United States for a speech in April 1959, President Eisenhower refused to meet with him; instead, Eisenhower went to Georgia to play golf.

The Soviets had not rushed to support or aid Castro's Cuba. It was more than a year after Castro came to power when the Soviets made their first commitment to purchase large amounts of Cuban sugar and to provide aid to Cuba. Relations between the United States and Cuba, which had already been tenuous, rapidly deteriorated and became highly polarized.

Castro's talk of exporting revolution greatly concerned American policymakers. The United States, which had been applying economic pressure, turned to a full economic embargo that was to remain in effect for years, and in January 1961 broke diplomatic relations with Cuba. For its part, Cuba was establishing stronger political, economic, and military ties with the Soviets.

ATTEMPTED OVERTHROW

Although the United States concentrated its efforts on economic and diplomatic pressure, within the government there were discussions about other ways of bringing down Castro. When John F. Kennedy became president in 1961, he was presented by the Central Intelligence Agency (CIA) with a plan that had been developed for invading Cuba. Kennedy allowed the planning to go ahead, possibly because he saw Cuba as a new Cold War battleground and a test of will. The CIA had engineered the overthrow of President Jacobo Arbenz, president of Guatemala in 1954, by training and supporting a group of Guatemalan exiles who invaded the country. Arbenz, democratically elected, had carried out a program of expropriation of unused land, legalized the Communist Party, and taken other steps that were seen by some in the United States as threatening American business and political interests in the area. In planning an overthrow of Castro, the CIA used the Guatemalan model.

In April 1961, some 1,500 Cuban exiles went ashore at the Bay of Pigs in Cuba. The CIA had underestimated Castro's preparedness, and the invaders did not get some air cover that they thought the CIA had promised. In any case, there was no popular uprising in Cuba in support of the invasion, and it was a total failure, actually strengthening Castro's hand. Indeed, as historian Hugh Thomas has pointed out, the very thing that Castro needed to consolidate control was an unsuccessful attack from without, backed, though not to the hilt, by the United States. Both the French and the Russian revolutions had been consolidated by unsuccessful invasions by exiles.

In consolidating the revolution, Castro also made extremely effective use of television, a medium not available to previous revolutionary leaders. Known for his lengthy speeches, often of several hours duration, Castro frequently utilized television to reach the masses throughout the country with his revolutionary messages. Having "defeated imperialism" at the Bay of Pigs, Castro went on television to review all the details of the triumph. Later, some of the captured invaders were paraded in front of the TV cameras. At times, Castro even talked and argued with the captives on television.

THE MISSILE CRISIS

If the Bay of Pigs invasion helped strengthen Castro's position in Cuba and further frustrated the United States, it also may have led to the tense and dramatic showdown between the United States and the Soviet Union in the 1962 Cuban missile crisis. After the Bay of Pigs, Castro was apprehensive about another invasion and said that Cuba had to be able to defend itself and repel any attacks. Castro's concerns were not unjustified. It was later revealed that the United States had sponsored a number of covert actions against Cuba, including sabotage, raids, and even assassination plots aimed at Castro. It was to deter a possible United States move against Cuba that the Soviets used as the rationale for installing missiles in Cuba. However, it is also likely that the Soviets saw an opportunity to alter the international balance of power, strengthening their overall strategic position relative to the United States. At that time, the United States still enjoyed a significant strategic advantage. Castro said that the purpose was not only to strengthen his country's defense, but "to strengthen the socialist camp on the world scale."[3]

The Cuban missile crisis (which is discussed

in Chapter 5) has been described as the point at which the world came closest to nuclear conflict. It was certainly one of the most harrowing periods in modern history. The showdown, which has been referred to as the week that shook the world, occurred in late October 1962, after an American U-2 reconnaissance flight photographed medium-range missile sites under construction in Cuba. This discovery set off somber deliberations within the United States government amidst an atmosphere of heightening tension. President Kennedy established an Executive Committee of the National Security Council to consider options. After much discussion, Kennedy decided on a naval blockade or "quarantine" of Cuba. Castro's island nation was at the center of the crisis, but matters were now largely in the hands of Kennedy and Soviet leader Nikita Krushchev. Fortunately, an actual military confrontation was averted.

Although the United States had prevented the establishment of a significant Soviet strategic presence in the hemisphere, the animosity between Cuba and the United States had only grown stronger. For a time after the missile crisis, relations between Havana and Moscow were strained. Castro resented the Soviets for having struck a deal with the United States to withdraw the missiles from Cuba and to refrain from deploying offensive weapons on the island. However, Krushchev informed Castro that Kennedy had pledged that the United States would not invade Cuba. In this sense the experience might be viewed as a victory for Castro. In any case, the breach between Castro and the Soviets didn't last. There were some indications that Kennedy sought to pursue the possibility of improved relations with Castro through secret channels, but, at the same time, the United States was organizing, through the CIA, efforts to sabotage the Cuban economy, hit-and-run raids on the Cuban coast, and repeated attempts to assassinate Castro. With improved relations with the United States apparently out of the question, Castro gradually repaired and deepened

relations with the Soviets. However, while Castro was in many ways dependent upon the Soviets, the relationship was a complex and sometimes contentious one. Castro also sought to identify himself and Cuba with the Third World and sometimes differed with Moscow's international priorities.

CASTRO AND THE THIRD WORLD

As noted earlier, Castro and some of his comrades (especially Ernesto "Che" Guevara, who was killed in Bolivia in 1967 while engaged in revolutionary activity), were involved in efforts to "export revolution." Also, Castro promoted Third-World "solidarity" in various international meetings and organizations. In 1966, he hosted the Tricontinental Conference of revolutionary leaders, and in 1979 the summit conference of the nonaligned nations. Despite Castro's close alignment with the Soviets, he managed to position himself as a leader of the Third World, serving as chairman of the Nonaligned Movement from 1979 to 1982. As Cuba's economic and political affairs became more intertwined with those of the Soviet Union, Castro was also closely tied to elements of Soviet foreign policy, particularly in Africa. It would be mistaken, however, to view the involvement of Cuban military forces in Angola and Ethiopia as simply an extension of Soviet foreign policy. Castro's African policy reflected not only Cuba's continuing role in the struggle between the superpowers but also Castro's attempt to be strongly identified with other Third-World countries, and with nationalism and anticolonialism.

Cuba's African involvement contributed to undercutting the possibilities for improved relations with the United States, which made moves in the early stages of the Carter administration to initiate a new phase in United States–Cuban relations. Cuba also began assuming a more active role in support of revolutionary movements in Central America. Castro was not prepared to forgo direct involvement in the

Castro attempted to establish Cuba as a champion of Third World revolutions, as in Angola where Cubans were also closely tied to Soviet foreign policy. Cuban forces aided an Angolan faction fighting to gain and maintain control in the southern African country. Cuban troops remained in Angola for more than 15 years before their 1991 withdrawal as part of a United Nations accord.

Third World in exchange for possible improved relations with the United States. He saw it as his duty to support revolution.

UNITED STATES FRUSTRATION

As Cuba remained the Soviets' leading Third-World ally, and Cuba remained heavily dependent upon Soviet economic assistance, the Soviets also retained a military contingent in Cuba. This became an issue in 1979 when there were reports of a new Soviet "combat brigade" in Cuba, at a time when the United States Senate was taking up the SALT II treaty between the United States and the Soviets. It turned out that there was not a new brigade, but the controversy stirred by the reports delayed Senate consideration of the arms treaty, which never was approved. Once again Cuba had become a major factor in United States–Soviet relations.

Castro remained a source of frustration for the United States, which was unable to deter Cuba from its close association with the Soviets, even though the United States used all sorts of pressure. United States support for attempts to intervene in Cuba or to overthrow Castro, or the economic pressures (such as eliminating Cuba's sugar sales to the United States), actually helped divert attention from Cuba's internal problems, and provided a rallying point for Cuban nationalism. Castro was able to use the United States as a scapegoat for Cuba's difficulties. He portrayed Cuba to his countrymen and to the world as a tiny, innocent nation threatened by its giant imperialistic neighbor.

Castro, who cultivated his romantic revolutionary image, often dressing in combat fatigues, became a hero to many in the Third World, especially in Latin America, because he had successfully defied the most powerful nation in the world. In some ways, Castro heavily influenced United States attitudes and policies toward Latin America. American presidents and policymakers were determined not to allow "another Cuba" in the hemisphere, and often attributed troubles in Latin nations to Castro's efforts and example. Thousands of Cubans who had been unhappy with Castro's government had fled the island and settled in the United States. Cuban-Americans, many of them strongly opposed to Castro, became an important factor in United States politics and helped keep Cuba as a high-profile issue.

In some respects, Castro conducted Cuba's foreign policy as if it were a major power. Castro also took up the cause of those Third-World nations, particularly in Latin America, which were burdened with massive foreign debt. He said that they should band together and collectively cancel their debts, much of which were owed to United States banks. Castro said the debts were the results of capitalist exploitation and were holding back economic and social development in the Third World. (See Chapter 10.)

Castro traveled frequently, particularly to Third-World nations. While Cuba provided military personnel and advisors in several countries, it also provided a significant number of doctors and teachers and workers on development projects. Castro, proud of Cuba's overseas contributions, said, "Our economic resources may perhaps be limited, but our human resources are unlimited."[4]

PROGRESS AND PROBLEMS

Castro took great pride in the achievements made within Cuba, where health services, education, and literacy programs received great emphasis. Sports were given a high priority by Castro and seen as important to Cuba's international prestige. In 1991, Castro was very visible at the Pan American Games hosted by Cuba and clearly relished his country's strong showing in the competition.

"In health, education, culture, and sports, we hold first place among Third World countries and rank higher than many industrialized countries," Castro proclaimed. He also boasted that on a per capita basis, there were fewer illiterates and semiliterates in Cuba than in the United States. And Castro insisted that Cuba was a more just society than the United States.[5] However, Castro had little to point to in terms of economic progress at home, with the country plagued by chronic inefficiency. Also, dissidents were not tolerated and the government held a tight rein on the mass media and free expression. The media, according to Castro, are "at the service of the revolution."[6] For example, he refused to allow information about Cuban casualties in Angola to be published.

CASTRO AND CHANGE

Fidel Castro succeeded, against very long odds, in retaining power in Cuba while consistently defying the United States. A series of American presidents—all the way back to Eisenhower—had to contend with Castro and his international activism. Cuba's location helped put Castro in a unique geopolitical position, and

he made the most of it. Castro symbolized a time of change in international affairs, a time when, although the United States remained the primary power in the world, it could not necessarily dominate all the nearby nations. Castro opened the door to Soviet involvement in the Western hemisphere.

Ironically, however, as changes swept the world in the late 1980s and many nations moved away from communism, Castro was seen as out of touch with the times and certainly out of step with the Soviet Union. He was critical of Mikhail Gorbachev's *perestroika*, considering it a corruption of pure socialism, and Cuban-Soviet relations became strained. With Soviet assistance diminished, Cuba's economic problems mounted. Although Castro had seen himself as in the vanguard of nations and of international change, many now saw Castro's Cuba as mired in an international backwater.

Nonetheless, though Castro had been closely aligned with the Soviet Union, he also symbolized the nationalistic aspirations of many Third-World peoples. By force of his personality and his revolutionary commitment, and by making Cuba a subject of dispute between the superpowers, Castro was able to become for a time a major player on the international scene.

NOTES

1. Fidel Castro, televised speech to the Cuban nation, December 2, 1961; text printed in *Revolucion* (Havana), December 2, 1961, and *Bohemia*, December 10, 1961; see "Cuba's Red Premier: Fidel Castro Ruz," *New York Times*, November 2, 1962; Tad Szulc, *Fidel: A Critical Portrait*, (New York: Avon, 1987), p. 629; Hugh Thomas, *The Cuban Revolution* (New York: Harper & Row, 1977), p. 595.

2. Edward Gonzalez, *Partners in Deadlock: The United States and Castro, 1959–1972*, report of the Southern California Arms Control and Foreign Policy Seminar, 1972; see

Castro became well-known for his lengthy and fiery speeches at large public rallies in Havana. At the July 26, 1990, celebration of the anniversary of the Cuban revolution, Castro was joined by Daniel Ortega (right), leader of the Sandinistas in Nicaragua and a frequent visitor to Cuba. Ortega was defeated in Nicaraguan elections in 1990, and Castro's international influence waned.

also Alan H. Luxenberg, "Did Eisenhower Push Castro into the Arms of the Soviets?" pp. 3–37 in Irving Louis Horowitz (ed.), *Cuban Communism* (7th ed.) (New Brunswick, New Jersey: Transaction, 1989).

3. Statement made by Fidel Castro in interview by Claude Julien, "Kennedy-Castro," *Le Monde* (Paris), March 22, 1963; see Raymond L. Garthoff, *Reflections on the Cuban Missile Crisis* (rev. ed.) (Washington: Brookings, 1989), p. 11.

4. See *Fidel Castro Speeches 1984–85: War and Crisis in the Americas* (New York: Pathfinder Press, 1985), pp. 135, 146; Diane Klein, "Tightening economic grip," *Houston Chronicle*, August 3, 1987.

5. Transcript of interview of Fidel Castro by Robert MacNeil, February 9, 1985; televised on the MacNeil/Lehrer News Hour, Public Broadcasting System, February 11–15, 1985.

6. *Ibid.*

SUGGESTIONS FOR FURTHER READING

Dinerstein, Herbert S. *The Making of a Missile Crisis: October 1962.* Baltimore: Johns Hopkins University Press, 1976.

Divine, Robert. (ed.) *The Cuban Missile Crisis.* Chicago: Quadrangle, 1971.

Dominquez, Jorge I. *To Make a World Safe for Revolution: Cuba's Foreign Policy.* Cambridge, Massachusetts: Harvard University Press, 1989.

Fidel Castro Speeches 1984–85: War and Crisis in the Americas. New York: Pathfinder Press, 1985.

Garthoff, Raymond L. *Reflections on the Cuban Missile Crisis*. (rev. ed.) Washington: Brookings, 1989.

Geyer, Georgie Anne. *Guerilla Prince: The Untold Story of Fidel Castro*. New York: Little Brown, 1991.

Horowitz, Irving Louis (ed.) *Cuban Communism* (7th ed.) New Brunswick, New Jersey: Transaction, 1989.

LeoGrande, William M. "Cuba: Going to the Source," in Richard Newfarmer (ed.), *From Gunboats to Diplomacy*. Baltimore: Johns Hopkins University Press, 1984.

Smith, Wayne. "Dateline Havana: Myopic Diplomacy," *Foreign Policy*, no. 48 (fall 1981).

Szulc, Tad. *Fidel: A Critical Portrait*. New York: Avon (paper), 1987.

Thomas, Hugh. *The Cuban Revolution*. New York: Harper & Row (paper), 1977.

CHAPTER EIGHT

Global Security Issues

The two preceding chapters have considered the role of the major military powers in the nuclear age and the causes and areas of conflicts in the international community, many of which are found in the Third World. In addition to the problems and issues discussed in those chapters, there are other significant ongoing and developing international security issues which merit major concern. These are matters that involve both the established powers and other nations, including some Third-World countries. Some of these issues were referred to within the context of regional rivalries or conflicts and international flashpoints, discussed in the previous chapter.

Among these issues are:

1. Nuclear proliferation;
2. Chemical and biological weapons;
3. The international arms trade and the diffusion of military technology;
4. Terrorism.

This chapter will examine each of these issues, all of which have important implications for the future of international security and global relations. There will also be consideration of other dangers related to the growing global militarization and of means of cooperation to guard against and limit military conflicts.

NUCLEAR PROLIFERATION

A major concern in international affairs is that nuclear weapons would come into the possession of or be developed by a number of nations around the world, greatly increasing the chances of nuclear war and adding a further ominous dimension to conflicts or potential conflicts among nations.

A network of agreements and safeguards has been established to attempt to head off nuclear proliferation. The principal elements of this network are the International Atomic Energy Agency (IAEA), affiliated with the United Nations and charged with monitoring the production and use of fissionable materials; the Treaty of the Nonproliferation of Nuclear Weapons or Nuclear Nonproliferation Treaty (NPT) of 1968, a multilateral agreement; and the Treaty of Tlatelolco of 1967, which established the Latin American nuclear-free zone. (See Figure 8-1.)

The IAEA, with more than 110 member nations, has responsibility for seeing that atomic energy is used for peaceful purposes. The agency has been effective in overseeing transfer of civilian nuclear technology to nonweapons states, but not as effective in dealing with nations suspected of developing nuclear weapons capability.

The NPT provides the general legal framework for the nonproliferation effort. It has been signed by more than 140 nations. Among the few not signing were France and China, which also refused to sign the 1963 Limited Test Ban Treaty. The test ban treaty banned nuclear weapons tests in the atmosphere, outer space, or under water, and prohibited underground explosions which caused release of radioactive debris beyond the testing nation's borders.

By 1991, under strong international pressure, both France and China said they would no longer be NPT holdouts and pledged to support the treaty, marking a significant step toward greater international arms-control cooperation. The NPT is the landmark agreement in the effort to prevent proliferation. It places responsibilities on both "nuclear weapons states" (the "haves") and "non-nuclear weapons states" (the "have-nots"). It prohibits

- the transfer by nuclear weapons states of nuclear weapons or other nuclear explosive devices "to any recipient";
- the assistance, encouragement, or inducement of any non-nuclear weapon state to manufacture or otherwise acquire nuclear weapons or devices; and
- the receipt, manufacture, or acquisition by non-nuclear states of nuclear weapons or other nuclear explosive devices.

The NPT, which created a framework for international inspection of nuclear facilities, has also provided a structure for the international

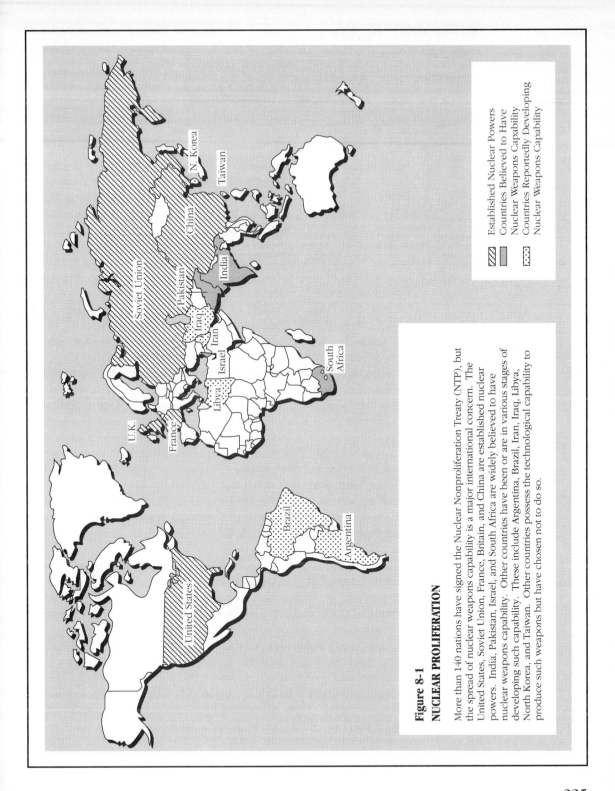

Figure 8-1
NUCLEAR PROLIFERATION

More than 140 nations have signed the Nuclear Nonproliferation Treaty (NTP), but the spread of nuclear weapons capability is a major international concern. The United States, Soviet Union, France, Britain, and China are established nuclear powers. India, Pakistan, Israel, and South Africa are widely believed to have nuclear weapons capability. Other countries have been or are in various stages of developing such capability. These include Argentina, Brazil, Iran, Iraq, Libya, North Korea, and Taiwan. Other countries possess the technological capability to produce such weapons but have chosen not to do so.

Established Nuclear Powers

Countries Believed to Have Nuclear Weapons Capability

Countries Reportedly Developing Nuclear Weapons Capability

transfer of *peaceful* nuclear technology. Concern over the spread of nuclear weapons capabilities could significantly limit international cooperation in this field if there were no reliable method to ensure that civil nuclear technology would not be diverted to military purposes. NPT adherence helps guarantee that civil nuclear technology is used for legitimate peaceful purposes.

Although the nuclear club has remained relatively small and has not grown as fast as some predicted or feared, the number of nations thought to possess nuclear weapons has gradually increased. The United States, the Soviet Union/Russia, France, Britain, and China are the established nuclear powers. Four additional countries—India, Pakistan, Israel, and South Africa—are widely believed to have nuclear weapons capability. Other countries have moved close to the nuclear threshold. Iraq's pursuit of nuclear weapons capability has been a matter of major international concern, and United Nations inspectors discovered after the 1991 Gulf War that Iraq had been relatively close to building such weapons.

The spreading of nuclear weapons to new states is referred to as "*horizontal*" proliferation, while "*vertical*" proliferation refers to the growth in the stockpiles of nuclear arms held by existing nuclear weapons states.

In a world where nations have covertly acquired nuclear capability, as Joseph S. Nye, Jr., points out, "the danger of mistakes grows." [1] Since some of the nations acquiring nuclear capabilities lack the political and technological capacity to control nuclear weaponry, the risk of leakages to terrorist groups or of unauthorized use during political turmoil increases.

Even at the height of their adversarial relationship, the Americans and the Soviets both seemed to realize that they had a common interest in curbing the spread of nuclear weapons. If nothing else, guarding against proliferation would help maintain the fragile balance the superpowers had achieved through deterrence. Those who possess nuclear weapons are always open to the charge that they want to maintain a monopoly or that they are being paternalistic. Indeed, some made this claim about the United States back in 1946 when it put forward the Baruch Plan to internationalize control of the atom, discussed earlier in this chapter. Although it was a generous offer, detractors pointed out that the United States would, at least indirectly, have maintained a monopoly on atom bomb technology.

From a common-sense viewpoint it seems apparent that it is destabilizing for more nations to acquire nuclear weapons and that the chances of war increase with proliferation. However, the argument is made by some, particularly from a field of study known as defense economics, that just as the nuclear arsenals of the Americans and Soviets had a deterrent effect on each other, in certain cases nuclear proliferation can reduce the chances of war. Obviously, this is a debatable proposition. This theory accepts that initial increases in the number of nations having nuclear weapons or large increases in the number of such nations might make the chances of war greater, especially in the latter case because of the heightened danger of accidents. However, in between these two extremes, according to this theory, for "small numbers" of nuclear weapons states, increases may, in fact, reduce the chance of war because of the potential countercoalitions effect. To back up this counterintuitive proposition, it is argued that the acquisition of nuclear weapons by France and China were valuable in making the Soviet Union more restrained, since it faced two additional nuclear powers.[2]

It is, nonetheless, hard to make a case for positive effects of nuclear proliferation, even though, as is discussed elsewhere in this book, power balances, coalitions, and alliances can be important factors influencing international relations and international security.

Nuclear Accidents

Although the nuclear powers take great precautions, the danger of accidents cannot be dismissed lightly. An accidental launching of a nuclear attack was the subject of a biting satirical film, *Dr. Strangelove or: How I Learned to Stop Worrying and Love the Bomb*, released in 1964. The film followed not long after the 1962 Cuban missile crisis, generally considered to be the closest the world has come to nuclear conflict. In *Dr. Strangelove*, a fanatic general, without presidential authorization, ordered a flight of B-52 bombers to attack the Soviet Union.

In one scene from the film, which conveys its black humor, the American president attempted to explain to his Soviet counterpart over the "hot line" what is happening:

> How are you? . . . Oh fine. Just fine. Look, Dimitri, you know how we've always talked about the possibility of something going wrong with the Bomb? . . . The Bomb? The HYDROGEN BOMB! . . . That's right. Well, I'll tell you what happened. One of our base commanders did a silly thing. He, uh, went a little funny in the head. You know, funny. He ordered our planes to attack your country . . . let me *finish* Dimitri.[3]

Both governments try to stop the attack, but as the movie ends the screen fills with mushroom-shaped clouds. Some critics of the film said that the implication that a nuclear accident *could* happen (also the subject of another film of the same year, *Fail Safe*) was not realistic.

By 1991, there was some concern about the security of Soviet nuclear weapons because of the political chaos there and as the republics that made up the Soviet Union became increasingly independent. The concern was not only about the control of those weapons as power and authority became more decentralized, but also that information and technical expertise about nuclear weapons might be disseminated to other areas.

Despite the existence of elaborate procedures within the established nuclear nations to guard against accidental or unauthorized launching or detonation of nuclear weapons or mishaps in the production, transportation, or storage of weapons, concern persists that somehow, somewhere, something might go wrong. The proliferation of nuclear weapons almost inevitably increases the chances, however remote, of such an occurrence.

Nonproliferation As a Priority

Even though the United States and the Soviet Union have both been committed to policies of nonproliferation, they have not always given it high priority. Some have argued that the United States has in certain cases undermined rather than strengthened the worldwide nonproliferation regime. Gerard C. Smith, a former United States arms control negotiator, and Helena Cobban, a scholar in international security affairs, contend that the United States "adopted a frequently permissive attitude" toward two friendly nations, Israel and Pakistan, which "allowed both states to reach or cross the threshold of nuclear weapons possession."[4] As part of the obligations of the NPT, the nuclear powers agreed to pursue arms reductions as a complement to the commitments from the non-nuclear states to forgo nuclear weapons. At NPT review conferences, many Third-World countries have criticized the lack of significant progress by the superpowers in arms control. Some analysts argue that the failure of the Americans and Soviets to restrain their own nuclear arsenals dooms efforts to stop horizontal proliferation. In fact, there are probably a variety of factors, including regional rivalries and balances of power, discussed in the previous chapters, which influence nations seeking nuclear capability. Clearly, however, the United States and the former Soviet Union can do much to set the tone and pattern in limiting the spread of nuclear weaponry.

Supporters of stronger nonproliferation efforts believe that greater political costs must be attached to proliferation, and that nations involved in transfer or development of nuclear capability should be subject to strong international sanctions. One step that might help strengthen the nonproliferation campaign is development of more regional agreements, such as the 1967 Tlatelolco Treaty, which established a nuclear weapons-free zone in Latin America. Regional agreements could encourage greater confidence among threatening neighbors.

Though proliferation is only a part of the larger problem of the existence of nuclear weapons, it is a matter of continuing concern. The spread of such weapons almost inevitably increases the chances of a conflict escalating to the nuclear level. There is always the danger of vengeful political leaders or terrorists getting access to nuclear weapons. Guarding against further proliferation will require constant vigilance. The established nuclear powers have an especially important role to play in this area.

CHEMICAL AND BIOLOGICAL WEAPONS

On April 22, 1915, a yellowish cloud appeared over the French lines on the battlefield near the Belgian town of Ypres. The deadly cloud was formed by chlorine gas, released by the German forces against the Allied troops in World War I. Later, the Allies retaliated with phosgene and chlorine gases, and in 1917 the Germans used mustard gas.

There was such an outcry over the use of these chemicals in World War I that in 1925 an international agreement, the Geneva Protocol, forbidding the first use of chemical and biological weapons, was adopted. Nations were still allowed to produce and stockpile weapons, however. (The United States did not ratify the Geneva Protocol until 1975.)

Chemical and biological warfare have long histories. In 600 B.C. the Athenians poisoned their enemy's water supply. In 1343, biological warfare was used by the Tatars, who catapulted bodies of plague victims into a besieged fortress in Genoa. Sailors from Genoa soon carried the disease all over Europe and millions died.

In the years since World War I there have been claims and counterclaims about the use of chemical and biological weapons. In some instances it is clear that such weapons were used; in other cases the evidence was murky. But, with rare exceptions, nations refrained from using chemical and biological weapons against other nations for 70 years after World War I. In the meantime, however, research continued, and chemical and biological weapons became much more sophisticated, even if rarely used.

Iraq's use of chemicals in its war against Iran in the 1980s was the most widespread use in recent times, and it focused renewed attention on this form of lethality. There was broad concern that Iraq might employ chemicals in the 1991 Gulf War, but that didn't happen.

In the 1970s there had been moves to further restrict chemical and biological weapons. The 1972 United Nations Biological Weapons Convention, prohibiting the manufacture and stockpiling of biological and toxin weapons, was signed by more than 100 nations. The United States and the Soviet Union also made progress toward agreement on destruction of existing stocks and on prohibition of manufacture of chemical weapons. However, the deteriorating political relations that derailed arms control also derailed those efforts.

In 1969, the United States had ceased manufacturing chemical offensive agents, but in 1982 announced resumption of chemical production.

In 1989, President George Bush helped put the issue of chemical weapons back on the international agenda with a speech at the United Nations in which he said it was time "to rid the earth of this scourge." He pledged that the United States would destroy 80 percent of its chemical weapons if the Soviet Union agreed to cut its chemical stockpile to the American level. Writing in 1983, defense analyst Edward Luttwak said that Soviet chemical warfare and defenses "are far more comprehensive than in any

Western army." [5] Bush promised to eliminate all American chemical arms within a decade if a treaty banning such weapons all over the world was signed. Eliminating chemical weapons is no easy matter, however, because destroying and disposing of them can be a highly expensive process which poses considerable environmental dangers.

Chemical weapons are compounds which are intended to incapacitate, kill, or seriously injure those whom they are directed against. A more advanced form of chemical weapons are the *binary* weapons, which require two chemicals to be mixed together. Separately they are supposed to be relatively harmless, but when they are combined they can produce lethal poison. Theoretically, the binary approach is safer from the standpoint of storage, since the inert chemicals are lethal only when combined.

Proliferation of chemical weapons differs from nuclear proliferation in several respects. The technology and materials involved are less expensive and more accessible than those necessary for nuclear weapons production. Chemical weapons have been referred to as the poorer nations' substitute for the atom bomb. Many more nations are believed to have chemical weapons or the probable capability to produce them than is the case with nuclear weapons. It is estimated that about 20 nations have chemical weapons or have been attempting to develop them. Libya, for example, is among those believed to be developing chemical weapons capability.

Indeed, much of the impetus for tightening of international restrictions on chemical weapons results from the spread of chemical warfare capability to Iraq, Libya, and various Third-World nations. This proliferation problem has led to the efforts to force back into its bottle this evil genie of horrific destruction.

Chemical weapons and the perhaps even more insidious biological weapons achieve their results by stealth. They are often invisible and odorless and can spread silently on the wind, lingering for days in some cases. They can be used by free-lance terrorists as well as by armies. Such weapons can kill or injure in a variety of ways, often by burning the skin or lungs or by simply putting the victim to sleep.

In 1985, the Geneva Protocol was informally supplemented by a new institution known as the "Australia Group," which involved 19 nations agreeing to impose tough export controls on chemicals that could be used in weapons manufacture. The United Nations Conference on Disarmament also has been engaged in efforts to negotiate a ban on production or stockpiling of chemical weapons.

Verification is a major stumbling block in an agreement restricting chemical weapons because of the relative ease of hiding a facility or of deception as to a facility's true purpose. There was great controversy over a facility in Libya which the Libyan government insisted was a pharmaceutical plant but which others strongly suspected of being geared up for chemical weapons production. Lacking on-site inspection, it is extremely difficult to verify the real purpose of such facilities. Even with on-site inspection there are probably much greater opportunities for deception than with nuclear weapons.

Biological weapons, as distinguished from chemical agents, are intended to cause disease in humans, plants, or animals. There are more than 30 known viruses, microorganisms, and toxins which can be used as weapons. Advanced biotechnology introduces the possibility of new types of weapons which were not necessarily envisioned in the 1972 United Nations Biological Weapons Convention. Signatories to that agreement pledged "never in any circumstances to develop, stockpile, acquire, or retain microbial or other biological agents or toxins of types and in quantities that have no justification or prophylactic, protective, or other peaceful purposes, as well as weapons, equipment, and means of delivery designed to use such agents or toxins for hostile purpose or in armed conflict."

Biological weapons have generally been of less immediate concern than chemical weapons. Even though the number of nations suspected of possessing or developing offensive biological capabilities has grown from four in 1972 to about ten, the proliferation problem has not been seen as being as serious as with chemical weapons. Biological weapons have been thought by most analysts to have less military utility than chemical weapons, although they have enormous destructive potential. Biological weapons have been considered more difficult to manage and store. Precise military use is made difficult by the danger, for example, of a change in wind directions which might render biological elements dispersed into the air as lethal to their users as to their intended victims. Problems of sustaining the living organisms in biological weapons for long periods have also limited their potential military utility. Even with these limitations, biological weapons have unquestioned capability for devastating effects, and, significantly, it is thought that new techniques may make it unnecessary to stockpile biological weapons because they can be produced in very short order.

These developments complicate the process of verification, which, again in the case of biological weapons, is a major challenge.

Considering the terrible effects that might result from chemical and biological weapons, it is encouraging that they have been used on an extremely limited basis. The agreement between the Americans and Soviets at the Bush-Gorbachev summit in 1990 was a step along the road toward banning chemical weapons. However, particularly with developments in biotechnology (including genetic engineering) and new chemical and biological agents, the danger remains that a renegade nation or demented dictator could make devastating use of such weapons or might try to hold other nations to ransom.

ARMS TRADE AND DIFFUSION OF MILITARY TECHNOLOGY

Just as the United States and the former Soviet Union, the nuclear super-powers, have dominated international security affairs with their massive arsenals, they have also played major roles, primarily through military aid and arms sales, in supplying arms to a number of nations around the globe, particularly in the Third World. Chapter 7 looked at some conflicts in the Third World and the role of the superpowers in those conflicts. Very closely related to that subject is the broader topic of international arms traffic, the role of the major powers in that arms traffic, the development of additional arms suppliers, and the impact of new military technology and weapons development on international relations.

Even though there has been some leveling off in international arms sales, worldwide military spending tended to continue to rise through most of the 1980s, and the developing countries accounted for much of the growth in military spending and in armed forces. By 1987, total yearly military spending by all countries reached $1 trillion. Although the 1990s brought some reduction in global military spending, many countries still devote significant portions of their national budgets to defense, and military spending exceeds combined expenditures for health and education in some Third-World countries. (See Figure 8-2.)

The heavy volume of arms sales to Third-World countries has traditionally been dominated by the Soviet Union and the United States. Although sales and military aid from the Americans and Soviets generally declined by the late 1980s, as did the overall volume of arms trade, several other countries were stepping up their sales or entering the market. It is certainly significant that in recent years Third-World nations purchased three-fourths of the arms that were sold internationally.

In the early 1990s, the United States jumped back to the top of the list of the world's weapons suppliers. Even with the Cold War concluded, United States sales more than doubled from 1989 to 1990, and for the first time since 1983, the United States ranked as the leading arms supplier to Third-World nations. Some of the increase was attributed to the Iraqi threat in the Persian Gulf, which accelerated arms purchases by Saudi Arabia in particular.

Discussing the role that arms trade plays in international relations, Andrew J. Pierre wrote, "Arms sales are far more than an economic occurrence, a military relationship, or an arms control challenge—arms sales are foreign policy writ large." There is little doubt that at the height of the American-Soviet rivalry, arms transfers became a critical dimension of the global policies of the major powers. Pierre refers to arms sales as "the common coin of contemporary diplomacy."[6]

While it would be misleading to suggest that the arms trade is not important to the defense industries of the United States and Russia, it is, nonetheless, fair to say that during the period of Cold War rivalry foreign policy considerations were primary factors in their arms transfers and

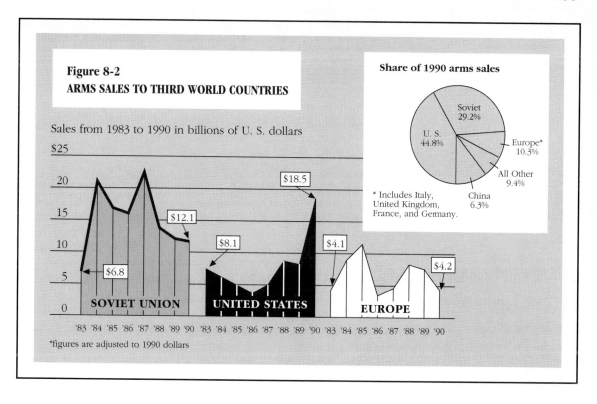

Figure 8-2
ARMS SALES TO THIRD WORLD COUNTRIES

Sales from 1983 to 1990 in billions of U. S. dollars

Share of 1990 arms sales

* Includes Italy, United Kingdom, France, and Germany.

*figures are adjusted to 1990 dollars

military assistance. While the United States and the Soviet Union tended to sell or provide weapons for political and strategic reasons, seeking to exercise international influence and power, various other suppliers have seen arms sales as more of an economic proposition. (In recent times that has also been more the case for the Soviet Union/Russia. Arms sales also became an important source of hard currency for the Russians. And, as the American defense budget declined, some United States defense contractors sought to increase their foreign sales.) France, Britain, China, Israel, India, and Brazil are among those who have been or are becoming most active in producing and/or selling arms.

Producing weapons for foreign sale, as well as for domestic needs of the producing nation, can help hold down the unit cost of a particular weapons system. In some cases, international sales are important to help sustain a production line seen as necessary for domestic security needs. China and Israel are examples of this trend. In a study on Third-World arms production, the Stockholm International Peace Research Institute (SIPRI) concluded that the primary reason for a developing country to establish its own arms industry was to free it from dependence on undependable external suppliers.

Some arms sales feature "coproduction" agreements. Under such agreements, a seller sells not only a weapons system but also provides the parts and helps build it in the buyer's country, or licenses the buyer to produce it. This enables the buying nations to obtain the know-how to service the weapons and to develop the capability to build the next generation themselves. This is how arms industries in many Third-World nations began. In some cases, after obtaining weapons from abroad, the technique of reverse engineering is used: the weapons systems are torn down, then rebuilt, and thereafter can be reproduced.

In the past, most of the arms transferred to developing nations were obsolete weapons which the major powers wanted to eliminate from their inventories to make room for newer, more advanced ones. Now, some of the developing nations are asking for the newer, more advanced weapons. The chief market for arms and military equipment has been the Middle East. South Asia has also been a growing market in recent years.

More than 40 different nations were reported to have made sales to Iran and Iraq during the war in the 1980s, with 27 nations selling to both sides. It has been called the largest arms buying spree in history, with more than $55 billion in arms delivered to the two nations between 1980 and 1987.[7] China was a leading supplier to both sides. It also sold $1 billion worth of longer-range (2,000-miles) CSS-2 missiles to Saudi Arabia. China's sales have helped finance a modernization program for its own military force.

In the Gulf War in 1991, Iraq used weapons that it had previously acquired from some of the nations allied against it. Indeed, Iraq imported $52.8 billion in arms from the five permanent members of the United Nations Security Council between 1974 and 1988. During that period, Middle East nations bought about $214 billion worth of weapons and military equipment, with more than 75 percent of it coming from the five Security Council permanent members.

Iraq's massive military buildup was, after all, only a magnified facet of an unrelenting trend which has poured billions of dollars of weapons into the Middle East. As a United States military official commented, "Iraq today is the nightmare example of what can happen in an atmosphere of virtually uncontrolled weapons and technology proliferation."[8]

Ironically, in addition to the fact that Iraq acquired many of its weapons from the nations that fought against it in the Gulf War, Saudi Arabia and Kuwait helped finance Saddam Hussein's weapons buying when Iraq was fighting Iran.

Iraq began its military buildup in the 1970s, purchasing weapons from the Soviets, who were eager to extend their influence in the Middle East. Iraq wanted to counter the United States–supplied arms buildup in Iran. When Western sympathies shifted against Iran after the 1979 Islamic revolution, Iraq began to have access to Western arms. As was pointed out previously, numerous nations made weapons available to Iraq during its war with Iran, including the United States. France proved to be an especially significant supplier. China, along with 26 other countries, was selling to both Iraq and Iran. The ceasefire in the Iraq-Iran war did not slow Saddam down; in the 18 months thereafter, he purchased another $2 billion in weapons. He played the international arms market deftly, knowing that he could keep his foes guessing by relying on a variety of suppliers. The Scud missiles fired against Israel and Saudi Arabia, for example, were bought from the Soviet Union but were upgraded with French guidance systems and German and Italian propulsion systems. The Scuds proved largely ineffective, but that was only due to the advanced United States Patriot missiles which were able to counter them. The antitank and antipersonnel mines which the Iraquis planted so widely in and around Kuwait were obtained from a number of sources, including the Soviet Union, Taiwan, and Italy.

Although the Gulf War led to calls for arms control in the region, in its aftermath there was a scramble for new weapons purchases by countries in the area, and there were a number of willing sellers, even though there was not any evidence of a new "threat." Several of the nations that were partners in the triumphant coalition looked to the United States to reward their efforts by supplying them with more advanced weapons and planes. A United States official said, "Countries in the Gulf will continue to have a legitimate need for modern means of self-defense" because "the Middle East will remain a relatively unstable area."[9] Arms sales, as has been suggested, have been a time-honored way of sealing friendships with other governments.

Although there have been a variety of proposals for limitations on arms sales, finding agreement is very difficult because so many nations have an interest in either selling or buying military hardware and technology.

The spokesperson for the United Kingdom told the United Nations General Assembly in 1990,

> It has become a truism that we are moving from a bipolar to a multipolar world. Proliferation of arms into regions of high political tensions is one of the most worrying developments of recent years. For the most part the United Nations has tended to look the other way.

Referring to Iraq's arms buildup, the United Kingdom representative said,

> The events in the Gulf demonstrate how unrealistic that has been . . . The United Nations cannot continue to pretend the problem of armaments is confined mainly to Europe and North America . . . If the United Nations is at last allowed to speak out unambiguously for restraint in the accumulation of armed power in all the regions of the world and especially in areas of tension, that in itself will give the voice of the international community a new authority.[10]

Ballistic Missiles and Technology Proliferation

Not only has the world witnessed dramatic increases in the number of nations producing arms and in the number of nations building substantial stockpiles of armaments, but also a significant increase in the sophistication and lethality of some of those weapons. A notable example is in the field of ballistic missiles. The spread of *ballistic missiles* is one of the major weapons proliferation problems facing the world today. Ballistic missiles are propelled by booster rockets, guided for part of their flight path, then pulled by gravity and wind toward their targets. When the booster burns out, the payload continues to its target as a ball does when it is thrown. The high speed and improving accuracy of the most advanced ballistic missiles and their ability to carry large and destructive warheads—including chemical or nuclear weapons—make them both dangerous and difficult to defend against. They can hit targets more than 1,000 miles away.

Concern about the proliferation of technology is not new. However, as Joseph S. Nye, Jr. points out,

> What is new . . . are the interactions between nuclear, chemical, biological, and ballistic missile technology, the increase in the number of states involved, and the new threats posed for national security. A critical question is what role the arms control process can play in coping with these new threats.[11]

It is estimated that more than 25 countries have ballistic-missile capability or have been attempting to develop it, giving them the ability to hit distant targets in a matter of minutes with any kind of weapon—conventional, chemical, or nuclear. At least nine Middle East nations have ballistic missiles. The missiles have become a kind of status symbol. According to one analyst, "The prestige of having long-range missiles is enough to motivate many governments to pursue these weapons."[12]

The war between Iran and Iraq helped call attention not only to the problem of chemical weapons but to the ominous reality of ballistic weapons as well. The proliferation of ballistic missiles led to the establishment of the international Missile Technology Control Regime (MTCR) in 1987. The MTCR is not a treaty but an export control understanding among seven nations that have the technology to produce ballistic missiles or related parts—Canada, France, West Germany, Italy, Japan, the United Kingdom, and the United States. The Soviet Union also agreed to adhere to the MTCR guidelines. In its original form the MTCR was clearly limited by its size and the fact that there is no administrative mechanism for enforcement and verification. Still, it is a significant multilateral step to begin to deal with the dangers inherent in the proliferation of ballistic missiles.

Global Militarization

Some of the Third-World countries have viewed controls—as some have seen other nonproliferation efforts—as discriminatory and an attempt to keep them powerless and dependent. Spokesmen for some of these countries have pointed out that they need to protect themselves against intervention by larger powers and against quarrels among other nations being extended into their countries.

Some in the Third World have criticized what they see as an excessive preoccupation among analysts in the industrialized world with the level of military spending in Third-World nations. However, the combined Third-World total for military spending has usually exceeded the total expenditures for health and education. Twenty-four nations, most of them in the Third World, devoted more than 10 percent of their gross national product to military expenditures in 1987. Included in this category were nations involved in war or where war or sporadic fighting was occurring, such as Vietnam, Cambodia, Laos, Afghanistan, Angola, and Nicaragua, plus others such as North Korea, Libya, Saudi Arabia, Israel, and Jordan.[13]

Of the nearly 30 million uniformed military personnel in the world, almost two-thirds of them are in developing countries. Having a strong national military may be seen as an important symbol of sovereignty. And if one nation in a particular region has a strong military force or acquires a new weapon, there will be pressure for the surrounding countries to follow suit. In some cases nations have purchased weapons systems which were too ambitious for their operational and maintenance infrastructures and for their limited number of trained personnel, although these nations resent suggestions that they have bought arms for prestige rather than for legitimate security needs.

An indication of the spread of weapons and the growth of the arms trade is seen in the increase in the number of countries importing weapons. Seventy-four countries imported weapons in 1968, while 20 years later there were 116 recipient countries. During the same period the number of supplier countries jumped from 21 to 45.[14]

It should also be noted that the "black" and "gray" arms markets have been significantly expanding as well. The black market illegally transfers military equipment through private dealers and covertly through governments. Terrorists and drug cartels are able to obtain weapons in this manner. The gray market includes equipment that is not classified in the military category but can have military application, such as police paraphernalia, vehicles, computers, electronics, and other high-tech equipment. Iraq, for example, obtained considerable equipment through back channels and in gray-market sales. Many countries also import "upgrade" kits for the older weapons in their arsenals. These purchases do not show up in the basic arms-sales statistics but are an important part of the arms trade.

The areas of conventional weapons sales and the growing problem of proliferation of weapons technology have largely been overshadowed by the issues related to superpower nuclear arms control. However, these developments are symptomatic of the diffusion of power in the world and will almost inevitably become more critical issues on the international agenda.

TERRORISM

Terrorism is an undeniably important factor in the contemporary world. By resorting to terrorist tactics, even very small groups can have a disproportionately large impact on international affairs. Reference has been made in earlier chapters to the use of terrorism and to the fact that it is often employed by those who lack traditional means of exercising power. They are, in effect, conducting a kind of psychological warfare, though the results of terrorist efforts are often horribly real. An important element in modern terrorism has been the frequent dependence on the international media to carry the messages of the groups employing terrorism and to help draw attention to their causes. (See Chapter 12.)

Terrorism is normally thought of as involving civilians or nonmilitary personnel, but in fact, the distinctions are not that clear and those engaged in terrorism may well be paramilitary forces or be connected with military or quasimilitary organizations. There is debate about exactly what constitutes terrorism, and making that determination is influenced by differing perspectives. It has been said that one person's terrorist is another's freedom fighter; it all depends upon point of view.

The term has been applied to a variety of acts which have ranged from urban guerrilla warfare to violent political protest. Most experts would agree that terrorism involves violence or the threat of violence to advance or call attention to a political or social cause. Usually terrorists are acting because of a perceived grievance. Many acts of terrorism are intended to have international consequences; for example, by aiming attacks at international travelers or representatives of foreign businesses or governments. In some cases the intent is to pressure a nation to change its foreign policy or to "punish" a nation for past policies. In other cases terrorist acts may be intended to polarize or provoke, and could be aimed at undercutting international negotiations or potential agreements.

Modern terrorism is often associated with the Middle East, and, indeed that area has been the focus of much of the terrorist activity, as was noted earlier in the chapter. However, terrorism is by no means limited to the Middle East. South America has certainly seen its share of terrorism. Germany has been plagued by terrorist acts against prominent public and business figures. Transnational groups have operated in Europe. North Korea has been involved in a number of incidents. The Philippines have been the site of a variety of terrorist activities. The list could go on.

Publicity and Drama   Nonetheless, the largest number and certainly the most publicized terrorist events have been in or been related to the Middle East and those nations adjacent to the region. As was mentioned earlier, a number of acts of terrorism have been associated with the Palestinian cause. One of the most publicized events occurred at the 1972 Olympic games in Munich, Germany, when a group of terrorists seized some Israeli athletes. The operation was carried out by members of a group called Black September, claiming to act on behalf of the Palestinians, and demanding release of some of their comrades imprisoned in Israel. The terrorists killed two of the athletes, and took nine hostage. All nine were later killed when a rescue operation miscarried. Five terrorists were killed in the action; some others who were captured were later traded for hostages taken in an airline hijacking. Although the numbers involved were relatively small, the spectacular nature of the action and the fact that worldwide television audiences were watching the Olympics assured massive publicity.

There have been a number of other spectacular events of terrorism: several major airline hijackings, including the 1985 hijacking of TWA Flight 847 to Beirut; the "shipjacking" of the *Achille Lauro*, an Italian cruise ship, carrying more than 400 passengers and crew off the coast of Egypt; bombings and suicide missions, such as the attack on the United States Marine headquarters in Beirut in 1983. In 1988, an explosive device detonated aboard a Pan Am jumbo jet bound for the United States, killing all 259 people aboard. The plane's remnants fell on the village of Lockerbie, Scotland, killing 11 more on the ground. Islamic extremists claimed responsibility for the action.

All of these events were highly publicized. Did such publicity encourage terrorists to take further action? British Prime Minister Margaret Thatcher said terrorists and hijackers are dependent on the "oxygen of publicity."[15] Few events have been more publicized than the case of "America held hostage," when the Iranian militants seized the United States Embassy in Teheran. Fifty-two of the hostages taken at the embassy were held for 444 days.

There have also been some dramatic, if not always successful, efforts to rescue hostages or otherwise thwart terrorists. Israeli commandos successfully rescued hostages held at Entebbe Airport in Uganda in 1976, and German commandos rescued passengers aboard a hijacked airliner in Somalia in 1977. In the Netherlands that same year, commandos successfully stormed a train and a school that had been held by terrorists from South Molucca. (South Molucca was seeking independence from Indonesia, a former Dutch colony.) British commandos were able to free hostages held at the Iranian embassy in London in 1980. However, there were tragic failures, such as the shoot-out at the airport in Malta when an attempt to rescue passengers on an Egyptian airliner left 60 dead. Then there was the failed American rescue mission, intended to free the hostages in Iran in 1980, which had to be aborted before it reached Tehran. The failure of that mission was seen as epitomizing the inability of the United States to use its power effectively against a smaller nation employing terrorist tactics.

The Role of States

Attention increasingly turned to what is called *state-sponsored terrorism* or *state terrorism*, referring to terrorist activity carried out by established governments. The Reagan administration gave great prominence to the problem of terrorism and particularly to state-sponsored terrorism. Libya, Syria, and Iran were accused of supporting terrorism beyond their borders, and Libya was the subject of several retaliatory attacks by the United States. State-supported terrorists were seen as "substantially more dangerous than those operating independently" because state sponsorship gave terrorists several advantages, including access to travel and identification documents, a ready source of weapons and a means to transport them, training locations, a place of refuge, and financial support.[16]

Some Western analysts ascribed most international terrorism to a "network" orchestrated from Moscow, another example of the tendency to see all international affairs through the Cold War perspective. While there is little doubt that some governments have been involved in direct and indirect support for terrorist groups and their actions, most terrorists operate in a murky, complex environment in the same way that covert intelligence agents and underground groups have traditionally operated. Some are undoubtedly linked in one way or another to governments; others clearly operate within their own shadowy structures.

Effects and Responses

Most nations have developed policies of no negotiations with or no concessions to terrorists, based on the belief that firmness is necessary and that making concessions would only encourage further terrorism. There have been various efforts at international cooperation, through the United Nations and other international organizations, to combat terrorism. Collective economic and political sanctions against offending governments may help reduce terrorism. However, the very nature of terrorism will always make it difficult to control completely. Further, individual nations have their own agendas and for a variety of reasons nations are sometimes going to go their own ways.

As a candidate and as president, Ronald Reagan was adamant: the United States must never negotiate with terrorists and hostage-takers. Yet, the Reagan administration engaged in an attempt to obtain the release of hostages held in Lebanon by trading arms to Iran, a country that the United States had branded as the leading supporter of terrorism. Not only was this a contravention of stated United States policy, but it also involved making a deal with a government (Iran) that had only a few years before been involved in the seizure of hostages at the United States Embassy. The deal with Iran, which at most resulted in the release of one hostage (while other hostages were being taken during the same period), was part of a complex series of secret transactions which became known as the Iran-Contra affair. Part of the scheme involved using profits from the sale of arms to Iran to fund operation by the *contras* in Nicaragua.

Although the United States effort to negotiate the release of hostages evolved into a fiasco, it is not unusual to see governments make concessions to try to obtain release of hostages. After all, human lives are at stake and emotions often run high. With extensive media coverage, some of these episodes become highly visible. Terrorists, of course, understand this, and that is why they utilize such tactics. Terrorism sometimes has the effect of forcing the United States and other developed nations to pay greater attention to turmoil in the Third World.

Terrorism can be seen as a kind of perverse equalizer, a way of enabling the weak to compete against the strong.

NEW CHALLENGES IN INTERNATIONAL SECURITY

Although some notable progress has been made in arms control, as discussed in Chapter 6, and the ending of the Cold War should increase prospects for more serious limitations and reductions in nuclear arms, there are daunting and growing challenges in arms control and international security affairs. Terrorism is always going to be difficult to control and many of the security issues that arose during the 40 years of East-West armed competition remain unresolved; meanwhile, there is growing global militarization, the spread of dangerous military technologies, and the militarization of space.

The specific achievements in arms control have been modest but not unimportant. At the superpower level, arms control has helped introduce an element of stability into international security relations and, because it was a focal point for official Soviet-American contact, has probably helped improve and build trust beyond the direct military agreements.

Throughout history there have been attempts to negotiate and stabilize balances of military power. The naval agreements negotiated among the great powers between the two world wars were an example of such efforts.

One of the problems in most balance-stabilization negotiations is the difficulty in finding a common basis for comparing the components of the competing forces. Not only do nations have different ingredients in their arsenals but distinctive factors such as a nation's geographical situation and alliance arrangements can dictate strategic approaches. As Seyom

Brown points out, a country with more than one important military adversary finds it difficult to settle for military equality with an adversary that does not have to worry about others, just as a nation with numerous smaller allies (to defend or rely on) has military requirements not really comparable with those of a nation with few allies. Considering that some of these basic differences between nations are always present, "arriving at the configuration of a mutually acceptable military balance of power is more of an art than a science," according to Brown.[17] These differences are sometimes referred to as *asymmetries*, a term that crops up frequently in arms control negotiations.

In a strategic sense, Henry Kissinger and others introduced the concept of "offsetting" asymmetries—the idea, for example, that the Soviet reliance on large, land-based ICBMs did not necessarily mean that Soviet forces were superior to or more dangerous than the differently constituted American strategic arsenal, which is based on the triad concept.

Achievements and Risks

Americans and Soviets found enough common ground to establish a basis for negotiation and a series of agreements. Those agreements, as noted, have provided a framework of stability in strategic arms competition. Indeed, enhanced predictability and reduced uncertainty are among the major benefits of the arms control experience. According to international security experts Albert Carnesale and Richard N. Haass, this benefit has been especially valuable to the United States because, in the absence of arms control agreements, United States knowledge of Soviet defense plans would have been far less complete than Soviet knowledge of United States defense plans.[18]

Arms control agreements do have the effect of locking in limitations or reductions and making their reversal less likely. If, as a result of international agreements, weapons are forgone or destroyed, it is obviously more costly and more difficult for governments to reverse course. Although most of the superpower agreements have been very limited in their reach, they do provide some momentum and a framework for deeper cuts. Incremental steps may represent the most realistic path to serious cutbacks; meanwhile, negotiated agreements can impose limitations and reductions in directions which will best contribute to strategic stability.

Overall, both Soviets and Americans benefited from the enhanced predictability the arms control process engendered, and without arms control the force levels on both sides would obviously be higher. The current strategic balance appears basically stable, with each side's enormous arsenal providing a potent deterrent.

It is the view of political scientist Kenneth Waltz that nuclear weapons dissuade states from going to war more surely than conventional weapons do. "Although the possibility of war remains, nuclear weapons have drastically reduced the probability of its being fought by the states that have them." [19]

Deterrence, as writer Leon Wieseltier observes, is more than a military dispensation. "It is a political dispensation, too. It permits nations that have the power to kill each other to prosecute their interests without killing each other." [20]

President Bush, commenting on the long period of peace in Europe after World War II, said, "There are few lessons so clear in history as this: Only the combination of conventional forces and nuclear forces have ensured this long peace in Europe."

However, when it comes to deterrence, the question, must be asked: how much is enough?

Indeed, as journalist Walter Pincus, a long-time observer of strategic affairs, has pointed out, the experience of the nuclear age also teaches us "about the waste of money on nuclear forces and how U.S. nuclear systems beget other nations' systems." [21]

Professor Stanley Hoffmann of Harvard University says the lessons of the nuclear age should be clear. First, neither side will allow the other to attain clear nuclear superiority—even if there is little any nation can actually "do" with such superiority—because such an achievement might lead the power that became stronger to take dangerous risks, or because of the way the other side's superiority would be perceived at home and abroad. Second, the race to prevent the adversary from achieving superiority, or from acquiring the capacity to prevail, has, according to Hoffmann, put both superpowers in serious economic difficulty and done much to precipitate their decline." [22]

And if the arms control process and deterrence have directly and indirectly contributed to a certain order and stability, there are still, as has been emphasized in this chapter, significant potential destabilizing factors.

First, of course, as was noted in Chapter 6, progress in strategic arms control is closely tied to the status of United States–Soviet/Russian relations. Europe will be a fertile field for arms reductions as long as there is the prospect for East-West accord.

At this stage, most analysts see the primary risk of major war coming not from direct aggression in Europe, for example, but from the escalation of a regional political crisis. Discussing her ominous view of what might happen under such circumstances if the adversaries have nuclear weaponry, historian Barbara Tuchman said, "Governments, like the rest of us, know that in a conflict of nuclear powers there can be no hard dividing line between conventional and nuclear warfare." In her chilling scenario, conventional warfare would slide inevitably into nuclear war "as soon as the choice for one side becomes either escalation or surrender." Once nuclear war is started, she said, it cannot be limited, "because the side that is losing will employ whatever remains in its silos." [23]

Building Cooperation and Guarding against Escalation

In addition to formalized bilateral and multilateral agreements on arms control and related matters, it is important to employ confidence-building measures and construct firebreaks in order to guard against such a spread or escalation of conflict.

Confidence-building measures (CBMs) are cooperative arrangements by which nations communicate with each other about their military activity. A number of these were introduced by the superpowers. They are meant to make arms-control agreements easier to verify and to reduce the danger of war occurring through miscalculation or misunderstanding. The Final Act of the 1975 Helsinki Conference on Security and Cooperation in Europe (CSCE) and subsequent CSCE agreements incorporate the notion that security can be strengthened by cooperative measures to build confidence in the peaceful intention of all sides. (The Helsinki Conference established the CSCE, which has 34 members, and is the most inclusive cross-Atlantic, pan-European organization. It has provisions for political, economic, and security elements.) Confidence-building measures have included such steps as giving prior notification of military movements or maneuvers. The bilateral Soviet-American dialogue on CBMs has been concerned primarily with avoiding accidents and miscalculations that might lead to war. The 1963 agreement, after the Cuban missile crisis, to establish a direct communictions link, dubbed the "hot line," was the first such measure. There have also been agreements about supplying each other with data bases and inventories of weapons covered by arms agreements.

Central to confidence-building and integral to the process of arms limitations and reductions is verification and inspection. As has been repeatedly noted, verification is a key issue in arms control and nonproliferation efforts.

Firebreak refers to the psychological barrier that inhibits escalation from one level of warfare or conflict intensity to another—especially from conventional to nuclear warfare. The term is borrowed from forest-firefighting where the technique of clearing or plowing land to stop the spread of fire is utilized. The idea is to prevent fire—or warfare—from spreading by limiting and containing it. The reluctance of responsible political leaders to cross that firebreak is a major constraint. Fundamental to the firebreak strategy is avoidance of actions that could be interpreted as expanding, not containing a war. Direct involvement by external powers or introduction of advanced weapons that might blur the distinction between conventional and nuclear war are the kinds of steps that might result in escalation.

Confidence-building measures and firebreaks are essential, although no substitute for significant arms limitations and reductions. Action on all of these fronts is necessary. New or improved structures for monitoring and dealing with international security issues will be needed, and some envision a greater role for the United Nations and for United Nations peace-keeping forces, perhaps realizing more of the role that the organization's founders originally intended.

BROADENING SECURITY ISSUES

The agenda of issues in the area of international security and arms control is getting larger and more complex. Bilateral superpower strategic issues no longer dominate the security agenda, and as the multilateral issues are increasing, a more integrated diplomatic approach is needed to deal with the range of problems, including nuclear proliferation and the spread of chemical and biological weapons and ballistic missiles, and sophisticated military technology discussed in this chapter.

As this book stresses, the concept of what constitutes national security and what bears on international security should be defined in much broader terms than in the past. By the 1970s, it was evident that international economics had become an increasingly important factor influencing security. Additional factors such as resource, demographic, and environmental issues, as well as technological development, are likely to become important components of national/international security and these topics are considered in subsequent chapters.

NOTES

1. Joseph S. Nye, Jr., "Arms Control After the Cold War," *Foreign Affairs* 68, winter 1989–90, p. 55.
2. Michael D. Intriligator, "On the Nature and Scope of Defence Economics," *Defence Economics* 1, 1990, pp. 7–8.
3. *Dr. Strangelove or: How I Learned to Stop Worrying and Love the Bomb*, Columbia Pictures, Stanley Kubrick, director; screenplay by Stanley Kubrick, Peter George, and Terry Southern, 1964.
4. Gerard C. Smith and Helena Cobban, "A Blind Eye to Nuclear Proliferation," *Foreign Affairs* 68, summer 1989, pp. 53–54.
5. Edward N. Luttwak, *The Grand Strategy of the Soviet Union* (New York: St. Martin's, 1983), p. 49.
6. Andrew J. Pierre, *The Global Politics of Arms Sales* (Princeton: Princeton University Press, 1982), pp. 3, 311.
7. *World Military Expenditures and Arms Transfers 1988*, U.S. Arms Control and Disarmament Agency, 1989, p. 21.
8. Rear Adm. Thomas A. Brooks, director of U.S. naval intelligence, quoted in David C. Morrison, "Still Open for Business," *National Journal*, April 13, 1991, p. 850.
9. Statement by Reginald Bartholomew, undersecretary of state for international security affairs, before the Committee on Foreign Affairs, U.S. House of Representatives, March 14, 1991.
10. "UK National Statement at the UNGA First Committee," *Arms Con-*

trol and Disarmament Quarterly Review, Foreign and Commonwealth Office, London, January 1991, p. 3.

11. Nye, p. 54.

12. Aaron Karp, "The Frantic Third World Quest for Ballistic Missiles," *Bulletin of the Atomic Scientists*, June 1988, p. 17. *See also* Aaron Karp, "Ballistic Missile Proliferation," in *SIPRI Yearbook 1990: World Armaments and Disarmament*, Stockholm International Peace Research Institute (New York: Oxford University Press, 1990), pp. 369–91.

13. *World Military Expenditures*, pp. 32–67.

14. "We Arm the World," *The Defense Monitor*, Center for Defense Information, vol. 20, no. 4, 1991.

15. "Thatcher Urges the Press to Help 'Starve' Terrorists," *New York Times*, July 16, 1985, p. 3; Margaret Genovese, "Terrorism and the Media," *Presstime* (Journal of the American Newspaper Publishers Association), August 1986, p. 30.

16. L. Paul Bremer III, "Terrorism and U.S. Policy," U.S. Department of State, Bureau of Public Affairs, October 15, 1987.

17. Seyom Brown, *The Causes and Prevention of War* (New York: St. Martin's, 1987), p. 188.

18. See Albert Carnesale and Richard N. Haass, "Conclusions: Weighing the Evidence," in Carnesale and Haass (eds.), *Superpower Arms Control* (Cambridge, Massachusetts: Ballinger, 1987), pp. 329–55.

19. Kenneth N. Waltz, "Nuclear Myths and Political Realities," *American Political Science Review*, vol. 84, no. 3, September 1990, p. 74.

20. Leon Wieseltier, *Nuclear War, Nuclear Peace* (New York: Holt, Rinehart and Winston, 1983), p. 80.

21. Walter Pincus, "Time to Tuck the Nukes Into the Deep Freeze," *Washington Post* (National Weekly Edition), May 21, 1990, p. 25.

22. Stanley Hoffmann, "The Perfect In-and-Outer," *New York Review of Books*, November 23, 1989, p. 17.

23. Barbara Tuchman, "The Alternatives to Arms Control," in Roman Kolkowicz and Neil Joeck (eds.), *Arms Control and International Security* (Boulder: Westview, 1984), p. 136.

CHAPTER NINE

International Economics: Structure and Power

Economic factors and forces are increasingly significant in international relations. Previous chapters have pointed to the growing importance of economic power, which is very much a part of the international power equation, just as economic problems are a major source of instability and political tension in the world.

International trade has a long history; it has always been an important part of international relations. In more modern times, international trade and industrialization have been closely tied. As Adam Smith pointed out in *The Wealth of Nations* (1776), the development of industry is dependent on the ability to trade widely. For many nations, progress is related to their ability to trade relatively freely with the rest of the world. John Stuart Mill, in *Principles of Political Economy* (1848), commented on the gains that result from "foreign commerce," and said that it enables "more efficient employment of the productive forces of the world."

In the current era, the continuing trend toward greater international interdependence both reinforces and reflects the significance of economic factors in global affairs. The gradual integration of local and national economies into the broader regional economies and into a global economy moves forward. As is discussed in Chapter 1, nations are regularly affected by economic policies and economic developments in other nations. National borders are steadily decreasing in importance in economic affairs, although nationalism can certainly be a major factor in international economics, as in other areas of international relations. Economic nationalism usually arises as a response to concerns about protecting

247

domestic interests and often takes the form of *protectionism*, which in most cases involves government regulation of the types or volume of imports which are allowed to enter a nation. The political pressure for protectionism is another example of how domestic affairs can affect international policies.

THE UNITED STATES AND THE INTERNATIONAL ECONOMIC STRUCTURE

For much of the period since World War II, security issues and concerns tended to dominate the international agenda. For much of that time the United States was not only a dominant military power but was also the foremost economic power in the world, especially in the first two decades after World War II. As has been suggested in earlier chapters, we now live in an era in which power is more widely dispersed, and it is in the economic realm that this dispersal of power and the trend toward a multipolar world are most evident.

The formal and informal international economic structure that was established after World War II has also undergone significant change in recent times. That international economic structure was to a large degree a result of the international political pattern. East and West developed fundamentally different economic systems. Eventually, however, political change, much of it economically motivated, hit what was a rather solid bloc of communist-controlled nations with their state-run economies. Many of those nations have abandoned much of their rigid, planned, highly centralized, socialist "command" economies for a market approach more compatible with and comparable to the economies of most western nations. This development further intensified the trend toward global economic integration.

The move toward greater economic integration can be seen as the outgrowth of actions taken at the end of World War II to establish a framework for international economic cooperation. In 1944, a meeting of representatives of 44 nations was held at Bretton Woods, New Hampshire, to organize a postwar international monetary system and promote world trade and economic cooperation. It should be remembered that the disintegration of the international economy and extreme economic nationalism in the years before World War II had helped set the stage for that conflict. Thus, it was deemed highly important to establish structures and mechanisms that would help avoid a recurrence of the economic disintegration and instability of the 1930s.

At Bretton Woods the World Bank (formally known as the International Bank for Reconstruction and Development) and the International Monetary Fund (IMF) were established. Both are specialized agencies of the United Nations. They were conceived as the twin pillars of the postwar economic order. These two bodies were to be funded by member-country contributions, with voting rights within the organizations allocated on the basis of the contributions. In the early years, particularly, the United States, as the largest contributor, exercised dominant influence. The Soviet Union attended the Bretton Woods conference but refused to participate in the institutions established at Bretton Woods and subsequently blocked participation by other nations of what came to be called the East bloc. To counter the Western institutions, and as an Eastern response to the Marshall Plan, the Soviets set up the Council for Mutual Economic Assistance (COMECON), which primarily served to coordinate East-bloc trade.

Another important part of the postwar economic structure was the General Agreement on Tariffs and Trade (GATT), which was created in 1947 and establishes rules for the conduct of trade among its member states. GATT subsequently became a multilateral forum for trade and tariff negotiations and its membership expanded to include more than 100 nations, eventually including Russia and other former East-bloc nations. GATT has helped facilitate the growth in international trade, which has increased 10 times over since World War II and has become a vital element in the economies of many nations.

Bretton Woods Breakdown

The system of institutions and agreements established at Bretton Woods functioned rather effectively for about 25 years, until changing conditions presented new challenges and brought an end to the old order. Under the Bretton Woods system, the price of gold had been fixed at $35 an ounce and the United States dollar was the standard for setting the value for all other currencies. During this period, as indicated earlier, the United States economy helped spur growth in other industrialized nations, particularly in western Europe, which was aided by the Marshall Plan, and in Japan. As the economies of these nations began to flourish, the dominance of the United States began to decline. For example, the United States share of the world market of manufactured goods dropped by 50 percent between 1952 and 1968. Also, by the late 1960s the United States was feeling the pinch of the "guns and butter" approach of the Johnson administration, which had attempted to fund a massive "Great Society" program of social welfare while also paying for the war in Vietnam. The United States was finding that its international role carried a high price.

Confronted with growing economic difficulties, President Richard Nixon in 1971, without consulting the other nations in the international monetary system, announced that the dollar would no longer be convertible into gold, which ended the system of fixed exchange rates. He also announced that the United States would impose a 10 percent surcharge on dutiable imports. These actions meant the end of the Bretton Woods period, although the Bretton Woods institutions, the World Bank and the

IMF, remained in place and continue to be important factors in international development and financial affairs.

The 1970s were a turbulent period in international economics, not just because of the decline in the financial supremacy of the United States. As discussed previously, the Arab oil embargo of 1973–74, which resulted in skyrocketing oil prices, had major international impact. Meanwhile, Third-World nations were clamoring for what in their view was more "equitable" treatment and for what is sometimes referred to as a New International Economic Order (NIEO), which will be discussed in Chapter 10. Some Third-World nations made significant economic progress, while others have been unable to move ahead, finding themselves trapped in poverty and falling further behind.

A New Framework?

The rough outlines of a new international economic framework have emerged. Most interpretations of these outlines detect what is basically a tripolar structure, with three major blocs dominating the world economy at a time when economic strength is taking on added significance in world affairs. The three blocs in this tripolar structure are the North American, led by the United States; European, led by Germany; and East Asian/Pacific, led by Japan. These might be referred to as the Dollar group, the Deutsch Mark group, and the Yen group.

Even though there is tripolar dominance, the world can also be seen in multipolar terms because of the variety of nations and regional groups that can have significant bearing on international relations and economic affairs. While the broad outlines of the new framework may have emerged, many questions remain and there are abundant variables. What, for example, of the one-time Communist giants, the former Soviet Union (and its republics) and China, which have attempted to reorient their economies? What about the Third World, where there are both enormous problems and promising prospects?

The general view is that international relations will look very different by the turn of the century as the result of the global transformations in economic power, and of the ascendancy of economic strength in relation to military strength as a factor in the world power structure. "The hierarchy of nations will shift considerably," economist C. Fred Bergsten has written. "The Big Three of economics will supplant the Big Two of nuclear competition as the powers that will shape much of the 21st century." [1] Some have even predicted that the twenty-first century will be marked by economic warfare. In any case, international affairs will be significantly altered by these changes.

The remainder of this chapter will examine the emerging framework and the problems and issues associated with international economic relations—trade, aid, development, investment, national economic policies, regional groups, and the role of international organizations—in a period of growing interdependency.

EVOLUTION OF THE INTERNATIONAL ECONOMY

Certainly one of the significant turning points in contemporary world affairs was when the United States helped in the economic recovery of Japan and the European nations after World War II. Japan and Germany were, of course, defeated in the war, and yet they have emerged two generations later as major economic forces in the world. Another significant post–World War II development was the decolonization of the Third World, discussed in previous chapters. The end of colonization brought a new set of economic issues to the world agenda. A third important development, discussed extensively in previous chapters, was the bipolar political system in the post–World War II era, with East and West divided into adversarial camps. These were, in many ways, hierarchical political *and* economic systems, headed by the United States and the Soviet Union. As was pointed out earlier, East and West developed separate economic systems, with the Soviet Union's Marxist-derived, socialist planned economy serving as the model for the East, and the liberal, market-oriented American approach shaping the Western economic order. In the case of the East, Moscow attempted to tie the other members of the bloc to the Soviet Union, making them economically dependent and keeping them isolated from the West.

Over the years, another set of developments occurred, helping to increasingly globalize the economy. Multinational corporations extended their reach and expanded their operations, and advances in technology, transportation, and communications facilitated and encouraged increased international commerce and connections.

As noted elsewhere, the relative decline of United States power, the growing strength of other Western nations—particularly in the economic sphere—the gradual movement toward superpower détente, and the assertiveness of some of the Third-World nations eventually resulted in significant transformation of the international economic system. Finally, the old isolation of the Eastern economies ended, as the Soviet model was increasingly rejected and nations formerly in the Soviet realm determined not to be left out of global economic relations. As a sign of the changing times, former Soviet republics sought membership in the IMF while they attempted to transform their economies.

MAJOR ECONOMIC POWERS

A variety of clusters and organizations have grown up around the economically advanced nations, one of them being the Group of Seven or G-7, which annually draws its leaders together for the economic summit. (See Chapter 5.) Within this group, the most potent forces are Japan, Germany, and the United States. At the 1990 summit in Houston, each had its own agenda and there was some disagreement on significant issues. Germany wanted to broaden economic support for Mikhail Gorbachev's Soviet Union, but Japan was opposed and the United States cautious. Japan, on the other hand, wanted to resume its large-scale loan program to China, which had been subjected to economic sanctions by most other nations following the 1989 Tiananmen Square crackdown. In the end, Germany and Japan went their own ways on these issues. Even though other nations didn't go along, they didn't stop Germany or Japan from pursuing their own interests. For many years the United States was usually in a position to get its way in such matters and to head off actions that it opposed, but no longer was the United States in a position to impose unity.

In many ways the prosperity and shared power among these nations is a tribute to the success of United States policy, which sought to build strong allies after World War II. American policymakers considered it to be in the interest of the United States to protect friendly countries against what was seen as a communist threat. Helping to rebuild and strengthen their economies would also guard against discontent, which might lead to domestic turmoil or demands for radical change in these nations.

As part of its global strategy, the United States undertook a large-scale foreign-aid program, entered into a number of security agreements, and developed a worldwide network of military installations. These were costly endeavors, but the United States viewed these expenditures as consistent with its interests. At the same time, the United States opened its markets more readily than other nations and, in some cases, accepted trade arrangements that put American exporters at a disadvantage.

However, as had already been noted, the extensive global role eventually became a burden for the United States, and, meanwhile, other nations began to grow economically stronger. The United States continued to expend massive resources for security and security-related purposes. Japan, on the other hand, having been, in effect, prohibited by the United States from becoming a military power once again, and having the protection of the American "nuclear umbrella," enjoyed the luxury of concentrating on developing its economy.

The governments of Japan and Germany have been much more directly involved in international business affairs than the United States government. The distinction between economics and foreign policy in those countries is far more blurred than it is in the United States, according to economic analyst Jeffrey E. Garten. "Partly because they are smaller nations and more dependent on the world economy, and partly because of constraints on their ability and willingness to have independent military capabilities," Japan and Germany "have learned to make economics an extension of politics by other means. It is a perspective not characteristic of America."[2]

United States Problems and Power

By the 1980s, the United States had become a chronic debtor (although not everyone agreed on how much of a problem this really was). The twin deficits in the federal budget and in the United States trade account with the rest of the world were, at a minimum, serious impediments on the ability of the United States to exercise international economic influence. The global role of the dollar is declining. As the world's largest debtor nation, the United States is heavily dependent on foreign financing to cover its deficits.

While these are serious problems and there is also concern about the United States becoming less competitive in the international marketplace, it remains by far the most powerful nation overall. There are many areas in which the United States economy excels, and the underlying strength of the economy is deep and broad. The United States still has substantial leverage in pursuing its international economic interests and a central role in determining the direction of the global economy.

However, more and more that role will be shared, or at least be subject to significant influence by others. The next section will look more closely at the two other major economic forces in the world, Japan and the European Community.

JAPAN

The rise of Japan as an economic power has been spectacular. From a nation in ruins at the end of World War II, Japan rose to the economic heights. As Japan became increasingly prosperous, it also began to be a major player in international affairs. This is all the more remarkable considering that Japan has a population about half that of the United States, living in an area smaller than California. The densely populated island nation has limited natural resources and for such needs as energy is heavily dependent on imports. Only about one-sixth of its land is arable, and even with high productivity, more than 30 percent of its food must be imported.

What came to be called the "Japanese miracle" was slow to be recognized by the rest of the world. Although a variety of factors contributed to the success story, not the least being the strong commitment of the Japanese people, it is important to note that the political and economic reforms imposed or inspired by the United States during its postwar occupation of Japan contributed significantly to Japan's rapid economic advancement and its emergence as a major force in international trade. The primary goals of the occupation were democratization and demilitarization of Japan.

Japan's 1947 constitution was largely dictated to the Japanese by the Americans who were administering the occupation. It is sometimes referred to as the "MacArthur Constitution" after United States General Douglas MacArthur who served as Supreme Commander of the Allied

Powers (SCAP) and played a key role in charting the path of postwar Japan. The constitution was part of a broad program of social, political, and economic reforms under the guidance of United States occupation authorities. The new constitution converted Japan from an absolute monarchy to a constitutional monarchy, transferring sovereign power from the emperor to the people. War and the maintenance of military forces were expressly renounced in article nine of the constitution, which came to be known as the "peace clause." It declared that "the Japanese people forever renounce war as a sovereign right of the nation" and that "land, sea, and air forces, as well as other war potential will never be maintained." (Later the clause was interpreted as permitting the maintenance of "self-defense forces.")

Although the occupation ended in 1952, the Japanese continued to reorganize and create structures and mechanisms for commerce and industry. The strategy centered, of course, around developing exports. In its early years of amassing economic strength, Japan benefitted from low labor costs and high productivity. Americans and others sometimes tended to cite factors such as low wages or government subsidies of various "unfair" practices as reasons for Japan's success. However, as Japan became more prosperous, wages climbed to levels comparable to other industrialized nations. As will be discussed later, there were legitimate and contentious issues between the United States and Japan concerning trade practices and related matters. However, Ezra Vogel, author of *Japan as No. 1*, which analyzes Japan's success, said, "Americans are peculiarly receptive to any explanation of Japan's economic performance which avoids acknowledging Japan's superior competitiveness."[3] Vogel cites such factors as Japan's continued modernization decades after rebuilding from World War II, effective organization, genius in adapting technology, patience in marketing, learning to operate effectively in other cultures, and a disciplined work force as primary reasons for the Japanese success.

In his book *The Reckoning*, author David Halberstam chronicles the rise of Japanese industry, particularly the automobile industry, at a time when many United States firms and the American auto companies were failing to adapt to changing times. In the early years after the war, Japan had a reputation for producing shoddy goods. However, as Halberstam points out, "What looked to most Westerners like a poor, ravaged, helpless society was becoming, by the early fifties, a disciplined one with a singular sense of national purpose."[4] He notes that even as the war ended, Japanese leaders were planning the nation's future, realizing that the dream of Japanese greatness through military power had proved to be false and destructive. There was recognition that a nation so limited in size and natural resources, so vulnerable to modern weaponry, could become strong only if it focused all of its energies on commerce. Halberstam relates an old Japanese legend about a man who wanted to become a great warrior, but who spent all of his money on arms and shields instead of food. More and more burdened by the weight of his armament and ever weaker, he was easily slain in combat. The point is clear: Japan must conserve its energies and derive its powers solely from its human and commercial strengths.

While Japan remained carefully focused on building its economy, the United States was engaged in a fierce arms race with the Soviet Union. As Halberstam observes, there was no small irony in this. By competing all-out in the arms race, the Americans were taking on the Soviets at what the latter did best; indeed, the defense sector was one of the very few strong points of the sluggish Soviet state economy. A result of this competition, says Halberstam, was to weaken an otherwise sound and dynamic United States economy, making the way much easier for the Japanese, who were under the United States military umbrella. "Those were Toyotas, Hondas, and Datsuns driving down the American highways, not Moskvas, and that was East Asia that America was losing jobs to, not Eastern Europe." [5]

Growth and Success = Power and Problems

Japan experienced extraordinary growth. For most of the 1950s and 1960s, the gross national product (GNP) grew at an annual rate of better than 10 percent. (GNP refers to the total value of goods and services produced by a nation's economy.) Even through the 1970s, which included the period of the "oil shocks" when rising oil prices hit the country hard, Japan continued to grow at a rate nearly double that of the United States and Western Europe. Japan also began to accumulate enormous trade surpluses as its exports far exceeded imports, and it became the world's largest creditor and the leader in many key technological fields. While the American GNP was still nearly twice that of Japan, the spectacular growth of the Japanese economy had steadily narrowed the gap.

For some years, despite its growing prosperity, Japan had relatively little international clout and held back from an active role in world politics. Although Japan had difficulty adapting to a leadership position in world affairs, it began to abandon its low profile by the 1980s and also became more openly and directly competitive with the United States, even though the two nations continued to cooperate in many ways. Trade friction between the two actually dated back to the 1960s when increased competition from Japan in steel and textiles began to be felt in the United States and cost American jobs. The United States remains Japan's number-one trading partner, absorbing more than one-third of all Japanese exports, while Japan has ranked behind only Canada among United States customers. Japan is still heavily dependent on American food, coal, and wood products.

It was the United States that originally insisted on the demilitarization of Japan and the constitutional prohibition of military forces. However, as early as the Korean war period in the early 1950s, the United States began to revise its position, supporting the creation of "self-defense" forces in Japan. (The Korean war also gave a considerable boost to the Japanese economy, as the United States placed large orders for armaments and other equipment from Japanese manufacturers.) As Japan grew economically powerful and as the United States was increasingly burdened by its security commitments, there was growing American pressure for "burden sharing" by the Japanese. Until 1987, defense spending in Japan was limited to 1 percent of GNP. (This compared to an average at the time of more than 3 percent by the NATO countries and 6-percent-plus by the United States.) Even though Japan has only modestly increased the military proportion of its budget, it has become the third-largest military spender in the world, ranking behind only the United States and the Soviet Union in total defense expenditures.

In 1991, there was a great debate in Japan about the extent to which the nation should be involved in supporting the multinational military coalition opposing Iraq. Japan did not send any support personnel to the area, but did, after much agonizing, contribute significantly to the costs of the military operation and later sent minesweepers to help clear the mines left in the Gulf area by Saddam Hussein's forces. Japan's hesitancy and what many saw as a limited contribution drew some international criticism, particularly because critics pointed to Japan's heavy reliance on Middle East oil for its energy supply. It should be noted, however, that after earlier "oil shocks," Japan has taken many steps to reduce its vulnerability, and its industries are less energy-intensive than those of most industrialized countries.

Japan, Paul Kennedy wrote in *The Rise and Fall of the Great Powers*, "has been able to enjoy all of the advantages of evolving into a global economic giant, but without any of the political responsibilities and territorial disadvantages which have, historically, followed from such a growth."[6]

The United States pressed Japan to increase not only its defense spending but to assume a greater role in providing aid to developing nations. Now Japan has surpassed the United States as the largest aid donor. In addition to its strong emphasis on Southeast Asia, Japan has provided assistance to a number of areas of particular importance to the United States, including the Middle East, Latin America, and the Caribbean. China and the Philippines have been two major beneficiaries of Japanese aid. (Foreign aid and development assistance are discussed further in the next chapter.)

Japan has also become much more heavily involved in international economic organizations such as the World Bank and in dealing with Third-World debt and other international economic problems. As noted earlier, Japan has become more assertive in economic summit meetings and other economic groupings. Still, there are those who insist that

Japan's power is essentially one-dimensional and limited because its economic might is not bolstered by either military, political, or ideological clout, elements usually considered essential for a nation to be able to exercise major international influence. Nonetheless, Japan's power is broadening.

Cooperation and Competition

Together, Japan and the United States account for almost 40 percent of the world's GNP and 25 percent of world trade, and their economies are closely tied. However, while the two nations share many interests, their interests may diverge and their economic policies come into conflict. Recognizing and acting on that has been difficult for both the nations.

Given the rapid pattern of Japan's growth and the manner in which Japanese industry and technology outstripped the United States in some key areas, tensions were inevitable. As was previously pointed out, friction in trade relations was already evident in the 1960s. By the 1980s, there was a bitter edge to the friction. American resentment over Japan's growing share of the United States marketplace, the widespread presence of Japanese consumer goods, concern about increasing Japanese investment in the United States (although Britain and the Netherlands had long been the leading foreign business owners in America), and widespread conviction that Japan engaged in "unfair" trading practices contributed to anxiety and antagonism in the relationship. There was, of course, some ambivalence in the American attitude: Americans were still driving Hondas and listening to Sony Walkmans.

Japan's government–industry alliance, (in which for some years the Ministry of Trade and Industry—MITI—played an especially important role) was a frequent target of United States critics, who sometimes referred to "Japan, Inc." Japan was accused of industrial "targeting," wherein the government allegedly selects certain high-technology sectors, protects them by imposing tariffs and other measures on potential competitors, and intensively subsidizes them for eventual export purposes. The Japanese argued that they did no more than other industrialized nations in this regard.

The United States clamored for Japan to "open its markets" and for "market access" in Japan for American products. Numerous negotiations were conducted between the two nations, but they were often unproductive, as was stated in Chapter 5. A pattern developed whereby both sides would announce that agreements had been reached which would ameliorate trade problems, but within a relatively short time there would be American complaints that nothing had really changed or that the problems had re-emerged in a different form. More than a decade of negotiations and currency realignments failed to reduce the United States trade deficit with Japan. Cultural differences and misunderstandings exacerbated the problems.

Increasingly, talks focused on "nontariff barriers" (NTBs) or "structural impediments," factors other than tariffs and actual trade regulations that were seen as impairing trade. Americans insisted that part of the reason for the trade imbalance was the lack of a "level playing field." The nontariff barriers were seen as tilting the field in favor of Japan. The Japanese bureaucracy erected the NTBs as part of the effort to rebuild the economy. Americans ignored the barriers for years, but they became objectionable after Japan enjoyed such great economic success. Faced with pressure from the United States, Europe, and the Third World, the Japanese gradually reduced many of the barriers. However, Americans still believed that NTBs were being used to discriminate against American products trying to enter the Japanese market. Health and safety standards, environmental and technical regulations, and procedural complexities are examples of nontariff barriers. Structural impediments are deeper economic and cultural barriers that affect trade relations. Japan complained that the United States did not do enough to reduce its budget and trade deficits, needed to encourage savings, and improve its educational system. The United States wanted Japan to tighten antimonopoly regulations, allow larger retail stores, and generally facilitate consumer access to foreign products.

The frustration in both countries over trade issues led to a tendency for politicians to engage in "bashing" of the other nation. "Japan bashing" became a popular sport among certain American officials and commentators, blasting "unfair" practices. (This was addressed in Chapter 4.) Some polls even indicated that, with the end of the Cold War, more Americans had a negative view of Japan than of the Soviet Union, and many considered Japan to be the major "threat" to the United States. Meanwhile, some in Japan labeled the United States a nation of crybabies, and insisted that America had lost its competitive edge.

The bilateral trade disputes are likely to continue, but there are also opportunities and compelling reasons for close cooperation between Japan and the United States. In any case, Japan has established itself as an increasingly powerful force in the global economy.

THE EUROPEAN COMMUNITY AND GERMANY

Regional integration in the economic sphere is aimed at drawing nations together for common benefit. There have been, are, and almost certainly will be further examples of regional economic cooperation. The most significant effort at regional integration thus far, and one that has significant international political, as well as economic, connotations, is the European Community (EC).

In some respects the idea of European integration grew out of the ashes of World War II. There had, of course, been previous efforts at uniting Europe forcefully, with one or several nations seeking to dominate the continent. But this time the idea was voluntary, cooperative union; one of the aims being to avoid the rivalries and conflicts that had torn

Europe apart in the past. Establishing a cooperative framework would also make Europe less vulnerable to external domination. Such integration was strongly encouraged by the United States in the aftermath of the war, and the initial agency for coordination was the Committee on European Economic Cooperation (CEEC), which worked with the United States under the Marshall Plan (European Recovery Program), discussed earlier in this book.

As the economic recovery of Europe began to advance, the first step toward establishing a supranational organization was taken with the establishment of the European Coal and Steel Community (ECSC) in 1951. French Foreign Minister Robert Schuman led the way in setting up a single authority to control the production and distribution of coal and steel within a common market. An important element of this effort was that it would draw France and Germany, traditional enemies, together in a cooperative framework. Six nations joined together in the ECSC—France, the Federal Republic of Germany, Italy, Belgium, the Netherlands, and Luxembourg. For the first time, these nations were entrusting part of their sovereignty to a regional authority.

Steps toward Integration

By 1957, those six nations of Western Europe had established themselves on even more solid economic ground and took a decisive step toward integration by signing the Treaty of Rome, officially creating the European Economic Community or Common Market. The treaty also set up the European Atomic Energy Community (Euratom). In 1967, the three organizations were merged into the European Community, with headquarters in Brussels, and all tariffs between the member countries were abolished.

This progress was significant, yet there was doubt in the minds of many that Europe would become a true common market and that the individual nations would yield enough of their sovereignty to allow for real economic and possibly even political integration. Leaders such as France's Charles de Gaulle (see Profile) had supported European economic cooperation, seeing it as in the interest of their nations and as something of a counter to United States economic power. However, De Gaulle was fiercely committed to France's independence and sovereignty and thus saw real limits on how far integration should go. De Gaulle was also opposed to British entry into the EC, in part because he believed Britain was too closely tied to the United States. Britain was itself ambivalent about becoming part of Europe and, even after eventually becoming a member of the EC, is a sometimes hesitant partner as integration proceeds.

By the early 1970s, the advantages of the EC were increasingly apparent and other nations, including Britain, became members, expanding the original 6 nations to 12. Other new members, in addition to Britain, were Denmark and Ireland, which also joined in 1973; Greece (1981); and Spain and Portugal (1986). See Figure 9-1.

Figure 9-1
THE EUROPEAN COMMUNITY

Twelve countries are members of the European Community, which provides the structure for economic integration among the member nations and is moving toward integration in other areas as well. The EC is becoming a major factor in international economics. The six original Common Market countries were France, Italy, Belgium, Luxembourg, the Netherlands, and the Federal Republic of Germany (West Germany) (1958). Ireland, Denmark, and the United Kingdom joined in 1973, Greece, 1981, and Spain and Portugal, 1986. With German unification in 1990, the former East Germany was absorbed into the EC. Other countries are seeking membership and still more are expected to seek entry in the future.

EC MEMBERS

ICELAND

NORWAY

SWEDEN

FINLAND

UNITED KINGDOM

N. IRELAND

SCOTLAND

IRELAND

ENGLAND

DENMARK

ESTONIA

LATVIA

LITHUANIA

SOVIET UNION

NETH.

BELG.

LUX.

GERMANY

POLAND

CZECH.

AUSTRIA

HUNGARY

ROMANIA

FRANCE

SWITZ.

YUGOSLAVIA

BULGARIA

PORTUGAL

SPAIN

ITALY

ALB.

GREECE

TURKEY

The EC also has a legal and political structure which may take on increasing significance in coming years. The *European Parliament*, with popularly elected representatives from member countries, has limited power but could become more important as the EC becomes stronger. Other institutions are the *Commission*, whose members represent the entire EC and recommend policy; the *Council of Ministers*, the EC's supreme body, composed of representatives from the 12 member governments, with final power to approve or disapprove actions; and the *Court of Justice*, based in Luxembourg, which deals primarily with trade and business disputes and determines whether actions by the EC and its member governments are compatible with the governing treaties.

Creating the European Market

It was not until 1985 that the member nations committed themselves to movement toward a *true* common market. That year they signed the Single European Act, which amended the Treaty of Rome to streamline the decision-making process, open up more areas to EC jurisdiction, and reinvigorate the movement toward European economic and political integration. The EC formally obligated itself to achieve internal harmonization of the markets of the individual member countries, removing all barriers and boundaries to trade among EC nations. This single internal market was to be established by the end of 1992. At first, not a great deal of attention was paid to this development within Europe or elsewhere. After all, the idea of a common market had been kicking around for decades. Gradually, however, there was recognition that this was an extremely significant breakthrough and that the establishment of the single market would make Western Europe a much more potent economic force in the world. There had been concern that Europe was growing stagnant. Some were even using the term "Eurosclerosis," suggesting that Europe was undynamic and declining. Indeed, the Europeans were galvanized into action by the recognition that they risked falling even further behind Japan and the United States in such key sectors as telecommunications, aerospace, computers, and biotechnology, and being at an even greater disadvantage in international economic competition.

Economic integration of Europe is not an easy process. After agreement on the single market was reached, the EC identified about 300 directives which each nation had to comply with in order to accomplish the practical steps necessary to achieve integration. This involved some difficult and complex areas such as tax-system uniformity, educational requirements, environmental and health standards, consumer protections, and public procurement.

Particularly since World War II, the United States has had very close economic relations with Europe. Trade between the United States and Western Europe has amounted to more than $160 billion annually. The United States has been accounting for about one-fifth of the imports purchased by the EC countries and about the same percentage of EC exports have gone to the United States in recent years. Combined direct investment by the United States in Europe and by the EC countries in the United States is estimated at more than $320 billion. As was noted earlier, two of the three countries with the largest direct investment in the United States (Britain and the Netherlands) are EC members.

An economically united EC clearly constitutes a major force in the international economy and carries added political clout as well. With the unification of Germany adding another 16 million people to the EC, the total population of the 12 members is more than 340 million, making it almost as large in numbers as the United States and Japan combined. The combined GNP of the EC members almost equals that of the United States and is well ahead of Japan. Clearly, the EC is well positioned to be competitive and to exercise major economic influence in the world. Some have suggested that what may result is a "fortress Europe," which would be purely inward looking and would aim to keep out foreign competition. While elements of this may appear in certain sectors, it seems highly unlikely that Europe would want to build walls around itself. In today's world, most nations and businesses are taking much more of an international approach, and recognize the importance of a global outlook.

GERMANY AS A POWER

Within the EC, Germany is in the position to be a dominant power; indeed, as has already been pointed out, Germany itself ranks as a major international economic power.

Like Japan, Germany arose from defeat in World War II to become a modern industrial giant. Germany was, of course, divided between East and West for 45 years after the war, and was the focal point of much of the East-West rivalry in Europe, as is discussed in earlier chapters and in the Berlin City Portrait.

The rebuilding of the Federal Republic (West Germany) was strongly aided by the Marshall Plan and other assistance from the United States. The United States, through NATO, also made a major military commitment in Germany, and the presence of United States forces, in combination with those of the other Allies, and, later, the West German military, helped assure the nation's security. West Germany, like Japan, benefitted from astute leadership and planning in the economic sector and a recognition that the nation needed to gear itself for international competition. Under the leadership of Konrad Adenauer, elected as the first chancellor of the new Federal Republic government, and his economics minister, Ludwig Erhard (who later succeeded Adenauer as chancellor), West Germany, like Japan, experienced an "economic miracle."

Erhard energetically promoted private initiative according to market economy principles. With the spark provided by United States aid through the Marshall Plan, the new German economy developed rapidly. As in

Japan, it was significant that the government had no military expenditures in those early years. West Germany did eventually develop its own armed forces, being admitted into NATO in 1955.

West Germany also had a large number of refugees from the East who were looking for work. Production figures and profits rose quickly, and so did incomes. By the early 1950s, full employment was achieved and the standard of living rose steadily. An enormous pent-up demand for consumer goods existed, and, at the same time, West Germany was building up its export markets, and soon became a creditor nation with one of the world's strongest and most stable currencies. The demand for labor grew so intense that it could only be met by importing foreign workers. The *gastarbeiter* or "guest workers" came in large numbers from southern Europe and particularly from Turkey as West Germany became an international labor market.

East Germany, Unification, and the EC

As it prospered, West Germany became a driving force in the European economy and worked especially closely with France, its former adversary, in building European cooperation. Meanwhile, the East German economy developed slowly in comparison with that of the West. Eventually, however, East Germany became a political and economic cornerstone of the East bloc. It was the most industrialized and developed economy in Eastern Europe, and its per capita GNP was by far the highest of the Eastern European countries. There is some reason to suspect that western analysts overestimated East Germany's economic strength, but by most international standards, East Germany was comparatively well off. One reason for the advances in East Germany's economy was the growing economic relationship with West Germany, as tensions between East and West were gradually relaxed. However, East German citizens became increasingly dissatisfied with the inefficiency of their economy, which was dominated by 126 state-owned monopolies. More and more, those in the East compared themselves to the more affluent West Germans.

It has been suggested that East and West Germany provided a sort of laboratory test for the world's two major competing ideologies and economic systems. There were no differences of language, no significant cultural and historical differences. They were only divided by man-made barriers. It was increasingly evident that the Western experiment worked much more successfully than the Communist command economy in the East, and recognition of that helped bring down the barriers that separated them. Indeed, there is strong reason to believe that one of the major factors in the revolutionary changes that occurred in Eastern Europe at the end of the 1980s was the realization that, particularly with the coming of the 1992 EC single market, East Germany and its Eastern neighbors were going to fall even further behind. Increased awareness of the economic, political, and cultural vitality of the West helped doom the inefficient, state-run East bloc economic and political systems.

The rapidity with which German unification occurred, once the East German Communist government collapsed, surprised everyone. In the short term, unification was costly for the West Germans, as they bore the expense of the merger. A treaty on currency, economic, and social union between the two Germanies set forth principles and terms for those aspects of unification. The treaty extended West Germany's free-market economy into the East and provided for the conversion of the Ost (East) mark into Deutsch marks. Basically, the strong West German currency (the D-mark) absorbed the weaker East German mark, and, took over the East's economy while at the same time dismantling it. Private property rights were guaranteed under the treaty, and price controls and state monopolies, which had been prominent features of the East economy, were abolished. The absorption of the planned economy into the market economy and the harmonization of the two systems is not only extremely costly but a highly complex process. Indeed, the costs of unification proved much higher than originally estimated by the West German government. However, in the long term, it should make for an even stronger Germany and European Community.

Even before unification, West Germany was the largest nation in the EC in terms of population and economic strength, and consistently ranked among the world's top exporting nations, generating a large trade surplus. With the addition of the East, Germany has nearly 80 million people and significantly increased economic potential. The prospect of more German power is, not surprisingly, a matter of concern to Germany's neighbors, given Germany's earlier history of seeking to dominate the region. However, German unification and the prospect of an even stronger Germany was made more palatable because it occurred within the context of the European Community.

Links with the East

The growing success and strength of the EC is attracting other nations which would like to become members or have some type of affiliation. The changes in Eastern Europe and the breakdown of the old Communist governments and economic systems offer new opportunities for economic cooperation, although the other Eastern European countries were far weaker than East Germany and lacked the immediate connection to the West. Nonetheless, for those countries, for the EC, and especially for Germany, the changes open up the possibility of replacing the old divisions in Europe with greatly expanded political and economic contacts. Germany was already a major trading partner of the Soviet Union, and economic ties with East Europe and Soviet European republics could grow significantly as those areas seek to be more involved in the international economy. Soviet attempts to play an increased role in international trade were long limited by the lack of convertibility of the Soviet ruble. If a nation does not have a currency that is readily exchangeable (with values established in the international market), there are definite limitations to the ability of that nation to function in international commerce. Some trade can be carried out through what are essentially bartering arrangements. For example, the Soviets provided oil to neighboring Finland in return for ice-breaking ships and industrial products. As long as the Soviet and East European nations had essentially closed economies, the governments could exercise much greater political and economic control by keeping the currencies unconvertible—or, if exchanges were allowed, the rates were set at unrealistically high levels. In any case, such matters were almost entirely government controlled, with little left to be determined by the market.

Expanding the EC's Role and Size?

Currency and monetary union among its member nations are among the goals of the EC. At the 1991 Maastricht (Netherlands) summit, the EC took further steps toward monetary and political union, including closer coordination of foreign and security policy. The Maastricht treaty includes provisions for a single European currency by 1999, with Britain retaining the option of not taking part in the currency agreement and certain other aspects. Such steps toward greater integration involve a major transfer of national sovereignty. Most nations are hesitant about yielding such sovereignty, and this has been especially true of Britain. To many, European monetary union (EMU), involving a European central bank—comparable to the United States Federal Reserve system—and a common currency seem to be logical steps. Even before establishment of the single market, the EC nations were using the "ecu" or European currency for certain transactions that basically involved bookkeeping.

As was mentioned previously, as the single market project moves forward and the EC's potential becomes increasingly apparent, EC membership or affiliation becomes attractive to a growing number of nations. Jacques Delors, the Frenchman who was a leader in the EC's move to a single market, expressed concern that if the EC became too large, it would threaten the goal of more political integration, which he and some other EC leaders favor. Delors suggested that rather than expand the EC, there should be several "concentric circles" around the EC. The first of these circles around the EC would be composed of members of the European Free Trade Association (EFTA). This group includes Austria, Switzerland, Liechtenstein, Finland, Iceland, Norway, and Sweden. Although Norway and Iceland were NATO members, this group has been somewhat more "neutral" politically. The outer circle would be composed of the East European countries, former members of Comecon, the Communist trading group, and possibly some of the Baltic states. Other nations such as Turkey, a NATO member, have sought EC entry. Some have suggested that an organization such as the Council of Europe, originally set up to promote democracy and human rights and which includes most EC and EFTA members and a number of other nations, could serve as an umbrella for cooperation among these different groups. A significant step toward enlarging the framework was taken in 1991 when the 12-member EC and seven members of the EFTA agreed to create the European Economic Area (EEA), which will embrace 380 million Western Europeans from the Arctic Circle to the Mediterranean Sea. The agreement allows for the free flow of most goods, services, capital, and people among the 19 nations, although the EEA will not be a full common market in the same sense as the EC. Undoubtedly, however, some of the EFTA nations viewed this agreement as an interim step toward EC membership.

It is clear that the EC will be a central factor in the new Europe, but it is less clear exactly how far European integration will go and how extensive the formal cooperation among European nations may be. Will the EC become an actual political federation, as well as an economic body? Will the future of Europe be more of a confederation, which would associate the member nations in a common organization, but with each nation retaining more independence and sovereignty? And what of the former Soviet republics' role and Mikhail Gorbachev's talk of a "common European home"? Gorbachev said, "The requirements of economic development in both parts of Europe, as well as scientific and technological progress, prompt the need for a search for some form of mutually advantageous cooperation."[7] In some respects Gorbachev's theme of a common European home echoed Charles de Gaulle's call more than two decades earlier for a "Europe from the Atlantic to the Urals" (referring to the Ural mountains in Russia). DeGaulle was a strong advocate of European cooperation, but not of federation, wanting to guard France's independence. (See DeGaulle Profile.) Political scientist Jerry Hough has suggested that the European home may become much more expansive. "We are moving toward a world in which there will be a common European home from Vladivostok to San Francisco," meaning that in an informal sense, at least, there would be a cooperative entity involving Russia, Europe, and the United States.[8]

The core EC group, with Germany in the lead, will, in any case, be a major factor not only in a broader European context but in the rapidly changing global economic environment. As this section has emphasized, the EC, Japan, and the United States rank as the three major economic forces in the world. An indication of the dominance of the major economic powers is provided by looking at the world's largest industrial corporations. Of the "Global 500" (the largest industrial corporations in the world in 1990 ranked by sales, according to *Fortune* magazine) 167 are United States companies, 111 are from Japan, 43 are British, 32 German, and 29 French. Of the top 50, 17 are American, 10 Japanese, and 6 German. While the United States still makes a very impressive showing in these rankings, it should be noted that ten years earlier 23 United States companies made the top 50, compared with only 5 Japanese.

Although power is shifting toward Japan and Germany, leader of the EC, no single nation or group is likely to be able to exercise global economic hegemony in the sense that the United States did in the early post–World War II period or as Britain did in earlier times.

There is the possibility, as suggested earlier in the chapter, that three regional economic superblocs may emerge. In such a case, the three could be engaged in a fierce competition against each other. They could be inward-looking and discourage broader international cooperation. However, there appear to be compelling reasons for extensive commerce and cooperation beyond the regional level. One important consideration, of course, is that although these are the three major economic constellations, much of the world is not included, or may only be on the fringes of one of the constellations. The economic powers do have a stake in the rest of the world—in some respects a very important stake. Even if inclined to do so, they are unlikely to be able to isolate themselves from other areas, as will be discussed in the next chapter.

NOTES

1. Fred Bergsten, "The World Economy After the Cold War," *Foreign Affairs* 69, summer 1990, p. 96.
2. Jeffrey E. Garten, "Japan and Germany: American Concerns," *Foreign Affairs* 68, winter 1989–90, p. 87.
3. Ezra F. Vogel, *Japan as Number One* (Tokyo: Charles F. Tuttle, 1980), p. 225.
4. David Halberstam, *The Reckoning* (New York: Morrow, 1986), p. 271.
5. *Ibid.*, p. 726.
6. Paul Kennedy, *The Rise and Fall of the Great Powers* (New York: Random House, 1987), p. 459.
7. Mikhail Gorbachev, *Perestroika: New Thinking for Our Country and the World* (New York: Harper & Row, 1987), p. 190.
8. Jerry F. Hough, "Perestroika and Soviet Relations With the West," in Donald R. Kelley and Hoyt Purvis (eds.), *Old Myths and New Realities in United States–Soviet Relations* (New York: Praeger, 1990), p. 27.

MARGARET THATCHER

Relatively few women have served as leaders of national governments and played major roles in contemporary international relations. One who has had a significant impact on world affairs is Margaret Thatcher, who served as prime minister of the United Kingdom of Great Britain and Northern Ireland from 1979 to 1990.

Other women, such as India's Indira Gandhi (1966–70; 1980–84) and Israel's Golda Meir (1969–74), led their nations and figured prominently in international affairs. Sirimavo Bandaranaike of Sri Lanka (formerly Ceylon) became the first female prime minister, serving from 1960 to 1965 and 1970 to 1977. In more recent times Corazon Aquino of the Philippines and Violeta Barrios de Chamorro of Nicaragua were chosen to head their governments in elections that drew major international attention. Yet other women who have served as national leaders include Benazir Bhutto of Pakistan and Gro Harlem Brundtland, who was elected as Norway's prime minister and has been a leader in international environmental efforts.

One of the developments that established British prime minister Margaret Thatcher's leadership was her strong action in the war with Argentina over the Falkland (Malvinas) Islands in 1982. Her forceful stand was credited with helping to strengthen British national pride. She is seen leaving 10 Downing Street, residence of the British prime minister in London, to report to Parliament on the Falkland situation.

THATCHER AND BRITAIN'S ROLE

However, it was Thatcher who became the first female political leader of a major Western government, and, indeed, was the longest-serving British prime minister of the twentieth century. Thatcher vigorously defended Britain's national interests as she saw them and expressed strong reservations about the extent of integration and "federalism" associated with the European Community. She continued to speak out on this issue, voicing concerns about Britain yielding too much power to the EC, even after she was replaced as prime minister— a move that was partially due to her opposition to the growing economic and political integration of the EC.

In her concern about the extension of the powers and role of the EC and the ceding of some of her nation's sovereignty to the Community, Thatcher echoed some of the views expressed earlier by France's Charles de Gaulle (see Profile), who favored European economic cooperation but didn't want to sacrifice any of France's sovereignty or national control. Ironically, it was De Gaulle who initially blocked British entry into the Common Market, although Britain did eventually become a member in 1973, after De Gaulle's death. Increasingly, Britain saw membership in the Community as in the nation's economic interests.

When Thatcher was elected prime minister in 1979, she was little known internationally. A major goal was to reverse her nation's economic decline. Not only was Britain in economic difficulty, but also the European Community was moving at a slow pace in building a common economic union, and the Western European nations risked falling further behind Japan and the United States in economic strength and competitiveness.

While Thatcher set about improving Britain's economic position and its international stature, the EC began to move toward true economic integration. At first Thatcher and Britain seemed in step with their European partners. However, as the reality of integration and the national policies required to achieve it became more apparent, Thatcher became more hesitant and reluctant to fully commit her country to the expanding goals of the EC.

RISING TO INTERNATIONAL POWER

Thatcher entered Parliament in 1959 and has always been identified with the more conservative element of the Conservative Party. The daughter of a grocer who was involved in local politics, she was educated as a chemist and later became a barrister (lawyer). She worked her way up through the political ranks, becoming party leader in 1975 and leading the Conservatives to victory in 1979.

Her international reputation began to develop in the early 1980s after she formed a close relationship with United States president Ronald Reagan, and it was furthered by her tough stance in the war with Argentina over the Falkland (Malvinas) Islands in 1982. (See Chapters 1 and 4.) Her forceful position and use of Britain's

military strength to defeat the Argentines was credited with helping to restore British national pride. She proclaimed that "Great Britain is great again."

Her tough domestic and international positions earned her the nickname of "Iron Lady," a sobriquet originally applied by the Soviet press because of her harsh denunciation of communism. Although she was unwavering in her opposition to communism, she was the first Western leader to signal that the West could "do business" with Mikhail Gorbachev.

While Britain's leading opposition party was advocating a disarmament policy, Thatcher took a prominent role in favoring the modernization of British and NATO nuclear weapons. In this effort she worked closely with Reagan, forming what has been called the most significant and successful period in the long history of the "special" relationship between Britain and the United States.[1] Reagan valued Thatcher more than any other foreign leader. According to Reagan biographer Lou Cannon, "Each of them seemed less lonely in international affairs because of the presence of the other."[2]

Thatcher's relations with George Bush began less cordially, but grew very close, and many credit her with exerting major influence on Bush's decision to confront Iraq's Saddam Hussein after the 1990 invasion of Kuwait.

Thatcher's backers also credit her with a leading role in bringing about change in Eastern Europe, particularly through her encouragement of Gorbachev's more liberal policies and in backing those movements for economic and political reform in the countries behind what an earlier British political leader, Winston Churchill, had labeled the Iron Curtain.

For all of her contributions and achievements, Thatcher is a highly controversial figure. On the domestic front she was criticized for what some claimed were uncaring and inequitable social and economic policies, although her supporters argue that her actions and strong advocacy of the market economy significantly improved Britain's economic position and ended talk of Britain being the "sick man of Europe."

Internationally, much of the controversy surrounding Thatcher relates to her attitudes toward the European Community and Britain's role in it. Indeed, as noted earlier, her resistance to the growing economic and political integration of the EC was a major factor in bringing an end to her prime ministership.

OPPOSING EUROPEAN POLICIES

Although Thatcher became an outspoken critic of European integration and especially of centralization within the EC, she had been a part of Conservative governments that had committed Britain to participation in European integration. Thatcher represented Britain in signing the Single European Act of 1986, which hastened and broadened European integration. Increasingly, however, she became a "Euroskeptic," advocating voluntary cooperation among independent sovereign states rather than a highly regulated structure with central control and a powerful bureaucracy.

Thatcher became known for her thunderbolts of opposition within the EC. She was particularly fierce in opposing a single European currency and greater political union, including the idea of a common European foreign policy.

Margaret Thatcher met frequently with European leaders such as President Francois Mitterand of France. While Thatcher favored cooperation with France and other European Community members on certain issues, she became increasingly reluctant to fully commit her country to the expanding goals of the EC.

However, as the British magazine, *The Economist*, put it, "To her fellow EC leaders, she has become a bore, a ranter, nothing more. The idea that she is defending British interests in Europe is now a pathetic delusion. British interests are not even being heard."[3]

More and more, Thatcher found herself at odds not only with EC leaders such as Jacques Delors, the primary architect of the 1992 single-market plan, but with key figures in her own party and government in Britain. It was this growing division within Britain's Conservative Party that led to Thatcher's political downfall. Several key members of her cabinet had already resigned over her stand on the EC. When Sir Geoffrey Howe, who served in several top positions under Thatcher, resigned in November 1990, he criticized the notion that Britain was "surrendering sovereignty" to the EC and said that Thatcher's position had become a tragic one—"the prime minister's perceived attitude towards Europe is running increasingly serious risks for the future of a nation . . ."[4] A short time later, opponents within the Conservative Party mounted a direct challenge to her leadership. When Thatcher failed to obtain the necessary margin on a first-ballot test, she announced her resignation and moved out of the prime minister's residence at 10 Downing Street.

Her successor was John Major, who was Thatcher's choice among the contenders. Although some of his detractors referred to him as "son of Thatcher," Major evinced a significantly different attitude toward Europe. Major expressed reservations about some aspects of European integration plans, but he said, "We must not—cannot—turn our backs on the construction of the New Europe. That is where our history points, and our interest lies."

"Sulking on the fringe of talks about the destiny of Europe cannot be the right role for Britain," Major said. He added, "Of course, there are frustrations in membership of the European Community, things on which one member will disagree with another . . . But the opportunities dwarf the disappointments. We have gained much, we can hope to gain more from membership of a thriving Europe."[5]

RAISING FUNDAMENTAL QUESTIONS

Although Thatcher pledged her support for Major, she continued to express her concerns about Britain's role in European integration and focused on some fundamental issues in international relations at a point in history when nations are being drawn closer together for economic reasons. Thatcher was raising questions about the future of the nation-state, and about sovereignty and nationalism in a world in transition.

In an impassioned plea to the British Parliament in 1991, just before announcing that she would not seek re-election to the House of Commons, Thatcher warned against plans for a single European currency and other steps toward political and economic union. Thatcher said that such plans were going far beyond what had been contemplated in the Single European Act and represented "a massive extension of the community's powers and competence into almost every area of our national life, and that of other member states." She cautioned that "once those powers were given away they would never be taken back."[6]

She argued that a single currency or monetary union was irrelevant to Europe's economic problems, but also emphasized that she saw the issue as a fundamental question of principle. Thatcher said that if Britain went along with such moves that it would amount to "the greatest abdication of parliamentary and national sovereignty in our history." She said that Britain must guard against a "federal Europe achieved by stealth,"[7] suggesting that negotiations began with vague commitments and ended in dangerous obligations. Thatcher rejected any notion of a common European defense and foreign policy, constantly emphasizing that Britain must not relinquish its sovereignty to the EC.

One of the critics of her strongly nationalist approach said, "Thatcher's gift has always been to make tap-room xenophobia sound like high-minded principle."[8]

Those disagreeing with Thatcher see her as on the wrong side of history, unable to face what is inevitable and ultimately in Britain's best interests. Indeed, some pragmatists would argue that ceding some of Britain's sovereignty to the EC is a good idea because that is the best way of making the nation stronger and assuring its economic future.

Thatcher also expressed concern about the possible formation of three major economic blocs. She said, "I see a real danger of that: a European bloc based on the European Community's proposed economic and monetary union; a western-hemisphere bloc based on a U.S.–Canada–Latin America free trade area; and a Pacific bloc with Japan and some of the East and Northeast Asia countries."[9] According to Thatcher, such an arrangement would encourage protectionism and stifle trade, even though others believe that the formation of the international trading blocs is probably inevitable and would be broadly beneficial.

She has argued against giving more powers to highly centralized supranational institutions, calling instead for structures which accommodate diversity and preserve national traditions and institutions. She said that the European Community should be open to the nations of Eastern Europe at the earliest feasible time and added, "They have not thrown off central command and control in their own countries only to find them reincarnated in the European Community."[10]

While some see a decline in the significance of the nation-state, Thatcher contends, "One of the lessons of the twentieth century is that the nation-state has triumphed. Those nations put together artificially are in difficulties. People in Eastern Europe are delighted to have recovered their national identity."[11]

Thatcher is a strong exponent of the sovereign state: the nation is paramount. Anything that undermines its supremacy or would add a layer of authority above it is unacceptable. However, her opponents question whether it is possible to create a free-trade area and common market without changing the political institutions.

A critic of Thatcher's position said that for the former prime minister, sovereignty "seems to possess an almost mystical quality," and that Thatcher's idea of sovereignty is that it is some indivisible whole.[12] However, it can be argued that the concept of sovereignty varies from nation to nation and over time. In recent decades, every European nation, including Britain, has experienced a decline in its sovereignty, partially as a result of the development of the European Community, but also because of the increasing globalization of the economy, which, as is discussed throughout this book, tends to make national boundaries less meaningful.

THE THATCHER IMPACT

"Europe was her downfall," editorialized the *Times* of London, "but it was also the battle in which she would have chosen to go down."[13] Thatcher was also noted, the *Times* commented, for her consistent stand against international bullies, "her steady criticism of the Soviet leviathan during the early 1980s when its weakness was not yet apparent," and for never taking the subjection of Eastern Europe for granted. A veteran journalist who covered Thatcher wrote, "With her soulmate Ronald Reagan and her sparring partner Mikhail Gorbachev there was a personal chemistry. They responded . . . to the sheer energy force."[14]

"During her premiership Thatcher acquired an almost legendary reputation abroad, as a leader of great firmness and directness," wrote Nicholas Ridley, a former colleague of hers. In his view, "no other British prime minister achieved so much at home and abroad."[15]

While Thatcher's nationalist views on Europe may not have prevailed and may seem outdated at a time of growing internationalism, there can be little doubt that she has been a significant figure during a period of major change in international affairs.

NOTES

1. See Geoffrey Smith, *Reagan and Thatcher* (New York: Norton, 1991).
2. Lou Cannon, *President Reagan: The Role of a Lifetime* (New York: Simon and Schuster, 1991), p. 465.
3. "The End?" *The Economist* (London), November 17, 1990, p. 14.
4. Excerpts from Sir Geoffrey Howe's resignation speech in the House of Commons, November 13, 1990; reprinted in *The Economist* (London), November 17, 1990, p. 74.
5. Prime Minister John Major, "Britain's Contribution to Europe," speech at Swansea, June 14, 1991.
6. Margaret Thatcher, speech before the House of Commons, London, June 26, 1991. See George Jones, "Thatcher: We must never surrender," and excerpts from speech text published in *The Daily Telegram* (London), June 27, 1991.
7. *Ibid.*; See also Robin Oakley, "Power steering from the Tories' backseat driver," *The Times* (London), June 27, 1991 and "She makes her stand," *The Economist*, June 29, 1991, p. 27.
8. Iain Macwhirter, "Old bruiser goes for a knock-out," *Scotland on Sunday* (Edinburgh), June 30, 1991.
9. Margaret Thatcher, speech in Aspen, Colorado, August 5, 1990; reprinted in Adam Daniel Rotfel and Walther Stutzle (eds.), *Germany and Europe in Transition*, Stockholm International Peace Research Institute (SIPRI), Oxford, England: Oxford University Press, 1991, p. 115.
10. *Ibid.*, p. 114.
11. John Rowland and David Hughes, "Thatcher launches plan for worldwide export of ideals," *The Sunday Times* (London), June 30, 1991.
12. Martin Jacques, "Thatcher's brave, wrong song for Europe," *The Sunday Times* (London), June 30, 1991.
13. "Less Than Retiring," (leader/editorial), *The Times* (London), June 29, 1991.
14. Robin Oakley, "Triumph of sheer will, zest and personality," *The Times* (London), June 29, 1991.
15. Nicholas Ridley, "The Thatcher effect: lasting freedom," *The Sunday Times* (London), June 30, 1991.

SUGGESTIONS FOR FURTHER READING

Birch, Anthony H. *The British System of Government* (8th ed.). London: Unwin Hyman, 1990.

Britain in the European Community. London: Foreign and Commonwealth Office, 1990.

Ingram, Bernard. *Kill the Messenger*. New York: Harper Collins, 1991.

Pearce, Edward. *The Quiet Rise of John Major*. London: Weidenfeld and Nicholson, 1991.

Riddell, Peter. *The Thatcher Decade*. London: Basil Blackwell, 1990.

Ridley, Nicholas. *My Style of Government: The Thatcher Years*. London: Hutchinson, 1991.

Shepherd, Robert. *The Power Brokers: The Tory Party and Its Leaders*. London: Hutchinson, 1991.

Skidelsky, Robert. (ed.) *Thatcherism*. London: Basil Blackwell, 1990.

Smith, Geoffrey. *Reagan and Thatcher*. New York: Norton, 1991.

Tugendhat, Christopher and William Wallace. *Options for British Policy in the 1990s*. New York: Routledge, 1988.

Wallace, William. *The Transformation of Western Europe*. New York: Council on Foreign Relations Press, 1990.

CHAPTER TEN

International Economics: Progress and Challenges

The previous chapter focused primarily on the major economic powers and the more prosperous and industrialized nations. Obviously, that is only part of the story. Other nations are in various stages of economic development and some are in desperate condition with little prospect for significant economic progress.

The concept of the Third World has been discussed in earlier chapters, and the point has been made that there is considerable diversity within what is generally referred to as the Third World. This is certainly true in terms of relative economic conditions among Third-World nations. They range from the newly industrializing countries (NICs), primarily in East Asia and Latin America, to what are sometimes termed Fourth-World countries—the poorest of the poor. These poorest countries—there are as many as 42 by some calculations—have populations that have difficulty even maintaining a subsistence economy. They mainly produce primary commodities and are generally dependent on outside assistance.

THIRD-WORLD CHALLENGES

It is important to keep in mind that the Third-World nations, sometimes referred to as less-developed countries (LDCs) or developing nations, constitute more than three-fourths of the world's population, and they are growing at a much faster rate than the more-developed nations. (See Chapter 11.) The combined population of the 12 members of the European Community, including united Germany, is still less than one-third that of a single Third-World nation—China.

The Third World, as has been previously noted, is also referred to as the South—meaning the developing nations, mostly located in the Southern Hemisphere—as opposed to the North—the developed, industrialized nations. All of this terminology is imprecise and risks overgeneralization and simplification. Nonetheless, for purposes of discussion and analysis, such categories serve a useful purpose and they are generally accepted in international relations.

As has been discussed in earlier chapters, many of the Third-World nations gained their independence in the period after World War II. They now constitute a strong majority in the United Nations and through the Group of 77 (G-77, which actually includes about 127 nations) and other organizations have sought to shape the international agenda and call attention to their economic problems. The North-South dialogue, which at times has seemed to be a dialogue of the deaf and to matter for little, refers to the ongoing discussions and negotiations about trade, aid, and development and economic issues. Efforts by some Third-World nations to bring about establishment of a New International Economic Order (NIEO) generated considerable rhetoric but not much in the way of results. The solidarity which has sometimes been evident among the nations of the South stems from recognition of being dependent on the North and unequal with it, and for many nations in the South there is also the common experience of having lived under colonial control.

Political instability often accompanies economic difficulty, and for many Third-World nations this has been the case. While some nations have made notable progress in both political and economic terms, economic progress has eluded others. Despite various initiatives, and substantial international assistance in some cases, many nations lack the social, political, and economic infrastructure to realize sustained economic growth.

The economic challenge, while at the center of many of the difficulties facing the developing nations, is only part of the problem. Many nations are still engaged in the process of nation-building. As discussed in earlier chapters, a number of nations are faced with the difficulty of pulling together diverse religious, tribal, racial, and linguistic groups within their borders. At the same time they are attempting to develop viable political institutions to govern and administer the nation. Further complicating and contributing to the problems in many of these countries is the rapid growth in population.

Although some of these nations have found themselves torn by internal conflicts or involved in regional turmoil (see Chapter 7), development has been and continues to be a primary concern of most Third-World nations. As many of them gained political independence, their leaders were faced with the challenge of giving material substance to that independence. There was in many cases what has been called a revolution of rising expectations, as citizens of newly independent nations expected political independence to bring economic prosperity.

Some of these nations did make significant strides. From the 1950s through much of the 1970s there was considerable economic growth among Third-World countries as a whole. However, a relatively small number of countries accounted for much of that growth. For many nations the economic progress they were making, however limited, came to a halt in the late 1970s and the 1980s. As development expert Jyoti S. Singh has written, there was a realization that the situation for many of the developing countries was actually getting worse as each year passed. "Prices of manufactured goods from the industrialized countries continued to climb, while the prices of raw commodities from the developing world have been subject to erratic fluctuations."[1] The rise in oil prices in the 1970s benefitted some Third-World nations at least temporarily, but most of those without their own oil suffered a severe economic blow. Recession and slow growth in much of the industrialized world, which meant a reduction in imports from the Third World, and less credit, combined with falling prices for commodities from the Third World, resulted in economic disaster for many of the Third-World nations.

The South and the Economic Order

Through a variety of organizations and institutions, particularly within the United Nations, Third-World countries have attempted to assert themselves and to exercise more influence in international economics and commerce. Mention has already been made of G-77, and previous chapters discussed some of the efforts by Third-World leaders to unite Third-World nations around political and economic issues, beginning with the Afro-Asian Conference at Bandung, Indonesia, in 1955. The demands for a new international economic order were voiced there and at subsequent conferences of the "nonaligned nations."

The first United Nations Conference on Trade and Development (UNCTAD) was held in Geneva in 1964, with 120 nations taking part, including 77 developing countries (which formed G-77). UNCTAD was then established as a permanent special body within the United Nations and became a major forum for the views of the developing nations. A chief goal of these nations was to secure what they considered to be fair and stable prices of commodities crucial to the economies of the Third World. At times the G-77 nations took a militant position, criticizing the developed nations for not doing more to assist them and condemning the international financial institutions for allegedly being concerned primarily with protecting the interests of the wealthier nations. In calling for a new economic order, the South is pushing for an international system that it believes will be equitable and not permanently tilted against it in terms of commodity prices, access to markets, credit, technology transfer, and, particularly, economic policy decisions, which are generally made in the North. They have also sought "reform" of the international financial institutions, discussed later in this chapter.

In many respects, what the Third-World nations are seeking is fully understandable: they want more control over their own economic destiny. This goal involves control over their own resources, which might be seen as another expression of nationalism and economic sovereignty, and the ability to regulate the activities of outside economic interests, including multinational corporations, operating within their countries. There have been various examples of nationalization of foreign-owned businesses, sometimes with little or no compensation. As pointed out in Chapter 7, this has resulted in major disputes in some cases. Examples of such disputes have been seen in Central America and in the Suez Canal, both mentioned in previous chapters.

One of the aims of the NIEO was to establish the right of Third-World nations to form producer associations or *cartels*. A cartel is intended to control the market for a particular primary commodity or product. Cartels have been formed around a variety of products, many of them without much impact. The best-known and most-effective example has been the Organization of Petroleum Exporting Countries (OPEC), which consists of 13 nations, primarily countries in the Middle East–Persian Gulf region, but also including Ecuador, Gabon, Indonesia, Nigeria, and Venezuela. Many of the oil nations, notably those in the Middle East, found themselves with incredible sources of wealth as the world shifted to an oil-based economy in the years after World War II. As discussed in Chapter 7, OPEC helped enable them to take control away from the Western oil companies and to begin imposing their own pricing policy. Oil was no longer merely an economic commodity but a source of political leverage and an object of security concerns by the industrialized nations. As was also discussed in Chapter 7, OPEC imposed an oil embargo following the 1973 Arab-Israeli war and engineered increases in international oil prices. The subsequent effect on the world economic order has been compared to that of the two world wars.[2] Henry Kissinger called it one of the most pivotal events of the twentieth century.

OPEC has, however, lacked cohesion at times and has been torn by internal rivalries. This was evident in Iraq's invasion of Kuwait in 1990 and the subsequent Gulf War. For a variety of reasons, oil prices have fluctuated. Nonetheless, OPEC and the oil-rich nations have undeniably had a strong impact on world economic and political affairs. (See Figure 10-1.)

OPEC's actions demonstrated that the industrialized nations could be vulnerable to collective pressure from Third-World nations and that the richer nations were in many ways dependent upon the Third World. Ironically, however, the rise in petroleum prices devastated many of the non-oil-producing countries in the Third World. Besides burdening them with high oil import bills, the OPEC actions helped trigger a global

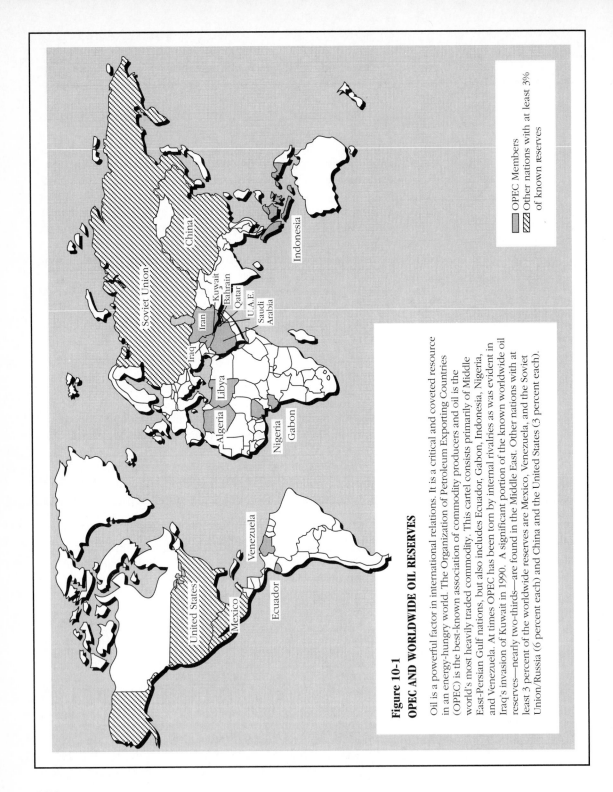

Figure 10-1
OPEC AND WORLDWIDE OIL RESERVES

Oil is a powerful factor in international relations. It is a critical and coveted resource in an energy-hungry world. The Organization of Petroleum Exporting Countries (OPEC) is the best-known association of commodity producers and oil is the world's most heavily traded commodity. This cartel consists primarily of Middle East-Persian Gulf nations, but also includes Ecuador, Gabon, Indonesia, Nigeria, and Venezuela. At times OPEC has been torn by internal rivalries as was evident in Iraq's invasion of Kuwait in 1990. A significant portion of the known worldwide oil reserves—nearly two-thirds—are found in the Middle East. Other nations with at least 3 percent of the worldwide reserves are Mexico, Venezuela, and the Soviet Union/Russia (6 percent each) and China and the United States (3 percent each).

recession that reduced demand for the commodity exports of many of the Third-World nations. It can be argued that OPEC's success in raising oil prices actually undercut the Third World push for a New International Economic Order by weakening the bargaining power of other Third-World nations.

There is a fundamental dilemma for Third-World nations seeking to improve their position and alter the economic order. As Robert Gilpin points out, the same nationalistic spirit that drives Third-World countries to attempt to change the operation of the world economy and improve their relative position "frequently undermines their efforts to cooperate with one another and to form an economic alliance against the developed countries."[5] Powerful and conflicting national interests can greatly weaken Third-World unity. In 1990, Iraq acted on its own, taking control of neighboring Kuwait and once again causing oil prices to jump dramatically. It was a demonstration of the impact that just one nation can have on the economy.

The resource-rich nations are one category of Third-World nations, and a rather limited one. As was stated earlier, there is a wide range in the relative economic positions among the countries of the Third World. At this point it is appropriate to look at several of these categories, the differing levels of development, and the problems and prospects facing some of these nations.

NEWLY INDUSTRIALIZING COUNTRIES

Despite the difficulties encountered by many of the Third-World nations, a small number of countries have experienced rapid economic growth and development and are considered as newly industrializing or industrialized countries—the NICs. The NICs include several Latin American and Asian countries, but particularly notable are the "four tigers" or "four dragons" of East Asia—Taiwan, South Korea, Hong Kong, and Singapore, all with rapidly rising economies. These four have been phenomenally successful in building up exports.

Several Third-World nations have made considerable progress in building a strong industrial base. India, for example, has become one of the world's largest industrial producers and is also advanced in certain technological areas. However, India has a huge population (about 850 million people) and a variety of developmental difficulties. Brazil and Mexico have also made considerable industrial progress, but face serious problems, including substantial foreign debts, which will be discussed later in the chapter. The real success stories have been the "four tigers" and, to a lesser extent, other East Asian countries, such as Malaysia and Thailand.

In many respects the East Asian nations which have been economically successful have modeled themselves after Japan. The export-led growth strategy begins with an import-substitution development strategy.

Guiding all this is a national industrial policy scheme, based on the Japanese model, emphasizing specific industrial sectors and with government playing a significant role in economic management, even though these are "capitalist" economies.

Import substitution emphasizes the development of domestic industries in order to achieve self-sufficiency in certain sectors and thus become less dependent on foreign goods. After the first stage, with its focus on import substitution, these nations move on to export expansion and an outward-looking approach. The East Asian NICs generally got the jump on other developing countries, as the field of countries pushing exports was not as crowded as it is now. What occurred in the case of the NICs was a shift in *comparative advantage*. In effect, they could produce and market goods more efficiently/cheaply than other countries, and thus enjoy a comparative advantage. Like Japan, several of the NICs began by manufacturing lower-cost consumer items and working their way up to more sophisticated and expensive exports. In some cases, as countries became more prosperous and as labor costs rose in those countries, advantage passed on to other countries. This happened, for example, with the manufacture of television sets, which has tended to move from one country to another.

Japan and the NICs have moved to the forefront or become highly competitive in a number of industrial sectors, including automobiles, textiles, shipping, steel, and petrochemicals, as well as in television sets and consumer electronics. In many cases the NICs have benefited from modernized production facilities in addition to lower labor costs and aggressive export policies. The industrial upgrading has been matched by astute market analysis and adaptability. As Steve Chan writes, "In the final analysis, the export competitiveness of the capitalist East Asian countries reflects not only the policies of their governments but also . . . the commercial adaptability of their manufacturers and entrepreneurs."[4] Just as understanding other countries is an important component of successful diplomacy, understanding foreign markets and their consumers is a key element in successful exporting. Japan and the East Asian NICs have often done a masterful job in this area, paying special attention to such matters as changing consumer tastes.

The NICs are, of course, heavily dependent upon open markets in the United States and elsewhere for their exports. And the success of those exports has resulted in increased political pressure for protectionist policies in some of the importing nations, including the United States, where there is concern about lost jobs and trade imbalances. The NICs, as suggested, also have to be concerned about being undercut by nations seeking to emulate them, nations which might gain their own comparative advantage due to lower labor costs.

Japan and the East Asian NICs have been compared to a formation of flying geese, with Japan leading the wedge formation, the NICs following behind, and with still other Asian nations to follow behind in a third and fourth wave. The wedge concept involves stages of linked development. Japan shifts labor-intensive industries such as textiles and consumer electronics to the "geese" behind it, as it moves into more advanced industries, and, in turn, the NICs do the same.

The East Asian NICs have been held up as an example for other Third-World nations to follow, just as in many ways the NICs imitated Japan's successful pattern. Can the success of the NICs be replicated? Many think not. As has already been noted, the world economic field has become much more crowded since the Asian NICs made their entry. Further, each nation is unique and there are distinctive features, in addition to timing, that helped create favorable circumstances for the four tigers. Certainly these four had serious obstacles to overcome, but they enjoyed advantages as well. All are relatively small areas, especially Hong Kong and Singapore, which are essentially cities. In fact, Hong Kong is a crown colony of the United Kingdom, most of which the British leased from China in 1898 for 99 years. In 1997, the territory will revert to Chinese control, although according to agreement between China and Britain, it is supposed to remain as a capitalist "special administrative region" for 50 years thereafter. Singapore is an independent republic, less than 240 square miles, one-fifth the size of Rhode Island, the smallest of the United States. It is a major port, strategically situated at the crossroads of Southeast Asian trade routes, with a long trading history. It was formerly a British colony, and for a brief time it was part of the Federation of Malaysia.

The Taiwan Case

Taiwan is yet another "special" case. As is discussed in Chapter 5, China claims, and most of the world agrees, at least technically, that Taiwan is a part of China. However, for many years, the United States and many others (including the United Nations) recognized Taiwan, known as the Republic of China, as *the* government of China. By the 1970s, most of the world had recognized the government in Beijing of the People's Republic of China as the legitimate Chinese government. The United States, in agreeing to the Shanghai Communiqué of 1972, and in later diplomatic recognition of the PRC, acknowledged that Taiwan was part of China. While Taiwan's political/diplomatic status may be murky, economically it has operated as if it were an independent nation and has done so very successfully. Because of its unusual status, Taiwan doesn't always show up as a separate entry in international economic statistical data. However, Taiwan's economic growth has been spectacular. For much of the 1970s and 80s, Taiwan's GNP grew at double-digit rates—better than 10 percent a year. By some measures it was the world's best economic performer during that period, when its economy expanded more than fortyfold, compared with a tenfold increase worldwide. If considered to be a nation, Taiwan ranks as the world's twelfth-largest trading nation. Beginning in 1955, Taiwan's trade tripled every five years, and increasingly its economy is based on capital-intensive and knowledge-intensive industries. Electronics replaced textiles as Taiwan's leading export, and it is a major exporter of microcomputers and computer parts, as well as a variety of other products. The standard of living in Taiwan is equal to that of many of the developed nations.

Despite its unusual political status, as John Copper, a specialist on Asian affairs, points out, "With trade and cultural contacts in nearly every country of the world, Taiwan held a commercial position of such significance that it was difficult for it to be ignored or isolated." In Copper's view, Taiwan's experience offers some special lessons. "With half its goods and services exported each year, mostly to Western countries, Taiwan has done what dependency theorists contended would lead to disaster."[5]

Dependence and Interdependence

The dependency theory maintains that Third-World dependence on the international market results in exploitation and domination of Third-World countries by developed nations and that this serves to thwart the development of the Third World.

There are different interpretations and variations of the dependency theory (also called *dependencia*), but its proponents basically see developed and Third-World nations in a neocolonial or neoimperialist relationship, with that relationship keeping the Third-World nations in a dependent position. As noted earlier, in the discussion of the NIEO, there are those who argue that there is a systemic bias against the less-developed countries and that the structure of the international economic order keeps them in a dependent status. The success of Taiwan and other NICs would seem to defy the dependency theory, but some would claim that what the NICs have achieved is not "true" development because they believe that it does not really lead to national economic independence, but results in a kind of "dependent development."

There is no doubt that there are nations which are in positions of dependency in varying degrees. However, it is clear that most of the NICs have made themselves factors in an *interdependent* international economy.

South Korea

Another of the economic success stories has been the Republic of Korea or South Korea, which experienced exceptional growth in the 1980s and moved into the top ranks of the world's trading nations. South Korea's economy did not really begin to develop until the 1960s. Under Japanese rule from 1910 to 1945, there was little industrial development in Korea. Following World War II, the country was divided into North and South. The Korean war, discussed in earlier chapters, further hindered development. As late as 1962, South Korea had a GNP of only $2.3 billion and a per capita GNP of $87. Twenty-five years later, the GNP had climbed to

$118 billion, with per capita GNP at $2,813, and continuing to grow. The key to success was an outward-looking development strategy that made exports the engine of growth. The United States and Japan have been South Korea's largest trading partners, although efforts are being made to strengthen trade links with Europe and with the members of the Association of South East Asian Nations (ASEAN).

In relatively short order, South Korea went from a basically backward, rural, primarily agricultural country, with very limited industry, to an increasingly urbanized, industrialized, and modernized nation. The 1988 Olympic Games in Seoul were a chance for the Koreans to show the world how much they had progressed, just as the 1964 Games in Tokyo provided a similar opportunity for Japan.

Commonalities, Concerns, and China

There are certain commonalities among the East Asian NICs that have contributed to their development. Mention has been made of the fact that most of them are very small. They have relatively well-educated populations, living mostly in urban areas. None of them were endowed with abundant natural resources, so there was a natural inclination to be traders.

A common experience shared by Taiwan and South Korea is that in the early stages of their modern economic development, both benefited from substantial economic and military assistance from the United States.

There are problems and uncertainties in the NICs, including political development. South Korea has had a history of political turmoil, repression, and military rule, but in both South Korea and Taiwan there are indications that economic development has helped open up the political process. In 1987–88, South Korea underwent considerable political reform.

A long shadow over the Asian NICs is cast by China, and, of course, this is particularly true for Hong Kong and Taiwan. China has itself attempted to become more integrated into the world economy, but economic reform has been a difficult and politically complicated process in the world's largest country.

China is looked upon as potentially being both a vast market and a significant force in the international economy. Japan, especially, and the United States and the other East Asian countries have been seeking to develop their economic ties with China. However, the 1989 Chinese government crackdown on the prodemocracy movement was economically damaging to the country. It resulted in pressure in a number of nations to restrict economic relations with China and caused hesitation among business interests about pursuing projects within China. Nonetheless, Chinese leaders made clear that they wanted to maintain an "open door" in terms of economic relations. Zhao Ziyang, who had been one of the leaders in opening up the Chinese economy before he was forced from power in the 1989 turmoil, had earlier said, "We are still at a quite backward stage because we lost too much time in the past. Closing one's country to external contacts results only in backwardness."[6] (See Profile: Mao Zedong, Deng Xiaoping, and China.)

Despite the government's apparent encouragement, many foreign businesses have encountered significant difficulty in dealing with China and operating within the country. Reaching clear agreements and coping with the complex government bureaucracy have been especially difficult for foreign businesses. Still, China's potential causes it to be of great economic interest to the rest of the world. Its future relations with two of the economic "tigers"—Hong Kong and Taiwan—could have some significant bearing on China's economic direction and development. For now, China remains in the category of low-income nations and faces an array of development challenges, including a growing population, which has been the subject of considerable government attention. (See Chapter 11.)

China at this stage remains far behind the economic status of the NICs and the high-income oil exporters, a small number of countries which constitute the upper ranks of Third-World nations in economic terms, even though some of them face their own difficulties and uncertainties. Like China, the vast majority of Third-World nations are low- and middle-income economies, facing awesome problems in their development efforts.

MIDDLE-INCOME NATIONS: DEVELOPMENT VS. DEBT

A number of Third-World nations have made some significant strides in economic development but are hindered by a variety of obstacles in advancing further or in even maintaining the standard already achieved. Some of the problems facing many of these nations, and those yet worse off—food, population, urban overcrowding—are discussed in the following chapter. According to the World Bank, about 60 nations fall into the middle-income category, but some of them are relatively well off. The upper level of this group includes some of the emerging NICs and others with economic standing equivalent to some of the "developed" economies. The biggest portion of the middle-income economies fall into the *lower middle-income* group, with 35 nations in that category. Another 37 are classed as low-income economies, and will be discussed in the next section of this chapter. (In listing the nations in each category, only those nations with populations of 1 million or above are included.) There are about 35 countries with populations of less than a million, including some which are very wealthy (Brunei, an oil-rich nation, has one of the highest per capita GNPs) and very poor (Guinea-Bissau is one of the poorest).

The middle-income category includes a group of nations which have experienced periods of growth, but which have found themselves saddled with high foreign indebtedness. About 20 of these countries have encountered severe difficulties in servicing their debts—that is, they have had difficulty even paying the interest on the money they borrowed. Brazil and Mexico are two countries generally listed, along with the rapidly growing East Asian countries, among the NICs. Both countries are large and have some highly developed industries and huge, modern, and sophisticated cities. However, they also have massive foreign debts, which limit their ability to make further economic progress.

Previous sections of this chapter have discussed some of the economic forces and trends that have affected Third-World nations in recent years. Generally speaking, the two decades between the early 1950s and early 1970s were marked by steady growth. Most developing countries shared in that growth, and many of them participated in the expansion of world trade. However, as has been pointed out, growth in much of the industrialized world slowed, particularly after the oil shocks of the 1970s, and there was a recession in the industrialized countries in the early 1980s. There have been variations in demand for the products of developing countries as output among industrialized nations has fluctuated. As growth rates in the industrialized nations fell, demand for goods from the developing countries declined. Certain sectors in some of the industrialized nations—especially agriculture, textiles, and clothing—were protected against exports from developing nations. Aid and investment from the wealthier nations became more limited or available only on unfavorable terms. There was a sharp rise in real international interest rates.

Figuring heavily in the problems encountered by the developing countries were the fluctuating oil prices and their resulting reverberations. They contributed significantly—directly and indirectly—to Third-World problems. The global recession of the early 1980s, brought on by the oil price increases of 1978–79, had an especially devastating effect on some of the middle-income countries, including Mexico, Brazil, and Argentina. These countries were expanding rapidly and had access to ample credit to fuel that expansion. As foreign exchange earnings declined because of the global recession and as interest rates increased, these countries found themselves caught in a squeeze. Mexico's situation was especially ironic, because much of its economic expansion in the late 1970s was spurred by its own oil revenues and the expectation of more. When oil prices began to fall in the early 1980s, Mexico was badly overextended.

The oil shocks of the 1970s were, in fact, major factors leading to the Third-World debt problem. While the non-oil Third-World countries were struggling to pay their oil bills, some of the oil-exporting nations, notably the Arab oil producers, were taking in far more than they could immediately spend. At that point the commercial banks entered the picture. Much of the surplus oil revenue was deposited in European and American banks, which then "recycled" the "petrodollars" as loans to the developing countries to help them finance development projects or meet increased oil costs. But many of these countries were borrowing their way into new trouble and, as they were hit by the economic slowdown and were unable to generate needed earnings from exports, could not meet their debt obligations. The oil shocks of the 1970s became the debt shocks of the 1980s.

The Debt Crisis

It was Mexico's problems that dramatized the debt crisis. In 1982, facing the financial abyss, Mexico announced that it would not be able to pay its debt. Soon thereafter, Argentina, Venezuela, and Brazil, all of which had been among the fastest-growing economies in the world, made similar declarations. The debt crisis sent shocks through the United States financial community, since many of the loans had come from American banks. In order to avert collapse of its economy, Mexico and the other nations had to take emergency steps and obtain additional loans, including assistance from the International Monetary Fund. At that point, the international institutions became more directly involved in attempting to deal with the crisis, and more will be said about the role of the IMF, World Bank, and other institutions later in the chapter. Brazil and Mexico both accumulated external debt in excess of $100 billion. Major debtors outside Latin America included Indonesia, Egypt, Nigeria, and the Philippines.

With strong urging from the IMF and other financial institutions and governments, most of the debtor nations—not always willingly—began to take steps to restructure their economies. The IMF functions as a sort of international credit union, borrowing from some members to provide help to others, while they attempt to overcome financial problems. While the World Bank makes longer-term loans for development projects, the IMF provides short- and mid-term loans to help countries deal with international payments problems. The debt crisis presented a major challenge for the IMF.

In order to obtain IMF assistance, a nation has to agree to an IMF-supervised stabilization program to reorganize its finances. This "conditionality" requirement, usually involving an IMF-imposed austerity program, has been the subject of great controversy among the nations being required to meet the conditionality terms. More than one leader of a nation faced with meeting IMF conditions has branded the IMF as the real ruler of the developing world. Typically, the conditions imposed upon debtor nations can include reductions in government spending, the elimination of various subsidies, and higher interest rates. These austerity moves are painful for countries already facing dire economic conditions. Brazil, Argentina, Peru, Mexico, and the Dominican Republic have all experienced major controversies over IMF conditions. Some countries have at times threatened not to even try to pay their debts, and a variety of proposals have been offered for reducing and restructuring the debts.

Mexico, as part of its agreement with the IMF, committed itself to ending or reducing a variety of subsidies on which many Mexicans had long relied, and to closing or selling inefficient state-owned enterprises. These were not popular moves and they created more unemployment, at least in the short term. In turn, Mexico got agreements from the IMF, the World Bank, the Inter-American Development Bank, and bilateral lenders for new loans to help Mexico service its debt (make interest payments) and for new investments in its strapped economy.

Latin American Dependence and Interdependence

Despite its proximity to the United States—or perhaps because of that proximity to the colossus of the north, Mexico often insisted on going its own way economically—a vivid demonstration of nationalism.

In 1938, Mexico expropriated the United States and British oil companies operating in Mexico and put the oil industry under a national organization—Pemex. Later, Mexico was one of the few nations that refused to join GATT, the body dealing with international trade regulations. The government was strongly protectionist. Foreign investment was generally discouraged and trading was limited by import quotas and licensing requirements, as Mexico sought to build a centralized, state-guided economy that, while capitalist, was also inward-looking. Bascially, Mexico ignored trends in the evolving international economy.

As is noted in Chapter 4, however, Mexico's concern about nationalism and independence is increasingly tempered by economic realism, particularly after the economic disaster of the early 1980s. Mexico has joined GATT and has taken steps to reduce many tariff barriers. Almost inevitably, the United States and Mexican economies grow more closely tied. Reference has already been made to the North American trading group or bloc, and some even foresee a hemispheric free-trade zone. Latin American nations are generally becoming less preoccupied with the issue of dependency, which has long clouded prospects for inter-American economic cooperation. The end of the Cold War, combined with the growing economic cooperation within Europe and Asia, have contributed to changing attitudes in some Latin American countries, where there is fear that the region might be left behind, in contrast to the economic dynamism of other areas. Most of the countries are more receptive to external investment and regard closer ties with the United States as more of an opportunity and less of a threat.

Mexico's Role

Creating a North American free-trade zone, or Yukon to Yucatan common market, is obviously a complicated process, but it would involve about 360 million people, slightly larger than the 12-member EC. There has been growing cooperation between the United States and Mexico, formally and informally. There have been a variety of commercial agreements and Mexico has become more open to United States products. A notable development has been the rise of the *maquiladora* industries on the Mexican side of the border with the United States.

The *maquiladoras* or *maquilas* are assembly plants where Mexican workers assemble parts for finished products which are then shipped across the border. Many leading United States and international firms have established such plants just across the border, where they have lower production costs, yet still enjoy ready access to the United States market. This is made possible by provisions in Mexican law that now allow for foreign ownership, and by United States provisions that waive the normal import duties on all but the value of the labor added on the Mexican side. While the *maquilas* have created thousands of new jobs in Mexico and aided Mexico's trade balance, not everyone is pleased with the development. In the United States there are complaints that jobs have been lost to the border plants. On the Mexican side, leaders recognize that these plants, with primarily low-paying jobs, do little to upgrade the nation's work force or its industrial capacity. Some favor development of additional joint enterprises involving more sophisticated industries.

Mexico's trade liberalization doesn't just involve the United States. The Mexicans are attempting to strengthen economic ties with a number of countries, especially Japan, and there is a growing Japanese economic presence in Mexico. Although there is still some strong resistance with Mexico, the developments there, particularly considering the nation's history of economic isolationism, symbolize the growing internationalization of the economy and the trend toward economic integration.

Problems, Potential, and the Poorest

Mexico and some of the other larger countries in the middle-income category still have major problems, including, for a number of them, massive foreign debt, which remains a major obstacle to growth and development. Without minimizing these problems, however, it is also fair to say that many of these countries do have considerable potential for economic advancement. For some of the poorest countries, the same cannot be said. These are the nations at the lowest end of the economic spectrum, producing mainly primary commodities and heavily dependent on outside aid. The World Bank counts as the poorest of the poor anyone living on $1 a day or less. By this measure, 1 billion of the world's 5-plus billion live in poverty.

LOW-INCOME ECONOMIES: THE FOURTH WORLD

Nearly 40 countries are in the category of the "least-developed" of the less-developed countries. By almost any economic measure, these nations, with low per capita incomes and low per capita GNP, are the poorest of the poor. Some of them have been referred to, unflatteringly and impolitely, as "international basket cases." These countries have GNPs per capita of only a few hundred dollars, a small fraction of that of the developed economies. They have little in common with those Third-World countries which have been economic super-achievers, and in most cases have little, if any, industrial development and figure very marginally in international trade. Many of them have not really become participants in the international economy. A number of them have only one export commodity. For all of these reasons, these countries might be considered as "Fourth-World" countries, well below the economic standard of even most Third-World nations. Some suggest that there should even be a "Fifth World" category, designating those countries mired in deep poverty. Most of these countries are facing serious food and population problems, subjects that will be discussed in the following chapter.

Mention has already been made in this chapter of India and China, both of which might be called special cases. They show up in some lists of the poorest nations, and by some measures belong in that category, particularly because of their huge populations—they are the two largest countries in the world. Many citizens of both countries do live in extreme poverty. However, despite major development obstacles, both India and China have made some significant progress. As was previously noted, India has some highly developed industries. India has some impressive achievements in agriculture too, as does China, which has reached a relatively high degree of self-sufficiency. Segments of the Indian population are well-educated, as is the case in China. These two countries still face awesome challenges, but they also have substantial assets.

Belts of Poverty

The largest number of least-developed countries are found in sub-Saharan Africa and in South Asia. The Independent Commission on International Development Issues, known as the Brandt Commission after its chairman, Willy Brandt of Germany, identified what it called "poverty belts," where most of the poorest countries are located. One extends across the middle of Africa, from the Sahara Desert in the north to Lake Nyasa in the south (between Malawi and Mozambique). The other, beginning with the two Yemens in the Middle East, stretches across Afghanistan and South Asia and some East Asian countries. These belts extend into other regions and parts of countries; for example, parts of Kenya in Africa, and, in Asia, Burma, Cambodia, Vietnam, and parts of India.[7]

These countries, as the commission noted, have different approaches to development and their economies have different degrees of openness. But each of them has a slim margin between subsistence and disaster. They are, the commission reported, circumscribed by their ecology and their dependence on market forces beyond their control. The Brandt Commission described the plight of these countries this way:

> They exist in a fragile tropical environment which has been
> upset by the growing pressure of people. Without irrigation and

water management they are afflicted by droughts, floods, soil erosion, and creeping deserts, which reduce the long-term fertility of the land. Disasters such as drought intensify the malnutrition and ill-health of their people, and they are all affected by endemic diseases which undermine their vitality. Their poverty, harsh climate, and isolation all make it harder to explore their resources, especially minerals.[8]

More will be said in the next chapter about the food-related problems that face these countries. Significantly, many of them have actually lost ground in terms of food supply and in other economic terms. During the 1980s, the Sub-Saharan region had negative growth rates by most economic measures.

Ethiopia, which has experienced severe drought, years of civil war, regional rivalries, and a long period of harsh military rule, is considered the poorest country in the world. Famine in the East African nation attracted worldwide attention and assistance, but at times critics accused the Ethiopian government of politicizing the relief efforts, thereby exacerbating the famine.

Others among the poorest nations, according to economic statistics, are Burkina Faso (formerly Upper Volta), Mali, and Mozambique in Africa, and Bangladesh, Bhutan, and Nepal in Asia.

Ghana's Struggle

Most of the Asian nations have recorded at least some economic progress, but many of the African countries have continued to lose ground. A case in point is Ghana in West Africa. As a British colony from the middle of the nineteenth century, it was known as the Gold Coast. It became independent Ghana in 1957 and was a leader in the struggle for African independence. Kwame Nkrumah led the peaceful resistance to British rule and became the first head of Ghana's government. He was a key figure among early Third-World leaders. However, his socialist government was unable to make economic headway. Corruption, mismanagement, limited technical resources, and lack of skilled personnel have been cited as factors contributing to the economic problems. The decline in the price of cocoa, Ghana's major export, and the rise in the costs of imports obviously were contributing factors. In 1966, Nkrumah was overthrown by a group of military officers, and since then Ghana has been struggling, without much success, to find a formula for economic progress. Recently, there have been some encouraging signs.

It is instructive to make some comparisons between Ghana's lack of progress over the past 25 years and that of South Korea, discussed earlier in the chapter. In 1957, when Ghana became independent, it was one of the richest countries in Africa, with one of the best-educated populations. It was the world's leading exporter of cocoa; it produced 10 percent of the world's gold and had diamonds, bauxite, and manganese, plus a thriving trade in mahogany. Its per capita income was almost exactly the same as that of South Korea at the time.

South Korea's success story has already been covered. By 1990, its per capita income was more than seven times that of Ghana, where the average income had actually fallen. By almost every measure of economic progress and living standards, South Korea has moved forward, while Ghana has done just the opposite, experiencing a loss in a number of categories, including a dramatic drop in exports, being hit particularly hard by the drop in cocoa prices. In some respects, Ghana represents an extreme case, but the situation there is not untypical of "Fourth-World" nations, many of which have less resources than Ghana.

Foreign Assistance

In a special session on African economic and development problems in 1991, the United Nations set a goal of doubling Africa's per capita income of $350 by the year 2015. The United Nations plan calls for diversifying national economies and exports and for increasing overseas development assistance to Africa by a 4 percent annual rate until 2000. Overall, Africa has experienced only a marginal increase in foreign assistance in recent years and in some countries the total has actually gone down. The United Nations noted that even with increased aid, many African nations are burdened by heavy external debts and said that steps must be taken to reschedule or write off the debts if some of the countries are to have any hope of economic progress.

Some of the poorer countries have already been heavily dependent on external aid from private agencies, national governments, and international organizations. Relatively speaking, Ghana has not been a major aid recipient, and in some years the total official aid received has actually declined. Ghana has been involved in programs with both the World Bank and the IMF to restructure and redirect its economy, and, as elsewhere, there has been some controversy about the conditions imposed by the international institutions.

The closing section of this chapter will examine bilateral and multilateral aid and the functions and role of the international financial institutions.

AID: BILATERAL AND MULTILATERAL

Aid and various forms of foreign assistance may be *bilateral*, from one nation to another, or *multilateral*, administered and disbursed by groups of nations or international organizations, such as the United Nations agencies. Most aid is in the form of *loans* (which may be on very favorable terms) or *grants* of funds or supplies/equipment. Some forms of aid are provided on a *concessionary* basis, meaning that the terms are extremely favorable or that there is no expectation of loans being paid. Aid that passes through government channels is sometimes referred to as official development assistance (ODA), particularly if it is intended for Third-World countries. Some aid is provided through nongovernmental organizations, especially through relief and disaster and emergency assistance organizations. Examples of such assistance have included projects to provide famine relief in Ethiopia or aid to earthquake victims in Mexico or cyclone victims in Bangladesh.

There are three major types of official aid:

■ Humanitarian assistance
■ Security or military assistance (discussed in Chapter 7)
■ Economic or development aid. (Sometimes "economic support" is a form of security assistance.)

For much of recent history, bilateral aid was often a part of or heavily influenced by the Cold War rivalry. The United States and the Soviets were major aid providers, and much of the aid went to countries of strategic significance.

United States Aid

Beginning with the post–World War II Marshall Plan, the United States set the pattern and the pace for foreign aid programs. As is discussed in earlier chapters, the Marshall Plan focused on Europe, and it was highly successful in helping to reconstruct Europe and in frustrating Communist aspirations. It has been suggested that the Marshall Plan's success, in contrast to many subsequent aid programs in the Third World, was because the task was clearly limited and defined; ample funding was available; and postwar Europe, even though badly damaged, already had the basis for a modern industrial economy.

Although the Marshall Plan was a magnanimous humanitarian gesture by the United States, it also served American foreign policy goals. After the Marshall Plan, the primary focus of United States aid shifted to Asia. As the economic and security problems of the emerging nations became more apparent, United States policymakers wanted to replicate the Marshall Plan in Asia. Two of the primary beneficiaries of United States aid, Korea and Taiwan, were ultimately very successful economically. Other American assistance was much less productive, and, of course, Vietnam was an especially costly experience for the United States.

In the 1960s, with the number of independent nations in the Third World significantly increasing, there was growing attention to their quest for economic development. At the same time, the Soviet Union was beginning to compete with the United States as an aid donor, particularly in India and Egypt, and this caused the rules of the game to shift. Nations that once aligned themselves with the United States as a precondition of aid now had a choice, and even enjoyed the luxury of being able to play one donor off against the other without making political commitments. Some Third-World leaders were especially adept at obtaining United States aid by invoking the Communist threat or by implying that they would take actions contrary to United States interests. Ferdinand Marcos of the Philippines was one who did this with great effectiveness.

With so much attention focused on the political-security aspects of aid, the development component sometimes received only scant attention. American aid policies were redesigned and were supposed to become more development-oriented, promoting economic growth and political stability, but in terms of financial commitment and overall emphasis, security concerns continued to be primary. Leading recipients of United States assistance over the years have been Israel and Egypt (after its peace treaty with Israel), Turkey, the Philippines, Pakistan, Greece, and, more recently, El Salvador. It would be hard to argue that "development" has been the primary consideration for aid to any of these countries, although certainly in Egypt, for example, United States aid has been vital to that nation's efforts to deal with its economic problems. Foreign aid has often been controversial in the United States, although the total of United States funds going for foreign aid, particularly for humanitarian and economic/development assistance, is a miniscule portion of the overall budget. Further, about 70 percent of the appropriations for bilateral foreign assistance is spent in the United States, not abroad. American firms supply commodities, equipment, and consulting services for foreign assistance projects.

The United States has strong economic ties to the Third World, as has been noted earlier. LDCs receive about 35 percent of United States exports, more than the EC and Japan combined. The United States is an important market for a number of Third-World nations and relies on the Third World for some vital raw materials. Trade is, of course, a greater source of foreign exchange for Third-World countries than assistance they receive from all donor countries combined.

The United States has played a leading role in the multilateral financial organizations, which are discussed in the next section. The Soviet Union, on the other hand, had little involvement with most of the multilaterals during the Cold War period.

Soviet Assistance

Soviet aid principally went to nations closely aligned with it. During the 1980s, Cuba, Mongolia, and Vietnam received the bulk of Soviet nonmilitary aid. Cuba and Vietnam also benefited from large supplies of arms. Afghanistan, Cambodia, North Korea, and Laos were other major Soviet aid recipients, and India has also been a large beneficiary, receiving aid on favorable terms in addition to arms deliveries. The Soviets also aided some of the poorest nations, including Ethiopia and Somalia. They also had their Third-World debtors, as nations such as Mozambique, South Yemen, Zambia, and Peru have had to postpone their debt repayments or have some of their obligations cancelled.

Cuba is an example of a country that became closely integrated with the Soviet Union and received vast amounts of Soviet aid. In addition to direct economic assistance, the Soviet Union subsidized Cuba in a variety of ways, amounting to a subsidy valued at about $2 billion a year. The Soviets paid considerably more than the world price for Cuban sugar and nickel, but they paid in "soft" (Soviet) currency, which meant that almost all Cuba could do was to use it for trade with the Eastern bloc. The Soviets supplied oil to Cuba at relatively low prices and allowed Cuba to sell for "hard" currency any oil left over from its allocation. In 1991, plans to end Soviet subsidies and withdraw Soviet military forces from Cuba were announced. As is pointed out elsewhere in this book, the Soviet troops in Cuba had long been a point of international contention.

When the Soviet Union began to concentrate more on its own economic difficulties and then moved into the postcommunist period, foreign assistance was curtailed. Indeed, some of the republics that were part of the U.S.S.R. as it was formerly constituted were themselves seeking foreign assistance from the West and Russia and others did receive some aid.

Unquestionably, the political realignment and restructuring and economic policy changes in the Soviet Union had profound implications for those Third-World countries that had been linked to and dependent on it.

Aid Donors and Targets

While Soviet aid to the Third World decreased, some other nations, notably Japan, have been increasing their aid. Japan, as noted in Chapter 9, has surpassed the United States as the world's largest aid donor. While the total amount of aid to developing countries has increased, it has fallen as a proportion of the GNP of the donor countries. There have been various calls by international groups for the donor countries to reach a target of 0.7 percent of their GNP for official development assistance. However, only the Netherlands, some Scandinavian countries, and a few of the oil-rich nations have regularly reached or passed the target figure. France is also a relatively large donor, primarily aiding former French colonies. German aid has also been increasing.

There have been efforts to see that a higher percentage of the aid goes to the least-developed nations, and there has been some progress toward that goal. Still, only a very small proportion of aid goes to these countries.

While the bulk of aid to developing countries is distributed bilaterally, bilateral aid is, of course, only one of the ways in which financial aid flows from developed to developing countries. Other ways include trade financing, loans from private banks or international institutions (such as the IMF), and multilateral aid through international organizations.

INTERNATIONAL ASSISTANCE AND ECONOMIC INSTITUTIONS

Much has already been said in this and the previous chapter about the role of international organizations and financial institutions in aid, trade, development, and economic affairs. Chapter 2 also includes some discussion of the international framework as it applies to economic relations and cooperation.

The distinctive roles of the World Bank, the IMF, and GATT have all been referred to earlier in this chapter. A number of the United Nations agencies are also involved with economic matters, including UNCTAD, discussed earlier; the United Nations Development Program (UNDP), which coordinates and administers technical assistance to help LDCs in their efforts to accelerate social and economic development; and five regional economic commissions which are part of the Economic and Social Council (ECOSOC). Other United Nations agencies—such as the Food and Agriculture Organization (FAO), International Fund for Agricultural Development (IFAD), and United Nations Industrial Development Organization (UNIDO)—are also concerned with development issues. The increasingly significant role of some of the regional economic groupings, particularly the European Community, has also been discussed, and it should be noted that the EC has a relationship with a number of developing nations which are affiliated with the Lome Convention. Nearly 70 African, Caribbean, and Pacific nations are part of the Lome group, which was originally established at a meeting in Lome, Togo, in 1975, and establishes a comprehensive trading and economic cooperation relationship between the EC and these developing nations, many of which are former British, French, and Portuguese colonies. This is the most important regional agreement providing special and differential treatment for a group of Third-World nations. There are also regional development banks, such as the Asian, African, and Latin-American Development Banks, intended to accelerate economic and social development by member states by promoting public and private investment.

Although many organizations and institutions are involved in economic cooperation and assistance, the key global groups in the areas of development and economic-financial cooperation are the World Bank, the International Monetary Fund, and the General Agreement on Tariffs and Trade. As was pointed out early in Chapter 9, the IMF and the World Bank were established by the Bretton Woods Conference and are specialized agencies of the United Nations. GATT was not intended to be an organization but was established in 1947 as a framework for tariff negotiations and has grown into a permanent structure. For most of their lives these organizations did not have the participation of the Soviet

Union and some of its close allies, but that began to change in the late 1980s.

Here is a brief summary of these organizations.

■**World Bank.** The World Bank is the leading source of long-term finance and policy advice for developing nations. It actually consists of three institutions:

International Bank for Reconstruction and Development (IBRD), which was the original institution founded at Bretton Woods. It makes loans at market-related interest rates to nations at more advanced stages of development.

International Development Association (IDA), established in 1960 to provide long-term, low-interest (or concessional) loans to the poorest countries.

International Finance Corporation (IFC), which supports promising private economic ventures in developing nations.

The United States has been the largest contributor to the World Bank, but there is broad participation in funding the Bank, and other nations have been assuming a larger share. Membership in the IMF is a prerequisite to World Bank membership. The Bank operates on a weighted voting system that is based on individual country subscriptions, but with the poorer nations being given a slightly larger than proportional share.

■**International Monetary Fund.** The growth of the IMF from its original 41 members to more than 150 is indicative of some of the dramatic changes that have occurred in international affairs and in the role of international institutions. The IMF provides a permanent forum for its members to coordinate economic and financial policies. Voting power, like that in the World Bank, is roughly dependent on the country's contribution to the Fund, based on a quota determined by its relative economic and financial strength. The IMF is not a bank and has both regulatory and financial functions. It was designed to promote international monetary cooperation, facilitate the growth of international trade, and to promote stability in foreign exchange. Today, as has been discussed in this chapter, the IMF is involved in a number of Third-World countries facing balance-of-payments difficulties. In response to the debt crisis, the IMF created new facilities and medium-term financing arrangements designed to support a borrowing member's efforts to improve its economic position. In working with countries in economic difficulty, the IMF has often imposed conditions for further assistance which have included reductions in government spending, elimination of various subsidies, higher interest rates, and increased reliance on market forces. The IMF also works closely with GATT.

When the Reagan administration took office in the United States in the early 1980s, there was initially a tendency to downgrade the importance of these multilateral institutions, including the IMF. President Reagan had been critical of the institutions and favored a decrease in United States financial support and participation in these bodies. However, after the scope of the international debt problem began to be apparent, there was a reversal of attitude, particularly toward the IMF, and the administration persuaded Congress to increase support for the organization. Without the IMF, the American financial and banking community would have been at much greater risk in dealing with the debt problem.

■ **General Agreement on Tariffs and Trade.**   Originally established to provide a temporary framework for tariff negotiations, pending the establishment of the International Trade Organization under United Nations auspices, GATT has become a permanent and important fixture in international economic relations. When formation of the ITO was indefinitely postponed, GATT was the only available instrument for seeking agreement on rules for the conduct of international trade and has continued to function as a multilateral forum for tariff negotiations. Over the years, GATT has played a significant role in providing the organizational basis for working out regulations on trade and reducing tariff barriers, although it has drawn criticism at times from Third-World governments for being too concerned with the interests of the industrial powers. In GATT, the process of negotiating reductions in trade barriers is based on the principle of reciprocity. Nations reduce tariffs with the understanding that other nations are making equivalent cuts. The combination of reciprocity for industrial nations and special and differential treatment for developing nations has meant that negotiations focused mainly on items of interest to the industrial nations.

The main success of GATT since 1948 has been the dramatic reduction in tariffs on trade in manufactured products. In more recent years, GATT has moved on to deal with new areas such as agriculture and trade in services. These were topics of the Uruguay Round of negotiations (so named because the meeting which initiated the negotiations was held in Punta del Este, Uruguay). Services have become an increasingly significant part of the international economy, involving such areas as transportation, travel, tourism, banking, and insurance, and are particularly important to the United States, the leading exporter of services.

CONCLUSION

Although the World Bank and the IMF have been criticized on a variety of counts and often appear to be overly bureaucratized, they are attempting to adapt to the needs of a changing world. In such critical situations as the onset of the debt crisis in 1982 and the collapse of the economies of the former Communist nations after 1989, the international financial institutions have responded and have shouldered a burden no other institutions could carry. Their new commitments in attempting to deal with the problems of Eastern Europe and the crumbling Soviet Union have imposed new demands and have further stretched their resources.

There have been a variety of proposals and suggestions for changing or expanding the international economic organizations and structure or creating new institutions. Despite many obstacles, however, these organizations have made a significant contribution. Nonetheless, in a world of "complex interdependence," major challenges remain and new ones are emerging, not just the restructuring of the economies of Eastern Europe and the old Soviet republics. On the one hand, there are the desperately poor nations described in this chapter, and on the other, there are the rising economic powers, the dynamics of regional integration, and the decreasing significance of national borders in economic relations, as companies and competition become truly international. The decrease in East-West tensions and the new tripolar international economic framework open up further possibilities for economic cooperation, and, perhaps, will lead to greater attention to the ongoing North-South economic issues. The remaining chapters will consider both the awesome problems that are limiting economic and social progress and the profound implications that advances in communications, transportation, and technology have for international development, commerce, and cooperation.

NOTES

1. Jyoti Shankhar Singh, *A New International Economic Order* (New York: Praeger, 1977), p. 2.
2. See W. W. Rostow, "Energy Target for the United States: A Net Export Position by 1990," *Orbis* 24, fall 1980, p. 459; and U.S. Congress, Senate, Committee on Energy and Natural Resources, Staff Report, *The Geopolitics of Oil*, December 1980.
3. Robert Gilpin, *The Political Economy of International Relations* (Princeton, N.J.: Princeton University Press, 1987), p. 300.
4. Steve Chan, *East Asian Dynamism: Growth, Order, and Security in the Pacific Region* (Boulder, Colo.: Westview, 1990), p. 52.
5. John F. Copper, "Taiwan: A Nation in Transition," *Current History*, April 1989, p. 199.
6. See Barry Kramer, "The Chinese Economy Appears to Be Firmly on the Reform Path," *Wall Street Journal*, May 14, 1987; also, Robert C. Byrd, "Report of Trip to the People's Republic," *Congressional Record*, p. S 9575, July 23, 1980, 96th Congress, 2nd Session; Zhao Ziyang, "The Opening of China," *The Atlantic*, December 1984, p. 24.
7. North-South: A Program of Survival, report of the Independent Commission on International Development Issues (Brandt Commission) (Cambridge, Mass.: MIT Press, 1980), p. 78; also, *Common Crisis—*

North-South: Cooperation for World Recovery, report of the Brandt
Commission (Cambridge, Mass.: MIT Press, 1983), p. 75.
8. *Ibid.*, (Brandt Commission, 1983), p. 79.

Particularly useful in providing statistical data on each nation is the annual *World Development Report* of the International Bank for Reconstruction and Development/The World Bank, published by Oxford University Press.

MAO ZEDONG, DENG XIAOPING, AND CHINA

Sometimes events deep within a single country, developments which may seem relatively unimportant at the time and which receive little attention, can, in fact, have profound international implications far into the future.

Such was the case with events that occurred in China in 1934–35. Encircled by the nationalist forces of Chiang Kaishek and threatened with annihilation, the Red Army of the Chinese Communists regrouped and launched a 6,000-mile trek into Northwest China. This journey became known as the Long March. It is estimated that more than 100,000 troops and supporters participated in the march (although estimates vary widely), while less than one-tenth that number survived the treacherous 368-day campaign that took the marchers across mountains, rivers, and deserts, through snow and heat, all the while facing ambushes from warlords and bombardment from the nationalist forces.

The Long March be-

It was in Tiananmen Square in Beijing that Mao Zedong proclaimed the establishment of the world's largest Communist nation in 1949. Forty years later, students in the "pro-democracy" movement constructed a symbolic statue of the goddess of liberty in the same square. The 1989 protests and the eventual crackdown by the Chinese government became a focal point of world attention.

came the crucible of the Communist revolution in China. This trek strengthened the dedication and spirit of those who survived. Out of this epic event came the leadership that would guide the world's largest nation and significantly affect world affairs for most of the remainder of the century.

One important result of the Long March was the clear emergence of Mao Zedong as the primary leader of the Chinese Communists. Mao made the army not only into an effective military force but also a strong political, economic, and propaganda force. The Communists didn't actually gain power in China until 1949, when the People's Republic of China (PRC) was established, and the nationalist government of Chiang Kai-shek, which had been supported by the United States, fled to the island of Taiwan.

Among the other survivors of the Long March who assumed positions of power in China was Deng Xiaoping. He was still the key figure in Chinese politics at the beginning of the 1990s. Deng and other veterans of the Long March were influential members of what had become the "old guard," the group believed responsible for ordering the crackdown on the student-based "prodemocracy" movement in China in 1989.

MAO, CHINA, AND THE WORLD

The most visible aspect of that crackdown occurred in Tiananmen Square. It was in that same square in Beijing where Mao proclaimed the establishment of the PRC in 1949. Mao served as China's leader until his death in 1976, having lived to see the opening of contacts with the United States in 1972 after more than 20

Mao Zedong led the Communists to power in China after long years of revolutionary struggle, including the epic Long March of 1934–1935. He is seen here proclaiming the founding of the People's Republic of China in Beijing's Tiananmen Square in 1949. Mao ruled China until his death in 1976, although in his final years his control over the nation was slipping.

years of frozen relations and hostile policies toward each other.

During his tenure, Mao led China away from its close relationship with the Soviet Union, ending the notion of "monolithic" communism. Indeed, the two Communist giants were often openly antagonistic.

The Chinese Communists decided that the Soviet development model, featuring heavy industry, was not applicable to China. Instead China sought to build development around collective units called *communes*, which Mao believed were consistent with Marxist-Leninist principles. The Chinese and Soviets also split over foreign policy and international issues. The Chinese wanted to develop their own nuclear capability and not be dependent upon Moscow. The Soviets stopped aiding China's nuclear program, but China proceeded on its own and exploded its first atomic bomb in 1964, further signaling its independence from Moscow. The Chinese also favored a more overtly hostile policy toward the United States and assertive identification with the causes of Third-World nations.

Some expected that this more independent China would emerge as a superpower. A major reason that didn't happen was because of China's difficulty in dealing with its domestic development and economic problems and the turmoil which engulfed the nation at several points.

As part of his effort to pursue an alternative to the Soviet development model, in 1958 Mao called for the Great Leap Forward, a scheme to increase production by greater human effort in the communes (which were increased in size) rather than from more investment or improved technology. This policy was short-lived and generally disastrous, with the problems heightened by several years of bad weather. There are some estimates that 20 to 30 million people died from 1959 to 1962 as a result of starvation and diseases caused by malnutrition.

Cultural Revolution, Chaos, and Change

In 1966, Mao sought to reinvigorate the Chinese revolution, which was clearly lagging. In effect, he was seeking a more modern version of the Long March when he launched the Great Proletarian Cultural Revolution, which he believed would restore revolutionary spirit. He feared that China was in danger of veering away from socialism. Mao called on China's young people to challenge authority, particularly "those revisionists in authority who are taking the capitalist road."

One goal of the Cultural Revolution was to rid China of foreign influence, particularly capitalism. "Capitalist roaders," intellectuals, bureaucrats, and individuals with foreign connections were targets. The term *capitalist roader* was a shortening of the phrase "one with power in the Party who is taking the capitalist road."

At the center of the Cultural Revolution were the young people who formed Mao's Red Guards. The zealous youths were soon rampaging through the country, harassing those who were deemed not sufficiently "revolutionary" and often turning violent. Posters and banners with Mao's picture or his sayings were ubiquitous. The Red Guards carried with them the little red books of Mao's quotations, as Mao's followers made him the object of a personality cult.

In a rather short period, China deteriorated into chaos. Finally, in 1969, Mao called a halt to the excesses of the Red Guards and they were disbanded. However, the chaos set in motion by the Cultural Revolution did not really end for some years.

Although Mao remained nominally in charge in China until his death, there was considerable infighting and turmoil in the country. Indications of a more pragmatic direction in Chinese policy were evident, however, from the changed attitude toward the United States in the early 1970s. Both China, under Chairman Mao, and the United States, under President Richard Nixon, saw it in their *realistic* strategic interests to end the hostile relationship between the two. As discussed in Chapter 1, an important factor motivating the two countries was their desire to balance off the Soviet Union. Both saw it as advantageous to let the Soviets know that they could no longer disregard the possibility of a Sino-American alliance. Many differences remained between China and the United States, but calculations of their respective national interests compelled them to downplay those differences. This was true even though Mao had built much of his career on his anti-American approach and Nixon had earned a reputation as a hardline anticommunist. Key roles in engineering this rapprochement were played by Nixon's national security advisor, Henry Kissinger (See Profile), on the American side, and Zhou Enlai for the Chinese. Zhou was another veteran of the Long March, who had worked alongside Mao for decades. Since the founding of the PRC he had served as premier and the leading diplomat.

DENG TAKES CONTROL

Mao and Zhou both died in 1976, and the struggle for control in China was out in the open. A more radical faction, led by the "Gang of Four," including Mao's wife, wanted to rid China of "capitalist roaders" and favored the continuous class struggle. They had been strong supporters of the Cultural Revolution. However, after Mao's death the Gang no longer enjoyed his protection (even though Mao became disenchanted with the radicals in his final years) and other party and army leaders had the Gang arrested within a month.

The individual who eventually emerged as the new power in China was Deng Xiaoping, although Hua Guofeng, a compromise candidate, initially succeeded Mao as chairman of the Chinese Communist Party.

Deng Xiaoping's rise to the paramount position in Chinese politics is a remarkable story. He ranks among the great political survivors, having twice been purged before returning to

In the years after Mao Zedong's death, Deng Xiaoping, known as a pragmatist and a "survivor" in China's internal political battles, emerged as the dominant figure in Chinese politics. Although a veteran Communist, he redirected China's international and economic policies. In 1989, however, he sided with the hardliners in cracking down on the "pro-democracy" protests.

become the most powerful figure in China. During the Cultural Revolution he was labeled a "capitalist roader" and was "struggled against" by the Red Guards. The radicals were determined not to let Deng gain power, considering him to be a "counterrevolutionary" who would alter Mao's rigid economic policies.

The diminutive Deng (only 4 feet, 11 inches) was, as noted earlier, another veteran of the Long March. He rose through the party hierarchy to become general secretary, remaining in that position from 1955 until he was purged in the Cultural Revolution in 1966. However, by 1974, Deng was speaking for China at a special session of the United Nations. (China had actually been represented in the United Nations by the Republic of China [Taiwan] government until the PRC was seated in 1971.) Indeed, it was Deng Xiaoping who spoke of Mao's "three

worlds" concept of international relations, asserting China's inclusion in and identification with the Third World. Zhou Enlai was largely responsible for rehabilitating Deng. Zhou, in failing health, wanted Deng, whom he considered to be a capable and trusted colleague, in a position of power; and by 1975, Deng became a vice-premier and chief of staff of the People's Liberation Army. However, Deng suffered a temporary setback during the political maneuvering after the death of Mao and Zhou. But, by 1977, at age 72, he had been restored to his posts, and he moved quickly to consolidate power.

While Mao was dogmatic and emphasized ideology, Deng attempted to be pragmatic and realistic. "I don't care about the color of the cat as long as it catches mice," said Deng, illustrating his practical, nonideological approach. He undertook to lead a modernization program in China, emphasizing science and technology, industry, and agriculture, and, to a lesser extent, defense. Most notably, Deng sought to redirect the Chinese economy.

By 1980, two of Deng's proteges, Zhao Ziyang (who replaced Hua Guofeng) and Hu Yaobang, had been installed in the top government and party positions. With Deng's backing, they introduced major economic changes, moving away from the centrally controlled command economy and encouraging decentralization, incentives, and a generally more open economy. On a parallel track, China opened its doors to international commerce and investment. Deng and his associates acknowledged that China had to have an "open door" policy and, in order to make economic progress, had to be part of the global economy.

For most of the 1980s, China made significant economic advances, including major increases in agricultural production. However, those who were pushing for a more open economy and, at the margins at least, for a more open society, were often under attack by the old guard Maoists, who considered China's new direction to be an abandonment of socialism. Deng Xiaoping skillfully balanced the competing forces, usually coming down on the liberal reform side economically, but sticking with the hard line politically. Not surprisingly, as China became more a part of the international community and there was more exposure to outside influence, there was, particularly among intellectuals, growing sentiment for political change and greater freedom. (This same pattern affected Eastern Europe and the Soviet Union.)

In addition to the growing political problems in the country, there was increasing trouble on the economic front. The reform policies were being undercut by soaring inflation and rampant corruption. This mix of political and economic currents created a volatile situation in the country, and this explosive combination was further fueled by two events during the spring of 1989.

CHINA'S DEVELOPMENT: TIANANMEN AND THE FUTURE

The two catalytic events were the death of Hu Yaobang, who had earlier been removed as party leader after heavy criticism from the old guard, and the visit by Soviet leader Mikhail Gorbachev. Hu Yaobang's death served as a rallying point for those seeking political reform and intellectual freedom. They began a series of demonstrations and launched what became known as the "prodemocracy" movement. As the movement gained momentum, it became increasingly antigovernment and generated growing international attention. One reason for all the attention was the presence in China of a large contingent of foreign journalists and telecommunications equipment to cover the scheduled Gorbachev visit. (See Chapter 12.)

Gorbachev's visit was to have been a great triumph for the Chinese leadership, especially for Deng. After all, Gorbachev was the leader of the country that had once dominated China and then became a bitter rival. And to some extent Gorbachev's attempted economic reforms in

the Soviet Union were following the example of China, as Gorbachev acknowledged.

But instead of being a triumphant moment for Deng, the Sino-Soviet summit was overshadowed by China's political unrest. Students treated Gorbachev—not Deng—as a hero. In many respects it was a humiliating occasion for the Chinese leaders. Ceremonies intended for Tiananmen Square had to be moved to avoid the protesters. With world attention focused on Beijing, the spotlight was not on Deng but on the protesters and Gorbachev.

It was a stinging experience for Deng. After Gorbachev's visit and when the protests did not subside, the government moved forcefully to end the demonstrations, and the brutal crackdown drew condemnation from much of the world. In the final analysis, Deng sided with the old guard who favored a hard line against the protesters. Zhao Ziyang, Deng's protégé, was pushed from power for being too sympathetic to the prodemocracy movement. With Zhao gone, the first generation of the Chinese Communist leadership, including veterans of the Long March, was clearly still in charge.

China found itself in a dilemma. Deng Xiaoping and at least some of his colleagues wanted to continue with China's modernization efforts and believed it important for China to continue increasing its involvement in the international economy. Chinese leaders insisted that they still had an "open door" policy for international trade and investment. In particular, China was seeking access to advanced technology from other nations. However, the widespread sense of outrage over the crackdown on the prodemocracy movement led a number of countries to suspend various economic, political, and military contacts with Beijing as a sign of their disapproval. As noted in Chapter 3, others argued that it would be a mistake to isolate China. This group said that a *realistic* approach required continued contacts with China, even if on a reduced basis, in order to keep China from turning inward once again. As the furor over the

The brave act of a lone protester symbolized the 1989 protest of Chinese citizens against the power of government and the military. This "man in the white shirt" stepped in front of a column of tanks and temporarily brought them to a halt. Captured by television and news photographers, the dramatic scene was relayed around the world.

Tiananmen events subsided, a number of nations, led by Japan, began to step up their economic dealings with China.

Deng and his colleagues argued that the Tiananmen crackdown was necessary to maintain stability and order and that otherwise there would have been chaos. The challenges within China remain formidable. Under Mao and then during the leadership of Deng, China has moved first in one direction and then in another, with many false starts and retreats along the way. China's long march is still under way and its future leadership will have a significant role in determining whether China moves closer to the role of a major international power that many predict for it.

SUGGESTIONS FOR FURTHER READING

Binyan, Liu. *China's Crisis, China's Hope.* Cambridge, Mass.: Harvard University Press, 1990.

Bonavia, David. *The Chinese.* New York: Penguin, 1983.

Dreyer, June Teufel (ed.). *Chinese Defense and Foreign Policy.* New York: Paragon House, 1989.

Hsin, Chi. *Teng Hsiao-Ping (Deng Xiaoping): A Political Biography.* Hong Kong: Cosmos Books, 1978.

June Four: A Chronicle of the Chinese Democratic Uprising. Fayetteville: University of Arkansas Press, 1989.

Karnow, Stanley. *Mao and China*. New York: Viking Press, 1982.

Oxenberg, Michel, Lawrence R. Sullivan, and Marc Lambert (eds.). *Beijing Spring, 1989, Confrontation and Conflict: The Basic Documents*. Armonk, N.Y.: M. E. Sharpe, 1990.

Salisbury, Harrison. *The Long March*. New York: McGraw-Hill, 1986.

Schaller, Michael. *The United States and China in the Twentieth Century*. (2nd. ed.) New York: Oxford University Press, 1990.

Snow, Edgar. *Red Star Over China*. New York: Grove Press, 1973. (Originally published in 1938.)

Terrill, Ross. *Mao: A Biography*. New York: Oxford University Press, 1980.

Wang, James C. F. *Contemporary Chinese Politics: An Introduction*. (3rd. ed.) Englewood Cliffs, N.J.: Prentice Hall, 1990.

CHAPTER ELEVEN

Food, Population, and the Environment

Political, economic, and security issues often dominate world news and relations among nations. However, another set of factors is interwoven among these issues and figures prominently in international affairs. These are the interrelated areas of food, population, and environment, and they must be taken into account in considering the issues and problems that affect and will affect world affairs.

By the year 2000, world population is expected to exceed 6 billion, having grown 1.4 billion in 15 years. About 5 billion of the world's people will be in Third-World countries, and many of the fastest-growing countries are among the world's poorest. Nearly two-thirds of the world population lives under conditions of poverty and deprivation. Population growth is a source of extreme pressure on many nations, contributing to instability and often to political upheaval. The growing population and its needs place added pressure on the world's environment and ecological support system.

For many of the world's citizens, the immediate, basic human needs—having sufficient food and a place to live—loom as far more important and more challenging issues than concerns about advanced weapons or the economic and political issues that might dominate the world's headlines and news programs.

In many respects, food remains at the core of international development issues. National governments, international organizations, and a variety of assistance programs have worked to increase the quantity and efficiency of food production and distribution. Although some significant progress has been made in international agriculture and in improving the levels and quality of food consumption, there continue to be major food-supply problems. Food problems are particularly critical in many of those countries referred to in the previous chapter as the Fourth World or the poorest of the poor. And world food prospects must be viewed against the background of the soaring world population.

As is the case with other issues and problems in international relations, the problem of hunger and an adequate world food supply cannot be viewed as a separate or isolated matter. Instead, it must be seen as a multifaceted problem involving production, distribution, research, and marketing, and also subject to being affected by a variety of forces and factors—weather and natural disasters, war, government policies, international politics, international economic trends, and, of course, population growth and environmental stress.

This chapter will take a closer look at the problems of food, population, and the environment and related issues, and will consider their impact on international relations.

FEEDING THE WORLD

Existing and prospective world food conditions pose a number of connected problems.

- First, the low productivity of agriculture in many less-developed countries makes them dependent on food imports.
- Second, instability in food production and its amplified effect on food price fluctuations contributes to insecurity and variability in food supplies.
- Third, there are the problems of chronic food shortages and widespread malnutrition which affect large numbers of the world's citizens.

Hunger and malnutrition are rife in many areas of the world. More than a billion people are reported to be seriously undernourished, including up to one-half of the children under the age of five in the Third World. About 700 million people, according to the World Bank, suffer from hunger. Food consumption has been declining in a number of countries.

Two-thirds of the world's chronically hungry live in South Asia and one-fifth in sub-Saharan Africa. As was discussed in the previous chapter, much of sub-Saharan Africa was self-sufficient in food in the 1960s, but the region has subsequently been plagued by a variety of problems which have seen agricultural production decline in some countries and, in any case, fail to keep pace with population growth. The inability of these countries to feed themselves results from a combination of factors: the high population growth rate; loss of arable land due to soil erosion and desertification; political instability and civil strife; limited transportation systems; and flawed development policies. Some in the developing nations would also point to the colonial legacy as a factor, arguing that the colonial heritage is responsible for much of their economic difficulty. As early as 1962, René Dumont, a French agronomist, wrote a book (translated in English as *False Start in Africa*) in which he lamented the failure of both the colonial officials and leaders of the newly independent nations to take the necessary steps to establish the basis for continuing agriculture development that would meet national needs. Regrettably, in many countries, little progress has been made in overcoming the false start.

Many of the developing nations have devoted much of their cropland to cash crops for export rather than to food crops intended for domestic consumption. In Senegal, one of the sub-Saharan nations, more than half of the cropland is devoted to growing peanuts for export to Europe. In some of the countries, productivity has been falling in both cash and food crops. Emphasizing cash crops for foreign sale might not be such a problem if the profits went toward strengthening domestic agriculture in the developing nations; instead, they often go for nonproductive purposes.

The World Bank has reported that "both the proportion and the total number of Africans with deficient diets have climbed and will continue to rise unless special action is taken."[1] Chad, Ethiopia, Mozambique, Somalia, Uganda, Zaire, and Zambia are among African countries which have had chronic problems of undernourished populations.

Per capita grain production, a major indicator of the status of food supply, has been falling in Latin America as well as in Africa, and this decline in food production per person seems likely to continue, thus increasing the number of malnourished people. While the situation is not as bleak everywhere, and even though there are some encouraging signs in other parts of the world in food production, many of the world's people are dependent on what is really a rather fragile balance. That balance can be threatened when there is a poor harvest in any of the major grain-producing countries. It should be noted that the United States and Canada control a larger share of the world's grain exports than the Middle East countries do of oil, and thus a significant decline in United States or Canadian crops can have significant worldwide implications. When droughts hit North America in 1988, and China as well, there was a major drop in production and in the worldwide food supply.

Even when the level of international food production is relatively high, nations which need to import food can still face serious difficulties. Many of the food-deficit countries are either poor countries and/or they are plagued by serious debt problems, as discussed in the previous chapter. Such countries are thus limited in what they can spend on food imports, and are in even more difficulty when grain and other basic food prices rise. It must also be noted that even when a fairly adequate food supply exists within a country, undernourishment may still persist because of gross inequities in income among its citizens or lack of efficient means of distribution. Agricultural development also requires an adequate infrastructure, particularly rural roads, and such an infrastructure has been badly neglected in many countries.

Progress and Problems

The world food and agriculture situation is a good news–bad news story. The favorable aspect is that, as has been mentioned, there have been some remarkable developments in agricultural techniques and capability and in cooperative international efforts to increase the world's food supply. The discouraging side is that, despite these advances, millions are still seriously undernourished, and there is danger that the numbers will continue to grow.

There have been advances in agricultural production not only in the United States and some of the other developed market economies but also in some of the developing countries. The "Green Revolution" helped bring about significant increases in food production. Research enabled development and introduction of new strains of wheat and rice, two of the world's basic foods. These hardy, high-yield grains were adaptable to a wide range of climates. Norman Borlaug, a United States agricultural scientist, was a leader in this field and received the Nobel Prize in 1970 for his contributions toward easing world hunger. He worked for many years in Mexico, under Rockefeller Foundation auspices, to develop these crops, which were then planted widely in developing countries. In those countries wheat yields increased by 84 percent and rice by 42 percent from the late 1960s until the mid-1980s. India has been particularly successful, with grain harvests more than tripling over the past 30 years and continuing to increase. Overall, production growth in the developing countries averaged 3.2 percent from the early 1960s through the 1980s. However, as has been noted, some regions, such as sub-Saharan Africa, actually suffered losses in production. The Green Revolution has had its major impact in Asia, with limited effect in Latin America (primarily in Mexico), and has not really reached Africa.

Progress in enhancing crop yields, spurred by the new strains of rice and wheat, and advances in agricultural mechanization, irrigation, fertilization, storage, and plant and animal disease control have to be balanced against the growing direct and indirect costs of agricultural production. There is a decline in available agricultural acreage due to such factors as urbanization and the loss of farm land to erosion and nonagricultural uses and damage to the ecology. Some of the gains in production were made possible by cultivating marginal land where the soil eroded rapidly, and the water supply used for irrigation could not be sustained. Another problem is the cost of petroleum. When oil costs rise, this has major ramifications because modern agriculture is heavily dependent on petroleum and petroleum-based products. Agriculture uses large amounts of petroleum for fuel for farm machinery and for fertilizer, pesticides, and herbicides.

While the Green Revolution helped ease chronic hunger problems and enabled some countries to become more self-sufficient, the increased production often involved extensive irrigation and heavy use of pesticides, with resultant environmental costs. Moreover, even where there have been considerable increases in production, it has already been pointed out that there often continue to be significant distribution problems.

Most research has tended to concentrate on market requirements, export crops, and on large-scale farming and Western agricultural methods, with relatively little attention paid to the needs of smaller farmers in the developing countries, whose production is an important factor in future food security. Despite the success stories and the dramatic advances that have occurred in certain countries, it is important to note that millions of people—990 million in Asia, 280 million in Africa, and 100 million in Latin America—raise food under difficult conditions and with yields that have not significantly increased. In many cases they are using cultivation and harvesting techniques that date back for centuries.

A further fundamental point that needs to be understood is that food problems are not confined to the Third World and less-developed countries. Sections of the former Soviet Union, for example, have had continuing difficulties with food production and availability.

Agricultural Trade Issues

Also, some of the wealthier nations have been involved in continuing controversy and diplomatic disputes over international agricultural trade. Food and agricultural issues have been major topics in international trade negotiations, including the General Agreement on Tariffs and Trade (GATT). (See Chapter 10.) These issues have been highly contentious among interested nations. Problem areas have included such issues as market access, export subsidies, and internal supports.

Because it is the leading agricultural exporter, the United States has pushed hard to increase its access to foreign markets. The United States and the European Community have frequently been at odds on these issues, particularly over the Common Agricultural Policy of the EC, which includes protection for the long-subsidized and traditional small farms in Europe. The United States has argued that such large-scale internal supports distort the international market. (Despite its internal supports, the EC constitutes the largest importer of food and agricultural products in the world.)

Another point of international controversy has been Japan's virtual exclusion of imported rice. Rice is a major item in the Japanese diet, but tradition and the political power of the Japanese farmers have severely restricted access to the Japanese market by other rice-producing nations.

FOOD AND POWER

In earlier chapters there was discussion of the factors that contribute to national power and security. The elements of national power cited by Hans Morgenthau include natural resources, and the most elemental of these resources, according to Morgenthau, is food. A country that is self-sufficient, or nearly self-sufficient, has a great advantage over a nation that is not and is dependent upon imported food. One of the great advantages that the United States enjoys is its agricultural strength. Conversely, one of the continuing weaknesses of the Soviet Union has been its inadequate food production.

Some Third-World countries have been seriously hindered in their efforts to become more politically independent and potent in world affairs by their inability to feed their own populations and their reliance on external food supplies. Several of the Middle Eastern countries that are richest in oil resources and can therefore exercise considerable economic clout are, on the other hand, heavily dependent on food imports because of the sparseness of their own agricultural output.

International Attention

A World Food Conference was convened in 1974 by the United Nations Food and Agriculture Organization (FAO) in an attempt to focus attention on food problems.

The FAO, established in 1945, is a specialized agency of the United Nations, the oldest and largest of the United Nations food agencies. Its headquarters are in Rome. FAO member countries pledge cooperative action to raise levels of nutrition, to improve production and distribution of food and agricultural products, and to raise the living standards of rural populations. FAO provides technical assistance to government and farmers in developing countries. It also serves as the chief forum for policy and program planning and as the main center for information exchange on food-related issues. The United Nations also has the World Food Program, which distributes food to needy nations and includes the International Emergency Food Reserve, which maintains large emergency food stocks.

The World Food Conference was a response to the growing recognition that population growth was exceeding growth in food production in a number of countries. At that conference the participating governments pledged to work together to eliminate hunger within a decade. Attainment of national food security for all of the world's countries was established as a goal. As part of that effort, the International Fund for Agricultural Development (IFAD) was created.

IFAD's efforts are aimed at helping finance food production and rural development projects in 69 poorer countries. The oil-rich nations of OPEC have joined the industrialized nations in providing the funds. Using the technical capacity of FAO to guide it, IFAD has had a good record of imaginative agricultural projects. Some of the IFAD projects have been aimed at helping the small farmer and at enabling more rural families to be self-sufficient in food. IFAD has backed such projects as a "motorbike bank" in Pakistan, where bankers travel by motorbike into remote regions to help provide financial credit and agricultural assistance to villagers who would otherwise have no contact with banks. IFAD has also supported a bank in Bangladesh that gives small loans to rural residents to help them buy a cow, a rickshaw, and some simple tools necessary for processing betel, mustard, and spices, or for paddy husking, working bamboo, or making brooms. In Africa, the fund, working with United States aid projects and others, has helped farmers in Burundi grow rice on irrigated land, initiated soil-conservation efforts on Rwanda's eroded hilltops, and helped create national agricultural research and extension services in Zimbabwe.

Despite these and other such efforts, however, the goals of the World Food Conference remain as distant targets. Many countries are even further from achieving food self-sufficiency and eradicating hunger and poverty than they were at the time of the World Food Conference.

The Soviet Case

Food supplies and agricultural production have been recurring problems in areas of the former Soviet Union. Although there are vast farmlands in the countryside, only 15 percent of the total territory is arable land, and the frigid northern latitude limits farming. While the climate has contributed to the agricultural problems, Soviet agriculture, dating back to Lenin and Stalin, was notoriously inefficient. Under Leonid Brezhnev and more significantly under Mikhail Gorbachev, there were major attempts to revamp the agricultural system.

Tsarist Russia was a grain exporter, but in recent times Russia has had to depend on imports, particularly for critical grain needs. Chronic shortfalls in planned levels of Soviet agricultural production meant that the government was unable to meet rising demands for food and fiber. By the 1970s, the Soviets were importing substantial amounts of grain from the United States, which was somewhat ironic in view of the generally adversarial nature of the relationship which existed between the two. In 1980, President Carter imposed an embargo on United States grain shipments to the Soviet Union, following the Soviet invasion of Afghanistan. President Reagan subsequently suspended the embargo. Other nations—particularly Argentina, Australia, and Canada—have also been sources of grain supplies for the Russians. Of course, importing grain is costly to

Russia in terms of foreign exchange, and the government would much rather have that currency for other purposes, particularly for high-tech equipment and machinery.

As the Soviet Union entered the 1990s, it was heavily dependent on food imports. The U.S.S.R even had to import potatoes, a staple of the Russian diet, from Germany. In one of the paradoxes of modern international relations, the Soviet Union, which had tried to starve West Berlin into submission during the Berlin blockade of the late 1940s (see Berlin City Portrait), received a large shipment of food and other supplies from Berlin in 1990. The food came from Berlin's Cold War stockpiles, which had been built up after the infamous blockade in case of another siege by the Soviets. With the Cold War over and the East-West divisions in Berlin and Germany having ended, the German government donated the food and supplies to ward off hunger in the Soviet Union in 1990–91. In another paradoxical development, India, a nation often identified with food shortages, was able to ship grain to Russia.

With the various republics that had constituted the Soviet Union struggling to work out new economic and political systems in the early 1990s, the food problem was especially critical in certain areas. The United States and the European Community provided some food aid during that period. United States aid included loans to help finance purchase of American food, mostly grain, and thus was helpful to American farmers.

A major factor hindering agricultural production and marketing in the Soviet Union and the republics has been the lack of adequate infrastructure. One indication of this inadequacy is that the total length of paved roads in the entire Soviet Union, as it was formerly constituted, is only equivalent to that of the state of Pennsylvania. This lack of infrastructure seriously inhibits the efficient transportation and distribution of produce. The severe food problems were a major source of political discontent within the Soviet Union and continue to trouble the sovereign republics. Even in the Ukraine, long referred to as the "breadbasket" of the Soviet Union, where there is an ample food supply, there have been problems with distribution and marketing. Also, some of the other republics that have been dependent on food from the Ukraine are no longer assured of that source of supply.

Any country or political entity that has difficulties feeding its own population is going to be limited in its ability to function as a major world power. This was true for the former Soviet Union, even at the apex of its military strength.

FAMINE AND FOOD AS A WEAPON

There have been a number of widely reported instances of severe famine in various sections of the world in recent years—and some instances not so widely reported. Televised pictures of emaciated children barely clinging to life can have a powerful impact in the more affluent nations.

In several of the highly publicized cases, citizens and groups around the world have rallied to the support of those facing starvation. Music groups, entertainers, and various charity campaigns have raised millions of dollars for famine relief. Meanwhile, there are, as noted earlier, numerous organizations within the United Nations, plus many national government aid and assistance programs and a large contingent of private organizations, that are devoted to dealing with international food and agricultural issues. Yet, the problems don't end, and the danger of further and more severe hunger and famine continues. The question is why?

Some of the reasons for these continuing problems have already been suggested and discussed. Structural poverty, the burdens of international debt, and the drop in prices for some of the primary exports of Third-World nations have all contributed to the desperate conditions which have plagued some of these nations. In some cases, they become caught in a spiral of worsening problems, and even if they make some progress, they are unable to keep pace with their needs. Their problems may be exacerbated by political and/or military conflicts.

Famine Factors

Before further consideration of the entanglements of food problems with war and politics, it is important to underline the fact that weather and environmental degradation are extremely important factors influencing agricultural productivity. Severe rain and storms or severe drought can wipe out crops and livestock. Some of the poorest countries seem to be hit most often by extreme weather conditions. However, as was pointed out earlier in the chapter, the United States, Canada, and other developed nations have at times suffered major crop losses as the result of extreme weather.

In the mid-1980s, some 22 African nations were hit by famine or near-famine conditions. Weather, primarily drought, and the loss of cropland due to environmental degradation were significant contributing factors. However, some of the nations were also victimized by political and military conflicts which seriously worsened food problems. Ethiopia, Sudan, Angola, and Mozambique are among the African nations where substantial numbers of people have experienced hunger problems, and all have been torn by internal conflict, with tens of thousands of citizens uprooted. For example, the long-running war in Angola, discussed in Chapter 7, has had a devastating effect on food production and supplies within the country. Such problems aren't confined to Africa. Afghanistan and Cambodia are examples of Asian countries where war has contributed to serious hunger problems.

For several decades Ethiopia was tortured by civil war, which, combined with superpower competition in the region, political pettiness, and periods of drought, has contributed to large-scale starvation. As the United States–Soviet rivalry died down, Ethiopia ceased to be a point of contention between the two, but political turmoil and the long struggle for autonomy or independence by the province of Eritrea continued, and at great cost. The conflict began in 1962 when Ethiopia ended the autonomy or self-rule that Eritrea had when it became part of a federation with Ethiopia in 1952. An Eritrean separatist movement began a guerrilla war that grew into a long-term conflict. The war grew more intense after the Ethiopian government of Emperor Haile Selassie was overthrown in 1974. Unrest resulting from famine within parts of the country, to which the wealthy emperor and his government seemed relatively oblivious, helped trigger the coup which overthrew him. Haile Selassie was replaced by a Soviet-backed military government, which held power for 17 years.

During the 1980s, the civil war continued, and in 1984–85 it was a major contributor to the death of more than a million civilian victims who died from famine and disease. Coverage of the famine on television in Europe and North America helped spur a massive food-aid campaign. However, in some cases the combatants and the Ethiopian government refused to allow the delivery of the international famine relief and medical supplies. Enough assistance did eventually get through to help alleviate the problem somewhat, but lack of rainfall and ongoing conflict left Ethiopia plagued by the continuing threat of famine.

Conflicts within and with neighboring countries have added to the problems facing the people of the area. In some cases, refugees from nearby nations have fled into Ethiopia. In other cases Ethiopians left for Sudan or Somalia, seeking relief from drought, civil war, and famine, only to find comparable difficulties in those countries.

The Sudan Case

The Sudan, one of Ethiopia's neighbors, has had problems similar to those of Ethiopia. Africa's largest country in terms of area, and the world's ninth largest, the Sudan is among the poorest. Most of the northern part of the country is desert, but there are fertile areas in the central and southern sections. Sudan has tremendous agricultural potential, and a variety of development schemes for the country have attempted to capitalize on the nation's greatest resource: the waters of the Nile river. However, in the early 1990s, drought even laid waste to the once-lush Tokar delta on Sudan's Red Sea coast, an area once expected to be East Africa's bread basket. Additionally, like Ethiopia, the Sudan has been plagued by long-running civil war, basically pitting Arab and Islamic Northerners, who have controlled the central government, against rebellious Southerners, who are mostly African and animist. Here, as in Ethiopia, the combination of recurring drought and continuing political turmoil have resulted in severe food shortages.

Moreover, both sides in Sudan's civil war attempted to use food as a weapon, blocking international food deliveries intended for those living in the opposing region. The United States and various international organizations charged that the government was leaving millions to starve in the south because it was blocking or diverting humanitarian assistance. Officials of the Sudan government claimed such reports were unfounded and charged that the United States and other aid donors were cutting aid for political reasons. Sudan government officials said their refusal to conform to Western political norms and the Sudan's support for Iraq's Saddam Hussein and close relations with Libya's Muammar Quaddafi were the real reasons for Western complaints. Whatever the domestic and international political factors, the reality was that millions were left with severely limited food supplies, and international assistance frequently could not reach those in need.

In spite of its own problems, the Sudan for some years accepted large numbers of refugees from nearby countries that were also troubled with war and famine, including Chad, Uganda, and, as noted earlier, Ethiopia. This influx and Sudan's own population growth rate, one of the highest in the world, added to the burden on the nation's resources.

While there is a clear record that the United States, through its government programs and private organizations, and other developed nations have provided generous amounts of food assistance to needy nations, there is no doubt that at times aid policies are influenced by political considerations. Cases of clear emergencies usually see the international community rally to respond to a humanitarian challenge, but, as noted, such assistance efforts can also become politically entangled at the recipient end.

Food Aid and Politics

Over the years, massive amounts of food have been transferred from one country to another to help deal with chronic and emergency food shortages. Under its Food for Peace program, since 1954 the United States has regularly sold food on very favorable terms to developing countries. In a number of cases of famine or where other urgent needs existed, food has been provided free. Food aid has served important humanitarian purposes, but like other components of foreign aid, it has a pragmatic political side and has often been seen as a means of assisting and rewarding friendly nations around the world. During the 1960s and early 1970s, for example, principal recipients of United States food aid included Israel, Turkey, Pakistan, South Korea, and South Vietnam, all of which at times were tied to the United States through mutual security interests. Concerned that the food aid program was being used primarily for political reasons, the United States Congress mandated that more of the food go to the poorest countries, particularly those in sub-Saharan Africa and Central America. Incentives were also added to encourage countries receiving food aid to strengthen their own agricultural development programs and to help their rural and poorest populations.

Despite the changes in the United States food-aid program, there has still been a strong tendency for aid to be related to political concerns, which is perhaps inevitable in a world where it is difficult to factor out such considerations in relations among nations. Food and agricultural assistance remain a relatively small part of overall United States foreign aid and of the aid programs of other nations.

In some cases, critics have charged that such food assistance has either distorted the international market, thus harming the export opportunities of other countries, or has undermined the agricultural sectors in recipient countries. The common criticisms of food aid are that it acts as a disincentive to local food producers by bringing down food prices; it reduces commitment to agricultural development in recipient countries; it does not reach the nutritionally needy; and it encourages eating habits which may be unrealistic in terms of domestic production capability. All of these criticisms may have had validity at various times. However, as the Brandt Commission (the Independent Commission on International Development Issues) pointed out in its 1983 study, "On all counts, everything depends on the policies of the recipient country and the availability of professional and administrative competence to carry them out. It is not food aid that should be objected to, but poorly used food aid."[2]

That such problems can arise or that food aid can be perceived as causing problems is simply one more indication of how the actions of one nation or nations can affect others, sometimes in ways not at all intended.

Despite all of the complications which can be involved in food assistance, or which may result, there is an obvious and continuing need for such aid. Some in the wealthier nations see providing aid to those in need as a moral obligation that goes beyond politics and economics. The network of public and private, national and international organizations involved in providing food assistance and agricultural development face a major challenge, made all the more daunting by the spiraling population growth.

THE POPULATION FACTOR

As stated at the beginning of this chapter, projections indicate that world population will surpass 6 billion by the year 2000, having increased by more than 1.4 billion in just 15 years. The previous section has emphasized the close link between food problems and growing population and the difficulties of producing and distributing enough food to keep pace with the burgeoning population. The relationship between population levels and the world environment and resource base is also strong and direct.

Two centuries ago, Thomas Malthus, an English clergyman and economist, expounded the theory that world population would increase faster than the food supply. In his *Essay on Population* (1798), Malthus put forward the view that population, when unchecked, increases in a geometric progression, while the food supply increases only in an arithmetic progression. According to Malthus, war, famine, and pestilence would be the checks that would prevent population from exceeding the means of subsistence. Some refer to Malthus as the founder of the "gloom-and-doom" school of population theory. They deride predictions that population will go beyond the capacity of the earth to sustain it.

Those in the current era who have warned about too much growth and overburdening the earth's "carrying capacity" are sometimes called neo-Malthusians. This group would include the authors of the report of the Club of Rome, who issued *The Limits to Growth* in 1972. This group of business leaders and scholars forecast major problems if there was not more conservation of nonrenewable resources and limitations to population growth. According to the Club of Rome's "Project on the Predicament of Mankind," the earth's interlocking resources—the global system of nature in which we all live—probably could not support existing rates of economic and population growth much beyond the year 2010, if that long, even with advanced technology. Also, biologists Paul and Anne Ehrlich raised concerns about "the population bomb" creating a demand on food, resources, and the environment that could not be supported. According to the Ehrlichs, "The explosive growth of the human population is the most significant terrestrial event of the past million millennia."[3]

Critics would argue that these dire predictions are not being borne out. Scarcity of resources has always been overcome in the past by the discovery of ways to derive more output from a declining resource base. Some insist that technological breakthroughs and such developments as the agricultural "green revolution" will see humanity through.

Economist Julian Simon is one of those who derides the concerns about population growth overwhelming the earth. In his view "economic life in the United States and rest of the world has been getting better rather than worse during recent centuries and decades." Moreover, he says, "there is no reason to believe that these trends will not continue indefinitely."[4] Simon and some others argue that population growth can stimulate productivity. A different viewpoint has been offered by such groups as the authors of the "Global 2000 Report," commissioned by the Carter administration, or of the annual "State of the World" reports of the Worldwatch Institute, who raise serious concerns about population exceeding the "carrying capacity."

Growth and Where It Is Occurring

It took 130 years for world population to increase from 1 billion to 2 billion. At current growth rates, a comparable increase occurs in 11 years. In the 1990s, an estimated 921 million people will be added to the world population, the largest growth ever for a decade. Every week the equivalent of another Houston is added to the world population; every year, another Mexico; every ten years, another India.

The overwhelmingly largest portion of this population growth is occurring in the Third World, much of it in some of the poorest countries. Nine out of 10 babies born today are in the developing world. In 1950, two out of three of the world's people lived in the developing countries. Now, three of four live in the developing countries and the proportion is increasing. Obviously, the continuing rapid growth in those countries places an increasing burden on some regions of the world already straining to cope with difficult economic, social, and development problems.

With increasing attention directed to the problems associated with rapid population growth, there has been some progress in scaling back the growth rate. The annual growth rate has dropped from nearly 2 percent in 1970 to about 1.7 percent. Even with this decrease, the total numbers of people are still increasing significantly each year.

The United States and those areas that have composed the Soviet Union are growing at around 1 percent annually and Europe is growing only half that fast. Asia has the world's largest land mass and is home to slightly more than one-half of the world's people, but Asia's share of world population is actually expected to diminish a bit in the next few decades. Latin America's growth rates have been declining in recent years, but with a projected growth rate still above 2 percent, Latin America's share of world population will continue to increase slightly. The largest percentage growth will occur in the Near East and in sub-Saharan Africa. The Near East and North Africa will grow at an annual rate of 2.8 percent through the year 2000. Sub-Saharan Africa, where many of the poorer countries are located, and where, as noted, many of the major food problems occur, is projected to grow at a 3.1 percent annual rate through the end of the century—twice the rate for the rest of the world.

The population growth of sub-Saharan Africa is a matter of increasing worldwide significance. Its population growth rate is 82 percent higher than the world average. The region's infant mortality rate is 42 percent higher than the world average and its overall death rate 58 percent higher. Projections indicate that in the period from 1987 to 2000, the population of sub-Saharan Africa will grow by about 50 percent, while the world's total increases by less than 25 percent.

As an example of the rapid growth in the region, Nigeria's population is expected to surge from 90 million in 1980 and 119 million in 1990 to 161 million by 2000 and at least 471 million by 2050. If projections hold true, Nigeria will have jumped from the thirteenth largest nation in 1950 to the third largest a century later. (Some demographers predict Nigeria's population will reach more than 500 million by 2050.) In 1950, Nigeria had just over one half of the population of Japan. By 1990, the population

Population and Projected Population for Regions and Selected Countries

(in millions) Region or Country	1950	1980	Year 1990	2000	2050
SUB-SAHARAN AFRICA	185.6	382.9	514.3	699.4	2,255.0
Ethiopia	20.8	38.6	51.4	71.2	243.6
Kenya	6.1	16.7	25.4	38.3	165.9
Nigeria	41.2	90.0	118.9	160.9	471.2
Tanzania	8.9	18.8	26.0	36.6	132.9
NEAR EAST/NORTH AFRICA	119.5	263.7	350.6	461.4	1,190.2
Egypt	21.2	42.2	56.2	71.2	142.4
Iran	16.4	39.2	55.2	73.9	251.8
Iraq	5.2	13.2	18.9	26.5	67.7
Turkey	21.1	45.1	56.5	68.6	120.5
ASIA	1,343.3	2,439.9	2,906.3	3,380.8	5,173.0
Bangladesh	45.6	88.1	115.8	144.9	265.9
China (P.R.C.)*	562.6	983.4	1,114.5	1,242.3	1,554.9
India	369.9	689.0	850.0	1,013.3	1,591.2
Japan	83.8	116.8	123.7	128.9	115.5
Pakistan	39.4	85.2	113.2	145.3	423.8
Philippines	21.1	50.9	66.7	85.5	204.0
LATIN AMERICA AND THE CARIBBEAN	165.8	364.7	454.9	551.1	966.8
Brazil	53.4	123.2	157.9	195.2	368.0
Mexico	28.5	70.1	86.9	104.5	169.2
Peru	7.6	17.3	22.4	28.1	56.7
NORTH AMERICA/EUROPE AND SOVIET UNION†	738.2	1,002.7	1,067.3	1,118.3	1,177.2
Germany (East & West)	68.3	78.3	77.5	77.2	61.2
Soviet Union†	180.0	266.4	290.1	311.6	386.5
United Kingdom	50.1	56.3	57.1	57.6	51.2
United States	152.3	227.8	250.0	268.0	299.2
OCEANIA	12.5	22.6	26.2	29.8	43.0
Australia	8.2	14.6	16.6	18.5	23.9

*Figures for People's Republic of China do not include Taiwan or Hong Kong

†Including all the republics that formerly constituted the U.S.S.R.

Sources: U.S. Bureau of the Census, *World Population Trends*; United Nations.

of the two was about the same. By 2050, Nigeria is expected to have four times the population of Japan.

Among the other rapidly growing nations are Ethiopia, Kenya, Iran, and Pakistan. China and India continue as the two most populous nations and, on the basis of their population alone, these two would have to be considered important factors in world affairs. Political scientist Jerry Hough, among others, believes that by the mid-twenty-first century India and China will have become superpowers.[5] There are some projections that suggest that India's population may surpass China's in less than 60 years, or before today's children in both countries reach old age.

In 1950, the population of the United States and Canada was equivalent to that of Latin America and the Caribbean (about 166 million). By 1990, the population for the Latin American–Caribbean region was 427 million compared to 270 million for the United States and Canada. By 2025, Latin America and the Caribbean will have grown to 789 million as opposed to 328 million for Canada and the United States.

As with the related issues of food and hunger, a variety of national and international organizations have focused on the population growth issue, and many of them have attempted to promote and encourage steps to limit or slow growth. Some analysts argue that certain nations are stuck in a "demographic trap"—that rapid growth outstrips their ability to advance economically and socially. This demographic trap involves the interaction of population, environmental, and economic factors.

As Lester R. Brown of the Worldwatch Institute describes it, "continuing rapid population growth eventually overwhelms natural support systems, and environmental deterioration starts to reduce per capita food production and income."[6]

According to Brown and others, polarized population growth rates are driving roughly half the world toward a better future and half toward ecological deterioration and economic decline. The world can be seen as divided into two categories:

■ Countries where population growth is slow or nonexistent and where living conditions are improving

■ Countries where population growth is rapid and living conditions are deteriorating or in imminent danger of doing so

Family Planning Programs

A number of nations and international organizations have emphasized family planning programs as part of an effort to slow population growth. Some of the programs have been controversial and the subject of political debates. Especially during the Reagan administration, there were disputes over United States bilateral aid and United States participation in multilateral family planning assistance. Part of the controversy centered around the issue of whether such programs were encouraging or supporting abortion.

The United States has been the largest donor to international family planning. However, at the 1984 International Conference on Population, the United States government representative said that population growth is, of itself, neither good nor bad and that the United States government did not believe that we faced a global population crisis. The United States reduced its funding for family planning programs, with funds going only to programs that provided freedom of choice in family planning and did not perform or promote abortion. United States contributions to the United Nations Fund for Population Activities were halted because of grants made to China, which some critics accused of pursuing a family planning program based on "abortion and coercion."

There have been some successful family planning programs in Third-World countries, and China's efforts have received particular attention. Singapore, Thailand, Cuba, and Indonesia are other countries where family planning programs have been relatively successful. The United Nations Population Fund reports that the percentage of couples in developing countries using birth control went from less than 10 percent in the 1960s to more than 50 percent by the 1990s. In some areas, however, the percentage remains extremely low.

Coping with Growth: China

China has recognized that rapid population increases can impose extreme burdens on a society. For a period during the 1970s and 1980s, there was a precipitous decline in the Chinese birth rate and a significant reduction in the population growth rate. The Chinese population control program combines education in family planning with such economic measures as material rewards for those who adhere to family planning regulations and penalties for those who do not. The Chinese program is aimed at one child per family, although the policy is not inflexible, and has been ignored by many. In fact, the goal of one child per family remains elusive. China came under fire from some quarters, however, because of charges that the program was punitive and coercive. The program was controversial both within China and internationally. Indeed, there were claims of female infanticide, allegations that in the rural areas, where males are considered valuable for agricultural work, some female babies were being killed.

The Chinese government has vigorously denied that the program is coercive. While stating that China "must keep the population growth rate within bounds if she is to better her people's material and cultural life," Chinese officials insist that the abuses in the program were stopped by government intervention and an aroused public opinion. As noted previously, the United States ceased contributions to the United Nations Fund for Population Activities because of its grants to China. Responding to charges that China's policy involved "abortion and coercion," a Chinese official said:

> . . . it is not part of official policy to encourage widespread use of abortion at all, much less forced abortions. But to set up and operate a family planning network among a billion people with widely differing circumstances is no easy task. In a few places the work was carried out in an oversimplified and arbitrary way by overzealous people. Once known, such abuses have been stopped . . . A few years ago some cases of female infanticide occurred in China's rural areas. This shocking survival of old, feudal ways horrified Chinese people quite as much as it did people elsewhere. The perpetrators were strongly condemned by public opinion and brought to trial as criminals.[7]

Despite the slowing of China's growth rate, the nation's population continues to mount. In the 1990s alone, China is expected to see the addition of at least 140 to 150 million people, roughly equivalent to the current population of Brazil. In China a child is born every 1.5 seconds.

China remains a predominantly rural nation, with millions of residents scattered across its vast terrain. However, China's cities are steadily becoming larger, consistent with a pattern of increasing urbanization around the world.

Urbanization and Megacities

Sometimes it seems that population growth takes on the character of background noise. Few give much notice to the burgeoning population, yet the relentless growth proceeds, with urban areas, in particular, becoming ever more crowded and densely populated. The dynamics of population growth, industrialization, and agricultural modernization are expected to keep urban population growth rates above the rural growth rates in all regions of the world.

The attractions of the city and the lure of jobs in urban areas draw increasing numbers away from the rural areas. Of course, the already overburdened cities can't cope with the growing rural migration and often what the new city dwellers find is misery and despair. Many large cities are surrounded by shantytowns, like the *favelas* (hillside shacks) of Brazil or the *callampas* (mushrooms) of other South American countries or the *bidonvilles* (tin-can cities) of Francophone Africa. These slum areas, which usually lack any amenities, are often nothing more than a collection of flimsy shacks just beyond the boundaries of municipal administration. Numerous cities have large street populations, individuals and families who have no homes other than the streets. The Indian city of Calcutta, for example, has a street population larger than the total population of many large cities.

Developed nations are more heavily urbanized, and by the year 2000 nearly three-fourths of the population of the developed countries will be in urban areas. However, the urbanization trend is clear worldwide. Latin America, already heavily urbanized, will have 77 percent of its population living in cities by 2000. Asia and Africa are much less urbanized, but Africa's urban population is expected to increase from 30 percent of the continent's total in 1985 to 41 percent by the turn of the century. In Asia it will jump from 28 to 35 percent. Overall, about half the world's population will live in cities by 2000, up from 41 percent only 20 years earlier. (See Figure 11-1.)

The number and size of "megacities" is growing dramatically in developing nations. By 2000, some 40 Third-World cities will contain more than 5 million inhabitants each; half of these may have more than 10 million, including Mexico City (26 million), Sao Paulo (24 million), Calcutta (16.6 million), and Bombay (16 million). Provision of jobs, housing, and social services to such massive urban populations is presenting difficulties previously unimagined by planners and governments. Areas such as public health, education, transportation, and communications are major challenges for Third-World cities. In Alexandria, Egypt, a sewage system built for 1 million now serves 4 million. Because the city lacks the resources to expand and upgrade the system, the city is at times awash in raw sewage, adding to the city's health problems. Similarly, it is estimated that more than 3 million inhabitants of Mexico City do not have access to the sewage system.

A study of the world's 100 largest metropolitan areas by the Population Crisis Committee indicated that 53 of the 57 cities in developing countries were ranked low in living standards. The analysis was based on statistical comparisons of urban life indicators, including such categories as infant mortality, air quality, and public safety. All 28 of the cities with the lowest ranking of "poor" are in the Third World. Only one city in an industrialized country—Naples, Italy—ranked as low as Third-World cities. The survey suggests that the cities of the world growing the fastest are also the cities least able to accommodate growth. Lagos, Nigeria, the world's fastest-growing city, ranked lowest in the study.

Cairo and Mexico City are two cities with long and proud histories. However, they also are among the largest and most rapidly growing, with populations that include large numbers of impoverished citizens. (See Mexico City Portrait.) They are both feeling the stresses imposed by rapid population growth and are struggling to deal with the myriad problems associated with this growth.

Cities of more than 5 million population can now be found on every continent. By 2000, 15 of the world's 35 largest cities will be in Asia. Cairo is the only African city in the 5 million category now, but by the end of the century, eight urban areas in Africa will reach that figure.

It should be noted that some of the urban areas in the Third World have become prosperous and have managed the problems of urbanization relatively well. The city-nation of Singapore in Southeast Asia is one example. Singapore's government has exercised tight control, and a

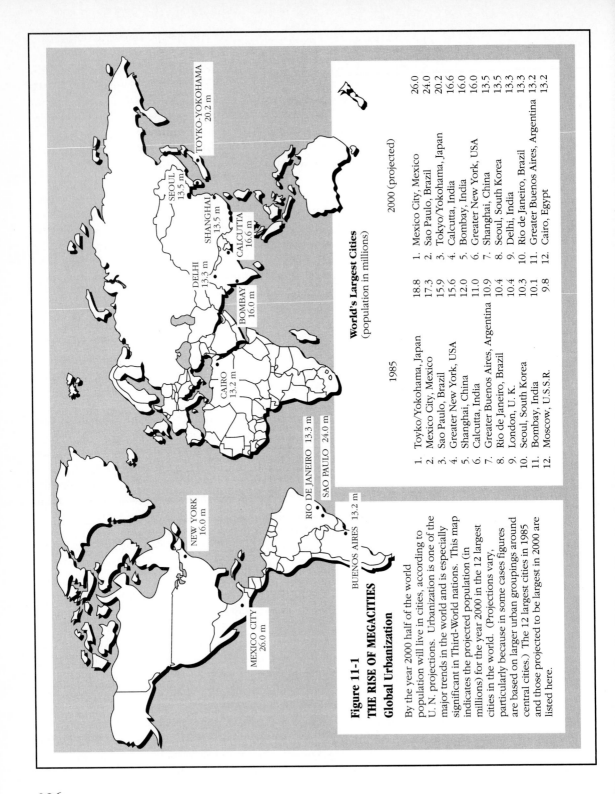

Figure 11-1
THE RISE OF MEGACITIES
Global Urbanization

By the year 2000 half of the world population will live in cities, according to U. N. projections. Urbanization is one of the major trends in the world and is especially significant in Third-World nations. This map indicates the projected population (in millions) for the year 2000 in the 12 largest cities in the world. (Projections vary, particularly because in some cases figures are based on larger urban groupings around central cities.) The 12 largest cities in 1985 and those projected to be largest in 2000 are listed here.

World's Largest Cities
(population in millions)

	1985			2000 (projected)	
1.	Toyko/Yokohama, Japan	18.8	1.	Mexico City, Mexico	26.0
2.	Mexico City, Mexico	17.3	2.	Sao Paulo, Brazil	24.0
3.	Sao Paulo, Brazil	15.9	3.	Tokyo/Yokohama, Japan	20.2
4.	Greater New York, USA	15.6	4.	Calcutta, India	16.6
5.	Shanghai, China	12.0	5.	Bombay, India	16.0
6.	Calcutta, India	11.0	6.	Greater New York, USA	16.0
7.	Greater Buenos Aires, Argentina	10.9	7.	Shanghai, China	13.5
8.	Rio de Janeiro, Brazil	10.4	8.	Seoul, South Korea	13.5
9.	London, U. K.	10.4	9.	Delhi, India	13.3
10.	Seoul, South Korea	10.3	10.	Rio de Janeiro, Brazil	13.3
11.	Bombay, India	10.1	11.	Greater Buenos Aires, Argentina	13.2
12.	Moscow, U.S.S.R.	9.8	12.	Cairo, Egypt	13.2

highly disciplined society in this thriving port city has built a modern and efficient community.

Singapore is, in effect, an urban nation without a countryside. Its development is not tied to a rural area. In many nations urban development in the past has been closely related to agricultural success. Today's urbanization trends in many Third-World countries are, however, often related to agricultural failure and rural problems, driven more by rural poverty than urban prosperity. Large-scale migration from rural areas is, as Lester R. Brown and Jodi Jacobson of Worldwatch Institute have pointed out, "a symptom of the severe imbalance that characterizes national economic strategies and the sheer weight of population growth pushing down rural incomes."[8] Such factors as rapid rural population growth, badly distorted and inequitable land distribution, the deterioration of agricultural prospects due to environmental degradation, and low or nonexistent government investment in agriculture all contribute to making even urban slums look more appealing than agrarian life.

The mushrooming urban population, with all the attendant problems, can pose major problems for both political and environmental stability.

ENVIRONMENTAL ISSUES

Environmental issues have found an increasingly prominent place on the international agenda, and there is every reason to believe that environmental matters will command even more attention in the future. (See Chapter 13.) Conditions already discussed in this chapter, particularly population growth, the expanding demand for land and resources, and urbanization have a direct relationship to the increased environmental stress. Air and water pollution are just two of the most obvious signs of today's environmental difficulties. And what can be referred to as the "global commons"—the atmosphere, the oceans, the forests—are threatened in a number of ways.

Especially relevant to international relations is the fact that, as was discussed in Chapter 1, environmental problems don't stop at national boundary lines. Transboundary pollution is a major concern, and many of the problems are truly global in scale. New and emerging environmental problems can span time periods and geographic areas that reach beyond the jurisdiction of existing political and social institutions. No single nation can preserve the planet's soils and forests, stabilize the earth's climate, protect the ozone layer, or reverse the pollution or acidification of rivers and lakes. Just as polluted air and water can cross national borders, pesticides and the hazardous waste policy of each nation can affect the environment of others. Climatic change, including the threat of global warming (discussed further in Chapter 13), and the shrinking of the stratospheric ozone shield—which shields us from the harmful ultraviolet rays of the sun—have implications for all nations.

Because of this international dimension to environmental issues, there is a compelling need for international cooperation. It has been said that we are all sharing the same lifeboat in the sea of space and, of necessity, we must cooperate. Since the 1972 Stockholm United Nations Conference on the Human Environment, the scope of international environmental cooperation has developed and expanded. It was to foster dialogue and provide leadership on these issues that the United National Environmental Program (UNEP) was established in 1972, and UNEP has served as a forum for the negotiation of key international agreements on protection of the ozone layer and transboundary shipments of hazardous waste.

Transboundary traffic in hazardous waste between industrialized countries had been a long-standing problem. Then, in the 1980s, growing concern developed about shipment of such waste to Third-World nations. In some cases, Third-World nations were willing to accept the waste in return for much-needed cash payments. However, charges of "toxic terrorism" and "garbage imperialism" were soon being leveled against the industrialized world. In 1988, the Organization of African Unity adopted a resolution declaring that the dumping of industrial waste in Africa is a crime against Africa and its people. It called upon African countries to refuse to take part in transactions involving such wastes. At the same time, the European Parliament condemned high-volume exports of dangerous wastes to developing nations.

Deforestation, Desertification, Degradation

Deforestation is a problem that is being experienced in both the developed and developing world for a variety of reasons and with a variety of serious implications. In some of the industrialized countries and their neighbors, industrial pollution is believed to have contributed to serious damage to remaining forests, as well as to lakes and aquatic life. Even though the German government has given considerable attention to preservation of its forest lands, it nonetheless became evident in recent years that there has been substantial damage to the forests. Industrial pollutants and the cumulative effects of chemical stress are thought to be the contributing factors. The more appalling problems are in Eastern Europe, where the abuses that occurred during a long period of unregulated industry turned parts of the region into an ecological wasteland. Through the period of Communist domination of the area, there was little regard for environmental protection. The years of heavy industrial output with few environmental safeguards left Eastern Europe with a legacy of poisoned water, smog-filled air, contaminated land, dying forests, and a high toll of cancer and respiratory diseases and a lower life expectancy for its peoples. Environmental issues played a part in the political upheavals that occurred in 1989–90; indeed, in some countries, notably Bulgaria, environmental pressure groups were an important part of the political opposition.

"We have laid waste to our soil and to the rivers and forests that our forefathers bequeathed to us," Czechoslovakian President Vaclav Havel said in his 1990 inaugural address. It was estimated that 70 percent of the nation's trees had been damaged by airborne pollution. Acid rain did major damage to forests in the former East Germany and in Poland, as well as in Czechoslovakia. The European Community's European Environmental Agency is working with Eastern European countries, and experts agree that the problems can only be solved with considerable financial and technological help from the West. The World Bank has estimated the cost of arresting pollution and dealing with related problems in Eastern Europe in the billions of dollars.

In the former Soviet Union, where the Chernobyl nuclear disaster occurred in 1986, there is a long history of environmental neglect. (Radiation emissions from the Chernobyl nuclear power plant accident reached a number of other countries. As mentioned in Chapter 1, this is indicative of how meaningless national boundaries are in such circumstances.) A broad range of environmental problems, including atmospheric pollution, endangered water resources, and soil degradation exist in the former Soviet states. However, with the economy under severe strain, little has been done to improve environmental protection.

Many of the more striking and devastating examples of deforestation and desertification have occurred in Third-World nations. Problems of land degradation related to agricultural production have already been discussed. "It is in the relentless push to produce more food that several decades of borrowing from the future are beginning to take a toll," the Worldwatch Institute warns. "In many countries, growth in the farm sector is pressing against the limits of land and water supplies."[9]

Northern Africa is an example of the problems of declining agricultural resources. Deterioration of its soils, forests, and water supplies has been heightened by rapid population growth, war, and unsound economic policies. In view of current conditions, it may be hard to believe that 2000 years ago fertile fields in Northern Africa served as the granary for the expanding Roman Empire. Today much of the area is desert and half of its grain is imported.

In many cases, the clearing of land for agricultural or related purposes or in certain countries for firewood, has set off a chain-linkage effect not only within countries but in other nearby countries. This deforestation has contributed to health problems, damage to the atmosphere, and erosion and loss of watershed, which can exacerbate problems of extreme weather and flooding. Deforestation is driving up firewood prices in many Third-World countries. Excessive soil erosion is contributing to reduced per capita food production in many more. Deforestation also contributes a significant portion of the increasing global emissions of carbon dioxide.

Rapid population growth, emphasis on cash crops, introduction of new technologies developed in other socioeconomic and ecological contexts, pressures to earn foreign exchange, and the unstable terms of trade for agricultural commodities have all been factors in upsetting the stability of traditional agriculture in many poorer countries. In turn, these factors are linked to soil degradation, deforestation, desertification, and growing scarcity of water.

The world's forests are diminishing at a rapid pace. At the present rate of deforestation, about 40 percent of the remaining forest cover in developing countries will be lost by the year 2000, according to UNEP. Tropical forests are being cleared both for their lumber and to make way for agriculture and development. The most rapid deforestation today is taking place in West Africa, Indonesia, and Brazil.

In South and East Asia and Latin America, deforestation in upland watersheds can cause increased downstream flooding in the rainy season. The flooding is followed by abnormally low water flow during the dry season, with severe damage to agricultural productivity in floodplains and valleys. In Bangladesh, tree cutting, overgrazing, and agricultural erosion in the Himalayan watershed make monsoons in the area increasingly disastrous. The plight of Bangladesh results, in part, from the clearing of forests in the neighboring upland countries of India and Nepal, as well as in the hilly areas of Bangladesh itself. The forests have been cleared to meet domestic timber needs and to provide firewood and building wood. Many believe that the catastrophic flooding in Bangladesh in recent years is directly related to the loss of vegetative cover in the upland areas. That cover used to absorb rainfall and moderate flooding.

Tropical countries with high population growth rates usually have deforestation rates well above the average, and the demand for land for agricultural and developmental purposes continues to grow. Some of that demand will almost certainly be met from present forest land. But many tropical soils are not suitable for continuous cultivation or intense grazing, and such agricultural expansion may cause ecological damage and loss of productivity. Much more than just trees are lost when a tropical forest is eradicated—an entire ecosystem is destroyed. Plant and animal species must adapt to their changed environments or perish. Human populations are displaced and their ways and means of living can be disrupted or lost. Fragile topical soils become infertile and prone to erosion. Regulated stream flows are replaced by alternating floods and droughts. Extensive deforestation can make the climate drier. Valuable sources of timber, food crops, medicine, and industrial goods are lost. These losses, in turn, can contribute to a range of social, economic, and political problems.

In some cases, tropical forests are exploited for timber exports, and nations may find themselves without enough wood for their own needs. With the world's highest deforestation rate, Ivory Coast may have lost more than half of its forest cover in two decades. And there are concerns that the Philippines, a leading timber exporter, may reach the point where it will not have enough timber for its own needs. Deforestation has been blamed as a leading factor in disastrous flooding in the Philippines, where nearly 8,000 died after a 1991 storm hit the islands. Southern Thailand has experienced similar problems.

The Cases of Brazil and Indonesia

Perhaps the most dramatic, significant, and controversial examples of deforestation have occurred in Brazil's Amazon region. The government encouraged settlement and economic development in the area. Part of the reason for the effort is that the major coastal cities are terribly overcrowded, and the government wanted to resettle large numbers in the inland forest areas. In 1988 alone, Brazil, using fires to clear land for farming and cattle ranching, destroyed more than 30,000 square miles of Amazon virgin forest, an area about the size of Maine. The burning was so extensive that it caused massive air pollution and is believed to have accounted for one-tenth of the global total of human production of carbon dioxide during the year.[10] Carbon dioxide is believed to be a primary cause of the "greenhouse effect" or global warming. The fires also generate millions of tons of methane and nitrogen oxides, which may help erode the earth's protective ozone shelter.

There has been an international outcry over the destruction of the Amazonian forests, and the Brazilian government has indicated that it would restrict subsidies for agriculture in the region, limit the export of logs, and place environmental controls on agricultural and industrial projects in the area.

A similar pattern has been seen in Indonesia. Sixty percent of the population lives on the island of Java, comparable in size to the state of New York. Yet while New York state has 24 million residents, Java's population is more than 100 million. The high population density on Java has led the government to undertake resettlement projects on less-populated islands, with vast amounts of tropical rain forests to be cleared. The forest industry is also important to Indonesia's economy. As the government notes, the industry increases job opportunities, supports other industrial development, and improves foreign exchange earnings through exports. However, the Indonesian government says that it practices "sustainable development"—which is aimed at reducing poverty and at the same time minimizing resource depletion and environmental degradation. Indonesian President Suharto said the nation is committed to preserving its rainforests, and said "our tropical forests constitute the lifelungs of the world."[11] Indonesia has pledged to take a number of steps to protect the forests and control the rate of exploitation, including setting aside some areas as "timber estates," banning the issuance of new licenses for the manufacture of plywood, extensive reforestation, and working with international agroscientists.

NATIONALISM AND THE GLOBAL ENVIRONMENT

Of course, each country has a right to manage and exploit its resources as it sees fit. Some in developing nations point out that the more-developed nations enjoyed the fruits of economic development without always worrying about the environment—so who are they to be setting standards for other countries? Brazilians, for example, have sometimes made the point that decisions about economic development of the Amazon are theirs to make.

While this kind of nationalism may be understandable, it is also very short-sighted and fails to take into account the realities of today's interdependent world. In the case of the forests, as has been discussed, they have a significant role in the global environment. And, as has been repeatedly emphasized, the actions of one nation often have significant effects on other nations.

Some leaders of Third-World nations used to regard environmentalism as a luxury that could be afforded only by wealthier nations. And some of today's worst environmental offenders, as has been discussed, are developing nations coming of age in a world that is growing much less forgiving of such abuse. Increasingly, leaders of these nations are accepting that development cannot be sustained without protecting natural resources.

A major concern today, then, is how nations, particularly those in the Third World, can undertake economic and industrial development without inflicting further damage on the environment. Mention has already been made of "sustainable development." The impact of growing population and economic activity has already diminished the resource base of many countries and poses increasing risks for the prospects of sustainable development. Fundamentally, this concept of development refers to meeting today's needs without compromising the ability of future generations to meet their needs.

Sustainable Development

The ability to carry out development in such a way that it meets both present and future needs can be increased by the use of scientific knowledge and ecologically sound technologies. Sustainable development requires changes in current growth patterns to make them less resource and energy intensive and more equitable. Inequities in international economic relations, combined with unsound economic policies in many countries, have contributed to environmental degradation and have otherwise limited the sustainability of development. Growth based on rapid resource depletion is neither economically nor ecologically sustainable.

Environmental stress is not just a result of the demand for scarce natural resources and the pollution and ecological damage resulting from rising living standards. Poverty also creates environmental stress. The rural poor, in order to survive, often degrade their immediate environment as they cut down forests for fire wood, abuse marginal agricultural land, and in many cases, as was discussed earlier, wind up leaving the rural areas for the deceptive lure of the cities—adding to the stress of urbanization. Many of the urban areas, as noted, are having serious difficulty in coping with their burgeoning populations, and in a number of cases extreme environmental problems have developed.

At the beginning of the 1990s, the World Bank identified five environmental problem areas that required special attention: (1) destruction of natural habitats; (2) land degradation; (3) degradation and depletion of freshwater resources; (4) urban, industrial, and agricultural pollution; and (5) degradation of the "global commons" as a result, for example, of atmospheric and marine pollution.[12]

Along with some of the other international financial institutions, the World Bank has drawn some strong criticism for not giving sufficient attention to environmental concerns in its support for development projects. In response, the bank has pledged to bring environmental strategy into the mainstream of its work and to increase lending for environmental and population projects.

Reference was made earlier in this chapter to the concept of "carrying capacity," which involves the long-term ability of the earth and its various regions to support their population without degrading their resources. The number of people, the quantity and nature of production and consumption, and the cumulative impact on resources and environment are all factors that determine an area's carrying capacity. As noted earlier, there are those who believe that some areas are in danger of exceeding that capacity. Environmental deterioration such as rapid soil loss or desertification or, in the industrial world, high per capita utilization of energy and raw materials that require major imports of resources, are seen as indications that the capacity may be threatened. Such trends underline the need for longer-range views in planning and development.

Progress toward sustainable development requires careful consideration of a range of social, economic, and environmental goals and the establishing of longer-term priorities. Some of these issues and emerging environmental problems will be discussed further in Chapter 13.

International Importance

What is particularly clear from the consideration of the environmental and related issues in this chapter is that international cooperation is essential. As was pointed out, some important international efforts are already under way. They deal with both more traditional environmental problems, such as water pollution, as well as problems of more recent vintage, such as the breaking down of the ozone layer. Many nations have agreed to limit production and use of the chemicals that are believed to deplete the ozone shield.

Environmental issues are moving away from the periphery of international relations and diplomacy and are receiving some of the attention once reserved for international security and economic affairs. "Green" matters are no longer dealt with merely as side issues, and national and international officials are increasingly involved in what might be referred to as "green diplomacy." It is not unusual to find environmental issues now on the agendas of important summit meetings. When Mikhail Gorbachev of the Soviet Union made a major address to the United Nations in December 1988, he mentioned the environment more than 20 times, comparing its degradation to such threats as war, hunger, and disease.

As has been indicated in this chapter, international environmental agreements have become more frequent, and in the future, as will be discussed in Chapter 13, there are likely to be further agreements as nations seek to cope with such issues as climate change. Between 1930 and 1959, the United States agreed to only a handful of treaties related to the environment, most of those on whaling. In the 1960s and 1970s, the numbers increased to five per decade, with endangered species and marine pollution becoming prominent issues. In the 1980s, the number increased to 11, including 4 related to air and 3 to marine pollution.

Environmental alliances to deal with specific transnational threats, as Lester R. Brown of Worldwatch Institute points out, are likely to become commonplace and far more numerous than the military alliances that were so prominent in the past.[13]

The problems of the environment and the earth's "carrying capacity" are shared among nations. Sometimes the problems affect a group of countries, as with the pollution of the Rhine river or with acid rain, two of the examples cited in Chapter 1 of problems that transcend national boundaries. The UNEP has declared that "States have . . . responsibility to ensure that activities within their jurisdiction or control do not cause damage to the environment of other states or of areas beyond the limits of national jurisdiction."[14] As with other issues discussed in previous chapters, nations are finding that it is no longer possible to draw a sharp line between foreign and domestic affairs.

NOTES

1. World Bank, *Report of the Task Force on Food Security in Africa* (Washington, D.C.: 1988); see also Lester R. Brown, Christopher Flavin, and Sandra Postel, "A World at Risk," in *State of the World, 1989*, Worldwatch Institute Report (New York: W. W. Norton, 1989).

2. *Common Crisis—North-South: Cooperation for World Recovery*, report of the Brandt Commission (Cambridge, Mass.: MIT Press, 1983), p. 131.

3. Paul R. Ehrlich and Anne H. Ehrlich, *Population, Resources, Environment* (San Francisco: W. H. Freeman, 1970), p. 1.

4. Julian L. Simon, *The Ultimate Resource* (Princeton, N.J.: Princeton University Press, 1981); also, Julian L. Simon, "Life on Earth is Getting Better, Not Worse," *The Futurist*, August 1983, p. 7.

5. Jerry F. Hough, "Perestroika and Soviet Relations With the West," in Donald R. Kelley and Hoyt Purvis (eds.), *Old Myths and New Realities in United States-Soviet Relations* (New York: Praeger, 1990), p. 28.

6. Lester R. Brown, "Analyzing the Demographic Trap," in *State of the World, 1987*, Worldwatch Institute Report (New York: W. W. Norton, 1987), p. 36.

7. Peng Zhiliang, "The Truth About China's Population Policy," *China Reconstructs*, May 1986, pp. 11–12.

8. Lester R. Brown and Jodi Jacobson, "Assessing the Future of Urbanization," in *State of the World, 1987*, Worldwatch Institute Report (New York: W. W. Norton, 1987), p. 42.

9. Lester R. Brown, "The New World Order," in *State of the World, 1991*, Worldwatch Institute Report (New York: W. W. Norton, 1991), p. 11.

10. Philip Shabecoff, "Suddenly, the World Itself Is a World Issue," *New York Times*, December 25, 1988, p. E-3.

11. "Indonesia: Unity in Diversity," supplement to *Washington Post National Weekly Edition*, September 17–23, 1990.

12. World Bank, *The World Bank and the Environment*, First Annual Report (Washington, D.C.: 1990).

13. Lester R. Brown, "The New World Order," in *State of the World, 1991*, Worldwatch Institute Report (New York: W. W. Norton, 1991), p. 18.

14. United Nations, *Global Outlook 2000* (New York: United Nations Publications, 1990), p. 105; see "Green Diplomacy," *The Economist*, June 16, 1990.

PROFILE
GANDHI AND INDIA

Among the major factors in international relations in the twentieth century has been the relationship between the industrial powers of Europe and North America and the nations of what is now called the Third World. And, as is emphasized throughout this book, among the major forces in world affairs is nationalism.

Many of the nations in the Third World are former colonies, having spent long periods under the dominion of external powers. In a number of cases, the struggle of the colonized nations to assert their nationalism and gain their independence was prolonged and intense. No case better symbolized this effort than India's long campaign for independence from Britain, and no one better symbolized that struggle than India's Mohandas K. Gandhi.

A small but dynamic man, Gandhi demonstrated that there are many ways to wield power in the world. He was the central figure in India's independence drive and his civil disobedience tactics put the powerful British government on the defensive.

COLONIALISM VS. NATIONALISM

Beginning with the British East India Com-

Emphasizing self-reliance, Mohandas Gandhi set an example for his fellow Indians. In this famous photograph by Margaret Bourke-White, Gandhi spins his own cloth. The spinning wheel became a symbol of the independent society Gandhi wanted India to become.

pany in the early seventeenth century, the British gradually expanded their presence in India. By the early eighteenth century, the British government had asserted paramount control over India, a land with a long and proud history.

As early as 1883, the Indian National Congress was founded, one of its goals being the achievement of national independence. In its early stages, the nationalist movement concentrated on securing for Indians a greater role in the administration of the country. However, the reluctance of the British to grant such a role helped spur demands for self-government. There were increasing efforts, some of them violent, aimed at ending or weakening British rule. After World War I, Gandhi emerged as the leader of the growing nationalist movement and launched a drive that would last nearly three decades, with India finally gaining its independence in 1947.

Gandhi emphasized that *sovereignty* could not rest with the colonial power but resided in the Indian people. Thus, he based his efforts on what he saw as both legal and moral rights of the Indians.

The concept of sovereignty, as discussed throughout this book, remains a powerful factor in international affairs.

Gandhi's Tactics

Gandhi was born in India in 1869. At age 18 he left to study law in England. After being admitted to the bar, he returned to India to enter the legal profession. However, in 1893, he was invited to South Africa to work on behalf of the Indian community there.

Shortly after arriving in South Africa, Gandhi was thrown off a train. He was riding in a first-class compartment, for which he had a ticket; however, because he was "colored," he was told to move to third class. When he refused to move, he was removed from the train. The Indians in South Africa were subjected to a wide range of discriminatory laws and practices, and Gandhi became the leader of the movement to change that. Intending to stay in South Africa just a year, he remained for 20, becoming engrossed in the antidiscrimination effort. It was here that he first employed his passive resistance approach, which he called *satyagraha*, translated as "soul force." He had some success and gained considerable respect, although, of course, South Africa was to remain a bastion of discrimination for many years.

In 1914, he returned to India and within a few years emerged as the leader of the Congress Party and of India's first *satyagraha* campaign. He became known as Mahatma or Great Soul for his efforts, much of which were concentrated on working in villages and with peasants. After the Amritsar massacre in 1919, when British troops fired on unarmed protesters, Gandhi temporarily withdrew, as he was to do on several occasions. He was imprisoned from 1922–24, accused of sedition. While he was in prison, communal rioting broke out between India's Hindus and Moslems, and this division was one of the problems Gandhi could never completely overcome. It was this division that led to the establishment of Pakistan as a separate, Moslem-dominated nation when India gained independence in 1947.

Through the years leading up to independence there were various negotiations between Britain and the Indian nationalists, and some concessions were made by the colonial power. However, some in India felt that Gandhi did not push hard enough and was too concerned with other issues, such as his efforts for better treatment of India's untouchables, those on the lowest rungs of society, on whose behalf he conducted a highly publicized fast and other actions. Gandhi also focused on the problems of poverty and the need for greater self-sufficiency among his compatriots. Wearing only a loincloth and shawl, he would work at a spinning wheel for a time each day, urging others to do the same. The spinning wheel became the symbol of the society Gandhi sought to achieve. He said that Indians should make their own homespun cloth rather than rely on shoddy manufactured goods.

His actions could be confounding, even to some of his most dedicated followers, but he had the ability to rally and inspire vast numbers of Indians. In 1930, he demonstrated this when he launched a campaign of civil disobedience, defying the government's salt monopoly, and protesting against the tax imposed on salt. He led a march from the *ashram,* or communal retreat where he lived, to the seaside 241 miles away. When they reached the sea, he and his followers took salt from the water, thus disobeying the law. The salt march had an extraordinary effect, leading to civil disobedience throughout the country. Thousands, including Gandhi, were eventually arrested. By working at the grassroots level and standing up for the rights of the poor, Gandhi forged Indian nationalism into a powerful, nonviolent force for Indian dignity and self-determination.

Jawaharlal Nehru was a colleague of Gandhi's, a political leader in the independence movement, who became India's first prime minister. Before Gandhi's civil disobedience campaign,

Gandhi's close associate in the Indian independence movement was Jawaharlal Nehru, who
became India's first prime minister. Gandhi,
through his civil disobedience campaign, forged
Indian nationalism into a powerful nonviolent
force while Nehru provided political leadership.
Both were frequently jailed for their resistance
to colonial rule.

Nehru said the alternatives were "just talking
and passing resolutions, or terrorist activity."
According to Nehru, "Both of these were set
aside and terrorism was especially condemned
as opposed to the basic policy of Congress." Instead, said Nehru, a new technique of action
evolved which, though perfectly peaceful, involved nonsubmission to what was considered
wrong and unfair. For the participants in this
movement, it meant "a willing acceptance of
the pain and suffering involved in this."[1] Nehru
was among those frequently imprisoned for his
participation in the protests.

Of Gandhi, Nehru said that he was "an odd
kind of pacifist, for he was an activist full of dynamic energy." He added, "There was no submission in him to fate or anything that he considered evil; he was full of resistance, though
this was peaceful and courteous."[2]

The outbreak of World War II brought a new
phase to the nationalist/independence movement. In 1939, British authorities, without con-

sulting Indian leaders, proclaimed India's entry into the war. The Congress Party condemned fascist aggression, but declared that India could not be part of the war effort against the fascists unless it was a free, independent nation. The British made some vague promises, but Gandhi believed they were not sufficient. In 1942, he demanded that Britain "quit India" or face mass civil disobedience. In response, the British declared Congress illegal and Gandhi and other leaders were again put in prison. Their arrests set off a wave of protest and by the end of the year about 100,000 people had been arrested.

When Gandhi was released in 1944, he tried to reach an understanding with Mohammed Ali Jinnah, leader of the Indian Moslems. To his disappointment, an agreement could not be reached. Jinnah and his Moslem followers were intent on going their own way and creating a separate nation, Pakistan.

Achieving Independence

When the Labor Party came to power in Britain at the end of World War II, the Indian drive for independence entered its final phase. Gandhi and his supporters kept the pressure on, and after a cautious beginning, the new British government indicated its willingness to allow full self-government in India. The question still remained: was it to be one free India or two? Gandhi continued to oppose division, insisting that Moslems and Hindus were one people. However, the tide was flowing the other way. In September 1946, Nehru took office as head of the interim government, and early in 1947 the British government declared that it intended to quit India no later than 1948. Lord Louis Mountbatten was appointed viceroy to arrange for the transfer of power. Mountbatten moved up the withdrawal date, and on August 15, 1947, India became an independent nation.

Gandhi's Impact

Gandhi had seen the achievement of an independent India, but he failed in his dramatic efforts to keep the nation from splitting into two. The early independence period was marked by communal rioting, as the territorial division left millions of each community on both sides of the India-Pakistan border. Gandhi repeatedly tried to stop the violence, sometimes resorting to fasts, but had only limited success.

In January 1947, seeing that even the capital city of Delhi was still unsafe for Moslems, Gandhi once again undertook a fast. Some Hindu militants denounced him, however, for his intervention on behalf of the Moslems. A bomb attempt was made on Gandhi's life, and then on January 20, 12 days after he had broken his fast, as he was walking to his daily prayer meeting, Gandhi was assassinated by a young Hindu extremist. Nehru said, "The light has gone out of our lives and there is darkness everywhere." Gandhi and the Indian independence movement helped inspire efforts for independence in other colonized nations, and in the years following India's independence a parade of former colonies began marching into the ranks of independent nations. India was a leader in the so-called nonaligned group of mostly Third-World nations, which sought to position themselves between the East and West blocs.

Although many of the independence efforts were marked by violence, such as that in Algeria (see DeGaulle Profile), or terrorism, Gandhi's commitment to nonviolence was adopted by, among others, Martin Luther King, Jr., leader of the civil rights movement in the United States. King and other civil rights advocates utilized Gandhi's tactics and principles in their campaign for equal treatment for American blacks. In Poland, Lech Walesa also employed Gandhian nonviolence in leading the way for the overthrow of Communist rule.

Sometimes referred to disparagingly as "the little brown man in a loin cloth," Gandhi was certainly one of the most remarkable figures of the twentieth century. He commanded no military forces and had no wealth, but he exercised great power. He made humility and simple truth powerful enough to move an empire.

Albert Einstein called Gandhi "the greatest political genius of our time." Said Einstein, "His work for the liberation of India is living testimony to the fact that a will governed by strong conviction is stronger than seemingly invincible power."[3]

INDIA AFTER INDEPENDENCE

In the years since Gandhi led his country to freedom, India established itself as a democracy, though not without difficulty and periods of repression. The Congress Party, though it split in 1969, with the dominant faction becoming known as Congress (I), has continued to dominate Indian politics and government.

Nehru served as prime minister until his death in 1964 and was a highly respected international figure. Along with such leaders as Gamal Abdel Nasser of Egypt and Kwame Nkrumah of Ghana, Nehru was at the forefront of the movement for neutralism and nonalignment among the newly independent nations.

Nehru was succeeded as prime minister by Lal Bahadur Shastri, but he had actually established a political dynasty which dominated postindependence India. When Shastri died in 1966, Nehru's daughter, Indira Gandhi, succeeded him. Mrs. Gandhi, though Nehru's daughter, was not related to Mohandas Gandhi. She had, however, been active in the Congress Party since her youth, and at age 21 she was arrested by the British authorities for her political activities and spent 21 months in prison. Her tenure as prime minister was marked by some major political turmoil. In 1975, she became embroiled in a controversy over alleged political fraud, and there were efforts to remove her from office. She declared a state of emergency, arresting hundreds of opposition leaders, curbing press freedom, and ruling by decree until the parliamentary elections of 1977, in which her faction was defeated by the Janata Party. However, in 1980, she scored a major comeback. Her Congress (I) Party won a landslide victory. A short time later, her son, Sanjay Gandhi, became secretary-general of the party and was being groomed to succeed her. Only days afterward, he was killed in a plane crash. At that point, Mrs. Gandhi turned to her oldest son, Rajiv, who had not been involved in politics, as her political heir.

Meanwhile, communal conflicts once again tore at India's national unity. The government faced mounting internal violence. This time the strife centered around the Sikhs, a religious minority with a strong sense of group identity. Concentrated primarily in the state of Punjab, where they were a slight majority, the Sikhs wanted autonomy for Punjab. On October 31, 1984, as she walked to her office from her adjacent home, Indira Gandhi was assassinated by two Sikh members of her personal security guard.

Indira Gandhi became India's prime minister in 1966. She was unrelated to Mohandas Gandhi but was the daughter of Prime Minister Nehru and part of a political dynasty. Her tenure was controversial and she was defeated in 1978. She was returned to office in 1980, but faced mounting communal violence. She was assassinated in 1985 and was succeeded by her son Rajiv, seen with her at a 1983 political rally. Rajiv Gandhi was defeated in 1989, and in 1991 while campaigning to return as prime minister, he, too, was assassinated.

Rajiv Gandhi succeeded his mother, but faced continuing Sikh terrorism in Punjab, as well as armed insurgency and communal violence in several other northern provinces. In a political surprise, he was defeated in the 1989 elections. However, he remained a major factor in Indian politics.

Then, in 1991, violent tragedy struck India once again, as Rajiv Gandhi was assassinated while campaigning in South India in an attempt to return to the prime minister's position. A reporter who witnessed the bomb explosion which killed Rajiv Gandhi, wrote, "In that blinding second of his death, he was walking toward a sea of people, a picture uncannily reminiscent of Mohandas K. Gandhi's last stroll in the garden in New Delhi moments before he was struck down . . ." [4]

In the years since Mohandas Gandhi led the way to Indian independence, making it one of the first of the colonies to attain self-rule, India can point to considerable achievements and is the world's largest democracy. In addition to the continuing communal divisions that have plagued the country, India has faced other major problems, including two basic ones: food and population.

India and the World: Progress and Problems

As discussed in Chapter 11, India has made some remarkable progress in food production. There were some serious food crises in the mid-1960s, and there are still major challenges in production and distribution. However, particularly during the 15 years when Indira Gandhi led the country, India, aided by the "green revolution," made significant strides in the agricultural area.

The growing population means a continuing challenge for India's ability to feed and house its citizenry. Nehru made the problem of India's overpopulation his special concern and was the first Hindu politician publicly to declare his approval of birth control. In subsequent years the

Indian government has supported an extensive family planning program. However, the program has been controversial, and some minority groups and some of the poorer, less-educated segments of the society have been most resistant to family planning. Despite the government's efforts, India's population continues to soar. At the time it became independent, the population was about 350 million. By the year 2000, India will have more than 1 billion inhabitants and, as noted in Chapter 11, some projections indicate that by 2050, India will overtake China as the world's most populous nation.

India has continued to follow the foreign policy course charted by Nehru in the early years of independence—not aligning itself with East or West but trying to pursue a more neutral path. At times some United States leaders thought that India was leaning toward the Soviet Union, and India did purchase major military equipment from the Soviets. At times, India justifiably, has seen the United States as tilting toward its neighbor and sometimes adversary, Pakistan. India's strained relations with China were another reason for closer India ties with the Soviets. The result of all of this has been that despite various pressures, India has generally managed to determine its own foreign policy.

As Mohandas Gandhi emphasized, India has an ancient culture and history that long preceded the colonial era. And in the years since he led India and the world into the postcolonial era, India's achievements have been considerable. In some respects, India, with its burgeoning population and communal strife, trying to achieve unity out of diversity and to fulfill the needs of the population, serves as a microcosm of the world and its progress and problems.

NOTES

1. Jawaharlal Nehru. *The Discovery of India* (Bombay: Asia Publishing House, 1946), p. 364.
2. *Ibid.*

3. Albert Einstein. *Ideas and Opinions* (New York: Bonanza Books, 1954), p. 166.
4. Barbara Crossette, "A Blast, and Then the Wailing Started," *New York Times,* May 22, 1991.

SUGGESTIONS FOR FURTHER READING

Brown, Judith M. *Gandhi: Prisoner of Hope.* New Haven: Yale University Press, 1990.

Fischer, Louis. *Gandhi: His Life and Message for the World.* New York: New American Library, 1954.

Hardgrave, Robert L. Jr. and Stanley A. Kochanek. *India: Government and Politics in a Developing Nation.* San Diego: Harcourt Brace Jovanovich, 1986.

Nanda, B. R. *Mahatma Gandhi: A Biography.* New York: Oxford University Press, 1981.

Nehru, Jawaharlal. *The Discovery of India.* Bombay: Asia Publishing House, 1946.

CITY PORTRAIT
MEXICO CITY

It is the world's largest city, a sprawling metropolitan area that will soon grow to a population of more than 26 million. It epitomizes the worldwide trend toward urbanization and it symbolizes both the promise and the problems of the Third World.

Mexico City is the oldest capital in the Americas, having been built in 1325 by the Aztecs (or Mexicas), who called it Tenochtitlan. It has a rich history, and the great eras and events in the life of the nation are encapsulated in the city. When it was an Aztec city it was conquered by the Spanish, who were colonial rulers for three centuries. The Spanish were overthrown in 1821, but in the early years of independence Mexico City endured brief occupations by the United States and by France and a period of dictatorial rule before the Mexican Revolution of 1910–1920, which marked the beginning of the capital's extraordinary growth.

As Mexico City's rapid growth continues, it has to deal with a variety of attendant problems. Among the more notable challenges Mexico City must cope with is the smog that often pervades the city's atmosphere and hangs over the area. The government is trying to improve conditions, but the problem is exacerbated by Mexico City's bowl-like setting and the millions of vehicles that crowd its streets and pour fumes into the thin air at 7,400 feet.

URBAN GROWTH AND CHAOS

With the population having climbed steadily throughout the twentieth century, Mexico City, as Alan Riding writes, "has become a case study in the chaos that awaits other developing nations where the rush to industrialize has stimulated a mass exodus from depressed rural to fast-growing urban areas, where the worst of underdevelopment has combined with the worst of overdevelopment."[1]

The city's unusual setting contributes significantly to its modern-day problems. It was built on an ancient lake bed, and the swampy soil is soft and slowly sinking. It is at an altitude of 7,400 feet and is ringed by mountains and volcanos. Because of this bowl-like setting, one of the city's most notable features has become the smog that almost constantly overhangs it, held in, it seems, by the surrounding mountains.

Mexico City is both sophisticated and

cosmopolitan, a center of culture and business, but it is also home to millions of impoverished citizens, many of whom have migrated from rural areas and small towns in search of jobs. A similar pattern has occurred in a number of other Third-World countries; Mexico City just happens to be the most extreme example. Often the newcomers to these cities settle in fringe areas, sometimes becoming squatters and living in the most rudimentary conditions since there is not adequate housing, even if they could afford it. This trend is one of the contributing factors to the rise of megacities around the world. Some estimates project that by the year 2000 half of the world population will live in cities, and there will be five "super-cities" of 15 million or more inhabitants, three of them in developing regions. The two largest, with populations of around 25 million, will be Mexico City and Sao Paulo, Brazil.

Pollution, Population, and Poverty

Like Mexico City, many of these urban areas find themselves overwhelmed and unable to provide the basic services and facilities needed to support such a population. Mexico City's basin location exacerbates the air pollution problems generated by industrial smokestacks, open-air burning, and snarled traffic. The poor air quality forced the closing of schools for a month in 1989.

Each day the population of the city increases by more than 2,000, due to the elevated birthrate and rural migration. This means that within a year Mexico City adds enough inhabitants to populate a city of the size of San Francisco. Even though more than 5 million of the city's population live in dire poverty, desperate immigrants from the destitute rural areas keep pouring into the city in search of opportunity. Millions of these new residents have begun life in the capital as squatters, setting up tents and cardboard and tarpaper shacks wherever they can find vacant space. Often they lack such basics as running water and electricity. This invasion has

contributed to the city's horizontal sprawl, as it has gobbled up surrounding countryside. At least three million of the inhabitants are said to lack access to the sewage system. All of this lack of services and infrastructure, including basic amenities, is not the result of particular government inefficiency, although Mexico City, like a number of other Third-World countries, has been plagued by corruption. The truth is that the scope and cost of the ever-growing needs for facilities and services in Mexico City would severely tax the resources of even the wealthiest of countries. Further, there are real limitations on the ability to expand services for Mexico City. Water is a special problem and is now piped in from as far as 55 miles away.

The lively, colorful streets of Mexico City are increasingly jammed—not just with the growing number of vehicles, which contribute so heavily to the pollution problem, but with the millions of street vendors and the jobless and homeless.

Decentralization?

Just as the government has attempted a variety of measures to reduce vehicular traffic, but with little success, there has been much talk and some efforts to decentralize government and industry, both of which are heavily concentrated in the capital city. Again, these efforts have led to little real change, even though there has been some success in spreading industry to other sections of the country. In fact, portions of the north are already heavily industrialized and the attractions of a North American Free Trade Agreement (NAFTA) with the United States and Canada would undoubtedly mean more industrialization in the north. Without more rigid environmental restrictions, however, any Mexican cities are likely to have severe ecological and pollution problems.

Almost all of the federal government and political power have been concentrated in the capital city, a pattern reflected in many Third-World countries. Few countries have been successful in dispersing governmental offices and functions to other areas. The most notable example is Brasilia, the "new city" which became the capital of Brazil in 1960. For years there was debate about moving the seat of government away from Rio de Janeiro and the heavily populated coastal area. Much of South America's largest country was underdeveloped, and it was reasoned that locating the capital in the interior would help open up a new region. It has been a moderately successful move. The modern capital city functions reasonably well as the center of government, but Rio and Sao Paulo continue to grow and serve as major business centers. More than one of every five Brazilians live in these two cities.

Moving Brazil's capital to Brasilia proved to be extremely costly, and even if other obstacles could be overcome, relocating major government functions in Mexico or other rapidly growing countries would probably be prohibitively expensive.

DEVELOPMENT AND DISINTEGRATION

An important factor in Mexico City's growth and resultant problems was national economic policy. Emphasis on industrial development pulled people from the rural areas to the city. Like many Third-World countries, Mexico came to rely on an "import substitution" policy, aimed at reducing the nation's dependency on goods from abroad. Instead, Mexico would manufacture its own products. With most of the industry concentrated in Mexico City, the migration from the rural areas was implicitly encouraged by the government. While focusing on economic development, little attention was given to urban planning or environmental concerns. Industrial wastes were disposed of with little thought to the ecological impact, creating a toxic nightmare. In Mexico, as in other Third-World countries, some argued that environmental protection and family planning programs advocated by international organizations and some of the developed countries were an

effort to slow Mexico's economic expansion. More recently, the leaders in Mexico City have realized how damaging some of the nation's policies have been and have attempted to deal more seriously with the mounting miseries of the megacity.

"Mexico City is an omen," said novelist Carlos Fuentes. "That jammed city of toxic air and leafless trees may be the first to know asphyxiation by progress." [2]

"Mexico City is beyond catastrophe," according to philosopher Ivan Illich, who sees it as a metaphor for all that has gone wrong with development. "That ancient city, founded on a lake in the pristine air of a high mountain valley, will have no clear air or water by the year 2000." [3]

One of the concerns about Mexico City is the division between rich and poor, between those who benefit from the expanding international economic order and those who are left out. "The equivalent of a new Berlin Wall is being built around the elites of Mexico City, Delhi, and Lagos, integrating them into the new order while disintegrating the majority of those demographically exploding populations." [4]

Mexico City's difficulties are symptomatic of the social and economic problems facing an increasingly urbanized world, especially in the rapidly growing developing nations. Despite its myriad difficulties, Mexico City endures and, in many ways, thrives. However, making it a livable city for the mass of its population constitutes a major challenge for the twenty-first century.

NOTES

1. Alan Riding, *Distant Neighbors* (New York: Alfred A. Knopf, 1985), p. 254.
2. Carlos Fuentes, "Asphyxiation by Progress," *New Perspectives Quarterly*, vol. 6, no. 1, spring 1989, p. 43.
3. Ivan Illich, "The Shadow Our Future Throws," *New Perspectives Quarterly*, vol. 6, no. 1, spring 1989, p. 23.

Exodus from rural areas into capital cities is a common phenomenon of the modern era, especially in Third World countries. In many cases the urban newcomers settle in fringe areas, sometimes becoming squatters and living in the most rudimentary conditions, as was the case with those who lived around a garbage dump in Mexico City and survived by salvaging from the dump. About 30 percent of Mexico City residents have no sewer service.

4. Jacques Attali, "Lines on the Horizon: A New Order in the Making," *New Perspectives Quarterly*, vol. 7, no. 2, spring 1990, p. 5.

SUGGESTIONS FOR FURTHER READING

Kandell, Jonathan. *La Capital: The Biography of Mexico City*. New York: Random House, 1988.

Riding, Alan. *Distant Neighbors*. New York: Alfred A. Knopf, 1985

CHAPTER TWELVE

Communications and Technology

A variety of important changes are affecting contemporary international relations, and perhaps nothing demonstrates this more vividly than the developments in communications and technology. Advances in these fields are having broad and dramatic impact on international affairs.

Significant developments in communications capability and technology, spurred by such innovations as microchips, computers, satellites, videotape, lightweight video cameras, and fiber optics, have opened up vast new possibilities for international communications, but have also created new problems and controversies, as the information and communications revolution is felt around the world.

MEDIA CHANNELS

The instantaneous communication of news and images over thousands of miles and the role of the media in interpreting and analyzing world affairs—and sometimes providing a channel for the conduct of international relations—bring new dimensions to diplomacy, politics, and commerce, and new issues for governments and media.

Increasingly, international affairs involve public relations, and, in some cases, a public relations competition or a war of worlds and/or battle of images, with the world communications media providing the forum for this competition.

Not only have we moved into the Information Age but also into an era of transnational communications and media diplomacy.

Censorship and efforts to control continue in some cases, but become more and more difficult to enforce. A key factor here is that telecommunications can transcend national boundaries.

347

In the case of television, its international impact is all the more significant and remarkable because of its ability to reach across borders and cultures and for images to be transmitted globally. Communications satellites, which can instantaneously beam signals around the globe, link much of the world together in one gigantic network. There are still many, primarily in the Third World, who do not have television, but it is becoming increasingly widespread. In China, for example, it is estimated that 75 percent of the population has access to television.

Television's Power and Reach: The Gulf War

The power and reach of television was vividly demonstrated in the coverage of the 1991 Persian Gulf War and related events. Technology, particularly satellite transmission, made it possible for viewers around the world to have live, instantaneous coverage of the war.

In the opening hours of the war, viewers could see the bright flashes of air attacks and tracer fire lighting up the skies of Baghdad. This was all the more extraordinary because television watchers in the United States and its allied countries were receiving reports from inside the enemy's capital city. The Iraqi government required nearly all journalists to leave Baghdad shortly thereafter, but did allow Peter Arnett, correspondent for Cable News Network (CNN), which can be received in many countries around the world, to remain. Arnett stayed in Iraq throughout the war and continued to transmit satellite reports, though they were subject to Iraqi censorship. Although transmitted by satellite around the world, in some countries CNN's audience is very limited. However, it also supplies a video feed that is picked up by many foreign networks. In any case, CNN's live coverage of the war was indicative of the possibilities of a true global network.

Because most of the war was carried out by air strikes and because there were government restrictions on both sides, television was limited in its ability to show the actual effects of the air war. Still, there was extensive coverage of this first full-scale war in an age of worldwide satellite communication. Air-raid or missile warnings, departures of bombers from bases in Saudi Arabia for attacks on Iraq, briefings by military officials, or statements from diplomats immediately resounded across the globe. There were, however, some false reports and misinformation, as the emphasis on speed sometimes resulted in news being aired before it could be confirmed. Nonetheless, the coverage of the war by CNN and other television services made clear the impact of international television.

New Issues in the Global Village

Just as in the case of the environmental issues discussed in the previous chapter, traditional boundaries lose much of their meaning when it comes to telecommunications. While there is much that is positive about these developments, there are, as mentioned earlier, new issues to consider—

for example, the question of trans-border data flow and "information sovereignty." Who controls the movement of information and data across national borders? And, of course, there are questions revolving around the tendency of the highly industrialized societies, and particularly the United States, to dominate the means and messages of international communications. Claiming that the international communications system is inequitable and imbalanced, some groups, especially from the Third World, have been calling for a New World Information Order (NWIO) or, as it is sometimes called, a New World Information and Communications Order (NWICO). These are some of the issues associated with what is referred to as the Information Age.

It was Marshall McLuhan, a Canadian professor and author, who popularized the term *global village.* McLuhan was referring to the interconnected world culture that, in his view, resulted from the rise of the electronic media, especially television. While the notion of a global village has become something of a cliché and can result in an oversimplified picture of a complex world, it is, nonetheless, a telling observation about the way in which telecommunications and other factors discussed in previous chapters have drawn the world closer.

International Images

There have been a variety of notable examples which have demonstrated the centrality of the media, particularly television, in today's diplomacy and international relations. One of the first such examples involved former Egyptian President Anwar Sadat's trip to Israel in 1977, dramatizing a sharp turn in Egyptian-Israeli relations. (See Chapter 5.) Tragically, four years later television cameras captured the assassination of Sadat by Islamic fundamentalists. (Sadat, with his bold foreign policy, like Gorbachev, enjoyed a strong international image, bolstered by the media, but had difficulties at home.)

The pictures of American hostages, blindfolded and with their hands tied behind them, being paraded before the media in Iran in 1979 and of the crowds of raging Iranians, chanting angrily at the gates to the United States Embassy in Teheran, had a powerful and traumatic effect in the United States. The American media focused heavily on the 444-day "hostage crisis," and that intensive coverage helped ensure that it was a crisis. It increased pressure on the Carter administration to act, raised questions about the post-Vietnam direction of American foreign policy, and, eventually, badly damaged the Carter administration and helped torpedo Carter's chances for reelection.

In addition to the Iranian events, television has been a major factor in a number of other terrorist/hostage scenarios, as was discussed in Chapter 8. Notable among these was the media's role in the 1985 saga involving the hijacking of TWA flight 847 by Shiite Muslim terrorists. The terrorists staged a series of media events, and television news people became directly involved in over-the-air discussions with the terrorists, in effect, serving as negotiators. Terrorists were asked, for example, what it would take for them to agree to release the hostages.

Some referred to what they saw as the ability of terrorists to manipulate television in order to gain attention as "terrorvision." As was mentioned in Chapter 8, former Prime Minister Margaret Thatcher said that the media provide "the oxygen of publicity" that sustains terrorism.

Television thrives on dramatic events and its strength is crisis coverage. And the reach of television is such that it can have extraordinary influence on developments around the world.

Philippine President Ferdinand Marcos, responding to a question on an American TV news program in 1985, announced that he would call elections early in 1986. Marcos was appearing on the program via a live satellite transmission from Manila. Marcos, who was drawing increasing criticism for his dictatorial rule, was seeking to portray himself as a democrat, and he understood the importance of doing so on American television. Viewers around the world had already seen, repeatedly, the video footage of the assassination of opposition leader Benigno Aquino upon his arrival in 1983 at Manila airport, returning from exile in the United States. (The assassination was apparently carried out by Marcos allies.) Aquino's widow, Corazon, became a candidate in the 1986 elections. Intensive international media coverage of the campaign, focusing on the corruption associated with the Marcos regime and Marcos's attempts to hold power by fraud, helped doom Marcos and helped propel Aquino and her "people power" movement into office.

Iraq's Saddam Hussein attempted to engage in media diplomacy following the 1990 invasion of Kuwait. He sought to alter his image in the rest of the world and to divert attention away from his military action. He appeared on television, mingling stiffly with the hostages he called "guests," and the media focused on the human dimension of the international crisis. The Iraqi leader was seeking to convince the world that he had no hostile intent and did not want to go to war against the United States and the alliance of nations opposing him.

MEDIA DIPLOMACY

Because the world is watching, television can help slow a rush to war or serve as a deterrent to expanded war. Indeed, some question whether earlier conflicts would have been as bloody or prolonged if the publics of the nations involved had been able to see the horrors of war on their home screens.

The world is watching, more and more. Television has become an electronic diplomatic courier by which messages are delivered and received. Public diplomacy, as discussed in Chapter 5, has become an increasingly prominent and significant component of international relations. Television often provides the forum for the international public relations competition which has now become an accepted aspect of world politics.

At the opening of the 1991 Middle East Peace Conference in Madrid, more than 4,500 journalists and media technicians were on hand to transmit news of the conference around the world. Representatives of several of the delegations from the Middle East gave numerous interviews and held press conferences, vying to get their viewpoints across to the world audience.

Mikhail Gorbachev was among those who best understood and utilized the international media. Gorbachev was effective at conveying through the media that he was a different type of Soviet leader. (See Gorbachev Profile.) The new international image that he established helped convince the world that Soviet policies were truly changing. In more tense Cold War times, Gorbachev's efforts would have been dismissed—and were still, by some—as a slicker version of Soviet *propaganda*. And, indeed, Gorbachev's "diplomatic offensive" and "charm offensive" could be seen in those terms. (International propaganda will be discussed later in this chapter.) Much of the Gorbachev public relations effort was aimed at Western public opinion and especially at Western Europe. During the United States–Soviet arms control negotiations in Geneva, it often seemed that the real bargaining was being fought out in the Western media and legislative bodies. Each side sought to convince Western public opinion that the other was not negotiating seriously.

Gorbachev's effectiveness at international public relations was in evidence on his 1989 visit to (then) West Germany. Given the history of hostilities between the two countries, Gorbachev's trip was of historic significance. He managed the visit masterfully, pushing all the right themes, and getting saturation television coverage. He stressed his desire for peace and cooperation with the West and emphasized the idea of a "common European home," as discussed in Chapter 9.

Gorbachev's mastery of media diplomacy was, as has already been suggested, of little value in dealing with the critical problems he faced at home, however. Indeed, in 1990, he was unable to leave Moscow to travel to Stockholm to accept the Nobel Peace Prize, one of the most prestigious international awards, and an occasion that would have given him highly favorable international attention.

International television coverage of the 1991 events when hardliners tried to seize control in the Soviet Union enabled the world to see the resistance and galvanized international opposition to the attempted *coup d'état* or *putsch*. (These French and German terms have similar meanings: a *coup d'état* is a sudden seizure of state power by a political or military group from within an existing system; a *putsch* is a suddenly effected attempt by a group to overthrow a government, and the term is usually associated with actions by right-wing or fascist groups.)

In the past, those seeking to seize power in the Soviet Union would have made a heavy-handed move to grab control of communications. This time, however, those involved in the *putsch* were relatively ineffective in controlling the media, and their own attempts to use the media were inept. Viewers around the globe could see the transparent totalitarianism of those involved in the attempted coup. As was the case with the totalitarian leaders in Eastern Europe earlier, the group that was trying to claim power in the Soviet Union found itself badly undercut by the technology, ingenuity, and proliferation of the global media.

Television not only served to inform the world, but also it again functioned as a hot line used by world leaders—notably President Bush and Russian President Boris Yeltsin—to communicate with each other and activate world opinion. In the age of media politics and diplomacy, the scenes of Yeltsin rallying Russian resistance to the *putsch*, and the pictures of Gorbachev returning to Moscow from the Crimean region, where he had been briefly held under house arrest, stirred international interest and support. Remarkably, from what was once a closed society, viewers and readers around the world then received extensive coverage of the debate in the various parliamentary bodies about the future of the Soviet Union and of the republics that were part of it.

Gorbachev was a factor in helping set in motion some of the more significant world events in recent years, events that have provided some dramatic visual images, particularly from Eastern/Central Europe and from China.

The opening of the Berlin Wall in November 1989, heavily covered by the media, was a striking symbol of the collapse of communism and the end of the old East-West divisions. (See Berlin City Portrait.)

PRIME-TIME REVOLUTION

Indeed, television's ability to cross borders helped bring an end to the East-West division. Although the wall separated East from West Germany for 28 years, it could not keep out television from the West. Even though by some standards East Germans were relatively well off, they could see from Western television that there were many products they couldn't buy and freedoms they couldn't enjoy. They could see the vitality and mobility of the West, characteristics that were missing from life in the East.

Walter Ulbricht, who was East German Communist leader at the time the wall went up and until 1971, said that the enemy of the people stood on the roofs, referring to television antennas. Despite efforts by the East German government to prevent reception of external TV signals, the citizens of the East continued to watch. It was estimated that about 85 percent of East Germans regularly tuned into West German television. At one point, the East German government was having difficulty finding workers for a factory in the city of Dresden, located in the far eastern section. Dresden was less attractive than other cities in East Germany because television reception from the West was not good.

Through television from the West, those in the East were able to keep up with political developments in West Germany and the world. They learned of Gorbachev's reforms largely through television. The East German government attempted to keep out printed information about changes in the Soviet Union. East German officials even prohibited some publications from the Soviet Union after they started reflecting Gorbachev's policies of *perestroika* and *glasnost*. As television producer Tara Sonenshine wrote, the East Germans "could keep Gorbachev out of the libraries, but could not keep him out of the living room."[1] From West German television came scenes of the Soviet leader in action—shaking hands with Margaret Thatcher and West German Chancellor Helmut Kohl, kissing babies in Britain, plunging into welcoming crowds in Washington, escorting Ronald Reagan through Red Square.

Through television the East Germans also saw reports about the tottering Communist governments in Hungary and Poland. They watched on their home screens as Hungarian soldiers helped crack the Iron Curtain by removing barbed-wire fences and other barriers on the frontier between Austria and Hungary. That development opened the way for East Germans to flee to West Germany in a roundabout way, traveling across the newly liberated borders of Hungary, Czechoslovakia, and Poland. That exodus dominated the television news coming from the West, as scenes of jubilant East Germans arriving in the West filled the TV screens. In turn, that encouraged still more East Germans to make a journey that had previously been impossible. This was an example of chain linkage through telecommunications.

These emotional and dramatic scenes, and others, such as those of young people dancing atop the Berlin Wall, almost certainly hastened the demise of the Communist governments in Eastern Europe. Television provided a window through which people could see for themselves that the Communist bloc was crumbling and could witness the revolutionary changes that were occurring. They could also see that much of what they had been told by Communist-controlled media about the West was not correct. Seeing all this emboldened many to act to bring about change.

Throughout history, the battle plan for war has often involved this strategy: seize the high ground, then attack the main garrison, palace, or government building. With the advent of radio, a new strategic goal was added: seize control of the radio transmitters. Often, when there has been a *coup d'état* or a revolution in a country, the radio station was a principal target. Television is, of course, even more strategically significant. The transmission tower has become the new high ground. This was evident in Romania, where the national television station was at the center of revolutionary events in 1989. Revolutionaries who succeeded in ousting dictator Nicolae Ceausescu set up headquarters at the station and broadcast on an impromptu basis.

The question might be asked: if Ceausescu was such a ruthless dictator, why wasn't he able to use television for his purposes? In fact, Ceausescu did rigidly control Romanian TV while he was in power. However, he did not enjoy a monopoly of communications, because external radio services—Voice of America (VOA), Radio Free Europe, and the British Broadcasting Corporation (BBC)—could all be heard in Romania and beamed in reports of the tumultuous events elsewhere in Eastern Europe. (The external broadcasting services will be discussed later in this chapter.)

Mark Wood, editor-in-chief of Reuters, one of the major international news services, said of Romania, "The revolution there was a video revolution. They weren't fighting for the palace, they were fighting for the television." [2] Such actions have been referred to as "videocracy."

CHINA AND MEDIA MISINTERPRETATION

Ironically, some in Eastern Europe said they had been inspired by the televised coverage earlier in 1989 from Tiananmen Square in China. It was ironic because, contrary to what later happened in much of Eastern Europe, the efforts to bring about change and a more democratic government in China were, after some weeks, brutally put down. But the events in China, particularly the activities of the "prodemocracy" groups there, did unfold before the eyes of much of the world as a result of intensive media coverage.

The presence of a large contingent of foreign journalists and state-of-the-art communications technology in China in 1989 meant an unprecedented ability to report news of China around the world. In another ironic angle to these events, the reason China permitted the influx of journalists and equipment was because of the scheduled visit of Soviet leader Gorbachev. However, Gorbachev's visit was increasingly overshadowed by the "prodemocracy" protests begun by Chinese students after the death of Hu Yaobang, former Communist Party leader. The protest movement became a focal point for media coverage in the United States and internationally, and in some respects the media, especially some of the Western commentators, were caught up in the euphoria of the antigovernment protests. Television, in particular, seemed to offer an overly optimistic view of the prospects for significant change in China. When the government brutally cracked down on protesters, many international observers and much of the public, particularly viewers of Western television, were caught by surprise, even though there were strong reasons to expect that the government would eventually react strongly to the continuing protests.

Suggestions that the Chinese leadership would fall at that time as a result of the protests seem to have been based more on wishful thinking than realistic analysis. While it is correct to note that some of the dramatic changes that occurred in Europe later in 1989 would have seemed improbable as well, they were part of a broader trend influenced by the significant redirection of Gorbachev's Soviet Union. They also quickly involved broader segments of the population and occurred in much more compact countries—with greater access to external media—than the sprawling China with its remote regions. And in some cases the pressure for change in Eastern European countries had been building for years.

The misinterpretation of events in China seems more comparable to what happened in Iran a decade earlier when many, but not all, experts and journalists in the United States were caught off guard or found the developments there difficult to explain. (The events in Iran were discussed in Chapters 5 and 7.) There are, of course, many examples of insightful reporting and analysis in the media of the United States and other countries where press freedom exists. And it should be remembered that many journalists and technicians have exhibited considerable courage and initiative in reporting from tumultuous locales, under difficult and sometimes dangerous circumstances.

Lack of Perspective and Context

Part of the problem with the coverage from China is a familiar shortcoming in coverage of international relations—the lack of context and perspective, the failure of journalists to understand and remind readers and viewers about the historical context, the political, social, and economic factors influencing events. The media are too easily seduced into concentrating on drama, personalities, and the excitement of the moment.

NBC-TV anchorman Tom Brokaw said of the China coverage, "I think that we were unsophisticated . . . I suppose what I fault us all on in China is that we took a really typical Western attitude toward it and failed to see it for its Chinese aspects, both culturally and politically."[3]

As mentioned earlier in this chapter, 1989 was the first time such a large contingent of journalists and sophisticated communications equipment were present in China. It was also the first time reporters and TV cameras were present in large numbers to record upheaval in China, even though such convulsions were hardly new or even unusual in the last 150 years. As Lucian Pye wrote in *China: An Introduction*, a standard American work on China, the story of modern China "is that of revolution—profound, intense, violent, and protracted." Pye notes that the Chinese have been caught up in the complex problems of modernization. "For more than 100 years they have been experiencing profound social change, and for decades they have lived through violence—political upheavals, civil wars, and foreign conquests."[4]

The lack of perspective and historical context in the case of China underlines the problems that can result from the rapidly roving media eye that focuses first on one trouble spot or international "crisis" and then suddenly moves elsewhere. In situations where there is intense and extensive coverage, television viewers may receive considerable information, but without context and perspective they gain relatively little understanding of the meaning of events. We know more than we understand.

Another weakness of the media focus is that while television deals well with drama, confrontation, and personalities, the more complex issues don't play as well. As discussed throughout this book, many of today's most important problems revolve around economic affairs. However, these stories are often glossed over and tend to be little understood.

CHARACTERISTICS OF THE MEDIA ROLE

The tendency toward episodic coverage, with the media's roving eye moving from one "big story" to another, often results, as noted, in the lack of historical perspective on world events. This is one of a set of general characteristics that mark the media coverage of and role in international relations. Some of these characteristics were suggested by James F. Larson in his study of the role of television in the Iran hostage crisis.[5] Here is an outline of the key characteristics, some of which have already been mentioned.

- *The media are increasingly transnational in nature*. Technology easily enables communication across borders. More and more it is possible for ideas, information, and images to be readily transmitted among nations.

- *Television's presence makes private or secret negotiations between governments more difficult*. It is not easy for officials to escape the media spotlight when attention is focused on a particular story or crisis. The intensity of media coverage often compels more communicative diplomacy.

- *In most cases, a nation's media coverage follows or reinforces policies of that nation's government*. This is true not only in countries where the media are controlled by government but is often the case in free-press countries too. Governments, by nature, even in free societies, seek to manage information. Normally the media will take their cue from government initiatives and policies. However, in some cases, especially in the United States, elements of the media may begin to question those policies, as in Vietnam, Central America, or the Persian Gulf. Those questions may be a reflection of and/or influence on questions being asked by the public and Congress. Although the media-government relationship is often viewed as adversarial, it is in many ways a symbiotic relationship, one of mutual dependency.

- *Media attention to a story, especially heavy television coverage, can put a story high on the international agenda*. Public officials are often obligated to respond to what the media deem as crucial. Conversely, some important stories and trends are largely ignored by media "gate-keepers" (those editors and news directors who determine what material will be used by the mass media) and don't receive the international attention they deserve. One reason this occurs is discussed next.

■ *Availability of or access to good visual images is an important factor in determining TV coverage.* If television producers don't have conflictual or telegenic footage, the importance of a story may be downgraded or it may be ignored altogether. At times officials succeed in quashing news coverage. This happened in South Africa for a period when the government banned cameras from protest demonstrations and large gatherings and imposed other media restrictions. (Nonetheless, there was enough foreign coverage of South Africa's apartheid policies that it kept up pressure for change in that country.) In the case of the Iranian hostage crisis, Iran wanted access to American and foreign television, and thus often encouraged certain coverage. As was discussed earlier, unique circumstances led to the large foreign media presence in China in 1989, and although the government eventually succeeded in cutting off much of the coverage, the Tiananmen Square story had become a staple of worldwide television.

■ *Television, in particular, becomes involved in media diplomacy, sometimes serving as a channel of communication between government officials or policy elites in different nations.* Mention has been made of the attempts by such figures as Sadam Hussein, Mikhail Gorbachev, and Anwar Sadat to engage in media diplomacy, and certain American leaders, notably Ronald Reagan, have done likewise. The media have also, as discussed, played a role in various hostage crises.

■ *Television's power to convey emotions and a sense of intimacy can become a strong force in international affairs.* The human and emotional dimension of stories involving hostages, famine, war, or discrimination can touch public opinion and bring pressure for action and influence foreign policies.

■ *The media's tendency toward episodic coverage, moving from one crisis to another, contributes to the lack of perspective and context.* As emphasized earlier in this chapter, television has a notably short attention span and it often brings viewers to an important international story with little or no frame of reference. Coverage of international affairs is usually event- and crisis-oriented, yet, as discussed throughout this book, economics, along with cultural and environmental factors, are major forces in the world. Change involves trends, not just events, and television is often at its weakest in dealing with trends.

■ *The media pay little attention to basic processes of social and cultural changes in developing nations and to the perspective of those nations.* This point is related to several of those mentioned earlier and is part of the reason that crises in the Third World are often not well understood. It is also part of a bigger problem that is especially felt in the Third World—the perceived distorted coverage of the Third World and the world communications imbalance between developed and developing nations. Mention was made earlier in this chapter of the calls for a New World Information Order (or New World Information and Communication Order). These have come mostly from the Third World and reflect the frustration of many in the Third World with the international media.

DIFFERING PERSPECTIVES AND INFORMATIONAL GEOPOLITICS

The divisions between North and South discussed in earlier chapters are by no means confined to economic, political, and security issues. They also extend to an important facet of the world's social-political-cultural context—communications. The calls for a New World Information Order paralleled the move for a New International Economic Order (NIEO), discussed in Chapter 10. Both took their impetus from claims that the international system is inequitable, imbalanced, and biased against the Third World. Some in the Third World have railed against what they call "cultural imperialism" on the part of the developed countries, and the United States in particular.

At the height of the controversy over the NWIO in the late 1970s and early 1980s, the Soviets and their allies often lined up with and, indeed, encouraged the Third-World nations in their complaints. Much of the debate occurred within the United Nations Educational, Scientific, and Cultural Organization (UNESCO), which has headquarters in Paris. UNESCO itself became a focal point of major criticism from the United States and some other Western countries. In 1984, the United States withdrew from UNESCO, having charged that the organization had become highly politicized and "exhibited hostility toward the basic institutions of a free society, especially a free market and a free press." Critics also pointed to the organization's bloated bureaucracy and budget.

UNESCO has had important achievements since its founding as part of the United Nations in 1946, with its goals including "full and equal opportunities for education for all" and "the unrestricted pursuit of objective truth" and "the free exchange of ideas and knowledge." It has made notable contributions in literacy programs, promotion of scientific cooperation, cultural exchange, and preservation of historic sites. However, as it became increasingly embroiled in the NWIO controversy, its critics charged that UNESCO was discouraging rather than promoting intellectual freedom.

In more recent years UNESCO has made some important changes in its organization and operations and the debate over communications issues has become much less heated. At the end of 1989, the general conference of UNESCO approved a six-year communications program that commits the organization to "encouraging" freedom of the press and the "free flow of ideas." It calls on UNESCO to promote "wider and better-balanced dissemination of information" between developed and developing nations, but states such an effort should be undertaken "without any obstacle to freedom of expression." The program also commits UNESCO to work for the strengthening of communications infrastructures in developing countries "in order to increase their participation in the communication process." Some in the West were still skeptical about UNESCO's direction and the view of the proper role of the media. Still, there has been a move away from the earlier polemical debates. And the divisive debate that did occur should not obscure the fact that some of the problems associated with the NWIO controversy are matters of valid and continuing concern.

Media and Cultural Dominance

The United States and some other Western nations have championed the free flow of information and unimpeded access to news and news sources by journalists. The free flow of information is seen as part of the concept of universal human rights. However, some in the Third World question the Western notion of the free flow of information, saying that it serves only those who control the networks of communications. If there is to be a free flow, it should, they say, be a free and *balanced* flow. A primary source of their concern is the dominating role of the major international news agencies, all based in industrialized nations. The "big five" press agencies—Associated Press and United Press International (U.S.); Reuters (Britain); Agence France-Press (France); and TASS (Russia)—control more than 80 percent of the world news flow. Some Third-World spokespersons have claimed that the structure of world communications perpetuates the old colonial system.

There is objection from the Third World to both the quantity and quality of news about developing countries. Additionally, some claim that the news coming into their countries—as well as films, television programs, advertising, and other examples of Western culture—often reflects alien values and amounts to cultural imperialism. (American cultural influence is especially strong, partially because American culture enjoys broad international popularity. Even Europeans have imposed various restrictions on American television programs in order to break the United States dominance and promote their own industry.) In his aptly titled book, *The Geopolitics of Information*, British author Anthony Smith examines how Western media and culture dominate the world. Smith notes that the dominance is "deeply rooted in history" and unlikely to change significantly. "Indeed," writes Smith, "the threat to independence in the late 20th century from the new electronics could be greater than was colonialism itself."[6]

The quantitative imbalance in the flow of information of which the Third World complains is in some respects simply a reflection of the historical dominance of the Western media, and particularly the Western news services. Although, as noted in the previous chapter, Third-World nations constitute a growing majority of the world's population, they often feel shut out of the international news flow and/or victimized by what they see as slanted coverage. Several attempts have been made to establish "alternative" news agencies, some of them based in the Third World. They have met with limited success.

Some of the complaining about news coverage and emphasis actually reflects a lack of understanding or acceptance of what constitutes news. After all, most of the Western media are in business. They are concerned not just with informing but with attracting readers, viewers, listeners, and advertisers—selling their product. Those in the Third World who criticize the media for emphasizing "negative" news, would find their criticisms echoed in the West.

Coups, Earthquakes, and the Need for Context

The press is accused of reporting coups and disasters, while ignoring "positive" stories and development efforts in the Third World. There is much validity to this criticism. Indeed, Mort Rosenblum, a veteran Associated Press correspondent, has written, "Coups and earthquakes are still perennial favorites of all editors." Discussion earlier in this chapter focused on some of the problems that plague international coverage, particularly the lack of perspective and context in reporting. Although there are some highly qualified and able international correspondents, their numbers are limited and sometimes what results is "parachute journalism." Like firefighters, the journalists are dispatched after the alarm sounds. A classic, though fictionalized and satirical account of such journalism is found in Evelyn Waugh's novel, *Scoop*, which tells of an inexperienced journalist being sent off to cover a civil war in an African country. Other than some preconceptions about "good guys" and "bad guys," the journalist had no notion of what was occurring or what it meant. According to Rosenblum, parachute journalism reinforces a pack mentality that has always plagued foreign reporting:

> Correspondents who hurry off to a new place tend to stick together, interviewing friends who arrived earlier and competing to find the most dramatic angle of the story. Wherever there are few residential correspondents, a Parkinson's Law of Journalism holds that news increases in direct proportion to the number of visiting reporters . . . For example, demonstrations in Jamaica in 1976 may have gone unnoticed except that they coincided with a major International Monetary Fund meeting. Scores of correspondents, taking a welcome break from analyzing sheets of figures, had a Caribbean-isle-in-flames story to cover. If any had been based in Jamaica, they may have judged the outbreaks to be

less significant than they appeared at first glance. But seen in isolation, they were a big story.[7]

Contemporary communications and transportation capabilities can in some cases make for better reporting and provide worldwide audiences with live, on-the-spot coverage, as has already been discussed. However, the nature of journalism is such that many of the problems are going to continue and many in the Third World (and elsewhere) will remain dissatisfied. As Gerald Long of Reuters has explained, "The prevalent school of journalism throughout the world is a journalism of exception. In other words, you don't report that everything is fine in Pakistan today. You report that there has been an air crash."[8]

Acknowledging that Western journalists, true to the Western concept of journalism, often seek out the aberrational rather than the normal, Anthony Smith points out that many Third-World news agencies adopt a similar attitude: reporting the gloom-and-doom stories from elsewhere while ignoring some home-grown problems. Various studies have tended to back up this point.

Governments, Development, and the Media

While the criticisms related to news coverage and emphasis and the lack of contextual reporting would find resonance in many quarters in many corners of the world, another aspect of the international debate on the role of the media is much more divisive. Much of the dispute centers around the proper role of governments in relation to the media.

In the United States there has traditionally been a strong separation between government and media, and this is true in varying degrees and with some exceptions in most other Western nations. On the other hand, totalitarian and other dictatorial governments have often used control of the media for propaganda purposes and to help maintain political control. Within the Third World, there are certainly examples of the media being used for such purposes, but in some cases another angle is involved— the proper role of the media in development. Some insist that developing societies are so fragile that they cannot withstand aggressive and critical reporting. Instead, they argue that it is the role of the media to be supportive of government and national development.

Responding to the Western concept of "journalism of exception," Dilip Mukerjee, an Indian journalist, wrote, "In our environment there is, and will be for a long time to come, much that is ugly and distasteful. If we follow up the Western norm, we will be playing up only these dark spots, and thus helping unwittingly to erode the faith and confidence without which growth and development are impossible." Mukerjee believes there should be a new style of journalism "which asserts that good news is just as newsworthy as bad."[9]

Rosemary Righter counters the arguments that governments in developing nations need a controlled press: "The media may occasionally undermine unified government support, but when that means highlighting corruption or publicizing an ill-executed government development project, to muzzle the press is to throw out the baby with the bath water."[10]

Some governments have indeed cited the need to protect national development as a basis for imposing censorship on their media and/or restricting or prohibiting access by external media. Although governments can clamp down on coverage, there have been encouraging developments in press access with the collapse of many totalitarian regimes. And, as discussed earlier, it is becoming more and more difficult for nations to wall themselves off from external communication. A reality of the age is that cultural, media, and information sovereignty or independence are very hard to maintain.

Even in the industrialized democracies of Western Europe, governments had a monopoly over radio and television services until recent years. These services, usually operated by public corporations, enjoyed relative degrees of autonomy—considerable in the case of the BBC, much less so in the case of French television, especially during the De Gaulle period, when the French president considered television to be an arm of government. Andre Malraux, who served as minister of culture under De Gaulle, reportedly asked President John Kennedy with some incredulity, "How can you govern a country if you don't control television?"

Various authoritarian governments have traditionally exercised tight control over their media. As has already been discussed, this includes some in the Third World. For many years in the Soviet Union the state and the Communist party had total control of publications and broadcasting. Gorbachev's *glasnost* and efforts toward democratization in the country opened the way for greater diversity and public debate in the media.

Although there were some flickerings of freedom in the Chinese media during the 1989 "prodemocracy" protests, the Communist authorities continued to maintain rigid control of the media. And China, because of its size and geography, is less accessible to external media than most countries. Although China and other countries can isolate themselves to a degree, it is increasingly difficult for any country to cut itself off from international telecommunications and still participate in international business and commerce. International direct-dial telephones, fax machines, and computers can all serve as important means of international communications.

Fax machines were heavily utilized by Chinese students in 1989 in sending and receiving information from abroad. These benign-appearing office machines can quickly transmit printed information and data. With a phone call and a push of a button, the information can be communicated across thousands of miles in minutes. Fax and photocopy machines and cellular phones were all utilized by journalists as well as citizens resisting the Soviet coup attempt in 1991.

Technological advances helped influence the break-up of government monopolies of the electronic media in Europe. The advent of cable, satellite-delivered programming, and other developments made it increasingly difficult for the national broadcasting services to retain exclusive control. The tendency toward privatization and deregulation (reduction or elimination of government control and/or regulation) gathered momentum in the 1980s, contributing to much greater diversification in such countries as Britain, France, and Germany. Although most nations maintain some limitations on the degree of foreign ownership of broadcast services, boundaries in the international communication business are increasingly blurred.

Multinational Multimedia

International media conglomerates are growing, crossing frontiers, and combining different media. Rupert Murdoch, who has been called the "Magellan of the information age," began with newspapers in Australia, expanded to the United Kingdom and the United States, and diversified into other publishing ventures, as well as television and a European satellite TV service. The late Robert Maxwell of Britain (born in Czechoslovakia) became an international media baron as he built a combine of British, American, Kenyan, Israeli, Hungarian, and German newspapers; an international book publisher; cable television; interest in a French television channel; and a European newspaper—*The European*, calling itself "Europe's first national newspaper."

There are many other examples of such international media entanglements. An Italian TV magnate has a substantial presence in French television. Bertelsmann, the German company that has international multimedia holdings that include a number of American book and recording companies, has been called one of the lords of the global village. A French company, which publishes books (including the *Encyclopedia Americana*) and is involved in radio and television, is the world's largest producer of magazines. Japanese companies, which have been so dominant in spreading the means of telecommunications, are increasingly involved in the international media business, especially film/video production and distribution.

While the global media barons have a significant involvement in the American market, many of them are simply responding to a pattern established by American media conglomerates. American media giants such as Time Warner continue to be major international factors. Time Warner has extensive international involvement in magazine and book publishing, film, and television. Its magazines have a worldwide readership of 120 million. (Significantly, two Japanese companies have purchased an interest in Time Warner's television and entertainment operations.) As mentioned previously, American influence has been powerful and pervasive, particularly in film, television, and popular culture. Much of the world watches such American TV shows as "Dallas," "Dynasty," "Hill Street Blues," and "The Cosby Show," though they may be versions dubbed into the local language.

To offset United States domination of TV programming, to promote European integration and foster European identity, and to help build the programming industry within Europe and make it more competitive internationally, the European Community has established quotas on television programming. In effect, the EC acted to limit TV imports from the United States, a move which drew strong American opposition. On the other hand, the expansion and commercialization of European television, following the American pattern, has made the market for foreign programming larger.

External Broadcasting

As discussed earlier in the chapter, there are cases, many in fact, where broadcasting signals from one country are easily received across borders or in neighboring countries. This was true in the case of West German television being watched in East Germany. There are a number of other examples, such as the United States and Canada, France and Belgium, or Jordan and Israel. This spillover effect, particularly with television, is one of the factors drawing people of different nations into the global village.

As has also been discussed, the development of satellite-transmitted television signals opens up much greater possibilities for transborder communications involving great distances. A notable example is Cable News Network, the American-based service which is received in many countries. Although in a number of those countries CNN is available only on a limited basis, usually in selected government offices, businesses, and hotels, it can still have great impact, serving in some cases as the kind of electronic diplomatic courier mentioned earlier in the chapter. The German newspaper *Die Zeit* commented, "CNN has taken Marshall McLuhan's famous phrase 'the global village' and made it real. Viewers get exactly the same information that their heads of state get. Television news has, to some extent, replaced classic diplomacy and espionage."[11]

CNN has demonstrated the considerable potential that exists for much broader transnational communications. The role of CNN in covering the Gulf War and related events has already been mentioned. As an example of what such international television can provide, on a day shortly before the war began, viewers around the world could watch live coverage of press conferences by the United States secretary of state and Iraqi foreign minister from Geneva, where they were holding discussions; by French president François Mitterand from Paris; by President Bush from Washington; and direct coverage from the United Nations, Baghdad, and Saudi Arabia.

GOVERNMENT SERVICES: INFORMATION/ PROPAGANDA

There is another category of external broadcasting—services operated by or supported by governments. Although there are some examples of external government television programming, and there are likely to be more, most of these external services have involved radio. Some of these have been looked upon as propaganda operations. Some have a reputation for integrity and fairness. In certain cases these radio services have been highly influential and have provided a major source of information to citizens of countries where the domestic media were under tight government control.

Propaganda was mentioned earlier in the chapter in connection with some of Mikhail Gorbachev's media diplomacy. Propaganda is often a "loaded" term which conjures up images of the "big lie" techniques associated with Hitler, Goebbels, and the Nazis, or some of the more heavy-handed efforts by the Soviets during the Cold War or the Chinese during the Cultural Revolution. Propaganda is communication aimed at influencing the thinking, emotions, or actions of a group or public. While there is a tendency to think of propaganda as false, distorted, or misleading information or manipulation of facts or data, that is not necessarily the case. Public diplomacy, discussed in Chapter 5, can be considered in some instances as propaganda, which basically involves an effort to present a cause, country, or an individual in a favorable or unfavorable light. Almost all major governments engage in public diplomacy and international propaganda efforts. However, it would be incorrect to view all government international communications activities as propaganda.

More than 80 nations operate official or quasiofficial external services, and the broadcasting is done in many different languages, with the programming sometimes targeted to specific countries, and/or language or ethnic groups. The best known of these have included the BBC World Service (originally known as the Empire Service), Radio Moscow, Radio Beijing, Deutsche Welle (German), Cuban radio, and the American external services. Short-wave radio signals can travel great distances and most external services utilize short wave. In some cases they also have networks of relay transmitters located in friendly countries. Short-wave broadcasting was especially intense during the Cold War, and at times external broadcasting services had significant audiences in the Soviet Union and other Communist countries.

United States–supported foreign broadcasting was for many years aimed primarily at the Communist world. Voice of America (VOA) is the official United States foreign broadcasting service. It began during World War II and was part of the Office of War Information. After the war VOA was continued and was eventually placed within the United States Information Agency, along with other United States international informational activities.

There have often been debates about how objective VOA should be and to what extent it should be an advocate rather than just a reporter of United States policies. Its programs have included not only news and commentary in more than 40 languages but some popular feature and music programs. Total audiences of regular listeners were estimated at as high as 130 million in the 1980s, with nearly half of those in the Soviet Union and Eastern Europe.

Interference?

For many years, the Soviet Union regularly jammed broadcasts from VOA and other foreign broadcasts aimed at its citizens. *Jamming* involves the creation of deliberate interference with incoming radio signals. The Soviets devoted considerable resources to jamming—at one time it was estimated that more was being spent to jam than the combined budgets of the United States–supported broadcasting services. Transmitters in the U.S.S.R., Czechoslovakia, East Germany, and Bulgaria were used to cause interference with the broadcasts of VOA, Radio Free Europe, and the BBC. Other nations, including Cuba, have also used jamming to try to block out foreign broadcasts.

Jamming such broadcasts was symptomatic of the Cold War rivalry and could be compared to construction of the Berlin Wall as an effort to isolate East from West and to shut out external information. The jamming was justified on grounds that the foreign broadcasts were pure propaganda, and aimed at sowing unrest among their listeners. During periods of improved relations between East and West the jamming decreased and finally ceased under Gorbachev's *glasnost* policies.

In addition to the VOA, the United States operated two other services targeted to Eastern Europe and the Soviet Union and one aimed at Cuba. Radio Free Europe (RFE) was aimed at audiences in Eastern Europe, while Radio Liberty (RL) was directed toward the Soviet Union. These stations were sometimes referred to as surrogate domestic services, the assumption being that citizens of the target countries were not being provided with full and accurate information about internal developments by the government-controlled domestic broadcasting services. From their founding in the early Cold War days until 1967, RFE and RL masqueraded as private operations supported by voluntary contributions from American citizens. In fact, the stations were largely funded and operated by the United States Central Intelligence Agency (CIA). When the CIA funding was disclosed, RFE and RL were placed under the jurisdiction of the Board of International Broadcasting. The board's members are appointed by the president and funding is appropriated by Congress.

More recently the United States government established Radio Marti and then TV Marti, both directed at Cuba and also intended to be surrogate domestic services. Although VOA had long been broadcasting to Cuba and Cubans could even receive United States domestic stations broadcasting (some in Spanish) from south Florida, Radio Marti began operation in 1985, intended to provide Cubans with the same kind of programming that RFE offered in Eastern Europe. (Radio Marti was named for Jose Marti, a nineteenth century Cuban independence hero.) Cuban President Fidel Castro denounced the broadcasts as "aggression" and took a variety of steps, including jamming, to impede them. Radio and TV Marti (begun in 1989) were born largely due to the efforts of Florida's strongly anti-Castro Cuban-exile community, which lobbied the Reagan and Bush administrations and Congress to fund the stations.

Impact of External Broadcasts

Another United States–supported radio service was RIAS—Radio in the American Sector of Berlin. RIAS aimed at East Berlin and East Germany and, particularly before West German TV became so pervasive in the East, helped breach the Berlin wall.

Many of those who lived behind the old Iron Curtain in Eastern Europe cited the external broadcasts from VOA, RFE, and BBC as having played an important role in providing information about what was going on in the world, especially in those tumultuous days of 1989 when communist regimes were collapsing. Mention has already been made of the role these broadcasts played in informing Romanians about the events elsewhere. Some Romanians said that the external broadcasts gave them hope and prevented the Ceausescu regime from monopolizing information.

Students in the "prodemocracy" movement in China in 1989 were able to obtain information about the international response to their efforts by listening to foreign broadcasts. When Mikhail Gorbachev was under house arrest in the Crimea in 1991, he was still able to hear the BBC, VOA, and Radio Liberty. Audiences in Russia and the other republics tuned to the foreign broadcasts to get reports of the resistance to the attempted coup, further undermining efforts of the coup plotters to control information.

In 1978, when his government was on the brink of collapse, the Shah of Iran was bitterly critical of the BBC, calling it "the mouthpiece of the opposition."[12] He said that many Iranians were listening to the broadcasts and receiving incorrect information. Since the media within Iran were tightly controlled and strictly limited, the BBC was one of the few sources Iranians had for news about the controversial developments within their country.

COMMUNICATIONS CROSSCURRENTS

Interestingly, the Shah was also being weakened by another form of communication. Ayatollah Khomeini, then in exile in France, made strong antishah pronouncements which were recorded on audio casettes and sent back to Iran, or in some cases played over long-distance telephone and recorded in Iran. The casettes were then duplicated in large numbers and distributed nationwide and played in mosques. Inexpensive casette players were plentiful in the country and thus the Shah's hold on mass communications were circumvented. It is also noteworthy that Ayatollah Khomeini, who railed against modernization and the Shah's role in attempting to modernize Iran, used these modern innovations to help bring down the Shah. Later he and his followers skillfully utilized foreign (particularly American) television during the hostage crisis, as discussed earlier.

Khomeini became involved in another international media-related controversy. Salman Rushdie, a British author (born in India), wrote a novel, *The Satanic Verses*, which generated strong protests from Islamic fundamentalists for what was seen as insulting treatment of the prophet Mohammed and the Muslim or Islamic religion. Khomeini pronounced a death sentence on Rushdie, offering a $1 million reward to his murderer, which, in turn, outraged many in the West. The death threat forced Rushdie into hiding and created enormous controversy. (Rushdie, who is of Islamic heritage, later sought to make clear that he had not intended to insult the religion or its believers.)

Politically, the Rushdie affair served to further isolate Iran from the Western world. It also pointed up the deep clashes in the value systems and ways of life between the West and much of the Muslim world. What to Westerners appeared to be a legitimate exercise of artistic expression was seen by strict believers in Islam as heresy, subject to strong punishment. This case exemplifies the cultural and political elements of the conflict between traditionalism and modernization discussed in Chapter 1. Shireen T. Hunter, an expert on the Islamic world, pointed out that Islamic forces are wary of the spread of Western secular values and see the West as intent upon undermining Islam. They see and fear Western economic and military supremacy and its cultural attraction for deprived Muslims. These fears help explain why the mere publication of a book was viewed as a grand Western conspiracy against Islam. Hunter wrote:

> As Muslim societies go through the pangs of growth and try to reconcile their Islamic values with the requirements of modernization and the need to live in an increasingly interdependent world, they are passing through turbulent times. As emerging nations, they try to assert themselves internationally, which often causes difficulties in their relations with others, including the West.[13]

The Rushdie affair demonstrates the impact of the crosscurrents of communication in today's world and underlines how explosive words and images may be in international relations.

INTERNATIONAL COMMUNICATIONS ISSUES AND COOPERATION

With all the nations of the world involved in telecommunications, it is imperative that there be some international structure for cooperation and technical regulation; otherwise, there might be complete havoc in international communications.

The International Telecommunications Union (ITU) can, in fact, claim to be the oldest intergovernmental organization, dating back to 1865. In that year, meeting in Paris, 20 nations signed its first convention, designed to facilitate transborder telegraphic communications. In 1947, ITU became an agency of the United Nations.

As new forms of telecommunications have come into being, the responsibilities of the ITU have expanded. Its membership has also steadily increased as an influx of Third-World countries has pushed the total to more than 160. The ITU serves as a forum for promoting interconnections of the world's telecommunications networks and for setting international telecommunications standards. The ITU has played a key role in administering the rational, efficient use of the international radio spectrum, seeking to prevent radio frequency interference. Without the ITU to oversee allocation of radio frequencies, there would almost inevitably be a cacophony of broadcasts by competing stations in different countries. More recently, the ITU has supported technical cooperation and assistance in the developing world by providing consultants and technical advice on telecommunications. The accelerating pace of technological change discussed in this chapter and the trend toward regulatory liberalization in much of the world have created complex new opportunities and challenges for the ITU.

The ITU holds a plenipotentiary conference every five to seven years to chart the general course for international telecommunications policy. With the telecommunications landscape constantly changing, there is a full agenda for the ITU. In between the plenipotentiary meetings, the permanent staff, based in Geneva, Switzerland, carries on the work of the organization. The ITU, like the International Atomic Energy Agency (IAEA), has had a reputation for professionalism and has mostly avoided polemical debates of the sort that took place in UNESCO.

There are periodic regional and international meetings of the important subgroups within ITU, including the World Administrative Radio Conference (WARC) and the World Administrative Telegraph and Telephone Conference (WATTC). Among the important problems to come before ITU and WARC in recent years have been questions related to communications via satellite, with the number and usage of satellites creating a new set of issues. Some of the Third-World countries have favored a system that would reserve some space frequencies and satellite "parking places" for the future when they might be able to utilize them, their concern being that a few industrialized countries would gain perpetual domination of satellite communications. Some of these matters are dealt with by Itelsat (International Telecommunications Satellite Organization Consortium), a cooperative venture among more than 100 countries to operate and coordinate communications satellites. Itelsat is open to all ITU members.

The WATTC has been increasingly involved with information services utilizing the new technologies.

The growing preoccupation of ITU and its subgroups with telecommunications involving advanced technology is indicative of the increasing significance of technological issues in global affairs.

TECHNOLOGY AND INTERNATIONAL RELATIONS

Throughout this chapter there has been consideration of how advances in communications and information technology are having an impact on world affairs. In particular, attention has been given to how technology affects news coverage and its transmission around the globe. There are, of course, many more manifestations of technology's impact and influence on international relations, and some of those have been discussed in earlier sections of this book. As discussed in Chapter 6, for example, technology and weaponry are closely related, and new weapons technologies have brought new dimensions to international security affairs.

High technology has also revolutionized international surveillance and intelligence-gathering. Sophisticated electronic equipment can be used to monitor or intercept another government's communications. In turn, governments often employ high-tech scrambling devices to thwart such electronic eavesdropping.

Satellites are used not just to facilitate and channel communications among nations. They have also greatly enhanced the ability of national intelligence agencies to monitor the activities in and around military installations and naval ports. High-resolution aerial photography can provide amazingly detailed views of such activities.

Information gathered through high-tech means is sometimes referred to in the intelligence community as *sigInt* (signal intelligence), as opposed to the more traditional human intelligence—information obtained by individual agents—made familiar in spy films and novels. When used for verifying compliance with arms control agreements, the high-tech monitoring from satellites and aircraft-based systems (such as radars and optical systems), as well as sea- and ground-based systems (such as radars and antennas), is referred to as "national technical means" of verification.

Technology: Power and Polarization

The effects of the significant strides being made in such areas as transportation, telecommunications, information processing, and biotechnology are being felt in many parts of the world, although there is concern that there will be a growing technology divide, that a new political/cultural polarization between the haves and the have-nots will result as we move further into what has been called the postindustrial society.

The steadily growing effects of technology and technological developments and the potential they offer and problems they may present for the future will be discussed further in the following, concluding chapter. However, as should be apparent from this chapter, technology-related changes and effects have already done much to link nations of the world more closely together. Technology changes the context in which relations among nations take place. And technological capability is becoming an increasingly important component of a nation's power in the modern world.

One of the key characteristics of contemporary international relations, as has been discussed in earlier chapters, is that the nature of power and security is being redefined. Some would suggest that technology or technological capability should be added to the elements of power outlined by Hans Morgenthau and others. Certainly, technological factors affect many of the recognized elements of power. National security is increasingly defined to take into account economic factors, with economic strength and growth, research and development, and access to needed resources among the important ingredients of security.

Professor Dennis Pirages uses the term "global technopolitics," which refers to the dynamics of an emerging postindustrial system which he sees as increasingly driven by the imperatives of technology. It is not, according to Pirages, that technopolitics makes military power unimportant, "Rather, the international rules of good conduct have changed so that the naked exercise of force has become much more difficult for mature industrial countries. And the focus has shifted away from gain by conquest to gain through technological domination and resource manipulation."[14] As Pirages points out, in a world characterized by growing interdependence and technopolitics, power will be a much more multidimensional concept.

The Soviet Dilemma

While the Soviet Union was an early leader in space technology and devoted massive resources to development of military technology, it lagged far behind in other areas. Problems in agriculture and related areas were discussed in Chapter 11. Gorbachev and others in the former Soviet Union recognized that to be competitive in the world, it was imperative to strengthen the economy and upgrade technological capabilities.

For many years the hyperconcern of the Soviet government about maintaining centralized control over information and technology within the country was a factor in holding back development. An example of the government's attitude was seen in its policy on broken-down or run-down photocopying machines. When the machines were no longer operative, they had to be destroyed so that it wouldn't be possible for the machines to be repaired or retooled for unauthorized use. (In China, access to photocopiers remains strictly limited.)

The computer industry within the Soviet Union did not develop very rapidly, and the Soviet Union was long denied access to some advanced computers and related technology from the West because of concerns about possible use for military or other security-related purposes. Those computers and other advanced technology that did get into the Soviet Union were usually subject to careful government control. However, it is hard for a government to harness the power of advanced technology without losing monopoly control over information. And earlier sections of this chapter indicated how difficult it is to shut out external communications and information in this era of transnational communications. Gorbachev's glasnost policies and improved relations with the West sharply increased the flow of high-tech equipment into Russia and other former Soviet states. Although the alleged "missile gap" or the Soviet lead in space travel were once matters of concern in the West, the "computer gap" contributed to the crumbling of the Soviet Union.

While the Soviet Union trailed far behind in technological capability, and the United States is a leader in technology and its utilization, other nations have made notable technological advances and contributions. Japan stands out as a technological-economic power, and technology has helped propel Japan into a central role in international economic relations. As was discussed in Chapter 10, others—including such newly industrializing countries as Korea, Singapore, and Taiwan—acquired new technologies and began to have their own impact on world markets that had previously been American domain. The dispersal of technological capability among nations has reduced economic and military preeminence.

Technology, Information, and Interaction

The interaction of technology with the international economy is far-reaching and has many dimensions. Transborder data flow and the growing internationalization of business affect and involve a wide variety of international transactions, trade, and movement of capital. The advances in information and communications technology make this possible and contribute to the steady interlocking of economies.

International computer networks are a key factor in the new pattern of global communications. According to Wilson Dizard, an American specialist on information and telecommunications policy, "Politically, communications are the nervous system for the interdependent world order . . . and particularly important to this world order are improved links between the industrialized and developing nations."[15]

Information is an extremely valuable commodity in today's global economy, and the ability to communicate quickly with other parts of the world is vital. As governments, business, industry, larger-scale agriculture, and education are increasingly internationalized, they are increasingly dependent on ready access to information from various points of the globe. Stock markets and commodity trading are more and more internationalized. Airline reservation services are on international computer networks. Multinational corporations have to be able to communicate detailed information between plants and offices around the world. Automobile manufacturers, as noted in Chapter 1, may utilize parts and components produced in a number of different countries. To be efficient, they rely on information technology to coordinate inventories, production schedules, and shipments among many countries.

The increasing number of *maquiladora* industries located on the Mexican side of the border with the United States must maintain transborder telecommunications with the company headquarters, often in the United States, and with other company plants and distribution centers.

As Professor Eugene Skolnikoff has written, "One of the characteristic effects of an increasingly technological world is to make interaction among nations more intense and at the same time unavoidable."[16] The application and potential uses of technology in business and in such fields as health, space, agriculture, weather, and environmental protection require international action to deal with its effects and/or to reap its benefits. The next chapter will explore these issues further and consider possibilities for applying technology to some of the critical problems facing the world. The growing need for cooperative action in these areas, combined with the border-breaching telecommunications and information discussed in this chapter, pushes these matters closer to the center of contemporary international relations.

NOTES

1. Tara Sonenshine, "The Revolution Has Been Televised," *Washington Post* (National Weekly Edition), October 8–14, 1990, p. 29.
2. *The Wall Comes Down*, Reuters, 1990. (Video report and publication based on Reuters coverage of the events in Europe in 1989.)
3. Quoted in David Shaw, "The Growing Trend of Pack Journalism," *Los Angeles Times*, September 24, 1989.
4. Lucian W. Pye, *China: An Introduction*, 3rd ed. (Boston: Little Brown, 1984), p. 2.
5. See James F. Larson, "Television and U.S. Foreign Policy: The Case of the Iran Hostage Crisis," in Doris A. Graber, *Media Power in Politics*, 2nd ed. (Washington: Congressional Quarterly Press, 1990), pp. 301–312.
6. Anthony Smith, *The Geopolitics of Information* (New York: Oxford University Press, 1980), p. 176.
7. Mort Rosenblum, *Coups and Earthquakes* (New York: Harper, 1981), pp. 12, 122.
8. Quoted in Rosemary Richter, "Battle of the Bias," *Foreign Policy* 34, spring 1979, pp. 124–25.

9. Roger Tatarian, "New Flows in the Third World: An Overview," in Philip C. Horton (ed.), *The Third World and Press Freedom* (New York: Praeger, 1978), p. 43.
10. Righter, "Battle of the Bias," p. 137.
11. Michael Schwelien, "CNN: Television for the Global Village," reprinted from *Die Zeit* (Germany) in *World Press Review*, December 1990, p. 34.
12. Report to President Jimmy Carter on Visit to Iran by Senator Robert C. Byrd, December 1978.
13. Shireen T. Hunter, "Rushdie Case Rooted in a Clash of Values," *Christian Science Monitor*, February 28, 1989.
14. Dennis Pirages, *Global Technopolitics* (Pacific Grove, Calif.: Brooks/Cole, 1989), p. 21.
15. Wilson P. Dizard, Jr. *The Coming Information Age*, 3rd ed. (New York: Longman: 1989), p. 184.
16. Eugene Skolnikoff, "Technology and the World Tomorrow," *Current History*, January 1989, p. 6.

CHAPTER THIRTEEN

Future World Order and International Issues for the Twenty-First Century

The previous chapters of this book have outlined and discussed the structures, forces, and issues which have shaped and are shaping international relations. It is evident that certain traditional problems and long-standing issues will remain as important factors in international relations. However, newer and emerging issues and forces are becoming increasingly significant. Additionally, there are prospective developments, problems, and issues that will significantly affect the international system and figure importantly in international relations of the future. This concluding chapter will examine some of the most notable of these and consider possible future trends, patterns, and directions in world affairs.

The twentieth century has brought many important developments and changes in international relations. The century was marked by two world wars and a number of other significant military conflicts. The world witnessed the development of highly sophisticated and immensely destructive weaponry, as well as the remarkable advances in communications and transportation which have served to draw the world closer together. World War II ended in 1945, and for much of the 45-year period that followed, the rivalry between the Soviet Union and the United States, or the East-West, Communist-noncommunist divisions dominated world affairs and cast long shadows over international structures and organizations, including the United Nations. The East-West division often extended into Latin America and to Africa and Asia where many nations were gaining their independence and struggling to provide sustenance for their growing populations and to attain political maturity.

THE SHAPE OF A NEW ORDER?

As we move toward the twenty-first century, momentous changes in the world order have occurred or are underway. The end of the Cold War and the diminished international thrust of Soviet communism have significantly altered world politics, but these developments did not by any means bring about the "end of history," as some proclaimed. A variety of important issues and conflicts existed or exist outside the realm of the East-West division, although some of them were entangled in or tangentially connected with the United States—Soviet rivalry. And, as has already been suggested, as the Cold War was winding down, a number of other trends were already underway or beginning to emerge, which were bringing some major alterations to international relations.

In the aftermath of the Cold War, there was much talk among diplomats and politicians and in the media and think tanks about an emerging new world order. However, even while some were proclaiming the arrival of a more tranquil and orderly world, the unpredictability of international relations and the persistence of instability in certain regions was vividly demonstrated by the Persian Gulf War following Iraq's invasion of Kuwait.

Predictability and Unpredictability— Old and New Issues

Francis Fukuyama stirred considerable debate with his 1989 article, "The End of History?" in which he wrote:

> What we may be witnessing is not just the end of the Cold War, or the passing of postwar history, but the end of history as such: that is, the end point of mankind's ideological evolution and the universalization of Western liberal democracy as the final form of human government.[1]

In his analysis, Fukuyama drew on the works of Georg W. F. Hegel (1770–1831), the German philosopher. Hegel, as Fukuyama described it, believed that "history" culminated when a "final, rational form of society and state became victorious." What Fukuyama saw as the triumph of the "Western idea" was, from his neo-Hegelian perspective, that end point.

Fukuyama tended to dismiss developments within the Third World as insignificant. He did acknowledge that religion and nationalism remain as important factors in the world, although, in his view, not as dominant ones. And he did say that terrorism and wars of national liberation will continue to be important items on the international agenda. "But," wrote Fukuyama, "Large-scale conflict must involve large states still caught in the grip of history," and in the posthistorical period that he believed was arriving, there would, he said, be no such conflicts.[2]

Some have contended that the "old order," centering on the United

States—Soviet rivalry, actually made the world more predictable. They argue that when international relations were essentially subject to bipolar domination, the world order was, in fact, more stable, less likely to experience violent lurches and conflicts. Professor John J. Mearsheimer of the University of Chicago believes, "We may . . . wake up one day lamenting the loss of the order that the Cold War gave to the anarchy of international relations." As mentioned in Chapter 7, Mearsheimer argues that the Cold War kept nationalism at bay in Europe, and that its end opens the way for a return to multipolarity and anarchy. According to this view, "untamed anarchy is what Europe knew in the 45 years of this century before the Cold War, and untamed anarchy—Hobbes' war of all against all—is a prime cause of armed conflict."[3]

Professor Samuel P. Huntington says that the end of the Cold War very probably does mean increased instability, unpredictability, and violence in international affairs and the end of what historian John Lewis Gaddis refers to as the "Long Peace" of the Cold War period. However, in Huntington's view, "The end of the Cold War does not mean the end of political, ideological, diplomatic, economic, technological, or even military rivalry among nations. It does not mean the end of the struggle for power and influence."[4]

While there are unquestionably new dangers and unpredictable consequences arising out of the crumbling of the old order, many would maintain that there are forces and factors at work that pull in the direction of greater international integration rather than disintegration. In this view, the pessimistic position, as taken by Mearsheimer, overstates the case and misreads the prospects for the post–Cold War world just as—in a different way—did the proclamations about the "end of history."

Fukuyama, in his "end of history" analysis, depicted whatever problems that lie ahead as little more than Third-World nuisances, lacking ideological content and context, and therefore lacking historical standing. A number of critics took issue with this notion. Tina Rosenberg, who writes about Latin American affairs, commented, "the end of history just hasn't caught on in Peru yet." She pointed out that history "is still going full tilt" in Peru, where *Sendero Luminoso* (Shining Path) guerillas and government forces have killed thousands while trying to eradicate each other.

Many of the revolutionary movements in the world, as Rosenberg notes, have little to do with either communism or capitalism. The motivation may owe much more to nationalistic, ethnic, religious, tribal, or racial factors than to ideology, and these movements are not important to Fukuyama's thesis because they do not represent a global ideology. "But that doesn't mean they are not important to the rest of us. The Third World is the site of most of the world's wars."[5]

As French political scientist Pierre Hassner points out, Fukuyama recognizes the persistence of war and poverty outside the West, but tends to see these problems as irrelevant and not of concern to the great developed nations. But, asks Hassner, can the developed nations remain unaffected? Indeed, Hassner suggests that we have growing evidence of increasing intolerance among nations caused by the shock of cultures and the overcrowding of the planet. "And are these conflicts not linked to internal stresses: at the economic level in times of crisis; at the political one if overpopulation and the competition for space make a strong, possibly an authoritarian state more likely; and, above all, within the soul of the individuals, where the thirst for absolutes and for community, for violence, and for hierarchy, may reassert itself?"[6]

As has been emphasized in earlier chapters, although the Cold War has ended, a catalogue of serious problems with global implications can easily be compiled. Some are old, some newer, and some emerging. They include long-standing border disputes, expanding populations, declining resources, ethnic conflicts, societal inequities, inadequate international institutions and cooperation, and struggling economies in developing nations.

Rather than marking the "end of history," some would argue that the culmination of the Cold War served to thaw out historical hatreds and rekindle old grievances, which had been frozen during the Cold War. Many of these involve ethnic or nationalist groups that had been subjugated by stronger forces. In some cases the grievances and enmities relate to boundaries drawn by colonial or other foreign powers, as discussed in earlier chapters. The Cold War did hold in check certain conflicts over these issues; in effect, some streams of history were dammed up during the Cold War and began to flow again as it ended—in some cases with torrential force.

Nations, Supranational Trends, and World Order

The framework of nation-states that existed during the Cold War, including one of the most dominant, the Soviet Union, helped subdue subnational tensions. Now, that framework of nation-states is being subjected to a variety of subnational and supranational pressures. Two seemingly contradictory trends are at work. From within, a number of nations, the Soviet Union prominent among them, have been challenged by ethnic and nationality groups demanding sovereignty and independence from the larger nation-states to which they were sometimes forcibly attached. At the same time, particularly for economic reasons (as discussed in Chapter 9), supranational groupings, such as the European Community, are becoming more important, and nation-states are ceding some of their traditional powers to those larger structures.

The nation-state has been the fundamental organizing unit in international relations. As was explained in Chapter 2, the Peace of Westphalia (1648) gave birth to the nation-state system. The sovereignty of individual nation-states over their respective territories was recognized, and that has remained as an enduring principle in international relations. Now, however, internal forces and the external attractions are placing new stresses on nation-states and creating new dynamics in international relations. In other words, both centripetal (inward) and centrifugal (outward) forces are operating, and their effects will not only alter the future world map but can also have a distinct impact on the time-honored concepts of nationhood and sovereignty.

Of course, at the end of both of the world wars of the twentieth century, there were those leaders and idealists who envisioned forms of world government, that would, if they worked successfully, result in member nations yielding some of their sovereignty to the international organizations. Both the League of Nations after World War I and United Nations after World War II embodied hopes for combining the nation-states into a cooperative world structure. First the League and then the United Nations were limited by the willingness of nations to accept their authority and to work within their frameworks. The end of the Cold War opened the way for the United Nations to assume a stronger role in international diplomacy and peacekeeping, moving closer to realization of some of the fundamental purposes intended by the organization's founders. And, as indicated earlier in this chapter, the end of the Cold War spurred considerable thought and discussion about a new global order.

What are some of the main ingredients of a possible new world order? Drawing on the ideas advanced by President Bush, as well as other proposals and developments, they would include[7]

- greater reliance on and a larger role for regional and international organizations;

- promotion of democratic values and free-market economies on a global scale;

- effective deterrence of military threats to the new order, based on the assumption that just as a democratic system of government requires police forces to ensure order, an orderly international system requires both a code of international conduct and ways to deter or, if necessary, resist and/or punish those who violate that code;

- cooperation between the United States and the other economic/political/military powers in the world, including the primary components that made up the Soviet Union;

- active diplomacy to prevent and resolve disputes, recognizing, as discussed in this and preceding chapters, that there are still significant political, economic, religious, and ethnic divisions in the world; and

- development programs to enhance support for and stakes in a more orderly international system.

In announcing the 1991 military action against Iraq, which had been approved by the United Nations Security Council, President George Bush said that the action was part of an effort to establish a *new world order.* "When we are successful, and we will be, we have a real chance at this new world order, an order in which a credible United Nations can use its peacekeeping role to fulfill the promise and vision of the U.N.'s founders."[8] Bush once said that such a world order, a durable system for peace, had been sought by a hundred generations in a thousand wars. Others feared that the war in the Persian Gulf area contained dangers of doing more to defeat the goal of a new world order than to attain it, with the United States—led international force relying on military strength rather than nonmilitary means to deal with problems in a turbulent region, and possibly unleashing unintended consequences and new problems.

Much of the discourse about the new world order centers around the prospect of larger roles for supranational organizations such as the United Nations, the European Community, and the Conference on Security and Cooperation in Europe (CSCE). Such organizations are moving more and more into areas that were formerly considered to be primarily the domain of individual nations—defense, human rights, and, of course, economics. Throughout this book, the increasing interlinking of economies has been emphasized. Further, such issues as the environment, drug trafficking, and terrorism require multinational attention and cooperation. Indeed, international or supranational organizations are best suited to deal with many of the issues on the future international agenda which are discussed in this chapter. As has been previously pointed out, unilateral action to deal with atmospheric or water pollution problems, for example, is often meaningless or ineffective because such problems cannot easily be contained within the boundaries of one nation.

Do the subnational tensions and supranational trends point to the demise of the nation-state and/or to a decline in its importance in international relations?

Pressures being placed on nations by ethnic, religious, or political groups are a major source of volatility in the contemporary world, as discussed in Chapter 7, and such pressures are apt to continue into the future. These groups are seeking autonomous rights within existing countries, or they are demanding their own separate countries, or reunification with kindred groups across borders. This drive for "self-determination" or self-government has proven to be a significant factor in late twentieth-century international affairs, with, as noted earlier, the end of the Cold War and the collapse of the Soviet empire opening the way for more assertive action by those seeking self-determination.

"It is easy to wax sentimental over the principle of self-determination," Ronald Steel, a writer on international relations, has said. "The notion that every nationality and ethnic group should have its own independent piece of territory sounds eminently sensible to most Americans." However, as Steel points out, the United States fought a civil war over the issue of whether a group of people, no matter how heartfelt their wishes, had the right to leave the American union. But columnist William Safire saw a striking difference between the American Civil War and the Soviet internal strife: "Lincoln believed in human freedom and Mr. Gorbachev was trying to perpetuate a system of political slavery."[9]

Part of the problem for the Soviet Union was that while the American colonies originally came together voluntarily, surrendering their sovereignty in the process, that was not the case for all the Soviet republics, nor were they cemented by a central and enduring idea or cultural heritage.

Steel notes, as does John Mearsheimer (referred to earlier in the chapter), that Eastern Europe's future may be like its pre–Cold War past. Steel is troubled by what he sees as the central premise of some of these self-determination efforts: that peoples of different faiths and ethnic compositions cannot live together in harmony. The destruction of existing nation-states, Steel believes, should not be taken lightly. "Do we seriously want to see the dismemberment of the Soviet Union?" Steel asked. "Will the world be a more stable and better place?" However annoying the Soviet Union might have been as a single unit, "it could be infinitely more troublesome when split asunder, ineluctably drawing neighboring countries into its quarrels."[10]

There is good reason to believe, writes international relations specialist Christopher Layne, that the breakup of the Soviet Union "would have a highly destabilizing impact on world politics."[11] Traditionally, nations try hard to maintain their standing in the international political system. An ebbing power perceived to be in decline or disintegrating is prone to try to stop or reverse that trend. A recent study of stability in the international system pointed out that the risk of war increases significantly when a great power believes that it is in danger of being rendered an "inessential player."[12] Layne suggests that those who believe that "history has ended" would do well to recall the lessons of the past, specifically the collapse of the multinational Austro-Hungarian empire, which plunged Europe into disaster in 1914.

Arbitrary Borders and Consequential Decisions

Even the future unity of a democratic and seemingly stable nation such as Canada could be in question because of the continuing conflicts between the English-speaking majority and French minority. The reality is that there are few nation-states where the two concepts (nation and state) come together neatly and fit within internationally recognized borders. Japan ranks as one of the rare cases that fall within this category.

As previous chapters have made clear, many of the nation-states of today's world are the result of borders drawn arbitrarily by colonial powers or from the fallout following the collapse of earlier empires. By the 46th annual session of the United Nations General Assembly in 1991, there were 166 members. As discussed in Chapter 2, more than half of them became independent or regained their independence in the years since World War II and the founding of the United Nations. (The three newly independent Baltic states—Estonia, Latvia, and Lithuania—that joined the United Nations in 1991 had been members of the League of Nations before World War II and their annexation by the Soviet Union.)

Many of the continuing problems in the world can be traced to jury-rigged borders and to efforts by groups/nations to break away from subjugation to larger units or to otherwise redraw boundary lines. Some of these borders, such as those in Africa agreed upon by the European powers at the 1884 Berlin Conference, were drawn with more attention to the balance of power in Europe than to the cultural, ethnic, and linguistic ties of the African peoples. Later, when the colonial powers withdrew from Africa, they left behind "cardboard countries without the glue of nationhood."[13] As was pointed out in Chapter 7, the arbitrarily fixed boundaries have contributed to a number of conflicts in African countries in recent times, including wars and civil wars involving Nigeria, Ethiopia, Sudan, Mozambique, and Angola.

Similarly, in the Middle East, where boundaries have shifted like desert sands over the centuries (see Figure 7-1), disputes about border lines have been a major factor in regional conflicts. In this century, colonial powers took part in establishing borders that would eventually become the subject of violent disputes, including conflicts between Arabs and Jews over the land sometimes known as Kuwait. The modern borders of Iraq, Kuwait, and Saudi Arabia were established by British imperial fiat at what became known as the Uqair conference of 1922. According to some accounts, in order to restrict Iraq's influence in the area, Britain deliberately limited Iraq's access to the sea when it redrew Iraq's borders in 1922. When Britain later withdrew from Kuwait in 1961, it created a vacuum in the area. Iraqis believed that a great injustice had been done because the nation had been denied a viable outlet to the Persian Gulf, while Kuwait, with its key location on the Gulf, became richer and richer from its oil resources. This long-festering indignation was a major factor in Iraq's war with Iran and the Iraqi invasion of Kuwait.

Such experiences indicate how decisions or actions can have reverberations far into the future. Short-term solutions can create long-term problems. There are numerous examples of groups or nations who feel aggrieved, often as the result of actions by more powerful (at least at the time) external forces. Nationalism, as has frequently been mentioned, remains a significant factor in international relations. A charismatic or demagogic leader can often channel such sentiments into a militant crusade, as history repeatedly demonstrates.

Also, history demonstrates, as Hannah Arendt wrote, that imperialism often eventually led to revolts and campaigns for sovereignty among those who were under imperial domination. "Wherever the nation-state appeared as conqueror, it aroused national consciousness and desire for sovereignty among the conquered people, thereby defeating all genuine attempts at empire building."[14]

INTEGRATION AND DISINTEGRATION

Europe's move toward integration through the European Community will be useful and instructive to watch, not only because it is a significant development in the alignment and distribution of international power (especially economic) but because Europe is a theater where the pushes and pulls of nationalism and transnational cooperation have often been played out. For two centuries, Europe, which gave birth to the nation-state, was often torn by nationalistic frays. At present, Western Europe is moving toward integration that will reduce the sovereign power of the member nations of EC, while on the other side, Eastern Europe is shaking off imposed consolidation, leaving old national grievances and ambitions exposed.

"What has to be prevented at all costs in tomorrow's Europe is the re-kindling of nationalism as the result of a renaissance of the nation-state," wrote Belgian Foreign Minister Mark Eyskens.[15]

One possible result, if separatist tendencies within states continue to develop, is that this could lead to a new, more intense multipolarity, with more dispersal of power. At the same time, new, small, and dependent nations could easily be dominated or victimized by larger powers in their regions. This leads back to the possible role of regional and subregional organizations, and in a scenario where such supranational organizations assume some of the characteristics of a federation, the result may be that there are fewer centers of power and that the regional framework will provide a more stable international structure.

What many of those in Eastern Europe and the former Soviet republics are seeking are arrangements that allow them autonomy and self-government within a larger framework of economic security. Supranational institutions, including federations or confederations, can provide a framework or structure for economic cooperation while leaving a large degree of political and social autonomy.

Indeed, some see the European Community and integration and related forms of continental cooperation as necessary alternatives to the possible *Balkanization* of Europe. (Balkanization is a term used to mean the breakup of an empire into small, usually ineffective, states.)

In any case, the moves toward disintegration on the one hand and integration on the other, seem likely to make the next century a flag maker's delight. Having kept busy during the decades of decolonization in the last half of this century, the map makers and flag makers should stay occupied as a result of the supranational and subnational trends. The new banners and shapes will reflect the two levels of development: regional groupings, many of them (at least initially) economy-based, such as the European Community and others likely to follow; and the smaller units resulting from break-up of some of the twentieth-century nation-states. This latter trend might be referred to as infranationalism.

Even though the nation-state's grip seems to be loosening, particularly in the economic area (and, as discussed in the previous chapter, advances in technology expedite this trend), the nation-state will remain the basic unit for the foreseeable future.

Economic Connections

As mentioned earlier, the development of the European Community will continue to provide an instructive example of integration, how broadly it develops (beyond economic cooperation), and the extent to which it serves as a model or inspiration for other regional integration efforts. One of the key issues, as suggested earlier, is the question of national sovereignty and the degree to which nations are willing to yield power to the center. Britain's Margaret Thatcher was one who had reservations about giving up much of her nation's sovereignty to further European economic and political union. She believed that Britain was being asked to yield too much of its control of its own destiny. (See Thatcher Profile.)

The reality is that on the economic level, sovereignty has already disappeared to a considerable degree. The telecommunications capabilities and rapid data transmission discussed in the previous chapter will stimulate further blurring of national boundaries. With information and money transmitted by electronic impulses, business and financial transactions flash speedily across borders and around the globe.

No nation can really be self-reliant economically. Events in one country, as has often been pointed out, can have dramatic and sometimes devastating effects on the economies of distant lands. The concept of chain linkage comes into play. Crop failures in one country can have repercussions around the world. An increase in oil prices, for example, can hit hard at Third-World countries already burdened with debt, making it more difficult for them to meet their financial obligations or to import products from nonoil countries. A significant effect of the 1990–91 events in the Persian Gulf region was that millions of foreign nationals working in the area lost their jobs and most had to return to their home countries. Not only did the home countries lose important income, since many of the paychecks of these workers had regularly been sent home, but it added to unemployment and potential instability in those countries. About 16 percent of Egypt's total work force was working in the Gulf area. A country as far away as the Philippines was affected, since large numbers of Filipinos worked in the Gulf region. These developments demonstrate both the growing mobility of the international work force and the chain-linkage effect in international relations.

It has been said that the nervous systems of the major national economies are linked like Siamese twins. Economic trends or fluctuations in Japan or the United States are quickly felt in Europe and vice versa. This interdependence in the global economy that has been emphasized throughout this book is certain to grow as a factor in world affairs in the future.

The economic imperative is one of the most compelling factors in the world today and is a driving force in the growing move toward economic cooperation and integration. Countries are getting together for good reason. World economic integration is being speeded up by growth in trade. Between 1950 and 1990, trade in goods and services increased by 13 times in real terms. National prosperity is increasingly dependent on international economic linkages. Single markets (such as the European Community) with no trade barriers between member countries offer the possibility of a much larger trading area and greater economic returns to those doing business. Border controls and national barriers frustrate trade and limit its benefits.

SECURITY AND POWER

Economic power is unquestionably growing in importance, or, to put it another way, power is increasingly tied to economic strength. As has been emphasized earlier, national security must be seen in much broader terms than military strength. Indeed, security is related not only to military and economic strength, but its definition must be broadened to include resource, environmental, technological, and demographic factors.[16]

Military power will remain important. Although some had forecast that wars involving the major powers were a thing of the past, the 1991 war in the Persian Gulf region demonstrated otherwise. When international pressure failed to dislodge Iraq's Saddam Hussein from occupying Kuwait, the United States–led alliance turned to military means. It was a notable example of a collective security effort, with the United Nations Security Council approving the use of force. Either the Soviet Union or China could have blocked the Security Council action; however, the Soviets voted to approve and China abstained. The vote was 12-2, with Cuba and Yemen casting the dissenting votes. The resolution authorized the use of "all necessary means" to achieve the withdrawal of Iraqi forces from Kuwait. Some saw this as a case of the United Nations finally realizing its potential for collective security action to maintain international order. As mentioned earlier, President Bush cited the action as a necessary step in the establishment of a new world order in which the United Nations could fulfill its peacekeeping role.

Thirty nations contributed in varying degrees to the allied military effort in the Persian Gulf, and others provided financial support and other forms of assistance; it was clearly a United States–dominated effort, however, just as was the United Nations–sanctioned action in Korea 40 years earlier. (See Figure 13–1.)

Some pictured the Persian Gulf War as an aberration, a last gasp of the

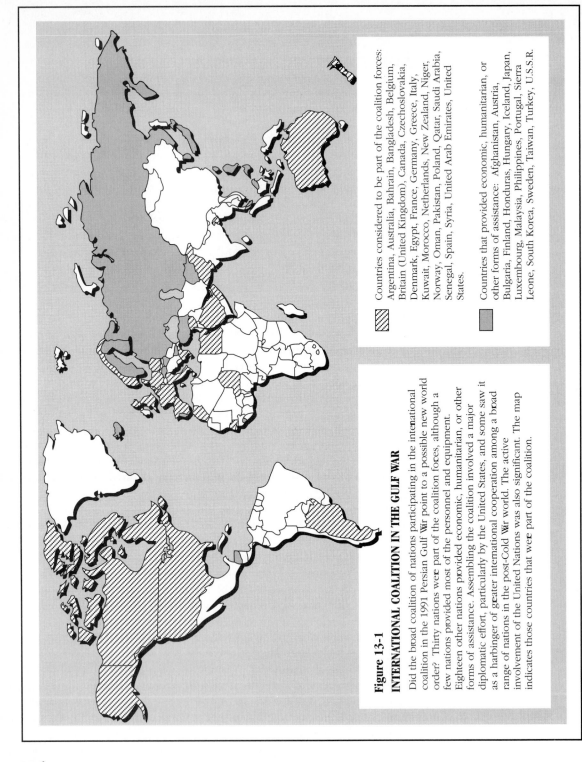

Figure 13-1

INTERNATIONAL COALITION IN THE GULF WAR

Did the broad coalition of nations participating in the international coalition in the 1991 Persian Gulf War point to a possible new world order? Thirty nations were part of the coalition forces, although a few nations provided most of the personnel and equipment. Eighteen other nations provided economic, humanitarian, or other forms of assistance. Assembling the coalition involved a major diplomatic effort, particularly by the United States, and some saw it as a harbinger of greater international cooperation among a broad range of nations in the post-Cold War world. The active involvement of the United Nations was also significant. The map indicates those countries that were part of the coalition.

Countries considered to be part of the coalition forces: Argentina, Australia, Bahrain, Bangladesh, Belgium, Britain (United Kingdom), Canada, Czechoslovakia, Denmark, Egypt, France, Germany, Greece, Italy, Kuwait, Morocco, Netherlands, New Zealand, Niger, Norway, Oman, Pakistan, Poland, Qatar, Saudi Arabia, Senegal, Spain, Syria, United Arab Emirates, United States.

Countries that provided economic, humanitarian, or other forms of assistance: Afghanistan, Austria, Bulgaria, Finland, Honduras, Hungary, Iceland, Japan, Luxembourg, Malaysia, Philippines, Portugal, Sierra Leone, South Korea, Sweden, Taiwan, Turkey, U.S.S.R.

old order. Others saw it as an indication that the United States intended to function as *the* world power, particularly in military terms. Contrary to all the discussions and predictions about a multipolar world, some interpreted this experience as evidence that the bipolar, Cold War world is giving way not to multipolarity, but to unipolarity, with the United States as the central power.

However, a unipolar world "is not the same as a hierarchical system dominated by a single power that creates the rules as well as enforces them," according to Professor Richard Spielman. "The European values that the U.S. endorses predate our existence and limit our imperial ambitions. We still live in an anarchic international order—one lacking an overarching government—although there is only one pole left." [17]

The notion of a unipolar world was echoed by Charles Krauthammer who said, "The most striking feature of the post–Cold War world is its unipolarity." According to Krauthammer, the end of the Cold War did not bring a multipolar world. "The center of world power is the unchallenged superpower, the United States." He believes that multipolarity will eventually come. "In perhaps another generation or so there will be great powers coequal with the United States . . . But we are not there yet . . . Now is the unipolar moment." [18]

These assertions about a unipolar world are based on the belief that only the United States has "the military, diplomatic, political, and economic assets to be a decisive player in any conflict in whatever part of the world it chooses to involve itself." [19] Others see the situation quite differently. William Pfaff, for instance, comments, "The collapse of communism has produced an unexpected result in the international order: the abolishment of superpower rivalry. Remove the rivalry and the category vanishes. Today there is not, as some argue, a single superpower, the United States; there are none." [20] Pfaff, along with many others, emphasizes that power is multifaceted and that economic strength is a key element. In his study of the rise and fall of great powers, Paul Kennedy reminded us: "To be a great power . . . demands a flourishing economic base." [21]

While the Gulf War provided ample evidence of American military strength, can the United States, even if it chooses to do so, afford to function as the world's policeman in the years ahead? The United States took the lead in all aspects of the Gulf War efforts—militarily, politically, and economically. However, the support of other nations was a critical ingredient in the formula that made success possible. It might be said that this international support simply demonstrated American power. However, it is a little more complex than that. Could the United States have exercised its power in the Persian Gulf without the political and economic coalition? It is important to note that in addition to the direct economic, political, and military cooperation of other nations, American forces in the Gulf area were dependent on other countries for key components for communications and advanced weapons systems. The globalization of high-technology industries provides further evidence of the growing international interdependence. United States troops in the Persian Gulf region found themselves dependent on other countries for the tiny semiconductor chips, transistors, and other electronic parts essential for some of their high-tech equipment. On several occasions the United States needed urgent shipments of crucial parts from other countries.[22]

Without the cooperation and support of other nations, including, of course, Saudi Arabia, which served as the base of the Gulf military operation, the diplomatic and financial costs would have been extremely high for the United States had it attempted to act alone. Japan and Germany, in particular, did eventually agree to make major financial contributions, but it seemed that the United States risked putting itself at even more of an economic disadvantage in relation to the other two major centers of economic power—the defeated military powers of World War II. Arguably, Germany and Japan have a greater stake in the Persian Gulf—at least in economic terms—than the United States because of their higher dependency on Middle East oil. In his study of national power, Paul Kennedy wrote that by going to war or devoting a large share of a nation's manufacturing power to expenditures on armaments there is "the risk of eroding the national economic base, especially vis-a-vis states which are concentrating a greater share of their income upon productive investment for long-term growth."[23]

The Gulf War and the Agenda Ahead

Before turning to further discussion of the economic implications and the future of international power alignments, there are some key points to be made about the Gulf War.

First, of course, is that the war was very clearly economic-related—it is the presence of the majority of the world's oil reserves in the Gulf region that make it so strategically important. Indeed, the war could be described as having been based on geoeconomics.

At the same time, it should be noted that the fundamental principle involved, according to President Bush and others who supported the action in the United Nations, was national sovereignty and that Iraq could not be allowed to take over the sovereign nation of Kuwait. Nonetheless, beyond the principle involved, what makes the area so important to the rest of the world is its oil resources. Iraq threatened to significantly increase the share of those resources under its control and to become the dominant power in the region. Iraq and Kuwait combined have nearly 20 percent of the world's oil, and Saudi Arabia has 25 percent. Chapter 7 noted the volatile mix of ingredients that make the Persian Gulf/Middle East region such a flashpoint, and Chapter 10 detailed the significance of the region's oil riches to the world's economy. Oil is not just any commodity, but the fuel on which many countries' hopes for growth and prosperity depend.

Whatever the Persian Gulf War tells us about the importance of military power in the future, it should serve as a potent reminder of some critical issues that complicate international security relations and jeopardize international stability. These issues deserve a prominent place on the international agenda.

- *Nuclear proliferation.* Although some significant progress has been made in superpower arms control, the problem of nuclear proliferation must remain a major international concern. Iraq's quest for nuclear arms capability should be a powerful reminder of the dangers inherent in the spread of nuclear weapons. Turmoil in the former Soviet Union and China, as well as in the Gulf region, raises questions about future security of existing nuclear weapons and the threat that such weapons could fall into the hands of renegade groups.

- *Chemical-biological weapons capability.* Iraq had already used chemical weapons in the war against Iran and the threat that chemical or biological weapons might be used in the Gulf War added a dangerous dimension to the conflict. Iraq managed to exploit weak control systems in the West to buy the equipment and materials needed to manufacture some horrifying weapons. Much of the technology and materials came from Germany. Efforts to control the proliferation of chemical and biological warfare capability were detailed in Chapter 8; however, more effective controls are clearly needed.

- *International arms sales.* Iraq acquired a massive arsenal of "conventional" weapons, purchasing arms from almost every arms-producing country in the world, including artillery from Austria, armored cars from Brazil, fighter planes from France, tanks from China, and helicopters from Italy and Chile. This is in addition to the large quantities of weapons supplied to Iraq by the Soviet Union in the days when the Soviets were angling for power in the region. And, of course, it must be remembered that during the Iran-Iraq war, Iraq became the American combatant of choice, receiving various forms of aid from the United States. Global military sales—government-to-government and through an intricate network of private operators—continue to be widespread and are frequently beyond the control of mechanisms established to prevent their spread. The Middle East area has been the prime recipient of such sales.

These problems, which are discussed at length in Chapters 7 and 8, have major implications for future international security and stability. Any consideration of a true new world order must include intensified efforts to restrict weapons proliferation. Further, Regina Cowan Karp of the Stockholm International Peace Research Institute states, the task of policy making in the post–Cold War world "is to recognize emerging opportunities that permit the evolution of security strategies that might make nuclear weapons increasingly less relevant in the conduct of states."[24]

Two other important issues with significant future implications have been given further emphasis by the Gulf War. Iraq's attempt to engage in what might be called environmental terrorism or ecoterrorism, deliberately spilling oil into the Perisan Gulf and setting the Kuwait oil fields afire, is a foreboding sample of what potential problems could be created by such premeditated pollution. Such problems could have devastating long-term effects and affect peoples of many nations. The Gulf War also reemphasized the heavy dependence of the rest of the world on Middle East oil. Despite the continuing instability in the region, the economic damage to many nations around the world as a result of rising oil prices, and the experience of the 1973 oil embargo, little progress has been made in developing alternative energy sources.

Vulnerability of so many nations to fluctuations in oil supplies and prices underlines the fact of international interdependence and the need for international cooperation to find alternative sources of energy. In the meantime, geoeconomics will keep the Middle East as a focal point for world attention.

ECONOMICS AND INTERNATIONAL TRENDS

While the fragility of the world's economy is exposed by such developments as the turmoil in the Middle East, and while military power and armed conflicts still figure prominently in international affairs, it is clear that economic factors are driving major trends in international relations and will be highly important in shaping the direction and alignments of the coming century.

There is a strong reason to believe that the economic imperative, the need for trade and economic interaction, will push nations toward greater economic cooperation and integration, which will, in turn, provide much of the major framework for international relations in the years ahead. Even though considerable military power and geopolitical leadership may be concentrated in the United States, as previous chapters have made clear, the world has already become much more multipolar, with economic factors, in particular, contributing to the dispersal of power. As the world grows more interdependent economically, the distinctions between domestic and foreign policy and between security policy and economic policy become more and more indistinct, and the connections between economics and politics more direct and apparent.

Moreover, not just economics but nearly all of the major issues on the international agenda involve the policies or efforts of a number of countries. Reference has already been made to the security agenda—arms control and nonproliferation of nuclear, chemical, and biological weapons and restrictions on the international arms trade. And, as will be emphasized later in this chapter, environmental concerns and social and health problems such as AIDS are clearly international in nature and require cooperation among nations.

Tripolar Framework

Many foresee the world's nations coalescing around three major trading blocs, as was discussed in Chapter 9. These three blocs would exercise considerable economic and political power, dominating international commerce and world affairs. The European bloc, led by Germany; the Asian bloc, headed by Japan; and a North American bloc, anchored by the United States, would be the three broad, predominant structures. (See Figure 13–2.) That something along these lines will develop seems fairly certain, although there is no certainty about the form this will take or how formalized this framework might be. And it must be recognized that other important factors will bear significantly on international relations. Also, when pointing to this trilateral power structure, it is important to remember that many of the world's nations and a substantial part of the world's population would not necessarily fall within one of these blocs. There are important questions, for example, about the future roles of China and sections of the former Soviet Union. However, there does seem to be recognition in these areas of the critical importance to their own interests of participation in the international economy. In China's case, isolationist tendencies are countered by the recognition of the needs for modernization and economic advancement, both of which require strong ties to the outside world.

There are, of course, many nations of Asia, Africa, and Latin America that would not necessarily be a part of the trilateral economic structure. Some of these nations are locked in the development struggle that was described in Chapters 10 and 11. Regardless of the preoccupation of the industrialized and newly industrializing nations with their own economic arrangements and advancement, the end of the Cold War and of the dominance of the East-West rivalry in world affairs opens the way for greater attention to the North-South division, which is in many ways a matter of the economic haves and the have-nots. The serious problems plaguing many Third-World societies, most of them related to or influencing the pace of the economic development, will require more attention from the developed world and international organizations. As Charles William Maynes, editor of *Foreign Policy*, points out, as the North-South divide increases in salience, "a new developmental paradigm is needed to garner the financial support in the North and the political support in the South necessary to make real progress."[25]

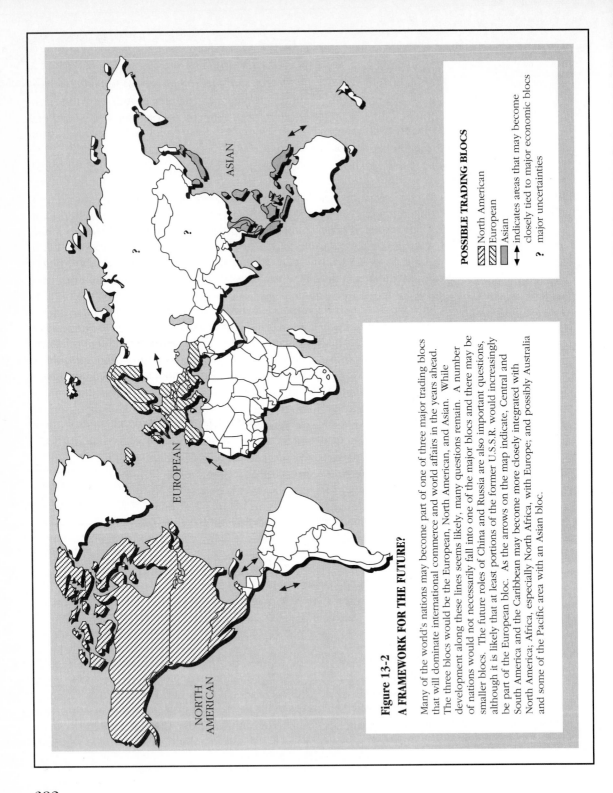

Figure 13-2
A FRAMEWORK FOR THE FUTURE?

Many of the world's nations may become part of one of three major trading blocs that will dominate international commerce and world affairs in the years ahead. The three blocs would be the European, North American, and Asian. While development along these lines seems likely, many questions remain. A number of nations would not necessarily fall into one of the major blocs and there may be smaller blocs. The future roles of China and Russia are also important questions, although it is likely that at least portions of the former U.S.S.R. would increasingly be part of the European bloc. As the arrows on the map indicate, Central and South America and the Caribbean may become more closely integrated with North America; Africa, especially North Africa, with Europe; and possibly Australia and some of the Pacific area with an Asian bloc.

POSSIBLE TRADING BLOCS

North American

European

Asian

← → indicates areas that may become closely tied to major economic blocs

? major uncertainties

ASIAN

EUROPEAN

NORTH AMERICAN

New Configurations and Complex Interdependence

Many of the countries in the Third World are experiencing rapid population growth, as outlined in Chapter 11, and in the twenty-first century those nations will constitute an increasingly dominant portion of the world's population. (See Figure 13–3.) Economic progress and political stability are often directly related, and, despite those who relegate Third-World affairs to the extreme margins of world politics and dismiss Third-World developments as relatively inconsequential, it should be evident that instability in the Third World can have a major international impact. The agenda of Third-World development issues is lengthy, complex, and daunting, but the industrialized nations do have an interest in helping the less-developed nations to confront these problems. If science, technology, and biotechnology can be applied to some of these problems, consistent with the principles of sustainable development, significant progress could be made.

Some of the nations that have been considered to be part of the Third World, as has been pointed out, are doing very well. Among these are some of the Pacific nations, particularly the Asian newly industrializing countries (NICs) such as South Korea and Singapore. Their progress is one of the reasons why there has been much talk of the twenty-first century as the Pacific Century, the notion being that in the years ahead the Pacific region will emerge as the center of economic power and activity. (The twentieth century was sometimes referred to as the American

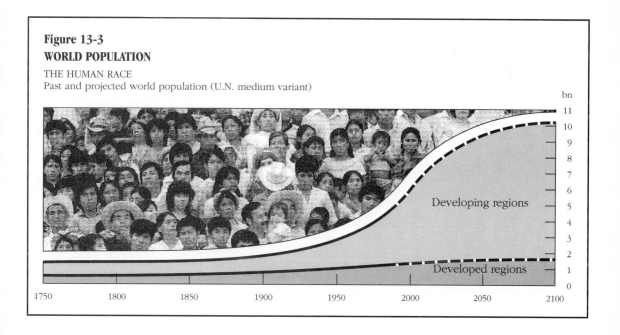

Figure 13-3
WORLD POPULATION

THE HUMAN RACE
Past and projected world population (U.N. medium variant)

Century. Publisher Henry Luce proclaimed this in the 1940s, and said United States leadership should create "a vital international economy" and "an international moral order.") As Robert Gilpin of Princeton University has written, "the Pacific is rapidly emerging as the world's most dynamic area, and its peoples are driving forces of global economics and international politics." [26]

Of course, the Pacific basin or Pacific rim takes in a significant portion of the world, including China, Japan, the Southeast Asian nations, Australia and New Zealand, as well as western America and Russia. Unquestionably, this constellation of nations will play a significant part in world affairs in the twenty-first century. Indeed, it was partially because of the increasing economic importance of and competition from the Pacific nations, led by Japan, that the Western European countries became more serious about their own economic integration and agreed upon the 1992 single market and further steps to assure that Europe would be an important force in the global economy of the future. In fact, the EC actions quieted some of the talk of a coming Pacific Century.

The probability, as suggested earlier, is that there will be a broadly trilateral international economic framework. However, there will be various centers of power, with some shifting and flexibility in alliances, and some overlapping, depending on the issues or circumstances; and in many respects it will be a multipolar world. As discussed in earlier chapters, authors Robert Keohane and Joseph Nye have used the term "complex interdependence" to characterize a world in which transnational actors and economic interdependence are increasingly important factors. Seyom Brown uses the term *polyarchy,* referring to a complex pattern of communities, spheres of influence, hegemonic imperiums, interdependencies, and trans-state loyalties.[27] Regardless of the configuration of power, influence, and cooperation in the years ahead, there is no doubt that the bipolarism of the Cold War era has ended.

Beyond the Bipolar World

Referring to the dramatic changes that occurred in 1989, which opened the way for the post–Cold War period, Czechoslovakia's President Vaclav Havel, a dissident playwright who only months before had been in political detention, told the United States Congress in 1990:

> The main thing is, it seems to me, that these revolutionary changes will enable us to escape from the rather antiquated straitjacket of this bipolar view of the world and to enter at last into an era of multipolarity in which all of us, large and small, former slaves and former masters, will be able to create what your great President Lincoln called "the family of man." [28]

While primary issues of the late twentieth century have included political security, self-government or self-determination, and economic development, in the twenty-first century important concerns will include economic security, environmental protection, and sustainable development, all of which require considerable international cooperation and which will be within the context of a world drawn much closer together by communications and technology, as outlined in the preceding chapter.

Indeed, a 1990 report from the Soviet Foreign Ministry summarizes and symbolizes the changing nature of the international agenda, and is particularly appropriate considering the long Soviet role as one of the bipolar powers. The Foreign Ministry report said:

> A dynamic economy based on new technologies, primarily electronics and information technology, is becoming a key source of influence in the world. Countries where traditional industries are predominant, especially those producing raw materials, are relegated to the role of involuntary tributaries of those whose might is based on investment in products of the human intellect.

The report further notes, consistent with the points made in Chapter 12:

> Global communications are giving rise to a single world information area. No frontiers can stop news or its interpretation from being transmitted immediately to any part of the earth. The information revolution has only just begun, yet its influence on the life of society and its every member is daily becoming more tangible. Attempts to shut out the rest of the world are particularly ineffective today, to say nothing of their unfavorable political consequences. . . . The ideas of freedom and democracy, the supremacy of law and order, and freedom of choice are increasingly taking hold of peoples' thinking. Individuals and peoples who are now in a position to compare things are demanding conditions and a quality of life that technological progress can provide.

Finally, there is the question, addressed earlier in this and in previous chapters, of what truly constitutes national security. The Soviet Foreign Ministry report concluded:

> No nation can consider itself secure unless it commands a powerful, dynamic economy. More and more, it is economic, technological, and monetary factors that are at work as sources of political influence and of secure national interests . . . Military means of procuring national security are giving way to political and economic ones.[29]

These statements are simply one indication of recognition of the changing concepts of security and national/international power and of the new driving forces in world affairs. The growing impact of transnational connections and interdependence, as Helga Haftendorn of the Free University of Berlin points out, increasingly forces states to adapt to international interaction. "In the West awareness has grown that security can no longer exclusively or predominantly be realized unilaterally. The provision of security necessitates cooperation rather than confrontation between states. Some challenges, such as the 'greenhouse effect,' can only be met on a global scale."[30]

A CHANGING AGE AND CHANGING AGENDA

As the world confronts the twenty-first century agenda and attempts to enter what Vaclav Havel called the "era of multipolarity," it is apparent that multilateral approaches are necessary to deal with that agenda. This is especially true with the environmentally related problems which are certain to grow in significance in the coming years. The world community—what Havel, invoking Lincoln, referred to as the family of man—will have to devote more attention to cooperative measures. Once again, it is important to emphasize that many of these problems are beyond the capability of any single nation-state. Such ominous problems as the spread of ocean pollution or the depletion of the earth's protective ozone shield clearly require multilateral efforts, as does nuclear proliferation and such basic problems as availability of energy and food supplies. A pragmatic vision of the post–Cold War era involves international organizations focusing on these problem areas, with cooperative problem-solving becoming a central element of diplomacy. This is sometimes referred to as "green diplomacy." Author Dennis Pirages suggests, "Existing international institutions must be strengthened, and new ones built to deal with the problems raised by the many dimensions of complex interdependence . . . Solving the global problems of the 21st century will require more multilateral action and less nationalistic posturing."[31]

Ecological Interdependence

The assumptions and institutions that governed international relations in the decades after World War II don't fit with the new realities. "Environmental strains that transcend national borders are already beginning to break down the sacred boundaries of national sovereignty," comments Jessica Tuchman Mathews of the World Resources Institute, noting that those boundaries had already been rendered porous by the information and communications revolutions and the instantaneous global movement of financial capital.[32]

The greatest threat to international cooperation on the global environment, according to Mathews, is the question of who will pay for the necessary changes, and that issue could provoke a debilitating North-South deadlock.[33] Some point to the shrinking Soviet military threat and the end of the Cold War as opening up the opportunity to redirect money and scientific and technological know-how toward solving the long-term environmental dilemma.

A new awareness of global ecological independence is filling the political space which used to be occupied by divisive Cold War concerns, according to Norwegian Prime Minister Gro Harlem Brundtland, who chaired the United Nations World Commission on Environment and Development. She points out that there are no ideological barriers to finding solutions to environmental problems and calls for new international scientific and political frameworks to deal with "ecological security."[34]

Rich and poor nations alike are degrading the earth and spewing hazardous substances into the air and water, as Chapter 11 detailed. Some of our major urban areas, such as Mexico City (see City Portrait), which has been called the world's most polluted and populous city, have enormous social and environmental problems. A generation ago, deforestation, ocean pollution, acid rain, thinning ozone, and global warming were not among the threats to international security. Now they are contributing to potentially serious predicaments in the global commons, and they must be high on the international agenda. Recognition of ecological limits and using technology to solve problems rather than create new ones should be high priorities. Technology can contribute to a bountiful future; it can also cause widespread damage and destruction.

Climatic Change?

The global environment is under assault in a variety of ways, as described in Chapter 11. One of the most worrisome problems, because it involves so many uncertainties, is climatic change and, in particular, the threat of global warming. Increasing concentrations of carbon dioxide and other trace gases in the atmosphere, largely as a result of human activities, may cause a significant increase in the earth's temperature over the next several decades. This would result in major ecological, economic, and social consequences, and it is apparent that the problem is of a nature and on a scale that makes it impossible for any one nation to solve.

Are we heading for the "greenhouse century?" Some believe that global warming may be the greatest environmental challenge of the coming century. The "greenhouse effect" is a phrase popularly used to describe the results of global warming. The warming of the earth's surface and lower atmosphere due to increased levels of carbon dioxide and other atmospheric gases is said to work like the glass panels of a greenhouse—letting the heat in but preventing some of it from going back out.

There is some dispute over just how serious the problem is, how responsible the greenhouse gases are for rising temperatures, and what the effects are likely to be. The United States has been criticized by many environmentalists around the world for its cautious attitude about agreeing to international controls intended to reduce the threat of climate change. Although the United States has imposed a number of standards for clean air and water, it is still the largest overall source of air pollution because of heavy energy consumption.

Predictions vary, but there is expectation that, particularly unless strong action is taken to control global warming, the average temperature of the earth's surface will probably rise about four degrees (Fahrenheit) and by as much as nine degrees by the mid-twenty-first century.[35] Scientists predict that the warming could change weather patterns and lead to droughts, coastal flooding, and other adverse effects on large areas of the planet. Deforestation is itself a major factor in the warming process. Clearly, the consequences of global warming cannot be assessed and addressed without strong international cooperation. The expected climate change would exacerbate the problems of desertification, deforestation, and soil erosion, and worsen the prospects for sustainable agriculture.

If present trends in energy use continue, according to the United Nations Environmental Program (UNEP), the concentration of carbon dioxide in the atmosphere is likely to continue increasing at a rapid rate, possibly a further 40 percent by the year 2050. The additional warming effect of other trace gases, especially methane, nitrous oxide, and the so-called chlorofluorocarbons (CFCs), is expected to be about equal to that caused by carbon dioxide. The CFCs are a principal cause of depletion of the ozone layer, which acts as a filter for harmful ultraviolet radiation emitted by the sun. CFCs are used in aerosol sprays and propellants and refrigerants. Steps have been taken to address the ozone problem, with the 1987 Montreal Protocol on Substances that Deplete the Ozone Layer and the 1989 Helsinki Declaration of the Protection of the Ozone Layer calling for drastic cuts in these greenhouse gases by 1999. These agreements can provide a model for international cooperation on global ecological problems.

While the more severe effects of these problems are expected in later decades, the UNEP believes that increased climatic variability already requires a greater buffer capacity in international food supplies than has been considered necessary in the past.

Innovations and Limitations

Many are betting on biotechnological innovations to help head off or alleviate some of the major food, health, medical, and environmental problems. There are, however, a number of contentious ethical, economic, and political issues and problems associated with biotechnology, which involves genetic engineering or manipulation of genes. Aspects of biotechnology, particularly those associated with genetic engineering, are creating technology transfer dilemmas. Biotechnology offers considerable benefits but raises significant risks.[36] In addition to the risk of innocent mistakes during research or manufacturing that might result in the release of dangerous organisms into the environment, the development of new biotechnologies could spread the potential for biological warfare capability. The potential to alter existing life forms or create new ones raises questions about what limitations should be imposed on biotechnology. Nonetheless, biotechnology is already making important contributions to medical treatment and agricultural production. For example, biotechnology can be utilized to develop new and more valuable types of fish and to enhance the fishery industry, to produce new pharmaceutical products, and to generate disease-resistant crops. Careful management of technology and biotechnology and global sharing of their benefits constitute major challenges and opportunities in future international relations.

PROGRESS AND THE CHALLENGES AHEAD

The catalog of issues and problems that has been outlined in this and earlier chapters represents an extensive agenda for the world. And the closeness and interdependence of the world exacerbates some problems, such as the scourge of AIDS and of drug abuse and drug trafficking. These problems certainly do not respect national boundaries. They require concerted international attention if significant progress is to be made in reducing their effects.

Looming over all of these issues, of course, is the matter of the earth's carrying capacity, the impact of rapid population growth (especially in the Third World), the need for development that does not simultaneously degrade the environment, and the ominous factor of nuclear arsenals and weapons proliferation, discussed earlier.

While the challenges are considerable, it is important to acknowledge and appreciate the remarkable progress that has been made on several fronts. Recent years have been notable for some dramatic advances in political freedom and human rights, particularly through the end of the division of Europe, and in strengthened international cooperation in a number of important areas and on some vital issues.

In reflecting on these developments and in assessing the prospects for the future, there are some key points to keep in mind, points that have been stressed in the foregoing pages. One is that not only do domestic factors remain important in influencing a nation's foreign policy, but also domestic politics can no longer really be isolated from international social, political, and economic currents. In the 1980s, it became clear that the Soviet and East European Communist regimes could not provide their citizens with the standard of economic and political life that they wanted, and could not keep pace with the technologically based progress in other countries. This became evident to the citizens of these countries because, increasingly, they had come to have a basis for comparison. Transportation and communications made this possible. As the isolation of those citizens gradually decreased, more were able to see for themselves, through travel or telecommunications, the political and economic vitality of Western society. It heightened pressure for reform in those countries and eventually compelled change. It was a triumph of example over precept or force.

A second point has to do with the role of leadership. As noted earlier in this book, some students and analysts of international relations tend to downgrade the importance of individual leaders. However, in the preceding chapters and the accompanying profiles, the point has been made that leaders do matter. Stanley Hoffmann reminds us that the changes in Europe were greatly influenced by the decisions of two men in particular, Soviet President Mikhail Gorbachev and German Chancellor Helmut Kohl.[37] Obviously, both men were dealing with powerful forces and sentiments, but, rather than allowing history to sweep by them, they responded to opportunities; provided leadership; and opened the way, even if their actions were more pragmatic than idealistic, for dramatic change. Both faced serious problems in accommodating their bold actions to domestic political and economic realities. In Gorbachev's case, he accelerated history and helped affect momentous international change, but faced extraordinary challenges and problems at home, had many critics, and was overtaken by events. (See Gorbachev Profile.) Kohl seized the moment and moved German unification at a pace quicker than anticipated; however, the cost and complexity of implementing unification was well beyond what most anticipated. Nonetheless, their leadership made a significant difference in moving the world into a new era.

Vaclav Havel, one of those who rose to lead Eastern Europe into the post–Cold War era, symbolizes the indomitability of the human spirit, and he tells us that it is a global revolution in human consciousness and a sense of international responsibility that must guide the world in dealing with the problems we face. Otherwise, the world cannot cope with the ecological, social, and demographic challenges outlined in the preceding pages.

The agenda is awesome. It will require skillful leadership and diplomacy, wise management of the earth's resources, and a broadened sense of international responsibility.

NOTES

1. Francis Fukuyama, "The End of History?" *The National Interest,* summer 1989, p. 4.
2. *Ibid.,* p. 18.
3. John J. Mearsheimer, "Why We Will Soon Miss the Cold War," *The Atlantic Monthly,* August 1990, p. 35.
4. Samuel P. Huntington, "No Exit, The Errors of Endism," *The National Interest,* fall 1989, p. 6.

5. Tina Rosenberg, "Thesis Disperuvian," *The New Republic,* October 9, 1989, p. 16.

6. Pierre Hassner, "Responses to Fukuyama," *The National Interest,* summer 1989, p. 23.

7. See Stanley R. Sloan, *The US Role in a New World Order: Prospects for George Bush's Global Vision,* Congressional Research Service, Library of Congress, Washington, March 28, 1991.

8. President George Bush, address to the nation, January 16, 1991. Text printed in *New York Times,* January 17, 1991, and *Congressional Quarterly,* January 19, 1991, pp. 197–98. See also address by President Bush to a joint session of Congress, September 11, 1990. Text printed in *Congressional Quarterly,* September 15, 1990, pp. 2953–55.

9. William Safire, "Gorbachev's 'Bloody Sunday,'" *New York Times,* January 17, 1991.

10. Ronald Steel, "Pax Sovietica," *The New Republic,* January 21, 1991, pp. 17–18.

11. Christopher Layne, "The Eclipse of a Great Power," *World Policy Journal,* vol. 8, no. 1, winter 1990–91, p. 66.

12. See Emerson M. S. Niou, Peter C. Ordeshook, and Gregory F. Rose, *The Balance of Power: Stability in International Systems* (Cambridge, England: Cambridge University Press, 1989).

13. Glenn Frankel, "Nation-State: An Idea Under Siege," *Washington Post,* November 11, 1990, p. 1.

14. Hannah Arendt, *The Origins of Totalitarianism* (new edition) (New York: Harcourt Brace Jovanovich, 1973), p. 127.

15. Quoted in Flora Lewis, "Nationalism Slow to Fade," *Arkansas Gazette* (*New York Times*), July 20, 1990.

16. See Jessica Tuchman Mathews, "Redefining Security," *Foreign Affairs* 68, spring 1989, pp. 162–77.

17. Richard Spielman, "The Emerging Unipolar World," *The New York Times,* August 21, 1990. See also Charles Krauthammer, "The Unipolar Moment," *Foreign Affairs: America and the World 1990/91,* vol. 70, pp. 23–33.

18. Charles Krauthammer, "The Unipolar Moment," *Foreign Affairs: America and the World 1990/91,* vol. 70, no. 1, 1991, pp. 23–24.

19. *Ibid.,* p. 24.

20. William Pfaff, "Redefining World Power," *Foreign Affairs: America and the World 1991,* vol. 70, no. 1, 1991, p. 34.

21. Paul Kennedy, *The Rise and Fall of the Great Powers* (New York: Vintage, 1989), p. 539.

22. *See* Stuart Auerbach, "The U.S. Achilles' Heel in Desert Storm," *Washington Post* (National Weekly Edition), April 7, 1991.

23. Kennedy, *The Rise and Fall of the Great Powers,* p. 539.

24. Regina Cowen Karp, "The Continuing Nuclear Challenge," in Regina Cowan Karp (ed.), *Security With Nuclear Weapons?* Stockholm International Peace Research Institute (SIPRI) (Oxford, England: Oxford University Press, 1991), p. 18.

25. Charles William Maynes, "The New Decade," *Foreign Policy* 80, fall 1990, p. 13.

26. Robert Gilpin, "International Politics in the Pacific Rim Era," in Steven L. Spiegel (ed.), *At Issue: Politics in the World Arena* (6th ed.) (New York: St. Martin's, 1991), p. 131.

27. Seyom Brown, *New Forces, Old Forces and the Future of World Politics* (Glenview, Ill.: Scott, Foresman, 1988).

28. Vaclav Havel, address to the United States Congress. See "The Revolution Has Just Begun," *Time,* March 5, 1990, pp. 14–15.

29. Report and documents from the Foreign Ministry to the Supreme Soviet, U.S.S.R., Novosti Press Agency, January 1990; See Max Jakobson, "Euro Future," *World Monitor,* December 1990, pp. 38–45.

30. Helga Haftendorn, "The Security Puzzle: Theory-Building and Discipline-Building in International Security," *International Studies Quarterly,* vol. 35, no. 1, March 1991, pp. 13–14.

31. Dennis Pirages, *Global Technopolitics* (Pacific Grove, Calif.: Brooks/Cole, 1989), p. 213.

32. Jessica Tuchman Mathews, *op. cit.,* p. 162.

33. See Jessica Tuchman Mathews (ed.), *Preserving the Global Environment* (New York: Norton, 1991), pp. 319–23.

34. Gro Harlem Brundtland, "From the Cold War to a Warm Atmosphere," *New Perspectives Quarterly,* vol. 6, no. 1, spring 1989, pp. 4–5.

35. See Stephen H. Schneider, *Global Warming: Are We Entering the Greenhouse Century?* (San Francisco: Sierra Club Books, 1990).

36. See Thomas C. Wiegele, "The Emerging Significance of Biotechnology for the Study of International Relations," *International Studies Notes,* vol. 15, no. 3, fall 1990, pp. 98–103.

37. Stanley Hoffmann, "The Case for Leadership," *Foreign Policy* 81, winter 1990–91, pp. 20–38.

GLOSSARY

actor(s)—term sometimes used to describe individuals, institutions, or organizations that play a role in international relations; realists consider the state to be the principal actor in international relations.

antiballistic missiles (ABMs)—defensive weapons designed to detect and intercept attacking missiles. The 1972 ABM treaty and its 1974 Protocol limited the number of ABMs deployed by the United States and the Soviet Union.

antisubmarine warfare (ASW)—active and passive measures used to reduce or nullify the effectiveness of enemy submarines.

apartheid—an Afrikaans word meaning "separateness," used to describe racial separation policies and laws in South Africa officially instituted in the late 1940s and maintained until laws and policies began to be changed in the 1990s.

arms control—explicit or implicit international agreements governing the numbers, types, characteristics deployment, and use of armed forces and armaments.

Association of South East Asian Nations (ASEAN)—established in 1967 to foster economic, social, cultural and political development and cooperation among member nations (Brunei, Indonesia, Malaysia, Philippines, Singapore, Thailand).

atomic bomb—weapon deriving its explosive force from the sudden release of nuclear energy through *fission,* or splitting, of heavy atomic nuclei.

balance of payments—an accounting of all economic transactions between one nation and the rest of the world; the net flow of funds into and out of a country due to all forms of international commerce.

balance of power—a term used in various ways, but the traditional concept involves creating/maintaining an equilibrium in the international order so that one nation/alliance does not become preponderant over others.

Balkanization—a term used to refer to the breakup of an empire into small, usually ineffective, states.

ballistic missile—a pilotless projectile launched into the atmosphere and pulled by gravity to its target.

bilateral—relations between two nations; for example, bilateral aid, trade, negotiations, or treaties.

biological warfare—the use of biological agents to cause disease, death, or debilitation among people or other forms of life.

biotechnology—the integrated use of biochemistry, microbiology, and chemical engineering intended to provide greater human control over genetic evolution, diseases, and the physical environment, with important potential applications in areas such as health care and agricultural productivity. Because of the far-reaching implications, such innovations can pose significant ethical, political, and economic questions.

bipolar—a world political system in which power is concentrated in two power centers.

bloc—French word used to describe groups or

combinations of states supporting particular military, political, or economic interests.

Bretton Woods system—the international monetary framework established at the end of World War II, named for the New Hampshire town where the 1944 financial conference was held.

capitalism—an economic system characterized by private ownership of property and commercial enterprise, competition for profits, and limited government interference in the marketplace.

carrying capacity—long-term ability to sustain or support the world's population or those people who live in a particular area.

cartel—an international agreement to restrict competition, usually through an attempt to control production and pricing of a commodity.

chain linkage—a term used to describe the chain reaction that can be set in motion by developments in or policies or actions of nations and by their impact on other nations; policies toward one nation or issue may have broad ramifications for relations with other nations.

chemical warfare—the use of asphyxiating, corrosive, poisonous gases, sprays, or smoke to produce casualties among humans and animals and/or damage to plants and material.

coercive diplomacy—the use of force or the threat of force as a diplomatic tactic.

Cold War—popular term used to describe the tension, hostility, and adversarial relationship that developed between the Western (noncommunist) and Eastern (Communist) blocs after World War II.

collective security—global security system based on agreement among states that an act of aggression against one state will be met by collective action; a fundamental principle of the United Nations.

colonialism—the rule of an area and its people by an external power; usually considered a form of imperialism.

command, control, and communications (C3)—facilities, equipment, and personnel used to acquire, process, and disseminate information needed by decision-makers to plan, direct, and control military operations.

communism—a political, economic, and social doctrine ideology, and/or system theoretically based on Marxist-Leninist principles aimed at a classless society in which there is common ownership of the means of production and subsistence; interpretations of communism and Marxist doctrine have varied widely.

comparative advantage—an economic asset (for example, resources, technology, labor) that enables a country to produce certain goods more efficiently than others.

conditionality—the conditioning of aid or assistance on a nation's adherence to certain requirements.

Conference on Security and Cooperation in Europe (CSCE)—sometimes referred to as the Helsinki Accord because of the agreement signed at the 1972–75 conference in the Finnish capital, with emphasis on human rights; subsequently, in the post–Cold War period, the CSCE, with 34 European and North American members, became the largest structure for cooperation on European security and related issues, with the 1990 Charter of Paris establishing a permanent secretariat.

confidence-building measures (CBMs)—sometimes referred to as confidence-and-security-building measures (CSBMs); cooperative arrangements through which military alliances notify or share information with others about activities and maneuvers so as to avoid misunderstandings and miscalculations.

containment—a guiding principle of United States foreign policy in the post–World War II period based on prevention of the spread of Soviet/communist influence.

conventional forces/weapons—military organizations or hardware that are not equipped with nuclear, chemical, or biological weapons having mass-destruction capabilities.

coup d'état—French term used to refer to a sudden and decisive seizure of state power by a political or military group from within an existing system; not necessarily a revolution since it may not represent a popular uprising or involve broad overthrow of political institutions.

covert—secret or clandestine actions or policies.

cruise missile—low-flying pilotless guided missile which can be equipped with nuclear or non-nuclear warheads. They can be ALCMs (air-launched cruise missiles), GLCMs (ground-launched cruise missiles), or SLCMs (sea-launched cruise missiles).

Cultural Revolution—social and political upheaval set in motion in China by Mao Zedong's attempt in 1966 to revitalize the communist revolution and rid the country of foreign influences; it resulted in chaos and hampered China's development.

dependence (dependencia)—a theory or interpretation based on the view that the developed/industrialized nations have created an international economic structure and relationship that keeps the developing nations in a condition of economic and political dependence.

détente—French term indicating a lessening or relaxation of tensions between nations; in modern usage has often referred to improved United States–Soviet relations.

deterrence—strategy of having a credible counterthreat so as to pose unacceptable risks to an opponent considering an attack.

diplomacy—the range of actions taken by a nation to represent and pursue its interests.

diplomat—an officially accredited agent or representative of a government who serves as a medium for the conduct of international relations.

entente—French term used in diplomacy to refer to an understanding or agreement between two or more nations.

escalation—an intensification or broadening of a conflict through the use of more powerful weapons, larger numbers of forces, or an expansion of the area involved.

European Community (EC)—the broad organization that includes the European Economic Community (EEC) or Common Market, the European Coal and Steel Community, and the European Atomic Energy Community (EURATOM); increasingly the term is used to refer to the regional economic integration of Western European nations.

extraterritoriality—exemption from the jurisdiction of local laws.

fascism—an authoritarian and/or totalitarian political system, often based on a corporate state and centering around a powerful supreme leader; usually emphasizing militarism and nationalism and characterized by regimentation, propaganda, and prejudice; normally associated with the extreme right; exemplified by the regimes in Germany and Italy before and during World War II.

firebreak—the psychological barrier that inhibits escalation from one level of conflict or intensity to another—especially from conventional to nuclear warfare.

first strike—the first move in a war; in nuclear war, refers to the ability to launch an attack eliminating effective retaliation by the opposition.

first use—the initial use of specific military

measures, such as nuclear weapons, during the conduct of a war.

First World—term sometimes applied to developed/industrialized capitalist nations, as distinct from the Second and Third Worlds.

fission—the splitting of an atomic nucleus of certain heavy elements (uranium or plutonium) accompanied by the release of large amounts of energy; the atomic bomb was a fission weapon.

flexible response—a multiple-option strategy based on meeting aggression at an appropriate level or place with the capability of escalating the level of conflict.

four tigers—term applied to four areas of East Asia with rapidly developing export-based economies—Taiwan, South Korea, Hong Kong, and Singapore; also called the four dragons.

Fourth World—a term sometimes applied to the poorest of the poor or the least-developed nations.

fusion—the thermonuclear process in which the nuclei of light elements combine to form the nucleus of heavier elements, releasing large amounts of energy.

General Agreement on Tariffs and Trade (GATT)—established in 1947 to promote free trade; has grown to more than 100 members and sets rules and policies for international trade.

geoeconomics—refers to the importance of a particular nation or region due to economic strength or the presence of valuable resources; the significance of economic factors in geopolitics and strategic considerations.

geopolitics—theories and concepts emphasizing location, size, and geographic factors as primary influences in international relations; contemporary usage refers to a broader concept involving locations, regional balances of relationships with great powers, presence of resources, and strategic factors.

geostrategy—the geostrategic approach emphasizes the security aspects and strategic planning, based on a geopolitical assessment.

glasnost—Russian term meaning openness.

green diplomacy—international negotiations and meetings related to environmental issues.

Green Revolution—dramatic increases in agricultural production in certain developing countries resulting from development and planting of hardy, high-yield grains adaptable to a wide range of climates. The increased production often involves extensive irrigation and use of pesticides, raising concerns about the effect on the ecosystem.

greenhouse effect—warming of the earth's surface and lower atmosphere due to increased emissions of carbon dioxide and other gases, primarily from the burning of fossil fuels and use of chlorofluorocarbons.

gross national product—total value of a nation's output of goods and services, usually per year.

Group of Seven (G-7)—the major economic powers (United States, Canada, Japan, Germany, France, United Kingdom, and Italy); leaders of these nations meet in an annual economic summit.

Group of 77 (G-77)—an economic caucus formed by developing nations, now numbering 127, to represent their interests in international economic affairs.

gunboat diplomacy—the use of warships as an instrument of diplomacy, usually associated with imperialism or domination by external powers.

hegemony—preponderant influence or dominance of one nation over other nations or regions.

horizontal proliferation—the spread of nuclear weapons from one nation to one or more others.

human rights—the concept that all human beings have basic rights and freedoms, regardless of what state they may inhabit; specific principles of basic human rights normally include freedom of expression, movement, religion, family life, and equitable treatment under law, as set forth in the United Nation's 1948 Universal Declaration of Human Rights and other multilateral conventions. Concerns about human rights have become increasingly important in international relations.

hydrogen bomb—powerful explosive weapon that uses the energy released through nuclear fusion; also known as the thermonuclear bomb. The first was exploded by the United States in 1952.

idealism—an approach to international relations based on the belief that moral principles and international cooperation should be guiding factors rather than considerations based purely on power and national interest.

imperialism—a policy or course of action through which a state imposes control over others.

infranationalism—refers to the break-up of nation-states into smaller units.

integration—the process and end result of creating a community of nations, usually with an economic and/or political basis and usually coordinated by supranational institutions.

intercontinental ballistic missile (ICBM)—a land-based fixed or mobile rocket-propelled vehicle capable of delivering a warhead to intercontinental ranges (generally considered in excess of 3,000 miles).

interdependence—the increasing interrelationship and mutual dependence among nations, especially in an economic sense.

intermediate (-range) nuclear forces (INF)—missiles and aircraft with ranges of less than 3,400 miles. Subject of the United States–Soviet treaty which was ratified in 1988.

international law—the body of legal rules considered binding upon states and other agents in their mutual relations, primarily on treaties and general principles and customs accepted by nations; may be considered as an approach to international relations.

intifada—Arabic term for uprising; the name given to the Palestinian uprising that began in 1987.

irredentism—an effort to unite certain people and territory in one state with another, usually on the basis of ethnic ties.

jihad—to strive or struggle to follow the precepts of the Islamic religion, sometimes interpreted as including a holy war in the defense of Islam.

just war—(*bellum justum*) the concept in Christian ethics and western tradition that war is justified under certain compelling conditions and circumstances.

launcher—the equipment used to launch a missile.

less-developed countries (LDCs)—a term applied to Third-World countries, referring to relative economic development and standard of living; the term *developing countries* is also used.

limited war—the concept that there can be armed conflict involving the use of nuclear weapons but not escalating to general war.

linkage—indicates the connections and effects of developments in or the policies or actions of nations on other nations; underlines the difficulty of separating a nation's domestic and foreign policies. In a related diplomatic sense, linkage refers to the tying of policies or agreements to a nation's international behavior.

low-intensity conflict—confrontations short of full-scale war, sometimes referred to as "unconventional" warfare.

maquiladora—Spanish term traditionally referring to the sharing of crops between landowners and workers or similar arrangements; now applies to a partnership or division of manufacturing activity ("twin plants") on both sides of the United States–Mexican border, with assembly plants frequently located on the Mexican side.

massive retaliation—strategic doctrine outlined by Secretary of State Dulles in 1954 which threatened a nuclear response to any military challenges.

megaton—the equivalent explosive power of one million tons of TNT, used as a measure of yield for nuclear weapons.

multiple independently targetable re-entry vehicle (MIRV)—offensive ballistic missile carrying multiple nuclear warheads, each capable of striking separate targets.

multipolar—distribution of power among several nations or blocs in the world political system.

mutual assured destruction (MAD)—a strategic doctrine of deterrence under which both sides are capable of absorbing a first nuclear attack by the other and retaliating by inflicting a high level of damage.

national interest(s)—those elements constituting a nation's most vital needs and objectives, including such factors as self-preservation, independence, sovereignty, territorial integrity, military security, and economic well-being.

national security—the survival, welfare, and protection of a nation-state and its interests and the well-being of its people; a broad concept related not only to the protection of a nation's sovereignty and identity but involving the relative military, political, and economic strength of a nation.

nationalism—identification with a group based on a sense of common heritage including some or all of these factors: language, ethnic or racial origins, religion, geographic location, or political base; also, the belief that the nation or nation-state merits political loyalty; often associated with the goals of self-determination and independence.

nation-state—the primary or fundamental unit in international relations, a political entity within a defined territorial area possessing legal and political authority over that area.

neocolonialism—a new, indirect form of colonialism resulting from economic, political, or cultural dominance.

New International Economic Order (NIEO)—refers to the efforts of Third-World or developing nations to revise global economic relations, creating what they would see as a more equitable international economic system.

New World Information (and Communications) Order (NWIO or NWICO)—refers to the efforts of some nations, primarily in the Third World, to revise the global information/communication system, creating what they would see as a more balanced system, believing the international system to be biased against and not understanding of developing nations; a subject of major debate within the United Nations Educational, Scientific, and Cultural Organization (UNESCO) during the 1970s and 80s.

newly industrializing/industrialized countries (NICs)—developing or Third-World countries which have experienced significant economic growth and have expanded their manufacturing sectors.

nonalignment—a foreign policy position adopted by some states, particularly in the Third World, of refraining from affiliating politically or militarily with major international blocs; this term had particular application during the Cold War period with nonaligned nations avoiding both the East and West blocs.

nontariff barriers—restrictions on trade other than through imposition of taxes; such obstacles can include quotas, legal or technical specifications or regulations, or government procurement policies.

North-South—terms used to distinguish between the advanced industrialized states of the northern hemisphere and the less-developed or Third-World states of the southern hemisphere; like other broad categorizations it is imprecise because the economic dichotomy between nations does not always follow north-south lines.

nuclear weapon—a bomb, missile warhead, or other deliverable munition that explodes as a result of energy released by atomic nuclei through fission, fusion, or both.

Organization of Petroleum Exporting Countries (OPEC)—an intergovernmental organization established in 1960 to coordinate oil-exporting policies and prices among Third-World member countries. OPEC has had varying degrees of success as membership in the cartel grew to 14 nations, and was most successful in the oil embargo directed against selected nations following the 1973 Middle East war.

paradigm—a framework, pattern, or model, often used for comparative purposes.

payload—the weapon and/or cargo capacity of any aircraft or missile system.

perestroika—Russian term meaning restructuring.

power—refers to the capability of a nation or nations to exert influence or dominance in international relations, usually through political, military, or economic means; often associated with the concept of realism, which emphasizes power as the central factor in international relations.

proliferation—the spread of weapons.

propaganda—communication aimed at influencing the thinking, emotions, or actions of a group or public.

protectionism—the use of tariffs and nontariff barriers, such as quotas and preferences, to reduce or restrict imports and give an advantage to or protect domestic producers.

public diplomacy—international public relations; policies, programs, or actions intended to present a favorable image for a nation, often through communications.

putsch—a suddenly effected attempt by a group to overthrow a government; the term is usually associated with actions by right-wing or fascist groups.

realism—a pragmatic approach to foreign policy/international relations, emphasizing national self-interest and based on the premise that power is the central factor in international relations.

realpolitik—a German term which has come to be used to describe policies or approaches to international relations based on realistic assessments or calculations of the prospects for those policies; usually based on the pursuit, maintenance, or use of power.

reentry vehicle—that portion of a ballistic missile which carries the nuclear warhead and reenters the earth's atmosphere in the final phase of flight.

sanctions—policies and actions seeking to compel a nation or nations to change policies or behavior by imposing economic and/or other restrictions against the target nation(s).

satyagraha—Sanskrit word meaning "faithful obstinacy," which Mohandas Gandhi translated as "soul force"; used to describe nonviolent or passive resistance in India and elsewhere.

sea- (or submarine-) launched ballistic missile—ballistic missile transported by and launched from a ship.

Second World—term sometimes used to identify the Soviet Union and socialist nations formerly aligned with it.

sherpas—aides who guide their national leaders through summit meetings and work out details of agreements; the name derives from the Sherpas of Tibet and Nepal who guide climbers to the mountain summits.

shuttle diplomacy—negotiations conducted by a middleman or mediator shuttling between countries, groups, or leaders; usually involves traveling between capitals of countries involved in negotiations or potential negotiations.

sovereignty—considered to be the enabling concept of world politics, whereby nation-states possess authority not only within their territorial entities but possess membership in the international community; implies equality among states (as, for example, in the United Nations), in the sense that there is equal capacity to acquire rights and be subjected to obligations.

Standing Consultative Commission (SCC)—A permanent United States–Soviet commission established under the SALT I agreements to oversee compliance with the SALT agreements.

Strategic Arms Limitation Talks (SALT)—Negotiations between the United States and Soviet Union begun in 1969 to seek to limit and reduce offensive and defensive strategic arms.

Strategic Arms Reduction Talks (START)—United States–U.S.S.R. arms negotiations begun in 1982 that emphasized reducing the number of nuclear weapons.

Strategic Defense Initiative (SDI)—space-based defense system proposed by President Reagan in 1983, popularly known as "Star Wars."

strategic weapons—long-range weapons, usually those nuclear weapons capable of striking the enemy's homeland.

summit—meeting of heads of government of major nations, may be bilateral or multilateral.

supranational—institutions or authorities that are above individual states; normally involves states yielding or delegating some of their sovereignty to an international organization.

sustainable development—economic development approaches or policies based on long-term considerations; meeting current needs without destroying resources that will be needed in the future.

tactical weapons—weapons used on battlefields, generally short-range systems, as opposed to strategic systems.

tariffs—taxes upon imports.

terrorism—the use or threatened use of violence by individuals or groups seeking to call attention to and/or achieve political objectives.

Third World—a broad categorization that normally refers to the nations of Africa, Asia (except Japan), Latin America, and the Middle East and other developing nations, many of which were formerly under colonial control; sometimes referred to as the South, most of the nations are part of the Group of 77. Although there are wide variations within the Third World, it is sometimes seen as an economic or political bloc in world affairs.

throw-weight—the payload capacity of a ballistic missile.

totalitarianism—a political system in which centralized control is held by an autocratic leader or hierarchy of leaders and the individual is subordinate to the state, which controls all aspects of life; coercive measures are used to maintain control and eliminate opposition.

transnational—extending beyond national borders.

triad—the basic tripartite structure of the United States strategic forces, composed of land-based ICBMs, the strategic bomber force, and the ballistic-missile submarines.

tripolar—a concept or world system in which power is concentrated in three major nations, groups, or blocs; in economic terms, many would see a tripolar world with the European Community, the United States/North America, and Japan/East Asia as the dominant forces.

unilateral—a nation acting on its own, independently, in the pursuit of its foreign policy objectives, as opposed to a bilateral or multilateral approach.

unipolar—a world system in which one actor or power is dominant.

verification—process of determining if parties to an arms-control agreement are complying with its provisions.

vertical proliferation—additions to the nuclear weapons already possessed by nuclear-weapons nations.

warhead—the part of a missile or munition which contains the nuclear or other explosive system or damage-inflicting agents.

xenophobia—fear, dislike, distrust, or intolerance of foreigners.

BIBLIOGRAPHY

Ardrey, Robert. *The Social Contract.* New York: Atheneum, 1970.

Arendt, Hannah. *The Origins of Totalitarianism.* new edition. New York: Harcourt Brace Jovanovich, 1973.

Aron, Raymond. *Peace and War: A Theory of International Relations.* (translation by Richard Howard and Annette Baker Fox) New York: Praeger, 1968.

Ash, Timothy Garton. *The Uses of Adversity: Essays on the Fate of Central Europe.* New York: Random House, 1989.

Attali, Jacques. *Millennium: Winners and Losers in the Coming World Order.* New York: Times Books, 1991.

Ball, George. *Diplomacy for a Crowded World.* Boston: Little, Brown, 1976.

Barston, R. P. *Modern Diplomacy.* London: Longman, 1988.

Bendahmane, Diane B., and John W. McDonald, Jr. *Perspectives on Negotiation.* Washington: Foreign Service Institute, U.S. Department of State/U.S. Government Printing Office, 1986.

Benedick, Richard Elliot. *Ozone Diplomacy: New Directions in Safeguarding the Planet.* Cambridge, Mass.: Harvard University Press, 1991.

Bill, James A. *The Eagle and the Lion: The Tragedy of American-Iranian Relations.* New Haven, Conn.: Yale University Press, 1988.

Blacker, Coit D. *Reluctant Warriors: The United States, the Soviet Union, and Arms Control.* New York: Freeman, 1987.

Booth, John A., and Thomas W. Walker. *Understanding Central America.* Boulder, Colo.: Westview, 1989.

Brodie, Bernard. *War and Politics.* New York: Macmillan, 1973.

Brown, Lester, et al. *State of the World* (annual editions). New York: (Worldwatch Institute) Norton.

Brown, Lester R. *World Without Borders.* New York: Random House, 1972.

Brown, Seyom. *The Causes and Prevention of War.* New York: St. Martin's, 1987.

Brown, Seyom. *New Forces, Old Forces, and the Future of World Politics.* Glenview, Ill.: Scott, Foresman, 1988.

Brzezinski, Zbigniew. *The Grand Failure: The Birth and Death of Communism in the Twentieth Century.* New York: Scribner's, 1989.

Brzezinski, Zbigniew. *Power and Principle.* New York: Farrar, Straus, Giroux, 1983.

Bulloch, John, and Harvey Morris. *Saddam's War.* London: Faber and Faber, 1991.

Carter, Gwendolen M., and Patrick O'Mera (eds.). *International Politics in Southern Africa.* Bloomington, Ind.: Indiana University Press, 1982.

Carter, Jimmy. *Keeping Faith.* New York: Bantam, 1982.

Chan, Steve. *East Asian Dynamism.* Boulder, Colo.: Westview, 1990.

Clapham, Christopher. *Third World Politics.* London: Croom & Helm, 1985.

Cockroft, James D. *Neighbors in Turmoil: Latin America.* New York: Harper and Row, 1989.

Common Crisis—North-South: Cooperation for World Recovery, report of the Brandt Commission. Cambridge, Mass.: MIT Press, 1983.

Cooper, Richard N. *The International Monetary System: Essays in World Economics.* Cambridge, Mass.: MIT Press, 1987.

Deutsch, Karl W. *Nationalism and its Alternatives.* New York: Alfred A. Knopf, 1969.

Dizard, Wilson P., Jr. *The Coming Information Age.* 3rd ed. New York: Longman, 1989.

Doughtery, James E., and Robert L. Pfaltzgraff, Jr. *Contending Theories of International Relations.* 3rd ed. New York: Harper and Row, 1990.

Dumont, René. *False Start in Africa.* (translated by Phyllis N. Ott) London: Andre Deutsch, 1966.

Dyson, Freeman. *Weapons and Hope.* New York: Harper and Row, 1984.

Ehrlich, Anne H., and Paul R. Ehrlich. *Earth.* New York: Franklin Watts, 1987.

Ehrlich, Paul R., and Anne H. Ehrlich. *The Population Explosion.* New York: Simon and Schuster, 1990.

Ehrlich, Paul R., and Anne H. Ehrlich. *Population, Resources, Environment.* San Francisco: Freeman, 1970.

Ehrlich, Paul R., Anne H. Ehrlich, and John P. Holdren. *Ecoscience.* San Francisco: Freeman, 1977.

Einstein, Albert. *Ideas and Opinions.* New York: Bonanza, 1954.

Emerson, Rupert. *From Empire to Nation.* Boston: Beacon Press, 1960.

Evans, Graham, and Jeffrey Newnham. *The Dictionary of World Politics.* New York: Simon and Schuster, 1990.

Fanon, Frantz. *The Wretched of the Earth.* (translated by Constance Farrington) New York: Grove Press, 1963.

Fontaine, Andre. *History of the Cold War.* (translated by D. D. Paige) New York: Pantheon, 1968.

Fulbright, J. W. *Old Myths and New Realities.* New York: Random House, 1964.

Furlong, William L., and Margaret E. Scranton. *The Dynamics of Foreign Policymaking.* Boulder, Colo.: Westview, 1984.

Garthoff, Raymond. *Détente and Confrontation.* Washington: Brookings, 1985.

Gilpin, Robert. *The Political Economy of International Relations.* Princeton, N.J.: Princeton University Press, 1987.

Gorbachev, Mikhail. *Perestroika—New Thinking for Our Country and the World.* New York: Harper and Row, 1987.

Gwertzman, Bernard, and Michael T. Kaufman (eds.). *The Collapse of Communism.* New York: Random House/Times Books, 1990.

Hackett, Clifford. *Cautious Revolution: The European Community Arrives.* New York: Praeger, 1990.

Halberstam, David. *The Reckoning.* New York: Morrow, 1986.

Hall, Edward T. *The Silent Language.* Garden City, N.Y.: Doubleday, 1959.

Hamilton, John Maxwell. *Entangling Alliances: How the Third World Shapes Our Lives.* Cabin John, Md.: Seven Locks Press, 1990.

Head, Sydney W. *World Broadcasting Systems.* Belmont, Calif.: Wadsworth, 1985.

Hellenier, G. K. *The New Global Economy and the Developing Countries.* Brookfield, Vt.: Edward Elgar, 1990.

Hough, Jerry F. *Russia and the West: Gorbachev and the Politics of Reform.* New York: Simon and Schuster, 1988.

Howard, Michael. *The Lessons of History.* New Haven, Conn.: Yale University Press, 1991.

Hurwitz, Leon, and Christian Lequense (eds.). *The State of the European Community.* Boulder, Colo.: Rienner, 1991.

Independent Commission on Disarmament and Security Issues. *Common Security: A Blueprint for Survival.* New York: Simon and Schuster, 1982.

International Bank for Reconstruction and Development/The World Bank. *World Development Report* (annual editions). New York: Oxford University Press.

International Commission for the Study of Communication Problems. *Many Voices, One World.* New York: Unipub, 1980.

Isaak, Robert. *Individuals and World Politics.* 2nd ed. Monterey, Calif.: Duxbury Pess, Wadsworth, 1981.

Jervis, Robert. *The Meaning of the Nuclear Revolution: Statecraft and the Prospect of Armageddon.* Ithaca, N.Y.: Cornell University Press, 1989.

Jorden, William J. *Panama Odyssey.* Austin: University of Texas Press, 1984.

Kaiser, Robert G. *Why Gorbachev Happened.* New York: Simon and Schuster, 1991.

Karnow, Stanley. *Vietnam: A History.* New York: Viking, 1983.

Karp, Regina Cowen. (ed.). *Security With Nuclear Weapons?* (Stockholm International Peace Research Institute—SIPRI) Oxford, England: Oxford University Press, 1991.

Kegley, Charles W., Jr. (ed.). *International Terrorism.* New York: St. Martin's, 1990.

Kegley, Charles W., Jr., and Eugene R. Wittokpf. *The Nuclear Reader.* 2nd ed. New York: St. Martin's, 1989.

Kelley, Donald R., and Hoyt Purvis (eds.). *Old Myths and New Realities in United States—Soviet Relations.* New York: Praeger, 1990.

Kennan, George F. *Memoirs, 1925–1950.* Boston: Little Brown, 1967.

Kennan, George F. *Memoirs, 1950–1963.* Boston: Little Brown, 1972.

Kennan, George F. *The Nuclear Delusion.* New York: Pantheon, 1983.

Kennan, George F. *Sketches From a Life.* New York: Pantheon, 1989.

Kennedy, Paul. *The Rise and Fall of the Great Powers.* New York: Random House, 1987.

Keohane, Robert O., and Joseph S. Nye. *Power and Interdependence.* 2nd ed. Glenview, Ill.: Scott, Foresman, 1989.

Kissinger, Henry. *White House Years.* Boston: Little Brown, 1979.

Kissinger, Henry. *Years of Upheaval.* Boston: Little Brown, 1982.

LaFeber, Walter. *America, Russia, and the Cold War,* 5th ed. New York: Alfred A. Knopf, 1985.

LaFeber, Walter. *The American Age.* New York: Norton, 1989.

LaFeber, Walter. *The Panama Canal.* New York: Oxford University Press, 1978.

Lincoln, Edward J. *Japan's Unequal Trade.* Washington: Brookings, 1990.

Lorenz, Konrad. *On Aggression.* New York: Harcourt, Brace & World, 1966.

Lowenthal, Abraham F. *Partners in Conflict: The United States and Latin America in the 1990s.* Baltimore: Johns Hopkins Press, 1988.

Luard, Evan. *Conflict and Peace in the Modern International System: A Study of the Principles of International Order.* Albany: State University of New York Press, 1988.

McCain, Morris. *Understanding Arms Control.* New York: Norton, 1989.

Mandelbaum, Michael. *The Fate of Nations: The Search for National Security in the Nine-*

teenth and Twentieth Centuries. New York: Cambridge University Press, 1988.

Martin, L. John and Ray Eldon Hiebert. *Current Issues in International Communication.* New York: Longman, 1990.

Mathews, Jessica Tuchman (ed.). *Preserving the Global Environment.* New York: Norton, 1991.

May, Ernest R. *"Lessons" of the Past.* New York: Oxford University Press, 1973.

Mazrui, Ali A. *Cultural Forces in World Politics.* Portsmouth, N.H.: Heinemann, 1990.

Merrill, John C. (ed.). *Global Journalism: Survey of International Communication.* 2nd ed. New York: Longman, 1991.

Montagu, Ashley. *The Nature of Human Aggression.* New York: Oxford University Press, 1976.

Morgenthau, Hans J. *Politics Among Nations.* 3rd ed. New York: Alfred A. Knopf, 1960.

Morgenthau, Hans J. *Politics Among Nations.* 6th ed., revised by Kenneth W. Thompson. New York: Alfred A. Knopf, 1985.

Newsom, David D. *The Soviet Brigade in Cuba.* Bloomington, Ind.: Indiana University Press, 1987.

Niou, Emerson M. S., Peter C. Ordeshook, and Gregory F. Rose. *The Balance of Power: Stability in International Systems.* Cambridge: Cambridge University Press, 1989.

Nolan, Janne E. *Trappings of Power: Ballistic Missiles in the Third World.* Washington: Brookings, 1991.

North-South: A Program of Survival, report of the Independent Commission on International Development Issues (Brandt Commission). Cambridge, Mass.: MIT Press, 1980.

Nye, Joseph S., Jr. *Bound to Lead: The Changing Nature of American Power.* New York: Basic Books, 1991.

Oberdofer, Don. *The Turn: From the Cold War to a New Era.* New York: Poseidon, 1991.

Oxford Analytica. *Latin America in Perspective.* Boston: Houghton Mifflin, 1991.

Palmer, Norman D. *The New Regionalism in Asia and the Pacific.* Lexington, Mass.: Lexington, 1991.

Pastor, Robert A. *Condemned to Repetition: The United States and Nicaragua.* Princeton, N.J.: Princeton University Press, 1987.

Peterson, M. J. *The General Assembly in World Politics.* Winchester, Mass.: Allen and Unwin, 1986.

Pfaff, William. *Barbarian Sentiments: How the American Century Ends.* New York: Hill and Wang, 1989.

Pierre, Andrew J. *The Global Politics of Arms Sales.* Princeton, N.J.: Princeton University Press, 1982.

Pirages, Dennis. *Global Technopolitics: The International Politics of Technology and Resources.* Pacific Grove, Calif.: Brooks/Cole, 1989.

Plano, Jack C., and Roy Olton. *The International Relations Dictionary.* 4th ed. Santa Barbara, Calif.: ABC-CLIO, 1988.

Poitras, Guy. *The Ordeal of Hegemony: The United States and Latin America.* Boulder, Colo.: Westview, 1990.

Porter, Michael E. *The Competitive Advantage of Nations.* New York: The Free Press, 1990.

Purvis, Hoyt, and Steven J. Baker (eds.). *Legislating Foreign Policy.* Boulder, Colo.: Westview, 1984.

Quester, George H. *The International Politics of Television.* Lexington, Mass.: Lexington, 1990.

Riding, Alan. *Distant Neighbors.* New York: Alfred A. Knopf, 1985.

Rosenau, James N. (ed.). *Linkage Politics.* New York: The Free Press, 1969.

Rosenberg, Tina. *Children of Cain: Violence and the Violent in Latin America.* New York: William Morrow, 1991.

Rosenblum, Mort. *Coups and Earthquakes: Reporting the World for America.* New York: Harper and Row, 1981.

Rotfeld, Adam Daniel, and Walther Stutzle (eds.). *Germany and Europe in Transition.* (Stockholm International Peace Research Institute—SIPRI) Oxford, England: Oxford University Press, 1991.

Rourke, John T. *Making Foreign Policy: United States, Soviet Union, and China.* Pacific Grove, Calif.: Brooks/Cole, 1990.

Russett, Bruce, Harvey Starr, and Richard Stall (eds.). *Choices in World Politics.* New York: W. H. Freeman, 1989.

Samovar, Larry A., and Richard E. Porter. *Communication Between Cultures.* Belmont, Calif.: Wadsworth, 1991.

Schmidt, Helmut. *Men and Powers: A Political Retrospective* (translated by Ruth Hein). New York: Random House, 1989.

Schneider, Stephen H. *Global Warming: Are We Entering the Greenhouse Century?* San Francisco: Sierra Club Books, 1989.

Seranton, Margaret. *The Noriega Years.* Boulder, Colo.: Rienner, 1991.

Singh, Jyoti Shankar. *A New International Economic Order.* New York: Praeger, 1977.

Sivard, Ruth Leger. *World Military and Social Expenditures.* (annual editions) Washington, D.C.: World Priorities.

Sloan, Stanley R. (ed.). *NATO in the 1990s.* Washington: Pergamon-Brassey's, 1989.

Smith, Anthony. *The Geopolitics of Information.* New York: Oxford University Press, 1980.

Smith, Charles D. *Palestine and the Arab-Israeli Conflict.* New York: St. Martin's, 1988.

Smith, Geoffrey. *Reagan and Thatcher.* New York: Norton, 1991.

Smoke, Richard. *The National Security and the Nuclear Dilemma.* Reading, Mass.: Addison-Wesley, 1984.

Spero, Joan Edelman. *The Politics of International Economic Relations.* 3rd ed. New York: St. Martin's, 1985.

Spiegel, Steven L. *At Issue: Politics in the World Arena.* 6th ed. New York: St. Martin's, 1991.

Stockholm International Peace Research Institute (SIPRI). *SIPRI Yearbook: World Armaments and Disarmament.* (annual editions) Oxford, England: Oxford University Press.

Stoessinger, John G. *Nations in Darkness.* 4th ed. New York: Random House, 1986.

Talbott, Strobe. *Deadly Gambits.* New York: Alfred A. Knopf, 1984.

Thomas, Hugh. *The Cuban Revolution.* New York: Harper and Row, 1977.

Tuchman, Barbara W. *The March of Folly: From Troy to Vietnam.* New York: Alfred A. Knopf, 1984.

Ulam, Adam B. *Dangerous Relations: The Soviet Union in World Politics, 1970–82.* New York: Oxford University Press, 1983.

Ullman, Richard H. *Securing Europe.* Princeton, N.J.: Twentieth Century Fund/Princeton University Press, 1991.

United Nations. *Global Outlook 2000.* New York: United Nations Publications, 1990.

United Nations Association of the United States of America. *A Global Agenda: Issues Before the General Assembly of the United Nations* (annual editions). Lanham, Md.: University Press of America.

U.S. Arms Control and Disarmament Agency. *Arms Control and Disarmament Agreements.* Washington: U.S. Government Printing Office, 1990.

U.S. Arms Control and Disarmament Agency. *World Military Expenditures and Arms Transfers* (annual editions). Washington: U.S. Government Printing Office.

Vanneman, Peter. *Soviet Strategy in Southern Africa.* Stanford, Calif.: Hoover Institution Press, 1990.

Vasquez, John A. (ed.). *Classics of International Relations.* Englewood Cliffs, N.J.: Prentice-Hall, 1986.

Viotti, Paul R., and Mark V. Kauppi. *International Relations Theory.* New York: Macmillan, 1987.

Vogel, Ezra F. *Japan as Number One.* Tokyo: Charles F. Tuttle, 1980.

Walker, Martin. *The Waking Giant: Gorbachev's Russia.* New York: Pantheon, 1987.

Wallace, William (ed.). *The Dynamics of European Integration.* New York: Columbia University Press, 1991.

Waltz, Kenneth. *Man, the State and War.* New York: Columbia University Press, 1959.

Ward, Barbara. *Five Ideas That Change the World.* New York: Norton, 1959.

Weintraub, Sidney (ed.), with Luis Rubio F. and Alan D. Jones. *U.S.-Mexican Industrial Integration: The Road to Free Trade.* Boulder, Colo.: Westview, 1991.

Whitaker, Jennifer S. *How Can Africa Survive?* New York: Council on Foreign Relations, 1989.

Winchester, Simon. *Pacific Rising.* New York: Prentice-Hall, 1991.

Woods, Randall B., and Howard Jones. *Dawning of the Cold War.* Athens, Ga.: University of Georgia Press, 1991.

Yergin, Daniel. *Shattered Peace: The Origins of the Cold War and the National Security State.* Boston: Houghton Mifflin, 1977.

INDEX